HOW CHINA ESCAPED
THE POVERTY TRAP

A VOLUME IN THE SERIES

Cornell Studies in Political Economy

Edited by Peter J. Katzenstein

A list of titles in this series is available at www.cornellpress.cornell.edu.

HOW CHINA ESCAPED THE POVERTY TRAP

Yuen Yuen Ang

CORNELL UNIVERSITY PRESS   ITHACA AND LONDON

Cornell University Press gratefully acknowledges receipt of a subvention from the University of Michigan Office of Research and the Department of Political Science, University of Michigan, which aided in the publication of this book.

First published 2016 by Cornell University Press
Printed in the United States of America

Library of Congress Cataloging-in-Publication Data

Names: Ang, Yuen Yuen, 1979– author.
Title: How China escaped the poverty trap / Yuen Yuen Ang.
Description: Ithaca : Cornell University Press, 2016. | Series: Cornell studies in
    political economy | Includes bibliographical references and index.
Identifiers: LCCN 2016014018 | ISBN 9781501700200 (cloth : alk. paper)
Subjects: LCSH: China—Economic conditions—1976–2000. | China—Economic
    conditions—2000– | China—Economic policy—1976–2000. | China—
    Economic policy—2000– | Developing countries—Economic policy. |
    Developing countries—Social policy. | Economic development—China. |
    Economic development—Developing countries. | Poverty—China. |
    Poverty—Developing countries.
Classification: LCC HC427.92 .A74 2016 | DDC 338.951—dc23
LC record available at http://lccn.loc.gov/2016014018

Cornell University Press strives to use environmentally responsible suppliers and materials to the fullest extent possible in the publishing of its books. Such materials include vegetable-based, low-VOC inks and acid-free papers that are recycled, totally chlorine-free, or partly composed of nonwood fibers. For further information, visit our website at www.cornellpress.cornell.edu.

Cloth printing   10 9 8 7 6 5 4 3 2 1

All photos are by the author.

For Chia

Every act of creation is first an act of destruction.

—Pablo Picasso

Contents

Figures and Tables

Figures

Tables

Preface

This book grew out of an earlier book I had abandoned.

Originally, I set out to write a book to explain why China could be a developmental (growth-promoting) state if it did not possess the Weberian (professional) bureaucracies necessary for effective growth promotion. On the surface, this was a good question, or so I thought.

But soon I realized the question was wrong.

First of all, are Weberian bureaucracies really a precondition for economic development? If good institutions like Weberian bureaucracies are necessary for market success, then where do these preconditions come from? Aren't they themselves dependent on the level of economic growth?

Second, is China indeed a developmental state and does it lack Weberian bureaucracies? Many observers credit China's local governments for strongly and proactively promoting growth. Yet others lambaste the same actors for the opposite problems: ineptitude and corruption. So who's right and who's wrong? In fact, depending on where and when you look within China, you can find every variety of political economy, from developmental to predatory, Weberian to patrimonial, modern to backward. In a country that changes so rapidly and varies so widely across regions, no single description is completely right.

Acknowledging that every part of the story was moving, I felt momentarily paralyzed.

Traditional concepts and tools of analysis work well when something can be held constant. In a simple example, when comparing a wealthy and a poor country, we look for variation in the two cases. If they are nearly identical in all respects except one, say, the quality of governance, we may infer that this factor is a likely cause of their economic variance.

Yet what if the cause is a consequence of the outcome? Clearly, institutions and governance are deeply influenced by the level of economic development. One may apply statistical techniques to isolate the causal effects of institutions on the economy (also known in technical parlance as "treat endogeneity"). But such techniques do not "resolve" the fact that the two variables are intrinsically interdependent.

Furthermore, what if both the cause and the consequence are moving targets that change over time? For instance, Shanghai was poor, messy, and corrupt in the 1980s, but by the 2010s it approximated the modern, developmental states of East Asia. Was it institutions that changed the economy or vice versa?

Analysts may try to get around these "problems" by tracing causation back to some deep causes that are presumably constant, such as geography or shocks that occurred in the past. But if factors like geography or history are primarily what determine present-day outcomes, then it suggests that successes and failures are predestined. If a country lacks the right geography or historical legacy, is it doomed? How can we explain the reversal of fortunes among some places that inherited poor geography or a traumatic past?

The more I thought about these questions, the more I wondered if we should—and could—study the world in a different way. The reality of political-economic development is that almost everything moves. Can we understand this reality without trying to hold things constant?

Thus I cast aside my original inquiry and restarted with a basic question: How did development *actually* happen? If we embrace reality as it is and simply follow the moving parts from point to point, what will we learn?

This book reports what I discovered from my detour into unfamiliar but ultimately more fruitful territory.

Acknowledgments

The creation of this book was an excruciating adventure, filled with surprises and rewards but also anxiety and toil. It would not have been possible to start and finish this long and winding journey without the generous assistance, encouragement, and opportunities provided by many individuals. First and foremost, my acknowledgment goes to mentors at Stanford University. My greatest debts are owed to Jean Oi, as it was Jean who prodded me back onto the path of a scholarly career when I had given up. It was also Jean who instilled in me an unconditional passion for studying politics on the ground; her tireless enthusiasm for fieldwork and interviewing was testimony to the intrinsic joy and scholarly duty of discovering what people really do. David Laitin's intellectual breadth and teaching sparked a lasting curiosity for big questions, and his sharp advice kept me on track at critical junctures. Alberto Diaz-Cayeros and Beatriz Magaloni showered generous concern both for my work as a scholar and for my happiness as a person; they were my role models of fine scholarship and kindness. Jonathan Rodden's comparative perspective pushed me to think about problems I would otherwise have taken for granted. Andrew Walder patiently listened to my ideas long before they made any sense. He deserves my utmost thanks for continuing to have faith in me and lending encouragement and support whenever it was most needed. More recently, a clarifying conversation with Jonathan Bendor, from whom I had learned about bureaucracies and principles of reasoning, helped me rethink some arguments.

Many other colleagues have influenced the evolution of this book. I wish to thank Atul Kohli, Deborah Yashar, and Miguel Centeno for including me in the Princeton Workshops on State Capacity in the Developing World. This series of workshops, which spanned years and took place in three different continents broadened my horizons and allowed me to test new ideas and receive feedback from esteemed colleagues as my questions and answers evolved. In particular, I thank Atul for inspiring me to take my work in a historical direction. At the workshop in New Delhi, he urged me to develop a "genetic" account, that is, to trace the origins of the institutions I studied. His suggestion sparked a new path and then subsequent ones, culminating in this book.

I was privileged to join the faculty at Columbia University's School of International and Public Affairs (SIPA). I am especially thankful for the warm welcome and collegiality of José Antonio Ocampo, Alfred Stepan, Victoria Murillo,

Jenny McGill, John Coatsworth, Andrew Nathan, and Isabela Mares. Colleagues and students at Columbia piqued my interest in international development and expanded the scope of this study in ways I could not otherwise have envisioned.

During my years at the University of Michigan, I have benefited from a supportive environment and exposure to new ideas. Mary Gallagher was an extraordinary comrade who once hosted guests at her place till midnight for a conference that I organized (and for this and more, Ken Duck, thanks to you too). She carefully read and commented on this book from its early to final incarnation. Pam Brandwein cheered me during good and bad times and was always there to remind me of what was important; without her unfailing support and abundant kindness, I would have given up many times. Learning about Robert Axelrod's pioneering work on complex adaptive systems was essential for reconstructing this book; otherwise I would have dismantled a previous project but would not have known what to do next. And it was also Bob who reminded me to write simply. Jim Morrow's incisive feedback pushed me both to clarify the substance of my arguments and to improve their framing; conversations with him motivated a substantial revision of the conclusion. Mariah Zeisberg and I shared mutual words of encouragement and many stimulating conversations despite our different fields of study.

In addition, I thank many people for their feedback on earlier drafts of the book. My gratitude goes to Elizabeth Perry, Robert Axelrod, Anna Grzymala-Busse, and Mary Gallagher for their advice at my book workshop. Despite the inchoate state of my project at the time, they were able to help me see its promise and point me in the right direction. At the workshop, Bob Axelrod suggested the title of this book, *How China Escaped the Poverty Trap*. Others provided useful comments on subsequent drafts: Jim Morrow, Charles Shipan, Pam Brandwein, John Padgett, Julia Strauss, Charlotte Lee, Martin Dimitrov, Vivienne Shue, Lee Benham, Dinsha Mistree, and Matthew Taylor. At various stages, conversations with Stephen Krasner, Kenneth Lieberthal, Nicholas Howson, Marty Powers, Francis Fukuyama, Scott Page, Jenna Bednar, Pauline Jones-Luong, Allen Hicken, Robert Franzese, Mark Tessler, Mika LaVague-Manty, Mariah Zeisberg, Mark Dincecco, Kenneth McElwain, Ann Chih Lin, Anne Pitcher, John Jackson, Jia Nan, Andrew Mertha, and Melanie Manion were all valuable. In 2014–15, I presented this work at the New Approaches to China Lecture Series at Stanford University, the Seminar on Development and Democracy at Princeton University, and the CCS Annual Conference at UM. I thank the participants at these events for providing stimulating feedback at an opportune time.

The field research on which much of this book is based would not have been possible without the kind assistance of colleagues in China. In particular, I thank Bian Huimin, Yu Xunda, Han Chaohua, Qiao Zhijian, and Yang Yan for their generous help in arranging interviews, especially knowing well the hassle and challenges of making such arrangements in China. A whole team of research assistants contributed to this project, but I can name only a few in this brief acknowledgment. In particular, Rosa Xie, Tong Lingao, Liu Bolei, and Wu Jundong deserve thanks for their persistence and dedication in conducting multiple rounds of interviews. I also thank Nicole Wu for her superb and timely research assistance at the write-up stage. I am also fortunate to have learned from and explored methods of field research with several of my peers at Stanford, especially Xuehua Zhang, Xiaojun Li, and Charlotte Lee. I must also not forget to thank the hundreds of interviewees who shared their experiences with me. Many had lived through the Maoist followed by the reform era and participated in the making of China's great transformation. I hope this volume does justice to their remarkable stories.

Finally, at Cornell University Press, my heartfelt thanks go to Roger Haydon for his enthusiastic support of the book even when it was only a fledging project. His expert shepherding of the whole process brought it to completion. I was especially fortunate to have two distinguished and perceptive reviewers. Peter Katzenstein and Kellee Tsai read through the entire manuscript carefully and suggested key structural revisions that improved the book immeasurably. In fact, Peter read more than two versions of this book. To be able to think and write freely under the guidance of expert advice was academic luxury at its best. I thank the entire team at Cornell University Press.

I gratefully acknowledge financial support for my research from the following institutions: Stanford University, Columbia SIPA, the University of Michigan, the Andrew Mellon Foundation/ACLS Early Career Program, the Chiang Ching-Kuo Foundation, the OYCF-1990 Institute, and the APSA Paul Volcker Junior Scholar Research Grant. At Michigan, the Center for Chinese Studies provided research, conference funding and a book subsidy. The Office of Research and the Department of Political Science provided subvention grants for the book.

Taking the starting point of this project back further, I would never have had the chance to study in the United States had Colorado College, my alma mater, not given me a full scholarship. My undergraduate advisor, Eve Grace, sparked my interest in political theory; the methods of systematic textual analyses she taught served me well years later when I had to think through complex concepts and unpack processes of coevolution. With two young children and with my husband often overseas, I simply could not have survived without the eager support and selfless help of my parents-in-law, Tang Hsien Teng and Liu Hsiu-Chen. Many friends at Stanford extended unconditional kindness when I most needed their help: Shawn Gaines, Mee Smuthkalin, Doug Kerr, Christina Gwin, Vicki Sherman, Charlotte Lee, Nik Crain, our "Saturday volleyball friends," among many others. My parents, Ang Tian Chan and Mary Ng, worked hard to make sure that my sister and I received the educational opportunities they did not have. Many thanks to my sister, Huiru, and our dear friends, Hsien Chen and Fiona Ng, for generously accommodating my whole family in Shanghai and in Hong Kong during my post-doc year. I extend my sincere gratitude to Dr. Taxin, who has prescribed both medicine to nurture our health and wisdom to nurture our minds. Together with the late Chinese philosopher Mr. Nan and the late Singaporean dramatist Mr. Kuo, they have taught me plenty about the art of creativity and learning through their lifelong practices.

Writing a book is such an absorbing activity that it spills over into family affairs. My children are wonderful companions who have grown cheerfully accustomed to my frequent absence. Justin read early drafts of the introduction and advised me to make it simpler. I've tried to comply. Jamie chirped a gentle reminder regularly, "How is your book coming along?" She won't rest until she sees it in print. My husband, Chia-Yu Tang, gave up his career so that I could have mine. Along with a career, he gave up many other things along the way. By example, he showed me what selfless love, purpose, and confidence mean. To him I dedicate this book.

HOW CHINA ESCAPED
THE POVERTY TRAP

HOW DID DEVELOPMENT *ACTUALLY* HAPPEN?

> **Providence has not created the human race either entirely independent or perfectly slave. It traces, it is true, a fatal circle around each man that he cannot leave; but within its vast limits man is powerful and free; so too with peoples.**
>
> —Alexis de Tocqueville, *Democracy in America*

> **The greatest fever of all was aspiration, a belief in the sheer possibility to remake a life. Some who tried succeeded; many others did not. More remarkable was that they defied a history that told them never to try.**
>
> —Evan Osnos, *The Age of Ambition*

Imagine a pauper who turns to two finance gurus for advice. Not only is he broke, this pauper is poorly educated and lives in a rough neighborhood. The first guru urges, "Earn your first paycheck. Once you start making money, your circumstances will improve, and you will eventually escape poverty." The second guru counsels differently: "Start by doing as my rich clients do: attend college, move to a safe town, and buy health insurance. You can only escape poverty by first creating the prerequisites for wealth."

The two gurus mean well, but the advice of both experts clearly falls short. The first guru provides no clue as to how the pauper might earn his first paycheck, much less how to sustain a stable income. Conversely, the second guru ignores the realities of poverty. If the pauper could afford to, he would have obtained the prerequisites for a better life long ago. Attaining such prerequisites is not the solution to poverty; the difficulty of attaining them is itself the problem.

The parable of the pauper and two gurus reflects a fundamental problem of development in the real world. All wealthy capitalist economies feature institutions of good governance, such as protection of private property rights, professional bureaucracies, modern courts, formal accountability, and pluralistic participation, which all seem necessary for successful markets.[1] Yet attaining these preconditions also appears to depend on the level of economic wealth.

So how can poor and weak societies escape poverty traps? Which comes first in development—economic growth or good governance?

Answers have been sharply divided. Modernization theory holds that "growth → good governance." The argument goes that as countries grow rich, a burgeoning middle class will demand greater accountability and protection of individual rights, leading eventually to capitalist democracies.[2] Similarly, others argue that countries succeed in modernizing public administrations and eradicating corruption only after they become sufficiently wealthy.[3]

Mirroring the first guru's shortfall, however, modernization theory does not explain the origins of economic growth. According to the Harrod-Domar model in classical economics, growth comes from capital investments. But how do impoverished countries secure investments? Economist Jeffrey Sachs argues that such investments should come from developed nations in the form of massive foreign aid.[4] He believes that once the Third World economy is jump-started, "all good things" will follow.[5] Yet many studies find the link between foreign aid and prosperity tenuous.[6] Some even contend that foreign aid has actually worsened corruption and brought more harm than good to the poor.[7]

A second widely embraced theory forcefully advances a reverse causal claim: "good governance → growth." International agencies like the World Bank and IMF, joined by many Western policy makers and academics, maintain that it is necessary to "get governance right" before markets can grow.[8] The logic is intuitive. All prosperous economies share a common set of strong, law-bound governmental institutions. Therefore, aspiring developers should first replicate the checklist of best practices found in wealthy democracies. Then, it is expected, growth will naturally blossom from good institutional soil.

Reminiscent of the second guru, however, this paradigm ignores the problem of how poor and weak states can meaningfully attain good governance. The term "meaningfully" deserves emphasis, for it is one thing to adopt the formality of best practices but another to actually implement them.[9] For instance, at the behest of international agencies, some developing countries have built courts and have written laws in books, but they have frequently lacked professional judges to adjudicate disputes, and citizens have routinely distrusted and avoided the legal system even after new laws were promulgated.[10] If achieving good governance were a mere technicality of copying best practices from the developed West, then late developers would have accomplished it long ago. In fact, as Pritchett and Woolcock, two leading voices on international development, lament, the imposition of good governance standards has been "a root cause of the deep problems encountered by developing countries."[11]

Going further, a third school points to history as the underlying cause of good governance or state capacity. This approach may be abbreviated as "history → good governance → growth." Following a path-dependent logic, several scholars posit colonialization as the root of present-day national inequalities.[12] In *Why Nations Fail*, Acemoglu and Robinson trace the stark divide between North and South America to their contrasting colonial legacies.[13] According to them, English colonizers founded settlements of equal opportunity and limited government on North American soil, paving the way for future capitalist success, whereas Spanish conquerors imposed unequal and exploitive structures in Latin America, stunting prosperity over the long term.

Although this third school reminds us of the enduring effects of history, it does not point a way out of poverty traps.[14] Rather, the authors of *Why Nations Fail* conclude that "different patterns of institutions today are deeply rooted in the past because once society gets organized in a particular way, this tends to persist." And they add, "This persistence and the forces that create it also explain why it is so difficult to remove world inequality and to make poor countries prosperous."[15] Their conclusion raises a troubling question: If the seeds of national successes and failures were indeed planted long ago and became rooted over time, what can nations lacking the right history do today?[16]

The observation that many poor nations fail *because* they suffer troubled histories and bad starts is correct, but by itself not particularly surprising. What is harder and more useful, instead, is to explain why some nations succeed *despite* ominous starting points and daunting odds, as witnessed most dramatically in China's rise from a socialist backwater to a global powerhouse since market reforms began in 1978.[17]

This book investigates how China escaped the poverty trap and made the Great Leap from a barren communist political economy into the middle-income, capitalist dynamo that it is today. More broadly, grounded in my analysis of China's metamorphosis, this is a study about how development *actually* happens. Is it really the institutions of good governance so keenly proffered to developing countries today that launch markets? Or is it growth that enables good governance? Or is history destiny?

My answer begins with a simple observation: development *is* a coevolutionary process. States and markets interact and adapt to each other, changing mutually over time. Neither economic growth nor good governance comes first in development. China's experience provides an especially rich illustration of the coevolutionary process of development, but this process is not unique to China. As we shall see by the end of this book, the rise of Western societies, too, actually followed a coevolutionary pattern,[18] as did the astonishing boom of the movie industry in contemporary Nigeria.

Although development as a coevolutionary process is intuitively observed (in my experience, it appears that the less formal training one receives, the more intuitive it is), analyzing mutual changes among many moving parts is far from easy. To this end, I lay out a framework for systematically mapping the coevolution of states and markets. This approach reveals surprising insights into the causal sequence of development and raises new questions about the sources of societal adaptation.

My answers to how China—and poor and weak societies in general—escaped the poverty trap are twofold. The first: build markets *with* weak institutions. My analysis reveals that the institutions, strategies, and state capacities that promote growth vary over the course of development, among countries and even among localities within countries. Even more surprisingly, I show that the practices and features that *defy* norms of good governance—normally viewed as "weak" institutions—are paradoxically the raw materials for *building* markets when none exist. By contrast, the "good" or "strong" institutions found in wealthy economies are institutions that *preserve* existing markets.

The idea that we can harness weak institutions to build markets carries tremendous political and practical import. Perhaps the one thing poor countries possess in abundance are so-called weak institutions. Examples of weak institutions featured in this study include the fusion of public and private interests (vs. bureaucratic professionalism), partial (vs. impartial) regulation, campaign-style (vs. routine) policy implementation, indiscriminate and uncoordinated (vs. selective) industrial promotion policies, incentives for petty fee extractions (vs. eradicating corruption), to name some.[19] Normally, we believe that the way out of poverty traps is to "quickly" replace such weak institutions with strong institutions that define advanced industrialized economies.[20] This book points to a different path. It illuminates the development potential that may lie hidden within apparently weak institutions.

The second answer: create the right conditions for adaptation. History is not destiny. Although past encounters determine starting points, any given legacy may be reshaped for destructive or constructive ends. Instead of attributing national successes and failures only to history or geography,[21] I emphasize instead the efforts of reformers to foster improvisation among ground-level agents, such that they may effectively utilize existing resources to tackle the problems of the poor, and thereby turn the typical *problems* of underdevelopment into the *solutions* to development.

Yet while improvisation is essential to the development process, improvisation does not occur automatically and indeed often fails. Instead of dispensing obvious advice like "avoid mimicry," "promote innovation," and "embrace experimentation," fashionable among some development pundits who invoke adaptive language,[22] I underscore the inherent challenges of achieving these goals. By studying how China tackled these challenges, we'll learn about some actions that may be taken to spur the coevolution of states and markets as well as the effects of particular measures deployed. Also, by unpacking the processes through which China escaped the poverty trap, we will also understand how China arrived at the particular problems that it faces today.

How Did China Escape the Poverty Trap?

Today, with news of China's spectacular rise repeated ad nauseam, it is easy to forget the dire circumstances confronting its reformers following the death of Mao.[23] It is also convenient to attribute China's transformation to the mis-impression of a "strong state" or that China was perhaps not so poor at the start of reforms. So a basic reality check is in order.

In 1980 China's GDP per capita was only US$193, lower than that of Bangladesh, Chad, and Malawi,[24] present-day "bottom-billion" countries.[25] In practical terms, an income per capita of US$193 means that average food consumption fell below basic nutritional standards. The Chinese people did not eat more or better food during the 1970s than they had in the 1930s, before the Chinese Communist Party (CCP) took power.[26]

Not only was China abjectly poor, the regime had oscillated between extreme dictatorship and political anarchy. In three decades under Mao's rule, China suffered two major political disasters. The Great Leap Forward (1958–1961) was Mao's frenzied scheme to accelerate economic production by political command, a campaign that culminated in mass starvation and claimed an estimated thirty million lives. Mao then tried to reconsolidate power by unleashing the Cultural Revolution (1966–1976), also nicknamed "ten years of madness."[27] Young red guards loyal to Mao went on a purge against alleged class enemies at all levels of government, including national leaders like Deng Xiaoping. In many official year-books, statistics during the period of the Cultural Revolution are missing,[28] for the bureaucracy was so devastated that it literally stopped counting. Mass killings spread to society and descended into what Walder describes as "virtual civil wars."[29] An entire generation of young people was deprived of formal education. Reflecting on the state of anarchy, MacFarquhar and Schoenhals conclude, "For a decade, the Chinese political system was first turned into chaos and then paralyzed."[30]

Granted, China was at least unified under the CCP when Deng and his reformist team took power. Nonetheless, the state apparatus they inherited hardly fit the description of a strong state. Add the fact that China was poorer than bottom-billion countries like Chad, and the starting point in 1978 bode ill.

Now, fast forward thirty-five years. China has become the world's second largest economy, the world's largest exporter, and America's largest foreign creditor. By 2012 China's GDP per capita had jumped thirty-fold from US$193 to US$6,091, leaving other bottom-billion countries far in the dust (in Malawi, GDP per capita nudged up by only $50 in thirty-two years, a typical case of being stuck).[31] Undergirding these impressive growth statistics is a radical restructuring of the economy. China today boasts legions of private firms, Fortune 500 companies, multinational investors, a booming middle class, and capitalist institutions like securities, e-commerce, and corporate governance standards.[32]

Politically, power remains firmly and solely in the hands of the CCP. Yet the absence of multiparty elections does not mean the absence of political change. Inside the dictatorial regime, the bureaucracy has undergone several makeovers that have altered the role of the government, its delivery of public services, and citizens' daily encounters with the state. In particular, although the reform-era bureaucracy remains notorious for corruption,[33] it is equally famous for being adaptive and entrepreneurial. China ranks among the world's most decentralized administrations. Local governments embrace capitalism, advance policy innovations, and compete to produce economic results. Under Mao, the bureaucracy was ossified and doggedly anticapitalist. But, today, as one Chinese official declared with a dash of irony, "Our nation cares about businesses. In fact, I feel that no capitalist state can match our devotion to the capitalist sector."[34]

For mainstream political economists, China's great transformation—both economic and bureaucratic—is intriguing but also troubling.[35] In *Why Nations Fail*, Acemoglu and Robinson struggle to make sense of China's rise. According to them, growth is preconditioned on the establishment of nonextractive and inclusive institutions, essentially, democratic institutions. But even today China is not a democracy. National elections are barred. Members of the judicial and legislative bodies are handpicked by the ruling party. Extractive practices are still rife in parts of China. During the early phase of reforms, there was no formal protection of private property rights.

In defense, Acemoglu and Robinson surmise that sooner or later, China's hyper-growth will run out of steam.[36] Yet even if growth slows, which is expected for any economy that reaches middle-income status, the burning question remains: how did China come *this* amazingly far? Their reply is that "a critical juncture," namely Mao's death, followed by Deng's efforts to build a reform coalition, turned China around. Furthermore, they claim, growth under extractive institutions was possible because an extremely poor country like China had plenty of "catching up" to do. Finally, they sum up: "Some luck is key, because history always unfolds in a contingent way."[37]

Luck, of course, influences any outcome. But assigning three decades of sustained economic and institutional remaking to luck is hardly satisfying. Moreover, all poor countries have ample room for "catching up," so why didn't they catch up the way China did?

Looking beyond luck and easy explanations, specialists of China have proposed a wealth of theories to account for its astonishing turnaround. All of these theories are valid and valuable, but, as we shall see, they form only parts of the grand picture of China's political-economic transformation that has been missing thus far. Let us first review some pieces of the puzzle.

For a start, some credit China's boom to loosened restrictions on capitalism in an economy that possesses basic growth factors, for example, abundant cheap labor and coastal cities poised to export.[38] There is no doubt that inputs like capital and labor are necessary for growth, but to conclude that such factors on their own will produce an economic miracle is like believing that eggs, sugar, and flour will turn into cake if left overnight in a mixing bowl.[39] Especially in a late-developing, communist context, how basic inputs are mobilized and distributed by the state is critical to the rise and shape of markets.

Shifting from economic to political factors, another set of explanations cites changes in bureaucratic incentives as the key to China's growth spurt. Under Deng's reformist agenda, local leaders who delivered prosperity were promoted,[40] and local governments were allowed to retain a sizable share of revenue earned.[41] These changes in incentives, it is argued, sparked local officials nationwide to pursue growth. These incentives, however, did *not* work equally throughout China. It is well-known that while some localities, concentrated on the coast, grew rich and built competent administrations, others remained poor and predatory.[42] These geographically limited theories not only mask wide variation in local outcomes within China, but more significantly, they underplay the role of regional inequalities in China's national reform success. As my study will show, unequal rates of political-economic coevolution across regions served to accelerate early takeoffs on the coast and late takeoffs among inland locales.

Still a third explanation looks to the incremental quality of China's reforms. As is well-known, Chinese reformers rejected the shock therapy approach of the former Soviet Union and instead chose to modify pre-existing institutions on the margins, such as by creating dual-track pricing and a system of hybrid property rights.[43] Some argue that such "second-best" and "transitional" institutional forms are sufficient to stimulate markets in the beginning.[44] Then, as predicted, once markets mature, early institutions "should eventually be replaced by more conventional, best-practice institutions."[45] My book extends this crucial idea that conventionally good institutions may not be necessary for early growth. But whereas the previous literature stopped at asserting that initial institutions "should" eventually be replaced,[46] this study presents historical evidence to identify *when, why,* and *how* institutional replacement occurs.

Yet a fourth body of literature lists various adaptive actions taken by the CCP-state as a cause of "authoritarian resilience" and reform success.[47] Examples include policy experiments,[48] eliciting and incorporation of social feedback,[49] party co-optation of private entrepreneurs,[50] bureaucratic initiatives in generating revenue,[51] and efforts to study the experiences of other countries.[52] This abundant literature describes various adaptive or entrepreneurial actions,[53] but it does not explain *why* China displays such exceptional inventiveness, especially in contrast to many other stagnant postcommunist systems and failed states. Moreover, China's apparent adaptive capacity cannot explain authoritarian resilience because such adaptability itself needs to be explained.

One notable effort to trace the sources of China's adaptability is Heilmann and Perry's *Mao's Invisible Hand*. They propose that post-Mao leaders inherited "guerrilla" norms of flexibility from the CCP's revolutionary past and applied these norms to market reforms.[54] I completely agree that the Maoist legacy has contributed to the current leadership's cache of rhetoric and tools.[55] Still it doesn't explain why reformers were persistently keen to reconfigure various elements, whether from the past or the present, to formulate new solutions and why many of these solutions successfully propelled change. A revolutionary legacy can lead down many paths. And the particular path China has taken—with distinct steps, achievements, and pains—is not neatly dictated by the past.

In short, existing accounts each highlight a different piece of the grand puzzle: basic growth factors, bureaucratic incentives, incremental reforms, historical legacies, and more. Every piece is essential, yet none can explain how the other pieces interacted and aggregated to remake an entire political economy within the span of a single generation.

Nor can existing theories account for three distinct patterns of China's capitalist revolution. First, the changes are *broad*. China's reforms are famously incremental; yet they culminate in a drastic economic and bureaucratic restructuring nationwide. Second, the methods are *bold*. State actors seemed unfazed by the use of extreme and unorthodox methods to achieve goals. Third, local outcomes are *uneven*. Coastal locales like Shanghai and Shenzhen sped ahead, growing markets and modernizing governance ahead of others. In China, national success is coupled with sharp regional inequalities not seen in East Asia or in other large countries like the United States.

Evidently, numerous factors were simultaneously at play in China's great transformation. A dynamic and comprehensive account, however, will have to go further to consider the underlying conditions that allowed multiple factors to interact and coevolve and to explain the distinctively broad, bold, and uneven patterns of change. To draw generalizable lessons from China's unique experiences, we must also answer this question: What is exceptional and not exceptional about the nature of adaptation in China?

Building this new and integrative account of how China escaped the poverty trap requires that we rethink some of the foundations of traditional social science analyses.

Complexity: An Alternative Paradigm

Development is more than a problem of growing from poor to rich. As the scholarship on poverty traps emphasizes,[56] the poor are simultaneously beset by problems of instability, corruption, patrimonialism, and weak policy enforcement that arise from and deepen poverty. No doubt, wealthy nations have their own share of problems too, such as obesity and aging populations, but these are problems that stem from material abundance. Cast more precisely in game theoretic terms, development is a problem of making the transition from one self-reinforcing equilibrium (poverty traps) to another equilibrium (rich and modern), a process that may be termed the Great Leap.

Existing frameworks and tools in social science are extremely useful for answering certain questions where endogeneity (mutual causation) is irrelevant, but they do not take us very far in understanding an inherently interactive and complex process like political-economic development.

Take for instance a state-of-the-art study by North, Wallis, and Weingast, which tries to explain how underdeveloped societies can make the transition to capitalism and modernity. They argue that this process requires several "doorstep conditions," including rule of law among elites and centralized control of the military. Once such doorstep conditions are in place, they hold, it is possible but not inevitable that "a transition proper ensues."[57] Needless to say, we must first arrive at the doorstep before we can step past any door. Although North, Wallis, and Weingast take us one major step back in the causal chain, their conclusion is still critically missing insights into the "incremental changes" that led to the doorstep or,[58] in Krasner's term, "the empty middle."[59]

Then consider the abundance of quantitative analyses that attempt to prove either the modernization theory or good governance as the primary cause of growth.[60] A debate between Kaufmann, Kraay, and Mastruzzi (creators of the Worldwide Governance Indicators or WGI) and political scientists Kurtz and Schrank is especially instructive.[61] Kaufmann and his colleagues have used the WGI, the most widely accepted measure of governance in the world, in many regression analyses to prove that "governance matters, in the sense that there is a strong causal relationship from good governance to better development outcomes."[62] Kurtz and Schrank refute this claim. Running regressions using the same data but with different empirical specifications, they reach the opposite conclusion: "good governance is in all likelihood a consequence, rather than a cause, of economic growth."[63] So who's right and who's wrong?[64]

Both conclusions are partial. The big, commonsense picture is lost in debates about whether growth or good governance comes first in development, as Przeworski acutely underscores in his sweeping review of the literature. He writes, "In the end, the motor of history is endogeneity. From some initial circumstances and under some invariant conditions, wealth, its distribution, and the institutions that allocate factors and distribute incomes are *mutually interdependent* and *evolve together*."[65]

My book takes the reality of "mutual interdependence" between growth and governance as the starting point and pursues two objectives:

1. Develop an analytic template and data-collection strategy to systematically map the coevolution of states and markets over time and across space.
2. Explore the conditions that allow and foster coevolutionary processes of radical change.

I adopt a paradigm that is different from the one we currently embrace. Our conventional paradigm (meaning the way we view the world) assumes a *complicated*—rather than *complex*—reality. The terms "complicated" and "complex" are often conflated in daily language, but in fact they describe two completely different worlds.[66] In a complicated world, collectives are made up of many separate parts that do not interact and change with one another, of which a toaster is a good example. A toaster is a machine made up of many separate parts. Press a button and it will produce a predictable action: toasted bread pops up. To study complicated worlds, we can parse out the different parts into separate categories of cause and effect and then try to pin down the linear effects of a hypothesized independent variable on a dependent variable. Much of our analyses have proceeded as if social worlds are complicated. In this view of the world, it makes sense to debate whether it is growth that causes good governance or the reverse.

Yet we all know that social worlds are not complicated; they are almost always complex. Complex systems comprise many moving parts that interact with one another and change together, triggering outcomes that cannot be precisely controlled or predicted in advance. Human bodies are an example of complex systems. Political economies, comprising many players, many institutions, and many interactions, are complex.

Traditional assumptions of causality and tools of analysis serve us well when studying complicated worlds, but "using these same tools to understand complex worlds fails," state Miller and Page, two leading theorists of the booming and interdisciplinary field of complex adaptive systems (which I term "complexity"). Why is that? They elaborate with an apt metaphor: "Because it becomes impossible to reduce the system without killing it. The ability to collect and pin to a board all of the insects that live in the garden does little to lend insight into the ecosystem contained therein."[67]

Fortunately, just as we don't always have to kill insects in order to study natural habitats, we don't have to reduce complexity in order to make sense of complex worlds. This book applies some concepts and tools from complexity studies to the political economy of development.[68]

Mapping Coevolution

My first and easier—but not easy—task is to develop a method for *systematically* mapping the coevolution of states and markets. As Pierson observes, "contemporary social scientists typically take a 'snapshot' view of political life."[69] For example, those who follow China may be inclined to draw conclusions from the most current events. The present, however, gives only a temporally limited view. Hence Pierson urges researchers to "shift from snapshots to moving pictures" by "*systematically* situating particular moments (including the present) in a temporal sequence."[70] My work extends this emphasis on time, and I seek to enrich this agenda by adding several new dimensions.

Without going into methodological details that will later be elaborated, here is a sketch of my approach. (1) I select two institutions or domains of activities (e.g., markets and bureaucratic functions, markets and state development strategies). (2) I specify the significant time periods of analysis, since we cannot obviously regress infinitely to the starting point of human development. In the case of China, the year of 1978, the official launch of market reforms, is a clear place to start. (3) I collect data to track the institutional traits of each domain studied. For example, to trace the market conditions of a city, I examine not only quantitative but also qualitative patterns, such as industrial makeup and the focus of economic reforms, at each significant time period.[71] My approach of recording state and market features over time generates a qualitative panel dataset for each case (observations of multiple dimensions repeated over time), rather than cross-sectional snapshots of several cases. (4) My final step is to locate and trace evidence of mutual feedbacks, where relevant, among the domains of concern in each case.

In examining mutual feedbacks, I focus on three signature mechanisms of coevolution:[72]

1. *Variation*: generation of alternatives
2. *Selection*: selection among and assembly of alternatives to form new combinations
3. *Niche creation*: crafting of distinct and valuable roles among heterogeneous units within a system

Each of these mechanisms raises concrete questions that guide our mapping of coevolutionary paths, as follows. *Variation*: Were new options and strategies being produced, and by whom? *Selection*: What shaped the motivation for selection at a given juncture? Was an adaptive choice retained or abandoned for a new selection, and why? *Niche creation*: Was a unit in question trying to differentiate from other members of the system or blindly replicating the strategies of others? Are their roles competitive or complementary? By attending to these signature mechanisms, we have a grounded basis for examining whether—and *exactly how*—states and markets coevolve.

One key distinction between my approach and the seminal work of Thelen, Mahoney, and other historical institutionalists on "institutional evolution" and "gradual institutional change" is my focus on mapping sequences of mutual adaptations.[73] I start with a precise understanding of evolution as an *adaptive* process that occurs through the mechanisms outlined above. As Holland, another leading complexity theorist, defines, adaptation is the process by which an agent "fits itself to its environment," including other agents.[74] A process of gradual change may *not* involve adaptation. For example, aging occurs gradually, but it is not the result of our adaptive responses to the environment. Nor are evolutionary processes always slow-moving;[75] microcosms can adapt and evolve within minutes. My analysis examines the processes of mutual adaptation—coevolution—among two or more populations or institutional domains in political economies, a process that is *not* synonymous with gradual or slow changes.

My empirical approach generates multiple snapshots of reciprocal feedbacks between states and markets. When these snapshots are strung in sequence, it reveals a causal logic that integrates and yet departs sharply from the conclusions of conventional theories. To get a feel for what I mean, consider five snapshots taken from my historical study of one coastal county in China,[76] reviewed in reverse order from its most current status.

Snapshot 1: Around 2002, the county government planned the construction of a central business district (CBD) and relocated businesses into state-designated zones. This forceful effort paved the way for an unprecedented economic boom.

For proponents of the developmental state, this snapshot illustrates the indispensable role of strong and autonomous states in accelerating growth among late-developing economies.[77]

Snapshot 2: During the late 1990s, as local industries flourished and the county became congested and chaotic, there was an increasing demand for urban zoning.

Now we learn that county officials initiated an aggressive zoning program in response to an earlier economic contingency and bottom-up demand for state interventions to address the problem, not because autonomous state planners came up with the initiative on their own.[78]

Snapshot 3: Between 1993 and 1995, collectively owned enterprises were privatized en masse. The state, at that time, limited its role to facilitating the creation of private property rights. It did not pick winners (favor some industries over others) nor had it conceived the idea of constructing a CBD.

This evidence would cheer the proponents of good governance, who advocate limited government and private property rights protection.[79] Looking at this snapshot in isolation, we would mistakenly conclude that the developmental state school was proven wrong.

Snapshot 4: Prior to 1993, the county achieved an initial growth spurt, but the expansion of existing collective enterprises were constrained by vestiges of state control and the lack of clear private property rights.

Again, proponents of good governance would cheer. Even prior to privatization, though, industrial production had already grown at a phenomenal rate (thirty-three-fold since 1978!), which disproves their assumption that private property rights are necessary for growth.

Snapshot 5: From 1978 onward, the county promoted the establishment of collectively owned township and village enterprises (TVEs), which sparked rural industrialization and early growth.

This snapshot illustrates that early growth can occur in the absence of private property rights and that "small initial changes can have a large impact."[80] With the benefit of hindsight, however, we know that such "small initial changes" were soon replaced by new institutions and development strategies.

So, depending on when (which year) and where (coastal or inland) we look in China, there is evidence for a whole variety of competing explanations for successful reforms: developmental vs. minimalist states, private vs. collective property rights, orthodox vs. unorthodox institutions.

What happens if we string the five snapshots in sequence, starting from 1978? Generically expressed, we obtain this causal sequence of *mutual feedbacks*: Pre-existing "weak" institutions (e.g., communes rather than private individuals and centralized states as political units)[81] → creatively adapted to build markets (e.g., creation of hybrid enterprises based on collective property rights) → market emerges → generates new pressures and resources for institutional change → market consolidates → generates new pressures and resources for institutional change again → market takes off and matures.[82]

Compressing the causal chain above, we arrive at a succinct three-step formula:

> harness weak institutions to build markets → emerging markets stimulate strong institutions → strong institutions preserve markets.

Although the particulars vary wildly from case to case, this is the long-term pattern of political-economic coevolution that I find at the national and sub-national levels in China. And as I will explore in the concluding chapter, such a pattern also emerges in the expansion of trade in late medieval Europe, the revolution of public finance in the antebellum United States, and the flourishing of Nollywood in contemporary Nigeria. To be clear, the causal pattern that emerges from my analyses does not suggest a teleological process that converges at the same end point. As is already well-known, even among advanced economies, good governance and strong institutions do not function and look the same.[83]

Rather, the value of extracting a coevolutionary causal chain lies in making clear what the study of development has critically missed. The third step of "strong institutions preserve markets" has been firmly established by the work of North,[84] North and Weingast,[85] Weingast,[86] and Acemoglu and Robinson,[87] among other leading political economists. The second step of "markets stimulate strong institutions" constitutes the domain of modernization theory.[88]

By comparison, with few exceptions,[89] we know woefully little about the *first* step of the causal chain: build markets *with* weak institutions. Even less is known about how these three essential steps connect in sequence. These are the gaps I seek to fill through a coevolutionary approach to development.

Fostering Adaptation

Mapping the coevolution of states and markets is the easier part of the book. Addressing the harder question comes next: What are the conditions that enable a continuously adaptive process of coevolution? Do these conditions result from exogenous forces or can they be created? In his thought-provoking book

Understanding the Process of Economic Change, Douglass North raises a similar question: "It is not sufficient to describe societal change; rather we must attempt to find the underlying forces shaping the process of change."[90] He dubs these underlying forces "adaptive efficiency." In his words, "Put simply the richer the artifactual structure the more likely are we to confront novel problems successfully. That is what is meant by adaptive efficiency; creating the necessary artifactual structure is an essential goal of public policy."[91]

What does this "necessary artifactual structure" look like? And how can we go about creating it? North proposes a causal link between individual beliefs at the cognitive level and adaptive efficiency at the societal level, but he does not indicate how we can bridge the overwhelming gap between the extremely micro and the extremely macro levels. Nevertheless, North's probing ruminations clearly indicate that the quest for understanding the underlying sources of adaptive efficiency is not wishful thinking. It marks the next frontier of development theories and practices, waiting to be explored.

To embark on a new intellectual journey to explore the creation of adaptive efficiency, we must find a different guide. Axelrod and Cohen's *Harnessing Complexity* provides an especially useful and concrete framework. Two founding thinkers of complexity, Axelrod and Cohen begin with the observation that adaptation is "both promising and problematic."[92] Not everyone would immediately agree with this observation. Normally we are inclined to think about adaptation itself as the solution to all problems. Thus popular literature readily invokes buzzwords from complexity and adaptation to accessorize slogans: "Embrace experimentation! Muddle through purposively! Promote innovation! Celebrate diverse solutions! And above all, don't fear change!"

Although adaptation is universally desirable, people often fail to adapt, and even if they try they may still fail. Experimentation and muddling through may not produce useful solutions or indeed any solution. Bottom-up participation may degenerate into shouting matches and gridlock, as is sometimes seen in democratic settings. And if promoting innovation were easy, then we would all have done it long ago, and all our problems would have been magically solved. Obviously it is easier said than done to adapt and to adapt effectively.

What precisely are some obstacles against effective adaptation? And what can we do about them? Drawing on the complexity paradigm, this book highlights three universal problems of adaptation, grouped into the themes of variation, selection, and niche creation. Interpreted in the context of reform China, these problems manifest as follows.

Variation: Central reformers want local agents to flexibly implement central mandates according to local conditions. But too much leeway may generate chaos. So one enduring problem in China's policy making and implementation is how to strike a balance between flexibility and conformity, variety and uniformity.

Selection: How agents adapt to particular situations is shaped by their criteria of success. In the corporate sector, success is defined by financial performance, so corporate agents adapt to make profits. Governments, on the other hand, typically have to cater to multiple and even conflicting goals and demands.[93] So how does the CCP state clearly define and reward success in the bureaucracy?

Niche creation: Diversity provides raw material for innovation and allows for niche creation.[94] In China, however, the sheer diversity of conditions across regions also leads to huge disparities that may impede national economic progress and foment political discontent. This generates a third problem of how regional diversity may be turned from a liability into a collective advantage.

China is not exceptional in the adaptive problems it faced; rather it is unique in the way it tackled these problems. Each of the remaining chapters in the book will be devoted to examining how the Chinese state, national and local, responded to the three adaptive problems named above.

Through this analysis, we will arrive at a dynamic picture of how China escaped the poverty trap. We will also understand why its transformative process has displayed three distinct patterns: systemic changes despite incremental reforms (broad), unusually entrepreneurial but also corruption-prone bureaucrats (bold), and wide regional disparities coexisting with national prosperity (uneven).

The Argument in Brief

Authors are often asked to give a one-line summary of their argument. Here is mine: Poor and weak countries can escape the poverty trap by first building markets with weak institutions and, more fundamentally, by crafting environments that facilitate improvisation among the relevant players.

It is tempting to search for a single "model"—a package of particular institutions and policies—that can be replicated across all contexts and believed to produce equal success. If such a model were to exist, it would be delightfully convenient. But this is a search for a mirage. In fact, whether in the capitalist-democratic West, the East Asian developmental states, or China at different periods of reform, no particular solution is universally effective or ideal. Particular solutions work only when they *fit* the needs and resources of particular contexts and the success criteria of the players involved.

Instead of aspiring to copy the exact actions taken by others, what is fundamentally needed for development are conditions that spur a productive and sustained search for solutions that fit different and evolving environments. Stated in North's terms, such conditions are "the necessary artifactual structure" that enables economic and political agents to "confront novel problems successfully."[95] And as Axelrod and Cohen emphasize, this process of confronting novel problems may produce endless possible solutions, "even without knowing in advance just what will change, or just what will be learned."[96]

China escaped the poverty trap by constructing a set of underlying conditions that fostered an adaptive, bottom-up search *within* the state for localized solutions. As China is a late-developing, single-party authoritarian regime, the state plays an oversized role in shaping adaptive processes and outcomes. Condensing various elements of its adaptive approach into a pithy maxim, I call it *directed improvisation*. Central reformers direct; local state agents improvise. The center does not direct by precisely dictating what local agents must do. Instead, it directs by tackling the problems of adaptation earlier outlined: authorizing yet delimiting the boundaries of localization (variation), clearly defining and rewarding bureaucratic success (selection), and encouraging mutual exchanges between highly unequal regions (niche creation). Within these centrally drawn parameters, local authorities improvise a variety of solutions to locally specific and ever-changing problems. It is this paradoxical mixture of top-down direction and bottom-up improvisation that lays the foundation for coevolutionary processes of radical change.

In other words, generalizable from China's market reforms are insights into the process of building markets with weak institutions and the strategies of directing improvisation, not the particular solutions that were improvised to solve particular problems at various times and places. Furthermore, such lessons need not apply only narrowly to other countries. Numerous organizations and groups share similar challenges of improvising with existing resources and making adaptation work.[97]

This book will focus on the processes of state-and-market coevolution and the conditions that enabled adaptive efficiency in the first thirty-five years of reform, starting from 1978. By the time the new leadership under Xi Jinping took office in 2013, China had ascended to middle-income status. Domestically and internationally, China also inhabits a different political environment. By exploring the adaptive processes that have taken China this far, we can better understand the origins of the particular challenges it faces today and assess whether its leadership can continue to tackle them in years to come.

Road Map

Here's how the rest of the book proceeds. Part 1 lays out the building blocks of my analysis in two chapters. Chapter 1, "Mapping Coevolution," introduces and previews my approach to mapping coevolutionary paths of development. In the style of a mini–analytic narrative, this chapter zooms in on the mutual emergence of industrial markets and professional bureaucratic traits in a modeled Chinese locality. As this chapter shows, a coevolutionary approach reaches sharply different conclusions about the causal relationship between growth and governance compared to linear and path-dependent theories.

A preview of *how* states and markets coevolve provokes the deeper question of *why* such processes could occur the way they did in China. Chapter 2, "Directed Improvisation," locates the answer in the way Chinese reformers tackled three key obstacles to effective adaptation, following the themes of variation, selection, and niche creation. The remaining chapters flesh out each of the three themes outlined in chapter 2.

Part 2 explores the role of central authorities in setting directions. Chapter 3, "Balancing Variety and Uniformity," investigates how the leadership empowered local authorities to boldly pursue change and flexibly tailor reforms to local conditions, while at the same time delimiting the boundaries of localized policy implementation. It locates the answers in the design of national reform packages and the articulation of central directives.

Chapter 4, "Franchising the Bureaucracy," examines how market reformers tackled the problems of weak incentives and muddled goals common to public organizations. Their solution, I show, is to run the bureaucracy like a franchised corporation, where local leaders are evaluated like CEOs and regular cadres (employees of the public administration) are paid like corporate employees. In combination, chapters 3 and 4 illuminate the strategies for influencing the amount of local variability and the selection criteria of bureaucratic agents.

Part 3 shifts to the improvising role of local governments. Working as a pair, chapters 5 and 6 chronicle the coevolutionary paths of three locales that are each defined by different geographic conditions and starting points. Chapter 5, "From Building to Preserving Markets," tells the life story of a city in Fujian province with a mixture of growth advantages and constraints. Applying the analytic template introduced in chapter 1, this chapter maps the reciprocal changes among markets, property rights, and developmental strategies from the 1980s to 2014. It documents the unfolding of a three-part causal sequence in thick details: harness weak institutions to build markets → emerging markets stimulate strong institutions → strong institutions preserve markets.

Chapter 6, "Connecting First Movers and Laggards," compares the coevolutionary paths of two unequally endowed locales: a coastal county in Zhejiang (a first mover) and a landlocked county in Hubei (a laggard). Expectedly, this analysis finds divergent speeds and outcomes of political-economic coevolution between the two cases. Unexpectedly, however, it also uncovers the different ways that first movers and laggards contributed to each other's economic takeoff at early and late periods of reform. Finally, I bring the central state back into the picture again, this time focusing on its role in regional niche formation and the evolution of its policies toward regional development.

The concluding chapter addresses the comparative question: Are coevolutionary processes of development unique to China? Extending my empirical approach, I retell accounts from late medieval Europe, America following independence, and Nigeria since the early 1990s from a coevolutionary perspective. These snippets provide further evidence that development *is* a coevolutionary process, not only in contemporary China but also in other national and temporal settings. Drawing on the cases analyzed, I summarize six lessons for constructing an adaptive environment. I also discuss some core obstacles that China must overcome in order to stay adaptive in the twenty-first century.

Through this book, I hope to show that we can study political economies as complex systems in coherent and constructive ways. Confronting the basic question of how development *actually* happens compels us to revise the theories we build, the analytic methods we use, and the actions we take to improve human lives.

Part 1

FRAMEWORK AND BUILDING BLOCKS

1

MAPPING COEVOLUTION

We do not need to be complex, however, just for the sake of being complex, but we do need to get over our simplicity hang-ups. Obviously, our theories will always be simpler than the worlds we study, or we are trying to reproduce these worlds rather than a theory of these worlds.

—Elinor Ostrom and Xavier Basurto, "Crafting Analytical Tools to Study Institutional Change"

My interviews with local bureaucrats in China deliberately included a question that has long been debated in academic circles: In your locality, do you think it was effective governance that led to growth or growth that enabled the government to improve? The bureaucrats were consistently astonished by the naiveté of this question. To them, the answer is obvious: causation runs both ways. One regular cadre in a city-level agency, who had no scholarly training whatsoever, gave a memorably insightful reply:[1]

> The economy and the bureaucracy interact and change together. If the economy is poor, then, inevitably, it will be difficult to improve governance. . . . In reality, we do what we must and then adjust as we go along. . . . There must be a process. It's impossible for a government to reform overnight.

More bluntly, another bureaucrat griped that the question posed was flawed. In his words, "To say that we should grow the economy and then improve the business environment or vice versa are both misguided. Obviously, we must pursue both at the same time, like the pursuit of material and spiritual development."[2]

These replies suggest that development as a coevolutionary process is a plain reality to many practitioners and probably lay observers too. It is no wonder that they dismissed the question as academic. I concurred heartily with their practical insights and then pressed further: "Could you tell me, from the beginning, how did this process of interaction unfold? How did growth affect the bureaucracy, and in turn, how did bureaucratic reforms affect the economy?" This time, even seasoned bureaucrats were stumped. "It's too complicated!" was the usual, exasperated response. Instinctively, the practitioners knew that the process of development is interactive and coevolutionary, but laying out and making sense of this entire process step-by-step is anything but easy.

The purpose of this chapter is twofold. First, I preview the steps I will take throughout this book to map coevolutionary processes of development. In order to chronicle *exactly* how states and markets coevolve, we must first spell out the steps of analyses. Second, I highlight new and important insights we can learn from a coevolutionary perspective that are obscured in standard linear and path-dependent accounts. At the outset, let me underscore three key insights:

1. Conventionally good institutions like formal property rights and professional bureaucracies are institutions that *preserve* markets after markets have already been built. *Building* markets, however, calls for drastically different institutions.
2. Market-building institutions typically look "wrong," that is, inconsistent with best practices, seemingly backward, and prone to corruption. Their developmental potential or role is therefore easily missed or even dismissed.
3. Institutions, once established, do not always self-reinforce. If initial institutions succeed to spur markets, increased wealth changes preferences and resources, which in turn motivate further institutional adaptation.

Before we survey the coevolution of states and markets across thirty years of reform and in thick contextual details, it helps to preview this complex process in a small and stylized setting. Following the style of analytic narratives,[3] I will apply my empirical approach to map the steps of a particular case of coevolution—the mutual emergence of industrial markets and professional bureaucracies—in a modeled local polity that I nickname Glorious County (in salutation to Deng's famous maxim "to get rich is glorious!"). Given the deliberately narrow scope of my analysis in this chapter, I call this a mini–analytic narrative. From this exercise, we'll extract general patterns of state-and-economic coevolution that will play out on a much larger scale in the remainder of the book.

Four Steps of Mapping Coevolution

The words "evolve" and "coevolve" are frequently invoked in social science analyses.[4] Coevolutionary narratives, however, are more than just statements that things evolved together or that incremental change occurred. These are intuitive statements that any lay observer can make, as my interviews with the local bureaucrats suggest. Coevolutionary narratives with teeth strive to reveal mutual causal influences between two (or more) domains of interest: for example, how a particular bureaucratic adaptation affects the economy, how subsequent economic changes feed back to the bureaucracy, so on and on, in a zigzag causal chain.[5] In particular, a useful coevolutionary account should pinpoint why particular institutions or strategies were selected at given junctures and whether or not these selections continued to fit the environment at later periods.

For the benefit of a general readership, I keep my methodological discussion in this chapter brief. For an elaboration, appendix A details my procedures of data collection, highlighting the design of fieldwork and interview questions to document changes across multiple institutional domains and over time.

The logic of coevolutionary analysis is straightforward: array the traits of selected domains over multiple time periods and then examine the influence of change in one domain on change in the other domain at each juncture. More concretely, I follow four basic steps:

1. Identify two (or more) domains of significance.
2. Identify significant time periods of analysis.
3. Identify dominant traits of each domain in the significant periods.
4. Identify the mechanisms of mutual influence at significant junctures.

While the logic of analysis is straightforward, the hard work lies in implementing these steps and collecting data to map coevolutionary paths. For a start, measuring qualitative changes across institutional domains, across regions, and over time is a formidable task in any national context, not to mention in developing and authoritarian countries, where there are few ready-made and precise datasets to download. In my study of China, nearly all the data had to be collected from scratch through extensive fieldwork and interviews, which generated more than a thousand pages of transcripts in Chinese (for more details, see appendix B). Using this cache of historical-qualitative data, I propose causal links on the grounds of plausibility. Precise testing of each of these numerous links is beyond the scope of this book, but the paths I sketch here lay the necessary groundwork for future ambitious efforts at collecting fine-grained panel datasets that may allow us to test more precisely *each* proposed link in *each* causal chain.

Any historical study in search of long-term interactive patterns will run into challenges of data collection. Such challenges are magnified when attempting to trace *multistep* and *multidirectional*—rather than linear—paths of change. Nevertheless, these obstacles should not stop us from reaching for a dynamic theory of development. My efforts at systematically mapping the coevolution of states and markets using the qualitative data I collected, I hope, suffices for readers as an essential and worthwhile step toward revisiting the fundamental question of how development *actually* happens.

The Norm: Good Bureaucracies and State-Led Growth

Studying the coevolution of states and markets is an exceedingly complex task. Both states and markets are large cluster domains, each containing multiple attributes. To preview a coevolutionary approach to the study of development, it makes sense to zoom in on one strand of each cluster. On the state cluster, I prioritize the bureaucracy. More specifically, I will focus on the emergence of professional bureaucracies organized along Weberian precepts or popularly regarded as "good" bureaucracies. Then, with respect to the economy, I will focus on the industrial sector, setting aside other higher-order spheres such as financial markets and corporate governance.

Especially in the study of late-developing economies, there is good reason to focus on good bureaucracies and industrial growth. This is because in poor and rural economies, the conversion of agriculture to industry is a (if not the) principal source of growth. And among late developers, interventionist state policies are crucial for accelerating the process of industrial catch-up, as persuasively argued by the developmental state school.[6] But in order for state intervention to successfully foster markets rather than breed corruption, proponents of developmental states stress that the right kind of bureaucracy must first be established.[7]

So what is the right bureaucracy for state-led development? The answers can be traced a century back to Weber's monumental essays, in which he spells out the characteristics of legal-rational, professional bureaucracies that depart fundamentally from—and more importantly are superior to—bureaucracies that prevailed in premodern times.

Among the list of attributes Weber identifies, two stand out.[8] First, professional bureaucracies perform specialized functions through technically qualified personnel. While nonspecialization was the norm in premodern and patrimonial settings,[9] modern corporations and governments all embrace functional specialization as a norm. Thus, Herbert Simon states as a matter of fact, "The administrative organization is characterized by specialization—particular tasks are delegated to particular parts of the organization."[10] Indeed, in public administrations across countries—including in China—every office is formally assigned a specialized function with a delineated scope of expertise and responsibilities (for example, the Commerce Bureau regulates commercial affairs, the Education Bureau administers education services, the Environment Protection Office enforces environmental regulations, and so forth). That specialization is superior to nonspecialization seems uncontroversial. Offices should be more efficient if they specialize in well-defined tasks than if they juggle multiple, overlapping responsibilities. Weber's observations are aligned with Adam Smith's emphasis on efficiency gains from the "division of labor" in capitalist economies.[11]

Second, inseparable from specialized functions is impersonality. Impersonality refers to the conduct of duties and exchanges with parties with whom we are not personally acquainted or related. When we say "keep it professional" in modern parlance, we mean such norms as not recruiting family members into workplaces and not discussing private affairs while at work.[12] For public agents, impersonality is associated with integrity. Public agents are expected to conduct their work on the basis of formal rules that are applied equally to everyone rather than in favor of particular individuals. Impersonality is a distinctively *modern* concept, premised on the meaningful separation of public and private spheres, which arises in communities large enough that people live among strangers.[13] From this modern perspective, we have come to mildly interpret the lack of separation between the two spheres as unprofessional, or worse as corrupt.

The Weberian traits of specialization and impersonality are taken-for-granted norms in Western public administration. Among East Asian developmental states, such characteristics are seen as indispensable for state effectiveness.[14] Chalmers Johnson's classic study of the developmental state in Japan features MITI (the Ministry of Trade and Industry) as the star. Staffed by top recruits from Japan's elite universities, MITI is a central ministry vested with sole authority to craft and execute national industrial policy. As Johnson observes, "[the] concentration of [vital powers] in [this] one ministry and the ministry's broad jurisdiction" accounted for its remarkable efficacy.[15] In another seminal study, Evans adds a social dimension to the character of East Asia's developmental bureaucracies, arguing that these agencies had combined Weberian coherence and discipline with collaborative state-business relationships, aptly captured in the label "embedded autonomy." Through this hybrid, Evans proposes, technocratic qualities may shield bureaucracies from corruption and direct capture by interest groups.[16]

Among the many tasks of growth promotion, recruiting foreign investment stands out as a top priority that must be delegated only to the most competent agents. In East Asia, the central assignment of investment promotion is assigned to specialized, elite agencies that are professionally equipped to woo investors as well as to coordinate investment policies for the entire economy. In Singapore, this specialized investment agency is the EDB (Economic Development Board), and in South Korea, the equivalent body is the KOTRA (Korea Trade-Investment Promotion Agency). At a speech delivered in Timor-Leste, Kishore Mahbubani, one of Singapore's leading diplomats, urged the officials of this newly independent state to emulate the efficacy of the EDB. In his words, "The EDB has been instrumental in Singapore's success by bringing in FDI [foreign direct investment]. . . . This is something which Timor-Leste can do as well. By setting up a one-stop specialized agency that focuses on foreign direct investment, Timor-Leste will also signal to the rest of the world that it means business when it comes to attracting FDI."[17]

Weberian bureaucracies like the EDB are clearly desirable, but how are they achieved? All developing countries want to have good bureaucracies, yet many fail to create them. Some observers credit the "political will" of strong leaders in East Asia,[18] such as Singapore's late prime minister Lee Kuan Yew, who forcefully stamped out corruption and installed a highly efficient civil service. Others, on the other hand, trace East Asia's remarkable bureaucratic capacity to the region's colonial legacies.[19] Indeed, Mr. Lee himself conceded that the British had left Singapore with "an administration that worked."[20] Despite disagreements about the origins of effective bureaucracy in East Asia, one consensus is clear: state agencies organized along Weberian precepts are universally ideal and a prerequisite for state-led economic success.

China's Anomaly: "Wrong" Bureaucracies and State-Led Growth

After reviewing the conventional wisdom, the surprise comes when we shift from East Asia to China. Whereas the states of East Asia are small and centralized, China is big, multileveled, and highly decentralized. In this context of extensive decentralization, developmental action in China is diffused across subnational bureaucracies, extending from the province down to the lowest level of village, rather than concentrated in a handful of powerful central ministries. Similar to their counterparts at the national level in East Asia, local leaders and even regular cadres in China are known to aggressively promote economic growth and industries in their locales. Their probusiness measures include drawing macroeconomic plans, constructing infrastructure, providing loans and subsidies to domestic firms, and even organizing promotional events for local industries. As Oi concludes, China showcases "a qualitatively new variety of developmental state,"[21] with "*local* governments in the lead role."[22]

Given their developmental qualities, are China's local states structured like the national states of East Asia, with professionals in economic agencies performing specialized roles? Although there are numerous references to the developmental behavior of China's local states,[23] surprisingly little is known about precisely which agencies conduct investment promotion and how targets and credit are allocated among them. If we read formal organizational charts, it appears that the structure of China's local states is similar to East Asia's national developmental states. Every locality (from province to county) features an Investment Bureau, whose nominal task is to attract investors and to craft investment policies. Based on the experience of East Asia, one expects China's local investment bureaus to be like Singapore's EDB or South Korea's KOTRA.

But in fact they are not.

Through my fieldwork, I uncovered the fact that local investment bureaus in China do not (or did not, depending on location) actually bear sole responsibility for investment work. Instead, *all* party and state offices, regardless of nominally assigned functions, are required and rewarded for participating in courting investors. Each agency has to perform its formal functions (e.g., environmental protection, law enforcement, personnel management), but at the same time they are all enlisted to prospect for investors for their home states. In some places, statewide efforts to woo investments is (or was) dubbed "the beehive campaign,"[24] and in others the slogan is (or was) "let all members join in courting investments."[25] In local China, the crucial developmental work of investment promotion is (or was) conducted by bureaucracies of all stripes; surprisingly, it is *not specialized.*

That's not all. Local governments make (or made) extensive use of the personal connections of public agents to attract investors. Instead of "keeping it professional," which we think should be the proper way to conduct official duties, the Chinese method of investment promotion fuses private and public spheres; it is deliberately *not impersonal.*

The Anomaly Up Close: Upstart County

To view the anomaly of en masse, personalized investment promotion in action, let me detail my findings from Upstart County of Jiangxi Province.[26] Among the five formal levels of government, the county is especially important. Not only do counties account for half of China's gross domestic production,[27] they also supply essential public services like education, health, and urban infrastructure.[28] Jiangxi is nestled between the coastal provinces of Fujian and Zhejiang and the central provinces of Hubei and Hunan. In terms of GDP per capita, Jiangxi ranks among the poorest provinces.[29] Hence the situation in Jiangxi is roughly representative of that in China's poorer inland regions.

The basic bureaucratic structure of local governments is nearly identical throughout China. Ministries at the central level are replicated at each administrative level and across all locales. The party and the state form two parallel hierarchies. In terms of formally assigned functions, party organs are generally responsible for political affairs (e.g., cadre appointments and propaganda), whereas state organs are in charge of regulation, economic management, and delivery of public services. In contrast to the formal separation of political party and state administration in democracies like the United States, party and state are deliberately fused in China's political system.

So in Upstart County, which organizations in the bureaucracy are in charge of investment promotion? First of all, consistent with previous studies,[30] my research finds that investment promotion targets are assigned to all townships and subdistricts within the county, which is the next lower level of administration.[31] This is not surprising as townships and subdistricts are levels of government and are therefore supposed to serve a variety of functions within their jurisdictions, including economic promotion. Instead, what I found surprising is that in addition to townships and subdistricts, virtually all agencies within the county party-state are *also* assigned targets to bring investors into the locale each year. To see the anomaly of this arrangement up close, see the translation of an official document in Table 1.1, issued in 2013 by the county Party Committee and State Secretariat, which lists the assignment of investment targets.

The list makes apparent that the Investment Bureau is only one among many agencies assigned the role of pursuing investors. Moreover, the assignment of investment promotion is not only limited to agencies with economic functions. Even agencies that obviously should not have economic functions are tasked to court investors, including the county Family Planning Bureau (in charge of enforcing birth policies), Audit Bureau (which audits the accounts of other departments), Department of Discipline (responsible for investigating corruption), and Department of Organization (which makes cadre appointment decisions). In addition to the agencies on the list, remaining county offices are "encouraged to court investors." These include party-led social organizations, such as the Communist Youth League, Women's Federation, Association for Culture, and even Association for the Handicapped. The names of these organizations alone clearly indicate that they should have no business in prospecting for investors!

Along with the assignment of targets, departments that meet and exceed targets are awarded bonuses and those that fail are penalized. As an additional monetary incentive, Upstart County devised a deposit scheme, requiring all agencies to submit a deposit of 50,000 yuan each year to the county treasury. Organizations that fulfill their targets receive a refund of the deposit in the form of extra budget allocations for administrative spending. Those that fail surrender their deposit to the county as a penalty. Compared to the norms of public administration, this arrangement is peculiar because we expect public agencies to receive funding from the county based on reported budgetary needs,[32] not on the amount of investments they attract. Submitting a deposit to the county and then receiving a refund based on performance makes these public agencies seem more like private contractors than bureaucratic subordinates.[33]

Similar to other localities I have studied, the agencies of Upstart County rely primarily on the personal connections of bureau chiefs and staff members to

TABLE 1.1 Document on investment targets assigned to county agencies, Upstart County, Jiangxi Province, 2013

AGENCY	INVESTMENT TARGET (10,000 YUAN)
Office of the Party Committee	1,000
Office of the People's Congress	1,000
Office of the County Government	1,000
Office of the People's Consultative Conference	1,000
Department of Discipline	1,000
Department of Organization	1,000
Department of Publicity	1,000
Department of Strategy	1,000
Department of Agriculture and Industry	1,000
Committee of the Industrial Parks	5,000
Committee of Urban Management	1,000
Office of Development	1,000
Technology Bureau	1,000
Environmental Protection Bureau	1,000
Private Enterprises Bureau	1,000
County Labor Union	1,000
Tourism Bureau	1,000
Agriculture Bureau	1,000
Culture and Education Bureau	5,000
Personnel and Labor Bureau	5,000
Health Bureau	5,000
Finance Bureau	5,000
Investment Bureau	5,000
Telecommunication Bureau	5,000
Family Planning Bureau	5,000
Reform and Development Bureau	5,000
Civil Affairs Bureau	5,000
Audit Bureau	5,000
Construction Bureau	5,000
Transportation Bureau	5,000
Forestry Bureau	5,000
Water Management Bureau	5,000
Land Bureau	5,000
Grain Bureau	5,000
Center for the Development of Services Sectors	5,000
Price Bureau	5,000

draw investors.[34] Local cadres tap connections with "friends, former classmates, and relatives," which locals describe as a way of "fully exploiting productive networks."[35] An officer at the Personnel Management Bureau of another county related, "Basically we rely on personal networks to attract investors. Whenever we meet our relatives and friends, we urge, hey, come to my county!"[36] Because Upstart County has a large outflow of migrants who left the county in search for work on the coast, some of whom succeeded as entrepreneurs, these natives form a promising source of investors.[37] Elsewhere, local officers called upon friends from other cities and overseas relatives in Taiwan and Hong Kong.[38]

One might ask how credit is assigned if so many agencies are enlisted to court investors en masse. The answer lies in the highly personalized nature of investment courtship: investors can clearly identify specific individuals as their intermediaries.[39] As one officer stated, "Our businesses are recruited by particular officials through affective relationships."[40] That is why in addition to awarding bonuses to departments, Upstart County also rolled out a bonus scheme for individual bureaucrats. Entitled "bonuses for intermediaries" (i.e., brokers), the policy is spelled out in fine detail in an internally circulated document. The program is divided by tier, and at the bottom of the bonus scheme are regular projects below a stipulated value, which entitles brokers up to 300,000 yuan (US$50,000) in bonuses.[41] For mega-size projects, brokers may receive up to 5 percent of the value of realized investments,[42] which could amount to a colossal sum. The potential size of these performance-based commissions completely overshadows the official wages of civil servants, usually less than two thousand yuan per month (more in chapter 4).

Such close personal ties between investors and bureaucrats, paired with a commission-based compensation system, can naturally breed special privileges and corruption. One official from Shanghai subtly acknowledged:[43]

> Recruiting investors requires good services but also affective relationships. The latter part operates within a black box, containing hidden promises of exchange between the investors and the recruiters. This process breeds corruption and tempts individuals to commit crimes.

Another economic bureaucrat from Upstart County elaborated more bluntly:[44]

> Officials and bosses are closely embedded with each other, and gradually this relationship will produce plenty of grease. For example, if an official pays the boss a visit, surely the boss would have to show some appreciation. At the same time, if the boss comes to invest in the official's locale, the official will lean toward this boss due to personal affective ties. It will be easier to negotiate preferential policies.

Even in the absence of corruption, agencies confront a fundamental conflict of interest between recruiting investors and enforcing regulatory rules. Another officer said, "The environmental protection bureau is supposed to be a regulator. But if you assign targets of investment promotion to this agency, then it will easily let enterprises pass and underestimate the environment costs of their projects."[45] Moreover, when all agencies are recruited to prospect for investors, it is nearly impossible to align individual actions with a collective development plan. Hence the quality of investments attracted is likely to be spotty.

The nonspecialized and personalized nature of investment promotion stands in sharp contrast to the professional economic agencies of developmental states in East Asia. Although elite bureaucrats in East Asia were criticized for snuggling too close to businesses,[46] those investors were generally not family members or personal friends of state bureaucrats. Nor were bureaucrats in EDB (Singapore) or KOTRA (South Korea) remunerated by commissions pegged to investment value. By contrast, in Upstart County, personal networks and bureaucratic functions are enmeshed.[47] Public agents deploy personal contacts and resources to perform official duties. And in doing so, they may obtain large bonuses and further solidify their individual connections with capitalist bosses.

The Puzzle Deepens: Upstart County vs. Other Counties

Just as you think the situation in Upstart County is odd, perhaps even disturbing, the surprise deepens. Comparing different localities, Upstart appears similar to some places yet different from others. Below are excerpts from two interviews conducted in 2012, the first in Fujian (a coastal province) and the second in Hubei (an inland province). Both quotes describe the *current* method of investment promotion in their locale.

> *Quote from Fujian (coastal) province*: We still have to promote investments, except, now, it is a routine. . . . Compared to ten years ago, we are more institutionalized, regularized. Investment promotion is a regular task, not a county-wide campaign like before. This is a change that happens as the economy grows. In the early stages, we went all out, en masse to pull in investments. Subsequently, our work became regularized, and the focus is now to guide and regulate investments.[48]

> *Quote from Hubei (inland) province*: Assigning investment tasks to all the departments can incentivize everyone to act together, fully utilizing everyone's networks and resources. We are now in the midst of a county-wide campaign to promote investment. Our county is a small

place, with no unique advantage in location or transportation. How can we develop economically if we don't pursue investments en masse? Anyway, the whole country is doing this.[49]

Comparing the two quotes, it appears that the two locations *lie on different points of a shared timeline*. The locality in Fujian has already transitioned from an earlier mode of nonspecialized, personalized investment promotion to "routine" work performed by the Investment Office, whose "focus is now to guide and regulate investments." Meanwhile, the locality in Hubei is still "in the midst of a county-wide campaign." The status quo in the second location mirrors what we currently find in Upstart County, which is also an inland county. The official in Hubei even *incorrectly* assumed that "the whole country is doing this" (en masse investment promotion). In fact, unbeknownst to him, parts of the country on the coast were *already finished* "doing this."

Findings from my fieldwork in China reveal a bureaucratic structure that is starkly inconsistent with Weberian norms of professionalism, of which specialization (each office is dedicated to an assigned function) and impartiality (separation of personal interests from official duties) are two defining traits. China's anomaly is striking when compared to public administration in the West and even more so when compared to the professional agencies of classic developmental states in East Asia. And that is not all: this anomaly *varies across space* and *changes over time*. Although the status quos clearly diverge across regions, the divergent regions appear to share similar processes of change.

A triple empirical challenge arises: What explains the origins of nonspecialized and personalized investment strategies among China's local states? How did these structural features evolve over time? And why did the evolution process diverge across space?

Limitations of Existing Explanations

Compared to a coevolutionary framework, prevailing interpretations of the absence of professionalized investment promotion will arrive at very different—and ultimately static and partial—conclusions. First, for those who consider legal-rational qualities as the norm and other practices as abnormal, the conclusion is that China's local bureaucracies "failed" to Weberianize.[50] Explanations will then center on why China is inherently deficient at modernizing.[51] For example, Lu argues that China's local bureaucracies, "rather than evolving toward regularization and rationalization, [became] indefinitely patrimonial."[52] He asserts that "the Chinese regime inherited an undisciplined, ineffective, and arbitrary bureaucracy by the time reforms began." Then, when market transition began, the bureaucracy became "more approximate to what Weber described as patrimonial officialdom, characterized by a lack of clear delineation of public and private spheres."[53]

There is no question that many practices of China's bureaucracies violate Weberian norms, but Lu's conclusion that these organizations are patrimonial and inferior does not square with the aggregate success of China's local state-led development.[54] Indeed, Upstart County, which we earlier saw, is currently in the midst of a growth spurt. This county started to court investments in an en masse and personalized fashion from around 2005, and it is also from this point that income and tax revenue rose (see figure 1.1). If this county failed to Weberianize, as Lu claims, then why has its failure coincided with an unprecedented economic boom? This is a paradox that those who equate deviations from norms of good bureaucracies with backwardness and corruption cannot resolve. Moreover, far from being "indefinitely patrimonial," these bureaucracies in fact continue to adapt over time and at different paces across regions.

Second, for those who adopt a more optimistic view, China's departure from specialization could be interpreted as a quirky adaptation or experimentation with nonconventional practices. Some argue that such "unorthodox" arrangements can work sufficiently well at an early stage of development.[55] Then, as Qian predicts, once market conditions mature, these second-best aberrations "should

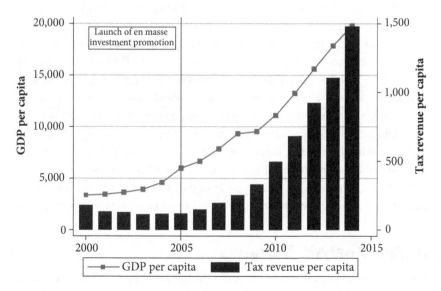

FIGURE 1.1 Economic growth and investment promotion in Upstart County. *City and County Financial Statistics* and *Upstart County Yearbooks*.

eventually be replaced by more conventional, best-practice institutions."[56] To Qian's credit, part of this prediction has indeed played out in wealthier locales I studied, where en masse investment promotion was eventually replaced by routinized work assigned to one specialized agency. Yet in other parts of China, like in Upstart County, the practices that are already obsolete on the coast have only begun to germinate. Many have observed the diffusion of successful policy experiments from "point to surface" (that is, from a pilot location selected by central reformers to the rest of the country) within a short time frame.[57] But what explains the *lagged* replication and replacement of practices across regions observed in my study, a process that does not appear to be centrally organized and planned? When and how did such a process occur? These are questions that those who noted the existence of "transitional institutions" have not yet asked, much less answered.

Adaptation is certainly part of the development story, but it is not enough to stop at asserting that adaptation occurred. To quote Holland, a leading complexity theorist, "the 'how' of this adaptive process is far from obvious."[58] By definition, adaptation is a response to a contingency. If so, what are the contingencies? Put differently, what problems are the assigners of the agencies' tasks responding to that may lead them to select nonspecialized and personalized investment promotion over other available options? What influences the range of alternatives in the environment? Over time, the practices I observed in some locales were not retained. Why not? What new economic contingencies triggered the modification of bureaucratic functions and practices?

The above are the types of questions that a coevolutionary framework raises. Because my framework does not assign a priori normative value to outcomes—namely, that Weberian bureaucracies are the gold standard—it explains institutional divergence as *divergence* rather than as *failure*. Because my approach attends to the mechanisms of variation, selection, and retention, I do not assume that adaptation will automatically occur but instead look for specific pressures that trigger and shape adaptation. I also do not assume that institutional forms in transitional contexts are temporary aberrations that will necessarily fade "once market conditions mature," because economic change is simultaneously dependent upon the existing matrix of institutions. Within China, so-called transitional institutions do not emerge and expire at uniform rates. To address the various new questions raised here, we need to map the process of coevolution step by step.

A Mini–Analytic Narrative

Part 2 of this book will chronicle the coevolutionary paths of three different localities in thick contextual detail. An initial encounter with so much detail, however, may overwhelm the reader and obscure the underlying logic of mutual change. Hence, in this section, I choose to strip away the details and instead present a coevolutionary path in abstraction, based on the modeled case of Glorious County. In mapping the development of Glorious County, the use of tense presents a tricky issue. Depending on where and when you look within China, the processes I trace will either *have taken place, are still occurring, have yet to occur,* or, lastly, *may never occur.* For consistency, I use the past tense, but please keep in mind that different tenses apply to different places.

Act I: The Starting Point

Like many other locales in China prior to reform, Glorious County began as a poor, agrarian, and closed economy, run by a Maoist bureaucracy and lacking the core capabilities of conventional growth-promoting states. How could Glorious County make the leap from a vicious trap of poverty and backwardness to becoming rich and developmental?

According to conventional wisdom, this transition might occur through two contrasting linear paths. Following the claim that good governance is necessary for economic success, Glorious County should "get governance right" before pursuing state-led development.[59] The county must first replace its pre-existing Maoist bureaucracy with a brand-new fleet of professional agencies and follow the best practices of Weberian administration. As this logic predicts, once elite and skilled agencies vested with monopoly power in vital economic tasks are combined with market-friendly policies, an influx of investments and high growth should follow.[60]

Conversely, according to arguments that it is economic growth that leads to improved governance rather than the other way around, what Glorious County needs is a massive injection of capital, such as foreign aid or central state investments.[61] The expectation is that once the locale crosses a critical capital threshold, it will be able to afford and create professional agencies. These two competing theories are schematized in figure 1.2.

The story I uncover, however, departs sharply from the predictions of either theory. Glorious County did not "get governance right" before pursuing growth. In fact, assessed in terms of Weberian standards, it got its structure of bureaucracy *wrong* as a first step. Glorious County also did not rely on handouts from the central or foreign governments to propel development. Instead, it pulled itself up by its own bootstraps. The coevolutionary path of development in Glorious County is summarized in figure 1.3.

At a start-up stage of development, Glorious County was poor and backward in that the county lacked a professional team of economic technocrats. Instead, the bureaucracy was staffed by cadres bequeathed from the Maoist era, many

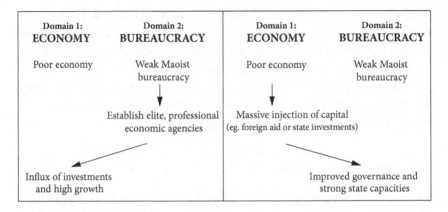

FIGURE 1.2 Two competing linear paths of development

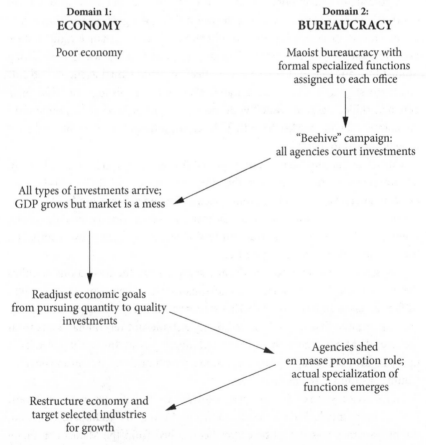

FIGURE 1.3 Coevolution of economy and bureaucracy in Glorious County

of whom had scant exposure to market activities and foreigners. In fact, during the previous decades under Mao, cadres perceived to have any capitalist dealing were severely punished. In terms of formal structure, the pre-existing party-state apparatus was composed of various offices that were each assigned a particular nominal function (e.g., Organization Department, Finance Bureau, Family Planning Bureau, Statistical Bureau, Communist Youth League, etc.).

A new contingency arose when the reformist leadership at the central government gave the green light for local governments to pursue external investments. What changes could Glorious County make to capitalize on this new policy opportunity? Who in the county could do the job of attracting investments, which the county had not done before?

Act II: Capitalizing on Market Opening

At this point, county leaders mulled over two alternatives: either assign one agency to specialize in attracting investors, or get all agencies to seek investment en masse to maximize the chances of getting a hit. Under normal—ideal—circumstances, the county should of course choose to build a competent and specialized team of investment officers, modeled after Japan's MITI or Singapore's EDB. These technocrats would draw up macro-economic plans, design county-wide investment policies, and seek investment opportunities that were in line with the county's long-term developmental vision.

Being poor and backward, however, influenced the selection of bureaucratic traits in two significant ways. First, a poor county is hungry for investors and capital *of any kind*. Second, Glorious County lacked the personnel to form a professional investment agency. Under Mao, recruitment into the party-state apparatus was based on political qualifications over technical expertise. Moreover, during the Cultural Revolution, lasting a decade before market liberalization, a whole generation of young people from the cities was sent to the countryside and deprived of education. Making matters more difficult, Chinese bureaucrats are entitled to de facto lifetime employment, even today. In short, the existing cadre corps was nowhere close to being technocratic and could not be fired.[62]

Yet although Glorious County lacked sophisticated know-how in market management, it had one key abundant resource: personal networks. An average county had more than twenty thousand cadres, each of whom had family members and friends, and even overseas relatives, who could supply capital and raw materials and provide a demand for manufactured goods.[63] What a backward rural setting lacked in terms of modern markets and technical expertise could be compensated for by strong personal ties and the affective power of such ties.

Now when the constraints and opportunities that define a start-up phase of development are reassessed, is it still obvious that a Weberian bureaucratic organization is the universal optimal strategy? In this context, en masse and personalized investment promotion—which some locals called the "beehive" campaign—actually presented a *better* fit than professional norms. Furthermore, I should stress that once the imperatives of early growth are underlined, the beehive campaign was not merely, as Rodrik terms, a "second-best" strategy that is not ideal but good enough for the time being.[64] Rather, for a county trying to take off with little financial and human capital but a strong traditional base of personal connections, the beehive campaign was a *first-best* strategy.

Unleashing an aggressive team of sales personnel to promote a county works, however, only if there is something credible to sell. Whether or not the agencies of Glorious County could recruit investors hinged critically upon the county's basic endowments, especially its geographical conditions. If Glorious sat on a steep hill or in the middle of nowhere, then it would have been impossible to build factories and export products. In that case, no matter how ambitious the quotas assigned, how strongly agencies were incentivized, and how hard they tried, a miracle would not happen. Conversely, if Glorious was located across the straits from Taiwan, with a ready flow of Taiwanese investors, then aggressive, en masse investment promotion would quickly bring visible results. This observation reminds us that arguments about the growth-promoting effects of revised bureaucratic incentives, whether through fiscal or career avenues,[65] are regionally limited and conditional upon the availability of feasible growth opportunities. (But the twist, as we'll see, is that such opportunities are not entirely static.)

Consider what would happen if Glorious County were located near the coast and therefore able to offer credible attractions to investors. A beehive mode of investment promotion would stimulate *more than* rapid growth. When every agency and cadre wooed investors without specialization, all types of investments arrived, some productive but others of low value. Also, without a central agency imbued with overarching powers to oversee the process, investments would be uncoordinated. For example, automobile factories might lack auxiliary producers of steel and tires, or polluting industries might locate alongside food manufacturers. In short, higher GDP was rave news, but the industrial structure was a mess. In evolutionary terms, a new bureaucratic trait (en masse and personalized investment promotion) would interact with the environment (coastal location) and trigger a new economic trait (high growth but a chaotic market).

Act III: No Longer Starving

Having kick-started early growth, economic change fed back to bureaucratic change. As capital accumulated, producing more industries and a larger tax base, the initial pressure to source investors indiscriminately subsided. As local cadres put it, during the start-up stage of development, their overriding impetus was to "eat," that is, to satisfy basic material needs.[66] When the county was no longer starving, however, it became pickier about what it ate. Consequently, a new contingency arose: how to restructure the economy to attract quality investments and to sustain growth. At this juncture, more sophisticated concerns about the complementarity of industries and the crafting of comparative advantages began to enter policy deliberation.

Changes in market conditions prompted policy makers to recalibrate the pros and cons of existing bureaucratic traits and to explore alternative bureaucratic traits. Glorious County no longer sought investments only in *quantity*; rather, it now valued the *quality* of investments. In other words, the success criteria changed as a result of economic change. At the earlier stage of growth, investment promotion en masse was advantageous in bringing in investors quickly and in large numbers, but the drawbacks of the method amplified as income grew. It distracted agencies from conducting their proper functions, created a conflict of interest between attracting investors and enforcing regulations, and obstructed centralized coordination of investment policy.

Moreover, there was a limit to the exploitation of personal networks to court investors. In particular, cadres in nonleading positions had only a certain number of friends and family members who were likely investors. Soon enough, they exhausted their familial networks and were drained by the beehive campaign. For these reasons, when the county sought to restructure and upgrade, rather than simply grow indiscriminately, specialized investment promotion *now* presented a better fit than the earlier beehive strategy.

In this environment, a new success criteria (the pursuit of quality investments) and new constraints (exhaustion of personal networks among nonelite bureaucrats) motivated the selection of a new bureaucratic trait (a professional mode of investment promotion). Moreover, policy makers were not the only actors who changed their preferences and adapted; businesses did too. As markets grew, mature entrepreneurs made investment decisions less on affective and personal ties and more on whether a given location provided quality infrastructure, predictable policies, and industrial clusters and complementarities that were necessary for profitable and sustainable production.

To supply these conditions for more sophisticated investors, the county leadership would require specialized economic agencies to plan and execute investment policies, this time placing greater emphasis on industrial coordination and selective investment promotion. In practical terms, this newly evolved imperative called for several bureaucratic reforms: redefine bureaucratic roles, remove en masse investment targets, and recruit more professionals. After shedding their role as a collective sales force, noneconomic agencies could better focus on the tasks of regulation and social services provision they were supposed to perform; they were subsequently able to build expertise in their specific domains. It was only by this juncture, several steps down the coevolution chain, that the bureaucracy began to acquire some of the characteristics of the Weberian ideal type.

To be clear, though, even as the bulk of the bureaucracy acquired more professional traits, personal connections and corruption were not eradicated; instead they took on more sophisticated and even legalized forms. Economic growth fed back to the *elite* segment of the bureaucracy by generating new avenues to exchange power for money. At early growth stages, corruption took the form of what some social scientists call *speed money*, that is, payments to bypass red tape and speed up administrative processes.[67] Then, as an economy matured, new opportunities to reap supersized profits by cashing in on emergent markets emerged, opportunities that were previously unimaginable when Glorious County was only a poor agrarian economy. One example is urban renewal projects that turned worthless parcels of land into pricey downtown properties; those given access to choice sites would later become billionaires. This structural conversion of the economy from rural to urban generated a new form of corruption that I call *access money*, that is, access to the game of fabulous wealth creation.[68]

The emergence of urban and industrialized economies altered the direction of greed among political elites who controlled access to markets. For them, it would be foolish to repel businesses through arbitrary extractive practices when forging partnerships with a select group of capitalists presented a far more beneficial alternative. Working hand-in-hand with businesses ensured continued growth for the county, while elite officeholders along with their capitalist partners could harvest the cream of prosperity. In short, during the Great Leap from a poor and backward to a rich and modern political economy, the revolution of the bureaucracy involved not only professionalization, as Weber observes, but also a fundamental shift in the nature of corruption.

Act IV: Regional Variation and Connections

The preceding discussion traced the steps of a coevolutionary trajectory under the condition that Glorious County could feasibly attract investors. But what if Glorious County was deep in the central region? Obviously, even if this less privileged reincarnation of Glorious County pursued en masse investment promotion, it would not generate an economic boom. Its cadres were not likely to have relatives in Taiwan and Hong Kong, nor would they have ready access to a network of local entrepreneurs. Moreover, even if they had such contacts, foreign investors were unlikely to invest in a remote county of central China when they could do so in attractive coastal locations.

In this scenario, if county leaders insisted that bureaucracies fulfill investment targets, regardless of whether they were realistic, this could backfire with disastrous outcomes. Local cadres would be pressured to falsify results in order to meet impossible demands. This was exactly what happened during the Great Leap Forward, where unrealistic targets for grain collection led to the starvation of millions of farmers. Again in the 1980s, we witnessed a similar fiasco when central and western locales joined a nationwide rush to set up township and village enterprises. Coastal locales succeeded spectacularly, but inland localities that lacked the basic endowments ended up deep in debt.

Fortunately and intriguingly, this is not where the story ends for the two reincarnations of Glorious County. When the nation initially opened its market, it was no surprise that foreign investors flocked to the coastal regions but ignored the interior areas. Thus the coastal regions were not only the first to grow rich but also the first to adapt and then phase out early bureaucratic traits, including en masse, personalized investment promotion. Once these areas were able to overcome the constraints of poverty, they then moved on to pursue the higher goals of economic restructuring and bureaucratic modernization. In short, these geographically endowed regions led the way in the coevolution of markets and bureaucracies.

When certain parts of China were no longer poor and backward in development, what happened next? In Deng Xiaoping's term, coastal locales that "got rich first" morphed into a rich source of investors for their laggard peers. While an inland county with no international visibility struggled to attract foreign investors, it had a far better chance of drawing *domestic* investors from Shanghai and Zhejiang. As the coastal areas restructured, they sought to dispose low-end manufacturers in order to clear the way for targeted industries and services on the higher-end of the value chain.

In a domestic flying geese pattern, the first-mover states turn to the neglected backyard in their country, belatedly bringing a new flow of investments into the inland regions. When these areas were able to attract domestic capital, the coevolutionary path that played out decades before in the coastal areas was then kick-started in locales that were previously left behind. These are some of the new dynamics in an evolving national system that propelled Upstart County in the interior of China to pursue en masse investment promotion *today*, a practice that coastal locales had abandoned many years before.

A spoiler alert: The story, however, does not end with happily ever after. Whether international or domestic, development is a moving train. Those who hop onto the train later than others may finally celebrate a chance to catch up, but the scenery outside the train has already changed, sometimes drastically so.[69] This analogy describes the present-day environment in China. Although many parts of the interior are experiencing late growth spurts, they face challenges and constraints of the twenty-first century that coastal first movers had avoided, such as restrictive national policies and regional competition from other low-cost manufacturing states like Cambodia. Whether and how laggards and first movers can adapt to evolving contingencies particular to their stage of development will collectively determine the sustainability of China's economic miracle.

Concluding Lessons

What difference does it make to study development from a coevolutionary as opposed to a linear and path-dependent perspective? I suggest that it makes a lot of difference. To highlight the explanatory power of my approach, let's compare the conclusions of my coevolutionary narrative of Glorious County—which is based on real-life cases that will later appear in chapters 5 and 6—to several tenets of conventional wisdom.

Conventional Wisdom 1: Good institutions of governance lead to growth.

Is it good institutions of governance (in this case, professional bureaucracies) that lead to capitalist growth? The answer is that it depends on *the stage of development*. When Glorious County reached a more advanced stage of development geared toward quality growth, it did require a bureaucracy consistent with Weberian norms of specialization and impersonality. When trying to build markets, however, the Weberian model did *not* fit best with the objective of achieving fast growth and maintaining political stability. It was not feasible to replace a Maoist bureaucracy with a technocratic fleet in one step. Equally important, a Weberian model would actually *fail* to take advantage of a unique and vital resource of pre-industrialized communities, that is, the personal connections of county cadres, as well as the mobilization power of a communist apparatus.

Conventional Wisdom 2: Growth leads to good governance

Conversely, is it economic growth that leads to good governance and state capacity, specifically the formation of a Weberian-style bureaucracy? Indeed, once Glorious County was no longer impoverished, it had increased impetus and resources to restructure its bureaucracy toward specialization and impersonality. Modernization theory, however, does not account for the drivers of initial growth. Nor can it explain why higher income leads to bureaucratic professionalization in the absence of civic demands for political change.

Mapping the coevolutionary process of development fills these crucial gaps. Contrary to the "Big Push" plans, Glorious County did not jump-start growth through massive foreign aid or central state investments. Neither foreign consultants nor planners from Beijing imposed comprehensive interventions. Instead, it was the bottom-up initiative of local governments in mobilizing existing resources that lured an initial wave of investors. We also learn that higher income led to bureaucratic professionalization not only because financial resources grew, but also because the preferences of policy makers changed. When poor, the goal of the local leadership was simply to "eat" (i.e., make ends meet). But when less poor, they aspired to eat better food.

Elite preferences change as the economy changes. This revelation forces us to rethink the assumption of fixed preferences among players that is commonly employed in game theory and dominant theories of political economy. It also reminds us that political change need not only take the form of formal democratization.[70] Within authoritarian regimes, bureaucratic change *is* political change.[71]

Conventional Wisdom 3: Developing countries should settle for "good enough" governance.

Acknowledging that it is not feasible to replicate an entire suite of good institutions within a short time, some development experts urge reforms in developing countries to settle for "good enough" governance. Grindle defines "good enough governance" as "a condition of minimally acceptable government performance . . . that does not significantly hinder economic or political development."[72] Krasner applies the same phrase when he proposes that American foreign policy should aim for "good enough governance," rather than consolidated democracy, in fragile postwar societies like Iraq and Afghanistan. By "good enough governance," Krasner similarly refers to minimal conditions like "the provision of basic levels of order," "some basic services" and "corruption, in which political leaders accumulate wealth for themselves, would be constrained."[73]

At first glance, the above recommendations seem to mirror the lessons of Glorious County's coevolutionary trajectory, but in fact they differ in significant ways. When experts like Grindle and Krasner say "good enough governance," they mean government performance that is only "minimally acceptable." Yet the story of Glorious County (and its real-life incarnations) clearly goes *beyond the minimal.* As we saw, the entire county bureaucracy, both elites and nonelites, was mobilized to promote growth, and they were all personally vested in the process of market building. These actors creatively reconfigured existing informal norms and communist institutions for the purpose of constructing capitalism from the ground up. Even though their initial strategies defied Weberian precepts, they worked spectacularly well for a takeoff stage of development. Hence it would be a mistake to reduce the unorthodox measures adapted in Glorious County to "good enough governance" that "[did] not significantly hinder economic development." To be clear, the measures taken *aided* economic development.

Without a doubt, the language of "good enough" and "second best" governance is a vast improvement over the one-size-fits-all assumption of good-governance reforms.[74] But this literature lulls us into the misimpression that early development merely requires *doing less*, when in fact it demands *doing things differently*, that is, by improvising with existing norms and even defying conventions.

> *Conventional Wisdom 4: Development is path-dependent, meaning that institutions and outcomes, once in place, self-reinforce and persist.*

Is the path of coevolution driven by path dependence? In my analysis of mutual adaptation, each step influences the next step, but the coevolutionary logic that I map is different from path-dependent arguments. The logic of path dependence is that an initial move generates self-reinforcing effects, precludes certain alternatives in future periods, and therefore becomes "locked in" over time. As Pierson states, in path-dependent analyses, the focus is on identifying the mechanisms that reinforce a given trajectory.[75] By contrast, as illustrated through my narrative, a coevolutionary approach makes no assumption that a given path will be reinforced; instead it can account for both *reproduction* and *replacement*. It does so by providing an accounting of changes that occurred at each significant juncture, so that we know when and why choices are made, retained, or replaced. As Glorious County's zigzag path sharply illustrates, an initial selection may modify the environment in ways that lead unintendedly to its demise and replacement down the coevolutionary chain. History does not always repeat itself.

If we string the snapshots of Glorious County's coevolutionary path from the beginning to the most recent, we find a three-step causal sequence: (1) *harness pre-existing weak institutions to build markets* (convert and combine personal connections and communist campaign-style enforcement into resources for investment promotion) → (2) *emerging markets stimulate strong institutions* (onset of early growth and chaotic markets spur the leadership to rethink the focus of development and to readapt the bureaucracy accordingly) → (3) *strong institutions preserve markets* (emergence of professional bureaucratic traits and replacement of petty corruption with institutionalized elite corruption provide a predictable basis for advanced markets). In sum, even within the same locale, the particular institutions and strategies that promote growth vary over the course of development with changing priorities and income levels.

We also learn that the effects of initial unorthodox measures (such as the beehive campaign) do not work equally and at the same time across regions. Be it standard good institutions or initial unorthodox institutions, the effects of *all* institutions are conditional upon the availability of basic growth opportunities, such as distance from export markets. Such opportunities, however, are themselves *dynamic*.[76] Although geography clearly plays a big role in determining any locale's starting growth opportunities, new opportunities may arise (or decline) as neighboring economies evolve.

Having reviewed the concluding lessons, we arrive at a final and important question: What allows coevolutionary processes of change to proceed in the way I traced in Glorious County? There is clearly plenty of improvisation involved. Central officials in Beijing did not dictate which specific bureaucratic practices and economic strategies should be enacted at various junctures of the county's development. In the process of improvisation, how do local policy makers know what to do and what not to do? If no boundaries are placed and every county is free to innovate, the situation will surely be chaotic. And yet, looking at the cases I have reviewed, there appears to be an order to the way localities across China evolved and diverged. What is the source of this mysterious order?

In addition, why might the officials in Glorious County care to adapt? Adaptation takes effort and thought; it even incurs risks. Why might these public agents not slack off or siphon off public funds into their private pockets without making any contribution in return? There are, of course, lazy and corrupt officials, but if the whole bureaucracy is run by such individuals, then China could not have achieved extraordinary state-led growth.

All these questions boil down to one key puzzle: *something* about China's environment makes on-the-ground agents seem unusually inclined and able to adapt. What is it? I turn to the answer in the next chapter.

2

DIRECTED IMPROVISATION

It is not sufficient to describe societal change; rather we
must attempt to find the underlying forces shaping the process
of change.

—Douglass North, *Understanding the Process of Economic Change*

As for directors, one can only advise them not to foist anything on
their actors . . . but to enthuse them. . . . Stimulate in an actor an
appetite for his part. This preserves the freedom of the creative
artist.

—Constantin Stanislavski, *An Actor's Handbook*

Effective adaptation is something we all love to have, but how do we get it? This is the question to be addressed in this chapter.

As the analytic narrative in chapter 1 suggests, states and markets coevolve through continuous responses among ground-level actors to ever-changing problems. Because China is an authoritarian, late-developing regime, state rather than social actors are the primary agents of adaptation. Nevertheless, the same questions may be asked of any context, be it states or societies that dominate: Under what conditions do agents adapt to changing circumstances? What defines and influences effective adaptation?

In order to answer these questions, this chapter draws on concepts from complex adaptive systems (complexity) to first define adaptation.[1] Rather than thinking about adaptation as a unidimensional process, it is better understood as a bundle of mechanisms (variation, selection, and niche creation) that collectively drives the process of evolution. Therefore, the conditions that foster adaptation are an assembly of measures taken to address certain problems inherent in each adaptive mechanism.

Two other important points will be explicated in this chapter. First, I underscore the differences between adaptation in biological and social settings. Natural environments feature a universal and uncontroversial yardstick of success and hence of effective adaptation: survival and reproduction. Among humans, however, the meaning of success is subjectively defined and sometimes fiercely contested. Therefore, theories of biological evolution cannot be imported wholesale into the study of societal adaptation.[2] The politics of defining success is central to the human evolutionary process.

Second, I differentiate between exerting *control* and exerting *influence*. Conventional theories rarely distinguish between the two actions. Theories of politics, including in Chinese politics, are predominantly theories of control.[3] This traditional emphasis on control, I propose, is predicated on a *complicated* world view, which assumes that those who seek to control know for sure what they want and take actions to achieve their goals. A world of *complexity*, however, is full of uncertainty. Even authoritarian leaders sometimes do not know what precise outcomes they prefer or what solutions may arise.[4] In a complex world, as we find in political economies, influencing processes of change and empowering ground-level actors to find their own solutions promises to be more fruitful than trying to control exact outcomes.

Focusing on the context of reform-era China, I will elaborate on three key measures taken by central reformers to influence adaptive processes, grouped under the themes of variation, selection, and niche creation. Briefly outlined, these measures include the following:

1. designing national reform packages and articulating central mandates in ways to balance variety and uniformity in policy implementation
2. structuring the cadre evaluation and compensation system in ways to clearly define and reward success within the bureaucracy
3. allowing regions to tap their natural comparative advantages but also intervening to connect the economies of first movers and laggards

Condensing these elements into a single label, I call it *directed improvisation*. Central reformers are most effective at fostering adaptation when they direct, not when they dictate. Akin to directors, the role of the central leadership is to construct a welcoming stage for improvisational responses from below. Then, as we saw in the analytic narrative of Glorious County, local state actors enter the scene and create their own stories.

Defining Adaptation and Its Implications

Like the word "evolution," the word "adaptation" is frequently used but seldom defined in social analyses. Expressed in biological terms, Holland defines adaptation as "the process where an organism fits itself to the environment."[5] Axelrod and Cohen provide a more generic definition: "When a selection process [leads] to improvement according to some measure of success, we call it adaptation."[6]

What are the mechanisms by which agents in biological and social systems adapt, that is, fit themselves to the environment? In this book, I highlight three key mechanisms: (1) *variation* (generation of alternatives); (2) *selection* (selection among and assembly of alternatives to form new combinations); and (3) *niche creation* (crafting of distinct and valuable roles among heterogeneous units within a system).

In chapter 1, I sketched these mechanisms in action through the analytic narrative of Glorious County. A quick review is helpful. Consider, for example, the processes by which the county officials adapted a pre-existing communist bureaucratic structure to attract capitalist investments.

> *Variation*: The process of adaptation began with generating and assessing alternative actions. For example, was firing the existing cadre corps inherited from the Maoist era an option? If not, could their targets be revised? What other existing sociopolitical features could be incorporated into investment promotion?

> *Selection*: Based on their initial criteria of success (i.e., achieve fast growth regardless of quality), county leaders selected and recombined campaign-style mobilization and personal connections to form a new investment recruitment strategy: "the beehive campaign."[7] After this selection was made, it was tested through practice. Where the strategy worked to attract investments, it was retained. But where it failed or when it became incompatible with evolved development priorities, the strategy was abandoned and replaced with a new selection: professionalization.

> *Niche creation*: Selections made by each locale can affect the performance of other locales and of the entire system. For instance, if all the locales competed head-to-head for the same investments, regardless of differing conditions, then, like monocropping, this could hurt the economy of each region and of the whole nation.

The above example illustrates that adaptation is not a unidimensional variable (i.e., either you adapt or you don't adapt); rather, it is a bundle of mechanisms. Collectively, these mechanisms drive the process of *evolution*. When two or more populations or domains adapt to each other, I call this a process of *coevolution*. Hence, importantly, evolution and coevolution should not be "confused with development, progress, gradualism, or indeed, any kind of change,"[8] as Lustick points out. This is because evolution is a *particular* type of change involving adaptive mechanisms outlined above.[9]

Social scientists have studied other types of institutional change that do not involve adaptive mechanisms. One variety is change via exogenous shocks.

Traumatic events like wars and colonial conquest abruptly and forcefully disrupt existing institutions and replace them with new forms.[10] Another variety is "gradual institutional change,"[11] which, I must stress, may or may not involve adaptation. Aging, wear and tear, and obsolescence are all gradual changes, but these processes do not entail learning nor are they driven by efforts to fit changing environments (instead it is the other way around; people are forced to adapt to inevitable processes of aging and wearing).[12]

Once adaptation and evolution are defined, two implications emerge. The first concerns the definition of effective adaptation in social contexts. As earlier mentioned, in biological settings, the definition of effective adaptation is straightforward; whichever selected strategy aids survival and reproduction is by definition effective. Through the mechanism of natural selection, selected traits that enhance survival and propagation in particular environments are retained and passed down to future generations, over time producing an astounding diversity of biological forms. Conversely, in social settings, quoting Axelrod and Cohen, "Clearly, different agents in a population may use different measures of success. So changes that are adaptations for some may not be for others."[13] Hence, analyses of societal adaptation must be prefixed by these questions: Who gets to define success? Is it the state, certain parts of society, interest groups, academics, aid agencies, foreign consultants, or others? And how do these different agents define success?

A second implication concerns the nature of indeterminacy and human agency in complex social worlds where interactions among many adaptive agents produce tremendous uncertainty. We face *risks* in complicated worlds but *uncertainty* in complex worlds.[14] Complicated systems like machines are made up of many separate parts that do not adapt to one another. Machines can be extremely intricate and pose difficult complications (try fixing even a simple machine like a broken toaster), but we normally do not expect the parts of machines to interact, recombine, and evolve into unexpected new entities, except in science fiction movies! Complicated systems pose *risks*, that is, the *probability* that certain anticipated outcomes may occur. For example, there is some likelihood that a toaster we buy today may break down a year from now; we may be annoyed when it does, but we would not be surprised if it happens.[15]

On the other hand, complex systems, exemplified by natural ecologies, human bodies, and political economies, are made up of many moving parts that adapt to one another and the environment. Complex systems can evolve and generate *uncertainty*, that is, *possibilities* that are beyond the anticipation and planning of agents within the system. Some possibilities are terrible, such as stock market crashes and outbreaks of war. Yet some possibilities are marvelous, such as scientific breakthroughs, artistic innovations, and the information revolution that we are currently experiencing.[16] To extinguish uncertainty is to extinguish possibilities, both terrible and marvelous.

Risks may be *predicted* and *controlled* to a varying extent, but possibilities may only be *imagined*.[17] Confronting risks in complicated worlds, we seek to exert control, to minimize the probability of undesired outcomes and to achieve specific desired goals. In the face of uncertainty in complex systems, however, control may be futile or even self-defeating,[18] because in our efforts to reach targeted destinations through particular preferred routes, we may well be missing even better possibilities and paths to these possibilities. Hence, rather than exerting *control*, which presumes knowledge of certain ideal outcomes or effective solutions, an alternative course of action is to *influence* the processes of adaptation and change. Axelrod and Cohen apply the term "harnessing complexity," by which they mean "seeking to improve without being able to fully control."[19]

Once the premises of complicated versus complex systems are clearly spelled out (summarized in table 2.1), it becomes clear that much of social science analysis is predicated on a complicated world view, with an accompanying focus on *control over outcomes* rather than *influence over processes*. Indeed, in his magisterial book *Understanding the Process of Economic Change*, Douglass North asserts on the opening page, "The central focus of this study, and the key to improving economic performance, is the deliberate effort of human beings to *control* their environment."[20] Control is not the right place to begin a study of adaptation. It is like a parent who aspires, "I want to help children unearth their potential and be creative. Let's start by thinking how I can control their behavior and mold them to fit my ideals." In order to explore the underlying conditions of "adaptive efficiency," as North terms it,[21] we'll have to move away from the conventional focus on control and instead ponder the exercise of influence.

TABLE 2.1 Complicated vs. complex adaptive systems

	COMPLICATED SYSTEMS	COMPLEX ADAPTIVE SYSTEMS
Characteristics	Collectives that comprise many *separate* parts that *do not adapt* to one another or the environment	Collectives that comprise many *moving* parts that *constantly adapt* to one another and the environment
Nature of causality	Dependent (outcome) vs. independent factor (cause)	Interdependent factors (both cause and outcome)
Nature of indeterminacy	Risk	Uncertainty
	Probability	Possibility
Nature of human agency	Control	Influence

Three Problems of Adaptation

A theoretically grounded understanding of adaptation is essential for advancing the implementation of adaptive approaches in international development. In recent years, there has been an encouraging shift away from "best practices" in the dominant good-governance agenda toward a localized "best-fit" approach in foreign aid and reforms.[22] Experts like Rodrik, Pritchett, Woolcock, Grindle, Fukuyama, Evans, among others, have argued that solutions in developing countries should be tailored to "local contexts,"[23] "local knowledge,"[24] and "particular situations."[25] Andrews prescribes the following rules of thumb in an approach he calls "problem driven iterative adaptation" (PDIA): instead of selling solutions to aid recipients, identify local problems first; instead of imposing best practices, use step-by-step experimentation; instead of making top-down plans, engage broad stakeholders.[26] Hardly anybody, I believe, would disagree with these prescriptions. The hard part, however, is *how* to put them into practice.

Some development specialists have tried to "operationalize" the task of promoting adaptation by reducing it to a technical or even ideological problem.[27] For example, Grindle tries to provide guidelines for achieving "good enough governance" by drawing up templates of "governance priorities" that allow practitioners to check off boxes and figure out what is good enough.[28] Recently, the Harvard Kennedy School initiated the signing of a "DDD [Do Development Differently] Manifesto" based on the principles of PDIA described above.[29] Those who sign the manifesto "pledge to apply these principles in our own efforts to pursue, promote and facilitate development progress." It is no doubt laudable that one of the world's leading public policy schools is actively enlisting practitioners to embrace an adaptive approach to development. Yet one cannot help, of course, but be reminded of Marx's communist manifesto. Chinese cadres and citizens, too, were once enjoined to pledge allegiance to Marxist principles, but, as we all know, such promises were thrown out the window as soon as Mao exited the scene.

The way to put adaptive ideas into practice is to begin by understanding that adaptation is "both promising and problematic."[30] Celebrating the promise of adaptation without appreciating its problems will lead nowhere. Embedded in the problems are clues to where and which appropriate actions may be taken to influence adaptive processes.[31]

Let's begin by exploring the first of three adaptive mechanisms highlighted: variation, that is, the generation of alternatives. As Axelrod and Cohen stated, "Variation provides the raw material for adaptation. But for an agent or population to take advantage of what has already been learned, some limits have to be placed on the amount of variation in the system."[32] If there are no alternatives at all, then no interaction and change can occur. Conversely, if there are too many alternatives, then the situation turns chaotic. Expressed in plain language, we experience option overload.

The above problem may also be viewed as a trade-off between exploration (inventing new ideas or objects) and exploitation (building on existing options). Between exploration and exploitation, one possible extreme is "eternal boiling," where agents switch too quickly from one selection to another, without sufficiently trying out and retaining inventions that work. The other extreme is "premature convergence," where agents settle too soon on a given option without sufficiently exploring other alternatives.[33] In short, successful adaptation requires a balance between uniformity and variety, that is, having some range of alternatives and experimentation, but not too much.

The above concepts and tensions are readily observed in international development settings. On one extreme, the good-governance agenda is premised on the belief that there is a universal set of good institutions, namely, institutions found in the capitalist West. This belief essentially suffocates adaptation at the point of origin: no variation is permitted. International benchmarks further entrench the belief that there is only one best option and that the quality of institutions in developing countries is measured only by its distance from one ideal type. Predictably, when aid recipients are pressured by conditional aid and international norms to adopt a set of golden standards, they have no choice but to pretend to do so, even if these standards do not fit their contexts.[34]

The converse of accepting only one option is to consider too many. This is commonly seen in the policy-making processes of young democracies, such as Thailand and the Philippines. When state leaders and bureaucrats are not insulated from popular pressures, they are pulled in every direction. Kohli describes a vivid example from India during the Nehru era.[35] Despite inheriting an elite and educated bureaucratic apparatus from British rule, the Nehru government was unable to pursue a coherent policy of industrial promotion because it sought to be a popular party at the same time. The Congress Party's espousal of nationalist and socialist values, as well as its accommodation of multiple ethnic groups within a federal system, fragmented state power and diluted developmental goals. This example reminds us that while buzzwords like "broad-based engagements" sound appealing, they do not always bring about effective adaptation.[36]

Next, consider selection, that is, choosing among available strategies. Measures of success determine how agents respond to particular situations, which has serious consequences in the policy world.[37] America's war in Afghanistan provides a striking case.[38] Should success in Afghanistan be defined as the wholesale transformation of this poor, war-torn country into a centralized and democratic state, complete with rule of law and protection of individual rights? Or should the attainment of a modicum of order suffice as a successful mission? In this instance, how success is defined affects whether the United States should hunker down for the long term or cut its losses short, shore up the central government in Kabul or strike bargains with regional warlords, continue to funnel billions of dollars and thousands of troops to Afghanistan, or withdraw American presence.

Defining success can be hard, very hard. It can be hard because leaders sometimes do not know exactly what success should look like. Or they may envision success to mean something so broad and idealistic that when the vision is translated into operation, front-line agents simply do not know what to prioritize and what to do. For example, some lament the Obama administration's "mission creep" in Afghanistan.[39] Not only do the U.S. armed forces have to fight terrorists, they also assume responsibility for building schools, reforming prisons, and even promoting agriculture business. This example again cautions against sanguine recommendations about "finding and fitting relevant reforms [through] purposive muddling."[40] For muddling to be purposive, success must first be concretely defined, and in practice this is a *political* challenge.

Finally, consider the third adaptive mechanism: niche creation, that is, the crafting of distinct and valuable roles among heterogeneous units within a collective. A niche refers to the relationship of a unit vis-à-vis other units within a shared environment.[41] For example, when describing a business, we say, "this company's product occupies a niche in the industry." Niche creation is a function of diversity: the greater the diversity, the more niches are created. Diversity can provide many advantages for interaction and adaptation. Specifically, diversity can enable agents to amass collective knowledge to cope with uncertainty, insure against catastrophic failures, and provide a range of skills and resources to tackle collective problems.[42] Given these potential advantages, it is no surprise that many organizations value diversity and champion it as a goal of personnel recruitment.

Upon closer examination, however, diversity is a double-edged sword; it may sometimes hinder system performance. As Miller and Page underscore, when there is too much heterogeneity, "the system might be too complex, with a tangle of shifting growth rates resulting in an incoherent structure that is impossible for the agents to exploit in any productive manner."[43] Simply explained, picture a classroom. At the college level, graduate and undergraduate classes are usually taught separately because the two groups possess unequal abilities and knowledge. Imagine if one had to teach a class made up of both college freshmen and advanced graduate students. If instructors insist on a uniform curriculum and teaching method, the class will be too hard for freshmen but too easy for graduate students. In these situations, some educators have exploited heterogeneous student composition to the advantage of collective learning. One method, popularized by Vygotsky, an educational psychologist, is peer tutoring. By having advanced students mentor younger students, this method is believed to accord mutual benefits to both learners.[44] In evolutionary terms, these students of uneven abilities each occupy a niche in the classroom, meaning a distinct role dependent on other roles.

Moving to the policy world, niche creation may take several forms: international, regional, and intranational. National economies craft niches in the international or regional markets to stay competitive. Within large countries like the United States and China, subnational economies may develop specializations in certain products and services. Yet while the advantages of niches may seem obvious, creating them is by no means straightforward. For example, with the onset of globalization, many middle-income countries find themselves stranded without a niche; they boast neither the technological prowess to dominate in high-end sectors nor cheap wages to compete in low-end manufacturing. For these countries, economic liberalization and openness have threatened to erode industries and jobs rather than deliver the benefits of a globalized market.[45]

In international aid policies, niche creation was even deliberately discouraged. Until the 1990s, the accepted wisdom had been that resource and factor endowments determined the comparative advantage of nations, which meant that developing countries should specialize only in lower ends of the production chain and leave skills and capital-intensive production to developed nations. Thus, as Evans relates, when South Korea requested a loan from the World Bank in the 1970s to build steel plants, the request was turned down on the grounds that Korea had no comparative advantage in steel production.[46] The potential role of the government in crafting niches for their economies was not recognized until the rise of the developmental state school in the 1990s.[47] These examples offer a sobering reminder that although diversity may seem universally desirable, leveraging intrasystem diversity for collective performance and staying competitive within a diverse environment are demanding challenges.

In sum, why do adaptive traits seem rare among many developing countries? The obsession with best practices and international benchmarks suffocate the generation of alternatives (variation). Vaguely defined or conflicting criteria of success confound the selection of strategies (selection). And national and local development policies often neglect to leverage interdependent ties among members of a system (niche creation).

Generically stated, the three problems of fostering effective adaptation are as follows:

1. Variation: how to balance variety and uniformity within a system
2. Selection: how to define and reward successful adaptation among agents
3. Niche creation: how to turn heterogeneity across units into a system advantage

These three problems are present everywhere, from small settings like classrooms to large and complex settings like countries. Once they are spelled out, it becomes clear that actualizing popular recommendations like developing best-fit reforms, engaging broad stakeholders, conducting experiments, muddling through, embracing diversity, and so forth, are *themselves problematic*, rather than solutions to building adaptive capacity.

Crafting Meta-Institutions to Foster Adaptation

The adaptive dynamics of variation, selection, and niche creation each presents a unique set of problems, but as Axelrod and Cohen indicate, "Organizations and strategies can be designed to take advantage of the opportunities provided by complexity."[48] In complexity thinking, the purpose of "design" differs markedly from that of standard political-economic theories and policy practices, in which institutions are designed to achieve specific expected outcomes. For example, in the late 1970s, World Bank consultants designed and implemented a modern irrigation system in Bali with the expectation of increasing agriculture production. But because this design was imposed upon a traditional cooperative system of water sharing among Balinese farmers, it ended up disrupting production.[49] From a complexity perspective, institutional design is motivated by a different goal: to empower local communities to improvise solutions that fit the particular needs of their environments, rather than to dictate to them what to do.

Stated differently, complexity theories point to the design of what I call *meta-institutions*. Properly defined, meta-institutions are higher-order structures and strategies that facilitate adaptive and learning processes. In educational psychology, the counterpart of meta-institutions is meta-cognition—the ability to think about and manage one's thinking—which is identified as the most critical learning skill and perhaps unique to humans.[50] Indeed, one of the distinct strengths of American higher education is that it prizes the nurturing of meta-cognition, more commonly known as "critical thinking."

My study is not the first to raise the idea of meta-institutions. Several prominent thinkers have pointed to deliberative democracy as a—or indeed *the*—meta-institution for channeling citizens' inputs toward collective problem solving and development. Applying the term "meta-institutions," Rodrik writes, "I would argue that the most reliable forms of such mechanisms are participatory political institutions . . . that elicit and aggregate local knowledge and thereby help build better institutions."[51] Similarly, Nobel laureate Amartya Sen proposes that societies choose their development goals primarily through public discussion and exchange of ideas. He states, "Processes of participation have to be understood as constitutive parts of the ends of development in themselves."[52] Concurring with Sen, Evans and Heller maintain that developmental states of the twenty-first century must learn to engage broad segments of society.[53] Evans hails the promise of deliberative democracy in "engaging the energies of ordinary citizens, increasing their willingness to invest in public goods, and enhancing the delivery of those goods."[54]

While I agree that deliberation offers intrinsic benefits, my perspective departs from the preceding arguments in several ways. First, it must be stressed that the presence of civil society and public participation does not always produce successful collective decision making. Free-for-all participation can easily degenerate into chaos and deadlock. Indeed, Evans acknowledges, "a public administrative apparatus with the capacity necessary to both provide informational inputs and implement the decisions that result from the process is a central element in making deliberation possible."[55] Effective public participation requires a blend of top-down authority and bottom-up participation.[56] Bottom-up participation alone does not magically produce adaptive results.

Second, democracy does not equate deliberation, even though the two tend to go together. Deliberative processes exist within authoritarian regimes, and likewise, restrictions on public deliberation may sometimes be found in democracies. Even though public participation is restricted in authoritarian China compared to democracies,[57] intense deliberation takes place *within* the bureaucracy.[58] Also, even among democracies, deliberation is not always directly open to the public. Evans' example of public participatory budgeting among village councils in India describes direct democracy.[59] Another variety is representative democracy, where citizens elect officials who deliberate upon and make decisions on their behalf in Parliament, as practiced in Britain.

Indeed, since antiquity, political theorists have debated the pros and cons of direct versus representative democracy.[60] As students of American politics know well, James Madison recommended representative over direct deliberative democracy. In the *Federalist Papers*, Madison cautioned against the dangers of "factions" (groups of citizens whose narrow interests may be contrary to those of the nation) in fragmenting and distorting decision making. Thus America has an Electoral College system, whereby citizens vote for a slate of electors who then elect the president. As Madison argued, elected delegates can better serve to "refine and enlarge the public view."[61] Expressed in adaptive language, Madison envisioned that representative institutions may work to limit the amount of variation and filter the quality of ideas in the political system. Evidently, even America—the global beacon of democracy—chooses to *restrict* direct public deliberation in certain arenas of decision making.

Third, direct public deliberation is not the only means of addressing the problems of adaptation earlier identified. Focusing on Western Europe, Katzenstein reveals a different set of mechanisms for limiting alternatives in political deliberation (the problem of "variation"). As he relates in *Small States in World Markets*, the small size of the Scandinavian countries renders them highly dependent on trade and hence vulnerable to international shocks. To adapt effectively to external turbulence, these countries "became convinced that they should pose strict limits on domestic quarrels."[62] To do so, the small states in Western Europe adopted a system Katzenstein calls "democratic corporatism," which has three characteristics: a national ideology of social partnership, highly concentrated interest groups, and continuous bargaining among businesses, state agencies, and political parties.

Turning next to the developmental states in East Asia, we find a different configuration of meta-institutions. To place limits on direct participation in politics, countries like Japan and South Korea relied on an elite bureaucratic apparatus that was insulated from populist pressures to make economic decisions.[63] Within these elite agencies, intense policy deliberation took place. In this sense, appointed bureaucrats in East Asia substituted for elected delegates in Western democracies. Governments in East Asia also took care to define and publicize measures of personal success, which is crucial for recruiting the brightest talents into the bureaucracy and for channeling the energy of citizens toward the developmental goals of the state.[64] For example, the government of Singapore awards state-funded scholarships to top academic performers, who are then required to return and serve in the public sector. By defining personal success as academic success, this system channels individual efforts toward formal schooling and scoring well in standardized tests. For better or worse, as state-sponsored scholars are selected based on academic ability and then trained in similar elite schools, the system churns out elites of similar types, which diminishes diversity and niches.[65]

Having reviewed various examples of nondeliberative meta-institutions that influence a society's capacity to adapt (generate alternatives, select strategies, and create niches), we may now turn to China. It is a mistake to think that leaders in a single-party autocracy can call the shots at whim and devise all the solutions necessary to govern the country. Autocracies can be dynamic, responsive, and open to change. But autocracies, too, have to tackle inherent problems of adaptation in order to harness complexity.

Three Problems of Adaptation in China

There are three basic conditions that define China, which in turn shape the problematic nature of adaptation and the available means to address these problems.

First, both in terms of land mass, population, and the number of party-state functionaries, China is extremely large. Such large size implies wide heterogeneity in resources, constraints, and starting points within the country. By comparison, countries like Japan, South Korea, and Singapore are much smaller and highly centralized. They do not have to contend with issues of immense scale and heterogeneity as China does.

Second, China is a single-party authoritarian state ruled by the CCP. Leaders and bureaucrats, whether national or local, are appointed to office by superiors at the next higher administrative level. Hence, compared to electoral democracies, state actors in a single-party hierarchical structure play an oversized role in improvising solutions and in shaping development. Social actors may exercise some influence too, but the power of the state far surpasses that of society. Moreover, in a single-party hierarchy, state actors look upward to their superiors rather than downward at voters for accountability. Local officials do face mounting pressures from an increasingly vocal civil society,[66] but bottom-up pressures remain secondary compared to pressures exerted by the higher levels.

Third, despite China's top-down authoritarian hierarchy, it is highly decentralized, both administratively and economically. Rather than the central leadership dictating precise plans and directly remitting resources downward, local governments are tasked to steer their own economies, collect taxes, finance and supply public services, and maintain law and order. Furthermore, China has five levels of government: central, province, city, county, and township. Each level governs the next lower level. This means that decentralization happens not only between the central party-state in Beijing and thirty-one provincial units, but also between subprovincial levels of government, forming a long nested chain of delegation. As Landry points out, China holds the distinction and paradox of being a "decentralized authoritarian" regime.[67]

These three basic conditions shape the nature of adaptive problems in China. I will elaborate upon three problems in the following order:

1. Variation: how to influence the agenda of change and amount of local policy variation
2. Selection: how to clearly define and reward success among bureaucratic agents
3. Niche creation: how to leverage wide regional inequality for national development

As discussed earlier, effective adaptation first requires striking "the right balance between variety and uniformity."[68] Theories of central-local relations in China have centered on problems of delegation and control, that is, how the leadership obtains local compliance with central directives.[69] This focus on control, however, misses the fact that central leaders do not always want uniform compliance with central policies. They often prefer that their subordinates adapt central policies to fit widely variant local conditions. Indeed, this desire for variability is frequently expressed in policy deliberations and central documents via a Chinese term: "tailor your methods to local contexts."[70] For development experts like Rodrik who advocate fitting reforms to "local conditions" and "local knowledge," there is no sharper illustration of this prescription than China.[71]

Localized policy implementation is desirable, but managing it is tricky. Before localities can proceed to make adjustments according to local conditions, central commanders must first authorize a national agenda of change. Yet formulating such an agenda is no easy task. Should change be initiated in a few policy domains, or in many? Should marginal changes be made, or radical ones? From the central perspective, such questions must be carefully considered, because once a national agenda is pronounced, like an emperor's edict, it forms the basis on which local adaptive actions are taken nationwide.

A follow-up problem concerns the degree of flexibility in different arenas of reform within a national agenda. In certain policy domains, the central leadership demands uniform compliance, such as issues concerning national security and political stability. But in other areas where local initiatives are more effective than higher-level dictates, such as strategies of growth promotion and social services provision, varying degrees of local variability are preferable. Moreover, central preferences for which policies should be flexibly implemented and to what degree are in constant flux. As conditions on the ground change, so too does central assessment of the balance between variety and uniformity. Once the challenges of managing localized policy implementation are underscored, it raises a crucial question: *How might the national leaders of a decentralized hierarchy influence the agenda of change and amount of local policy variation?*

The challenge of managing variation takes us to the next problem: influencing the selection criteria of bureaucratic agents. As earlier elaborated, how success is defined in any system powerfully shapes the choices agents make as they adapt. Because bureaucrats are the primary agents of adaptation in authoritarian China, the key problem of selection is one of defining and rewarding success *within* the bureaucracy. This problem is sharper in public organizations than in private corporations. As Wilson, an authority of American bureaucracy, asserts, "Whereas business management focuses on the 'bottom line' (that is, profits), government management focuses on the 'top line' (that is, constraints)."[72] A typical public agency faces multiple principals (bosses who can impose demands) and constituents. As a result, goals in the public sector are usually "vague or inconsistent,"[73] making the objective measurement of performance notoriously difficult.[74] Furthermore, public agencies are normally forbidden from employing their revenue to reward employees. Bound by legal restrictions, these organizations also cannot easily fire weak performers. In sum, the norms within governments are that success is vaguely defined and rewards for taking initiative to adapt and innovate are weak.

Once the general conditions that constrain bureaucratic adaptation are spelled out, the abundant observations of adaptive and entrepreneurial behavior among bureaucratic agents in China becomes deeply puzzling. In my own fieldwork, I have encountered numerous instances of creative, even audacious, methods of problem solving. Consider some examples: the chief of a county-level administrative services center pioneered a partnership with private service providers to help businesses complete complicated licensing applications; a school principal convinced his teachers to mortgage their private property to obtain a huge loan to finance the school's refurbishment; the city of Chengdu was among the first to trade "land quotas" on the market (quotas provided by the central government to turn farmland for urban use), well before central authorities even conceived of such an idea. As these varied examples suggest, adaptive behavior is not limited to political elites. Even rank-and-file cadres are observed to proactively devise ways to overcome operational and budgetary constraints. This raises a second crucial question: *Why do agents at all ranks of China's bureaucratic hierarchy seem exceptionally willing to take initiative and even risks to solve problems?*

Finally, the challenges of managing vast regional diversity are apparent. Territorially speaking, China is a collection of First World, Second World, and Third World states. When Deng Xiaoping famously said "let some get rich first," he in effect signaled the green light for what Miller and Page call "heterogeneous adaptation."[75] Concretely, Deng chose to let the regions tap their respective comparative advantages, a decision that completely reversed Mao's policy of suppressing growth on the coast and funneling industrial projects to the central and western regions. Once markets were opened to the world, coastal regions were clearly advantaged by their location and long entrepreneurial histories (a proximate result of location). As reforms proceeded, they raced further and further ahead in competition, leaving large swaths of the country behind.

Although regional disparities are widely regarded as a troubling issue,[76] it is far less noticed that such inequality may offer certain advantages for national development. The conventional response to regional inequality is to redistribute income from the rich to the poor through fiscal transfers.[77] Complexity theories, however, suggest a different approach: in any collection of diverse units, we must explore how "the system might develop enough structure so that the agents can find productive niches."[78] As an official from the National Development and Reform Commission (NDRC) remarked, unlike the smaller and more homogeneous East Asian economies of Japan and South Korea, China's economy features "sharp tiers across the regions," which provides "plenty of room for maneuvering."[79] This suggests that instead of trying to equalize disparities through redistribution, hold back rapid growth on the coast, or pit regions in competition against one another,[80] pairing the rich and the poor could be an alternative avenue for central powers to exercise influence. This potential raises a third crucial question: *What are some ways of leveraging wide regional inequality for national development?*

The underlying challenges of constructing adaptive capacity are not unique to China. What is unique about China is how these problems manifested in three major arenas of its political economy: national reforms, cadre evaluation and incentives, and regional development policies. Also unique is the ways in which state actors, national and local, responded to these problems. My next task is to examine their responses.

The Hardware and Software of Adaptation

Observations of the Chinese regime's adaptive capacity abound. Summing up the early phase of reforms, experts hailed the success of China's "muddling through" and incremental policy making over sweeping "big bang" reforms conducted in the former Soviet Union. As McMillan and Naughton observed, "The reforms have proceeded by trial and error, with frequent mid-course corrections and reversals of policy; the reformers were probing into the unknown. China has muddled through."[81] Even after the Tiananmen crisis in 1989, when the CCP regime perched precariously on the brink of collapse, the party bounced back. Surprising many observers, not only did the CCP leadership reconsolidate its power, it pursued capitalism with even greater fervor than before. This led Nathan to characterize China as an exceptional case of "authoritarian resilience," where "increased institutional complexity, autonomy, and coherence . . . equip the regime to adapt more successfully to the challenges it faces."[82] Since the 1990s, more adaptive labels of the Chinese government and its economy have proliferated, including terms like "adaptive governance,"[83] "adaptive informal institutions,"[84] "adaptive authoritarianism,"[85] "responsive authoritarianism,"[86] "structured uncertainty,"[87] and more.

Although the adaptive qualities of the Chinese regime are widely observed, however, few have attempted to specify its sources. One notable exception is Perry and Heilmann, who sharply ask, "But why has China alone benefited from such [informal and adaptive] institutions?"[88] The deeper source of China's flexibility, they argue, is the CCP's history as a revolutionary party, including its experiences in guerrilla warfare and in mobilizing the masses for support. My analysis in chapter 1 concurs with this argument. As we saw, local officials adapted campaign-style policy enforcement to the contemporary agenda of investment recruitment.

Precisely stated, though, this does not mean that CCP's revolutionary history is a *cause* of China's adaptive capacity. Rather, it means that revolutionary language and practices have contributed to the *variation* of alternatives from which current-day leaders may choose. Following this logic, one may point to other sources of variation, such as China's pre-1949 economic history and lessons that the CCP imbibed from studying foreign experiences.[89] Contributing to a stock of raw materials for innovation, however, does not equate causing innovation.

Another set of explanations for China's adaptability turns from history to structure. This strain of scholarship claims that by combining political centralization with economic decentralization, China achieved an optimal outcome of control and flexibility.[90] Politically, local officials are appointed by higher-level superiors in a nested chain of command reaching from the center down to the townships. Economically and administratively, ground-level agents are granted significant autonomy in making decisions and allocating resources. Landry concludes, "Each layer of local government is critically constrained by the capacity of a hierarchically superior unit to appoint, remove, or dismiss the leading officials in the locale in question. Personnel management is the glue that turns the fragments of the Chinese local state into a coherent—albeit colorful—mosaic."[91]

The combination of political centralization (through the personnel appointment system) and economic decentralization is certainly an enabling structural basis of China's adaptive reforms. But, on its own, the structural explanation sounds too easy to be sufficient for effective adaptation. If mixing top-down hierarchy and the delegation of power was what it took for the Chinese regime to adapt successfully, then why did other authoritarian regimes not copy this structure? Could it be that only China's leaders were smart enough to see the benefits of a mixed structure while other leaders failed to notice?

In tracing the construction of conditions for adaptive capacity in China, my argument builds on earlier structural accounts, but I go beyond them in one important respect: I argue that structure provides only the *hardware* of adaptation. For a comprehensive understanding of whether and how adaptation works, the *software*—namely, how key agents respond to core problems of adaptation within a given structure—needs also to be specified.

In terms of its hardware, I propose that not only is China a decentralized authoritarian state, but that it follows, more specifically, a franchising mode of decentralization.[92] Different from directly owned firms, franchises are hybrid organizations, fusing hierarchical corporate relations (between franchisor and franchisees) with high-powered incentives (franchisees are entitled to a share of store profits). McDonald's is a prime example of franchising; a central franchise leases the company's brand name and business model to entrepreneurs willing to join the partnership.[93]

A major advantage of franchised structures is that they are uniquely adept at adapting to diverse local environments while maintaining a unified brand and operational model. Anywhere we go in the world, we recognize McDonald's because certain features of the company are consistent. Yet local menus vary according to regional tastes. Methods of procurement, operation, and marketing are also localized. In the case of the CCP state, the challenge of balancing a coherent national reform model with adaptations to highly variant local conditions bears striking similarities with the basic operational concerns of franchised companies like McDonald's. But clearly, having the external trappings of a franchise alone does not ensure success; otherwise, all franchises would be profitable. It is the management practices—the software—developed within the hardware of a franchise structure that harnesses the advantages of franchising.

China's reformers combined top-down hierarchy with decentralization to tackle the three central problems of adaptation earlier identified. In broad strokes, I outline their responses to each of these problems, which will be elaborated upon in the next four chapters.

First, how did national leaders influence the agenda of change and amount of local policy variation? They did so through the design of national reform packages and the articulation of policy directives. Reforms initiated by central authorities generated a template of alternatives for the entire nation. In this regard, China's central authorities opted to design national reforms that were wide in scope (i.e., reforms happen simultaneously across multiple domains) but incremental in step (i.e., they build on the pre-existing system). This combination of qualities—wide and incremental—deserves emphasis because it is often assumed that incremental reforms are also narrowly targeted reforms.[94] Contrary to this assumption, China's experience suggests that a gradual approach may actually work better when it is comprehensive in coverage. Then, within a template of national reforms, central leaders fine-tune the degree of flexibility in selected policy areas by issuing a fluid mixture of clear and vague commands. Contrasting the legal and formalized system of rule making in matured democracies like America, where state mandates are inked unambiguously in parchment, central authorities in China's command hierarchy deployed ambiguity to serve adaptive purposes. This argument will be elaborated in chapter 3, "Balancing Variety and Uniformity."

Second, how do higher-level authorities define and reward success among bureaucratic agents, bearing in mind that the Chinese public bureaucracy is a gigantic organization with more than fifty million employees? Answering this question requires, first and foremost, a disaggregation of the bureaucracy into two basic layers: a layer of elite bureaucrats (i.e., officials at the rank of county leaders and above), numbering about 500,000 individuals, followed by tens of millions of regular bureaucrats who work under these elites. Once the distinction is drawn, the answer to my second question may be clarified: the Chinese bureaucracy operates like a quasi-firm. The success of party-state elites is defined in concrete and primarily economic terms through the cadre evaluation system, a report card that lists the targets assigned to each locality and the points earned from achieving these targets. Like corporate CEOs, local leaders care literally about the bottom line. Regular cadres, on the other hand, who have few opportunities for promotion, care mainly about compensation. Like corporate employees, they are paid according to economic output, namely, the amount of revenue generated by their respective agencies and local states. Through these measures of corporatization, the Chinese bureaucracy overcomes the usual barriers of inertia and weak incentives in the public sector. Troublingly, however, it also engenders an excessive focus on making money. This second theme will be examined at length in chapter 4, "Franchising the Bureaucracy."

Third, what are some ways to turn wide regional inequality into a national competitive advantage? On niche creation, China has a decidedly mixed record. During the 1980s and early 1990s, China's economy was plagued by duplicative industries and overcapacity across regions.[95] In the end, it was not central policy interventions but the market forces of competition that eliminated weak copiers and prompted increased regional specialization.[96] But I find that since the 2000s, regional development has evolved toward a new and unexpected direction. It is already well-known that coastal regions sprang ahead in development, growing wealthier and modernizing governance sooner and quicker than in the interior regions, thus widening regional disparities. It is little documented, however, that businesses on the coast started to invest en masse in underdeveloped inland economies, bringing new opportunities to areas that were previously left behind. Reactively rather than proactively, central authorities rode on this new wave by intervening to encourage—but not engineer—this twenty-first-century phenomenon of industrial relocation within China. These patterns form a *domestic* version of "flying geese," a phrase originally coined to describe the tiered system of development among economically unequal countries in Asia.[97]

Hence my comparison of the coevolutionary trajectories of locales across China in part 2 of the book yields an unusual story of *both* divergence and connection. A comparison of the status quo of coastal and inland locales will find marked differences in outcomes, not only in terms of income but also in the quality of administration, policy preferences, and actual practices within local governments. While wide divergence in outcomes across regions is no surprise, similarities in processes by which markets and bureaucracies coevolve are surprising, as previewed in chapter 1. Within localities, niche creation (i.e., the selective cultivation of targeted industries) only becomes a priority after initial growth has taken off. This sequence departs from the East Asian developmental model, where national governments selected winning industries and sought to craft niches for their economies as soon as they launched industrialization drives. This third theme will be laid out in chapters 5 and 6 through three historical cases.

We may now summarize the ways in which Chinese reformers, both national and local, responded to the three key problems of adaptation inherent in the processes of variation, selection, and niche creation, as shown in figure 2.1. Collectively, these responses constituted the meta-institutions that fostered adaptation

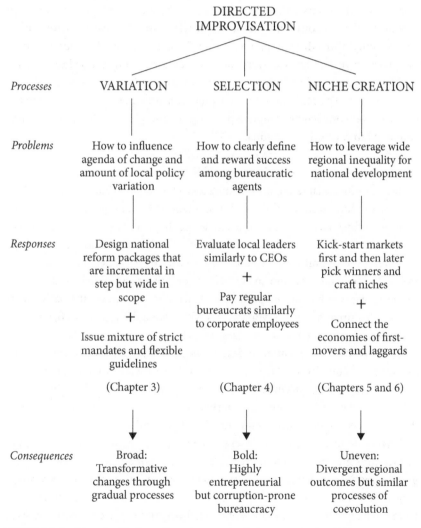

FIGURE 2.1   Meta-institutions that shape adaptive processes in China

in China's political economy. As we may see, meta-institutions need not only take the form of democratic and public deliberation. Rather, the design of national reform packages, methods of policy articulation, bureaucratic evaluation and compensation schemes, and regional development policies can also function as meta-institutions that shape the generation of alternatives, the selection criteria, and niche formation. Furthermore, these meta-institutions are not static structures. Over time, as economic and social conditions evolved, state responses to the essential problems of adaptation also evolved.

My analysis of the sources of adaptive capacity disaggregates adaptation into its composite processes, specifies their inherent tensions, and then examines state responses to these tensions. A key advantage of this analytically precise approach is that it sharpens our understanding of why China's great transformation has exhibited three distinct patterns: transformative changes through gradual processes (broad); highly entrepreneurial but corruption-prone bureaucracy (bold); divergent regional outcomes paired with similar processes of coevolution (uneven). The remaining four chapters will systematically lay out how the distinct—yet connected—adaptive processes taking place in different domains combined to revolutionize China.

We may now sum up the key lessons for the generic question that motivated this chapter: Effective adaptation is something we all love to have, but how do we get it?

First and foremost, what is effective adaptation? The answer depends on how a society defines success and who gets to decide the criteria. What counts as effective adaptation in one society may not be effective in another society. In China, as power is concentrated in the hands of the CCP, the party decides what success means for the country. And in the reform era, the party understands success to mean principally *material prosperity*, which also constitutes the basis for its political legitimacy. Not everyone agrees with such a definition. Mao, who had dedicated his life to continuous class struggle, would be aghast. Sen envisions political freedom as essential to development. Social democracies in Western Europe prize equality as much as prosperity. Nevertheless, CCP leaders choose to view success as the accumulation of national wealth. From this vantage, the efficacy of adaptation is assessed in terms of the effects of selected strategies in enhancing economic growth and maintaining political stability.

Having defined success in a society, the next issue concerns what assembly of measures may be taken to influence each process of adaptation, which I have grouped under the themes of variation, selection, and niche creation. My disaggregation of adaptation into its composite mechanisms differs in significant ways from others who trace the sources of societal adaptive capacity to past historical experiences or particular political structures. Past experiences add to a society's variation of alternatives in the adaptive process, but history does not by itself address problems of adaptation; it is people who exploit and reconfigure past experiences to do so.[98] Likewise, political structures may provide an enabling hardware for adaptation, but it still takes human intervention and constant tinkering to generate the necessary software for adaptation to work.

The overall approach of fostering adaptive governance and development in China may be summed up as *directed improvisation*. At first blush, "directed improvisation" seems to be a contradiction in terms, as we normally think about "directed" as controlling and giving top-down orders and "improvisation" as decentralized and free-flowing. Indeed, these two polarized modes of action have each dominated ideas in development. On the one hand, some emphasize the role of the state in planning and exerting control to achieve specific desired ends. This perspective is evident in the good-governance paradigm (copy best practices from the West), Sachs's Big Push proposal (combine massive foreign aid with comprehensive interventions), and the developmental state school (select winning industries and execute promarket policies). On the other hand, those who hail adaptive approaches urge deliberative democracy, decentralization, broad participation, experimentation, and so on. Whereas the former underscores the role of top-down planning, the latter champions the merits of bottom-up initiative.

In fact, as this chapter argues, direction and improvisation are not substitutive actions but necessary complements. A skilled director is not one who dictates to actors what exactly they should do; rather, he or she enthuses and empowers them in the creative process. To be clear, I am not saying that the Chinese government never exercises control; of course it does. Examples abound. It seeks to exert control over restive ethnic minorities in Xinjiang and Tibet; it seeks to control information on the Internet through censorship; it also controls organized civic actions through policing. But when the CCP exerts control, it inevitably meets resistance. Conversely, when the CCP acknowledges the limits of its control and knowledge and instead tries to influence processes of problem solving within the vast bureaucratic hierarchy, it displays remarkable flexibility and resilience that are unmatched even by many democratic regimes.

We can deepen the study of adaptation by grounding our analyses in a theoretical framework provided by complexity studies. The move toward localized, adaptive approaches in the development field is extremely promising, and such approaches are richly illustrated by China's reform experiences. In order to move this agenda forward, we need to learn more about the ways of combining direction and improvisation. The next four chapters will elaborate on how directed improvisation is done in China.

Part 2
DIRECTION

3

BALANCING VARIETY AND UNIFORMITY

When the central government makes a firm decision, that decision will trigger seismic changes across the country.

—City official, Fujian Province

No, absolutely not.

—Central official, on whether the central leadership intended market reforms to turn out the way they did

Reminiscent of emperors in dynastic regimes, central leaders in contemporary China wield awesome power. Huang's biography of a village party secretary in *The Spiral Road* provides a sharp illustration of the momentous impact of central-level decisions. As the author recounts, in March of 1978, a village party secretary in Fujian Province named Ye proposed a bonus system to the commune party secretary, arguing that if production teams could keep the surplus of their production as a bonus, it would incentivize villagers to work harder. Not surprisingly, Ye was reprimanded by his superior, who threatened to fire him if he dared to raise such audacious ideas again. Then in December of 1978, Deng Xiaoping, the newly anointed pre-eminent leader, announced the party's decision to "reform and open" at the Third Plenum of the Eleventh Party Congress. As soon as the announcement was made, only months after issuing a stern warning, the commune party boss turned around and congratulated Ye for his enterprising proposal. The bonus scheme was promptly implemented with resounding success.[1]

Yet as powerful as central leaders in a communist dictatorship may be, they suffer mortal limitations like everyone else. As the second quote above underscores, central leaders are not prescient. They are often surprised—sometimes even alarmed—when they learn about the unintended consequences of their decisions. Central leaders also lack knowledge of on-the-ground situations, especially in a vast and heterogeneous country like China. Sometimes leaders are even unsure about their own policy preferences. It is not uncommon for them to waver and fudge on difficult problems as the rest of the nation awaits their commands.[2]

The purpose of this chapter is to provide a fresh reinterpretation of the role of the central leadership in China's dynamic reforms. Following game theoretic and principal-agent models in political economy,[3] the assumption of agency is that central leaders (or principals in general) have clear and fixed preferences. Therefore, to many, the central problem of a command hierarchy is basically a control problem: how to ensure that local officials (or agents) will faithfully follow and implement the preferences of the central party-state.[4]

But this chapter stresses that central leaders do not always have clear and fixed preferences. Nor do they merely seek to control local officials and keep them strictly in line with central mandates. Instead, the reality in a complex environment is that higher-level authorities want their subordinates to exercise varying degrees of flexibility when implementing central goals. This is because ground-level agents typically know better than their superiors the particular problems of and possible remedies to problems in their localities. But in delegating problem solving to the grassroots, how did authorities at the top direct the process of local improvisation without exercising micro-control?

By recasting central-local relations from a purely control to an adaptive problem, this chapter illuminates a different role of the central leadership in the reform process: namely, its role in agenda setting and in influencing the amount of policy variation within a vast command hierarchy. Specifically, I will examine two instruments the center uses to authorize and yet delimit the boundaries of localized policy implementation: the design of national reform packages and the articulation of policy directives.

How Incremental Reforms Actually Work

In a single-party hierarchical regime, reform packages designed by the central leadership determine a common agenda for change throughout the chain of command. Many have noted that local governments frequently initiate policy experiments within their jurisdictions,[5] which may feed back to national policy making.[6] But, as clearly illustrated by the opening anecdote of the village party secretary, local experimentation is only possible if the central leadership has already signaled a decisive ideological shift and kick-started a national restructuring program.

As one local official explained in figurative terms, the entire Chinese bureaucracy operates like a stack of briquettes (a block of flammable materials with holes, as used in Chinese cookers). He said, "It is very difficult for a local government or department to initiate reform on its own. Air needs to flow from top to bottom, as in briquettes. If the top briquette has only 10 holes, but the bottom briquette has 12 holes, then air cannot flow."[7] This analogy implies that to launch a transformative path, central authorities must first decide the structure of the briquette—the configuration of reforms—and only then can local governments exercise autonomy and improvise within this authorized agenda.

Given an understanding of the seismic impact of national reforms in China, it is essential to ask: What are the characteristics of these reforms? How were they formulated? One immediate answer that comes to mind is that China's reforms are characteristically "incremental."[8] Contrasting the "big bang" reforms of the former Soviet Union that ambitiously sought to replace central planning with a capitalist system based on private ownership, China's reforms "used and built upon the existing structures of society."[9] And instead of following a predesigned blueprint, Chinese leaders had "proceeded by trial and error" and "muddled through."[10] Such incremental qualities are aptly captured in one of Deng's signature expressions: crossing the river by touching the stones.

Hence, to many observers, China's reforms compellingly testifies to the merits of incrementalism. More specifically, its success is widely interpreted to mean that the *opposite* of big-bang reforms—which were conducted "rapidly and on a broad front"[11]—is preferable. By this logic, incremental reforms should also be narrow in scope. Indeed, beyond China and postcommunist studies, there is growing consensus among development experts that reforms in developing countries should be taken step by step and, at the same time, should target only a few pressing issues. For example, Jomo and Chowdhury, both development experts at the United Nations, assert, "The only feasible and desirable governance agenda may be to incrementally improve developmental governance capabilities *on a smaller scale*."[12] Quoting a report by the United Kingdom's Department of International Development (DFID), they add, "A more modest incremental approach involving *a few important but feasible reforms* . . . may be more pragmatic and likely to succeed."[13] Echoing these statements, Grindle, a leading advocate of "good enough governance," advises,[14] "It is unlikely that much can be accomplished when such countries are overloaded with commitments to change large numbers of conditions at the same time. From this perspective, it is better to . . . *target fewer changes*, and work toward good enough rather than ideal conditions of governance."[15] In similar language, Rodrik also calls for the "targeting of reforms on the most binding constraints."[16]

At first blush, the above recommendations are, of course, sensible. Facing many constraints, developing and transitional countries should be pragmatic. And to be pragmatic, we normally think, means to make gradual *and* few changes. But intuition can be deceiving. In fact, I argue, China's reforms suggest a different lesson about how incremental reforms *actually* work. China's reforms are incremental in the sense that changes are made on the basis of pre-existing structures rather than invented from scratch, yet, as I will demonstrate, they consistently spanned an ambitious scope of policy domains. Contrary to intuition, China's experience suggests that *incremental reforms may actually work better when they are comprehensive in scope.*

To stylize the characteristics of incremental reforms in China as compared to other approaches, picture a row of squares and the alternatives for changing it, as depicted in figure 3.1. The big-bang approach advances reforms that are abrupt, broad, and aimed at replicating a predetermined ideal: a capitalist system as found in the West. Pictorially represented, this mode of reform aspires to turn a row of squares into a row of circles with the wave of a policy wand (the top row). In practice, this approach falters because it underestimates the complexity of engineering a wholesale reconfiguration of multiple institutional arenas in one big leap. The whole irony of the big-bang reforms is that the reformers tried to plan a free market through top-down designs, and in doing so they faced constraints similar to the communist state planners they sought to replace.

Given the failings of the big-bang approach, the intuitive alternative is to follow the direct opposite tack: conduct reforms that are both gradual and narrowly targeted. Pictorially, this method is equivalent to adding only one side to one square and leaving the other squares intact (the middle row).

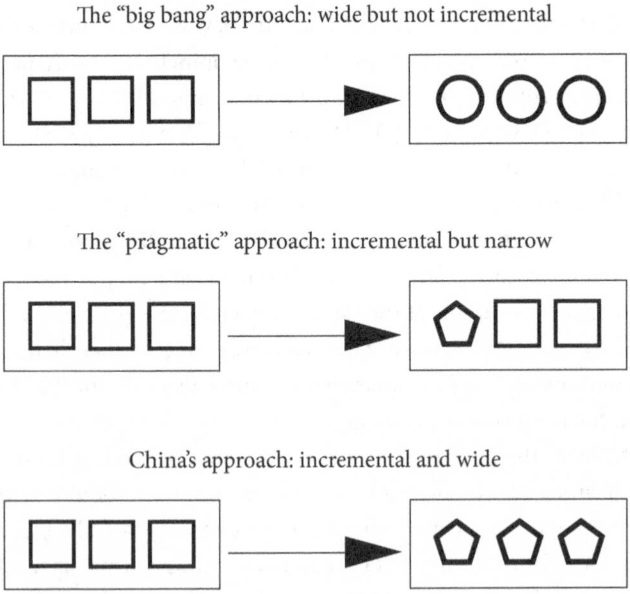

The "big bang" approach: wide but not incremental

The "pragmatic" approach: incremental but narrow

China's approach: incremental and wide

FIGURE 3.1   Three approaches to reform

China's incremental reforms are represented neither by the top nor middle row but instead by the bottom row: all the squares are modified marginally at the same time.

Why might a combination of gradual and broad changes work best to produce transformative results? The answer is embedded in the notion of "institutional complementarities," a term invoked earlier by Aoki and later popularized by Hall and Soskice in their seminal volume *Varieties of Capitalism*.[17] Hall and Soskice argue that even among mature market economies, we observe distinct complementary clusters of economic and governing institutions. According to their definition, "Two institutions can be said to be complementary if the presence (or efficiency) of one increases the returns from (or efficiency of) the other."[18] Extending their logic of cross-national structural variation to the dynamics of restructuring, one may reason that change in one domain is more likely to be effective if it is accompanied by complementary changes in connected parts of the system. Initially, conducting gradual reforms in narrow pockets may seem like the most pragmatic approach, but such reforms are unlikely to transform the system if other related pockets remain stuck. Indeed, in my interviews with central and local officials in China, they frequently invoke the Chinese word for "complementarity" when discussing reforms.[19] The term implies that for a reform to work in one policy arena, it is essential to activate reforms in other coupled arenas.

Below I trace the making of China's national reforms, highlighting the incremental-in-step but wide-in-scope quality of these reforms, as well as the unintended consequences they produced. My purpose is not to give an exhaustive account of China's reforms over thirty-five years of history. Instead, I will focus on the linkages and spillovers across three broad domains: the economy, the bureaucracy, and public finance. In terms of timing, my narrative will be divided into two distinct phases: before 1993 and after 1993. Prior to 1993, reforms under Deng consisted of market reforms on the fringes of the pre-existing planned economy. After 1993, the Jiang-Zhu leadership articulated and embarked on a bold vision to create a modern market economy. Even as a single national case, it is as if two different Chinas have evolved since 1978.

Phase I: Growing Out of the Plan, 1978–1989

The Chinese Communist Party (CCP), led by Mao Zedong, officially took power and established the People's Republic of China in 1949. During the first thirty years of rule under Mao, economic, bureaucratic, and state financial institutions were structured on the basis of the command system. The economy was centrally planned. Rural households were collectivized into communes, which had to surrender their grain production to the state. In the urban sector, state planners dictated to the state-owned enterprises what to produce and at what prices. By deliberately suppressing the prices of agricultural produce and inflating the prices of urban commodities, state planners channeled resources from the rural to the urban sector, thereby feeding an ambitious heavy industrialization drive. Revenue was remitted upward by local governments to the central level and then reallocated to the localities based on a centrally designed budget.[20] As the bulk of public revenue came from the profits of state-owned enterprises, there was little need during that time to construct a modern tax collection system.[21]

Coupled with the planned economy and centralized budgeting was a Maoist bureaucracy. In terms of personnel selection criteria, Mao valued "red" (professed political loyalty) over education and expertise.[22] As a result, unqualified opportunists were often placed in office,[23] the most notorious instance being the Gang of Four. Mao and his radical followers condemned entrepreneurial activities and incentives as bourgeois capitalism. Those who were accused of having capitalist leanings, be it top leaders like Deng or the village party secretary in Huang's account, were subject to persecutions, which culminated in the decade-long violence of the Cultural Revolution.

Deng's rise to power, following the death of Mao and the ouster of Hua Guofeng (Mao's handpicked successor), marked a critical turning point. After securing the reins of power, Deng announced the historic decision to "reform and open" at the Third Plenum of the Eleventh Party Congress in December of 1978. But even prior to this announcement, Deng made several decisive moves to alter the political environment, paving the way for reforms. In evolutionary terms, no adaptation is possible without variation. Hence the first step Deng took was to activate the creation of new alternatives by urging his comrades to "emancipate our minds." His call for emancipation was vigorously advanced through his speeches, party documents, and the state media.

Once the process of variation was activated, the next important step was to decide who in the political system had the authority to propose new policy visions and reforms. One painful lesson the party elders, including Deng himself, had learned is that the concentration of power in one dictator—Mao—can lead to abuses and disastrous consequences. Thus, even though Deng was widely recognized as the new paramount leader, the party patriarchs, including Chen Yun (a cautious planner) and Ye Jianying (a top military marshal), reached an unspoken agreement to rule China as a small collective leadership.[24] Even Deng would not have absolute power. Indeed, throughout his tenure, the highest offices Deng formally held were that of vice party secretary, vice premier, and chairman of the military commission. Instead of exercising power through titles, Deng appointed his trusted protégés to key offices, including Hu Yaobang as the general party secretary and Zhao Ziyang as premier. Vogel sums up the power structure in corporate terms: "Deng was the chairman of the board and chief executive officer, and under Deng, Hu and Zhao were the active presidents of the two separate divisions, the party and the government."[25]

Another key step taken by Deng was to advance a different set of criteria for evaluating societal success. Again, stated in evolutionary terms, effective adaptation and learning is premised on the definition of success. In his trademark straightforward style, Deng's method of evaluating success was encapsulated in the phrase "to seek truth from facts." If a given strategy relieves starvation, generates employment, and creates wealth for the country, it is successful. Expressing this logic in a folksy analogy, Deng famously said, "It doesn't matter whether it is a black or white cat, as long as it catches mice." Deng's clear-cut and pragmatic criteria for judging success presented a radical departure from Mao, to whom success meant adhering to his political ideology of continuous class struggle.

Once variation was activated and the selection criteria were redefined, Deng and his team proceeded to remake the economy. The reformers knew well that replacing a web of Maoist institutions with a web of alternative institutions was a politically delicate and complex task. They chose to implement economic reforms without political reforms as well as to "play to the provinces" by decentralizing power to the localities and ensuring that communist officials would benefit from the process of market reform.[26] Additionally, they opted not to dismantle the preexisting web of Leninist institutions, but instead to weave strands of capitalism onto the fringes of a centrally planned economy. Hence Naughton aptly labels Deng's style of economic reform "growing out of the plan."[27]

During the 1980s, market mechanisms were injected into *multiple* realms of the economy. Among them, I highlight six: rural households, collective enterprises, state enterprises, the price system, small private businesses, and special economic zones. To be clear, Deng did not assemble this package of reforms in the manner of a grand master planner. Instead, he delegated his protégés to tackle particular problems that arose in their respective domains under the guiding principle of "seeking truth from facts," that is, judging success by economic results.

One of the first catalytic changes took place in the impoverished countryside, which Coase and Wang describe as "the weakest part of the socialist economy, where resistance to reform was non-existent,"[28] Wan Li, who was appointed the party secretary of Anhui Province, spearheaded rural reforms. Years before the central leadership announced its decision to decollectivize communes and to contract rural production down to households, the poorest villages, driven by desperation, had already experimented secretly with private farming. In what later came to be known as the household responsibility system (HRS), after submitting grain quotas to the state, farmers were allowed to sell the reminder on the market, which incentivized production. The textbook case of private farming initiated by starving peasants happened in a village of Anhui Province. Wan's job was to deliver and communicate proven results from this bottom-up experiment in order for Deng to endorse it as a national policy.

Another astonishing development in the rural sector is the rise of township and village enterprises (TVEs), enterprises that were collectively owned and managed by township and village governments. The TVEs were neither state-owned enterprises under the charge of higher-level governments nor enterprises owned by private individuals. And it was precisely this hybrid status that allowed TVEs to thrive in a transitional economy. Because state enterprises remained shackled by state planning and controls, while private enterprises were politically ostracized, TVEs became the surrogate entrepreneurial force in vast areas of the countryside. By 1987, industry overtook agriculture as the main source of rural income, inspiring the oxymoronic phrase "rural industrialization."[29]

Deng expressed utter surprise at the proliferation of TVEs. He once said, "In the rural reform our greatest success—and it is one we had by no means anticipated—has been the emergence of a large number of enterprises run by villages and townships. . . . This result was not anything that I or any of the other comrades had foreseen; it just came out of the blue."[30] Commenting on TVEs at another occasion, Deng told a delegation from Yugoslavia that it was "as if a strange army had appeared suddenly from nowhere." And he candidly admitted, "This is not the achievement of our central government."[31]

Although Deng did not take credit for directly creating the TVEs, he and his reformist team had in fact created the underlying conditions that facilitated the rise of these enterprises. The Deng-era TVEs were not totally new inventions. They were spun off from commune and brigade enterprises established in the 1950s as part of Mao's drive for rural industrialization; many of these enterprises made up the "backyard furnaces" of the Great Leap Forward.[32] Why did rural enterprises fail miserably under Mao but succeed spectacularly under Deng? One answer lies in the creation of positive fiscal incentives by the reformers.[33] Under Mao's centralized budgeting system, local governments had to surrender all their revenue to the higher levels. As soon as market reform was launched, the central government introduced fiscal contracting, wherein each level of government remitted a negotiated amount of tax revenue upward and was allowed to keep the excess. In addition, profits generated by TVEs could be kept entirely at the local levels. This part-plan, part-market logic mirrored the contracting arrangements of the household responsibility system in the farming sector, and it had the similar effect of incentivizing local officials to set up TVEs as a vehicle for maximizing revenue.

Inseparable from the restructuring of public financial rules were changes in bureaucratic evaluation and rewards. The higher levels of the bureaucracy designed performance targets that assessed and rewarded lower-level governments based on their abilities to generate enterprise profits, collect revenue, and expand GDP.[34] Bureaucratic compensation practices were also adjusted along a part-plan, part-market logic, as I will later detail in chapter 4. Although formal wages were centrally fixed at a pittance rate, supplemental compensation (e.g., performance bonuses and nonmonetized perks) soared as state actors dove headlong into entrepreneurial activities.

Such new criteria and rewards of bureaucratic efficacy had a direct impact on local officials' selection of particular production strategies. Under Mao, local cadres adopted "crackpot" methods propagated in the state media, such as packing seedlings tightly to increase yields and melting household pots into useless blocks of steel.[35] These actions seem crazy, of course, but people chose to do crazy things because the political system under Mao defined good cadres as agents who demonstrated blind faith in Mao. At the launch of the Great Leap Forward, a front-page report in the *People's Daily* trumpeted, "The more courage you have, the greater the yields." By contrast, under Deng, success was judged by practical, material results. Thus local cadres chose to promote industrial production in rational ways,[36] rational in the sense that they were guided by facts, not faith.

On the urban front, Premier Zhao Ziyang took the lead in reforms. Like in other planned economies, the state enterprises in China had long been plagued by passivity, red tape, and inefficiency.[37] Led by Zhao and his staff at the think tanks, in May of 1984 the State Council issued a document to "further expand the autonomy of state-owned enterprises."[38] To incentivize state enterprises to take initiative and to produce more efficiently, they were allowed to sell surplus goods on the market after meeting stipulated quotas. Once again, note that this part-plan, part-market contracting arrangement was also paralleled in the farming and public financial sectors. State enterprises, rural households, and local states each had to fulfill their roles in the planned economy—deliver assigned targets—but once they had done their part, they were free to engage in the market.

A necessary corollary of the rural and urban reforms was a reform of the pricing system. After all, if prices were strictly controlled by state planners, disconnected from market demand, farmers and enterprises would have limited drive to sell on the market, even if they could. But instead of abruptly liberalizing prices across the board, as was implemented in Russia with destabilizing effects,[39] China's reformers devised a hybrid system of dual-track pricing: state planners fixed some prices but let the market determine the rest. As producers focused more on making goods that were sold profitably at market prices, state planners gradually liberalized price setting.

Meanwhile, two other major experiments were simultaneously unfolding in the economy. Daringly, Deng's reformist team proposed the revival of small private businesses, which were eliminated after collectivization in the mid-1950s. This proposal was the political equivalent of stepping into a minefield, given the lethal association of private businesses with capitalist exploitation under Mao. But Deng offered a compelling justification that even the party conservatives found hard to reject: job creation. In 1978 and 1979, an estimated 6.5 million "sent-down youths" had returned from the countryside to the cities. To avoid urban unrest, employment had to be created for these young people, and one easy solution was to allow private individuals to set up small businesses.[40]

Simultaneously, as millions of private entrepreneurs started small businesses, big businesses starting brewing in the coastal cities. Reformers at the helm, in partnership with enterprising provincial leaders like Ren Zhongyi (governor of Guangdong) and Xi Zhongxun (party secretary of Guangdong and father of current president Xi Jinping) carved out special economic zones (SEZs) in selected cities on the coast, where special exemptions and greater autonomy were granted to encourage export-oriented foreign investments. The SEZs became China's capitalist incubators, where cutting-edge economic practices and ideas were first innovated and then diffused to the rest of the country.[41]

It is worth taking a pause at this point to reconsider the incremental qualities of China's first decade of market transition. Looking at the scope of institutional changes, the reform package of the 1980s hardly fits the DFID's recommendation of a "modest incremental approach involving *a few* important but feasible reforms" or Rodrik's prescription of targeting reforms "on the most binding constraints." One may counter that all six realms of reforms reviewed constitute "the most binding constraints," but if so, they cover nearly *all* the economy, certainly not just "a few" changes! While it is clear that the reforms during this initial stage grew out of the pre-existing planned economy, they were *expansive in scope*. Importantly, too, the reforms across multiple arenas were *complementary*. For example, contracting arrangements could not have effectively spurred rural and urban production unless the pricing system was also partially liberalized. Nor could TVEs flourish unless the rules of public finance and cadre evaluation were also altered. In short, incremental reforms do not equal piecemeal reforms; the former works only when connected pieces of the system are simultaneously modified.

As Vogel relates, Deng's popularity peaked on National Day in 1984, when students at Peking University spontaneously greeted Deng on the streets with a banner that read "Hello, Xiaoping!"[42] Riding on his popularity, at the Third Plenum of the Twelfth Party Congress in 1984, Deng proposed the slogan "socialism with Chinese characteristics" to sum up the theme of the reforms conducted to date. He emphasized that socialism should aim to achieve prosperity for the whole society, not egalitarianism at the expense of wealth creation. This slogan was endorsed by Zhao Ziyang, who had been promoted to general party secretary, at the Thirteenth National Party Congress in 1987.

The first decade of reform boasted significant accomplishments. GDP per capita grew at an annual rate of 7.5 percent, and living standards visibly improved.[43] The early successes, however, bore the seeds of economic problems that, to use Shirk's phrase, "boomeranged, returning in the form of political resistance."[44] Rapid growth and investment sparked inflation, made worse by Deng's haste to accelerate price liberalization. The unexpected boom of TVEs eroded the competitiveness and profits of the large SOEs, threatening the interests of the working class. The emergence of rich private entrepreneurs provoked social envy. Partial market reforms and dual-track pricing created tempting opportunities for public managers and bureaucrats to exploit their privileges for private gain, such as by procuring scarce products under the plan and then selling them at inflated prices on the market. Social discontent, goaded on by a loosened political atmosphere, motivated large-scale protests in the spring of 1989, which congregated in Tiananmen Square in Beijing but soon spread to other major cities. On June 4, fearing that protests would run out of control, the central leaders made a fateful decision to order military troops to clear the square by force. The troops fired upon the protesters, injuring and killing possibly thousands. The first decade of reform had lifted millions of people out of abject poverty, but it ended tragically in massacre in 1989.

Phase II: Building a Socialist Market Economy, 1993–Present

The first few years in the aftermath of the Tiananmen incident represent a harrowing interlude in China's contemporary history. The killing of protesters tarnished China's international reputation. Foreign investors fled the country in droves. The event empowered the conservative faction in the CCP, whose worst nightmares about Deng's bold reforms had come alive. As powerful as he was, Deng, the paramount leader, was forced to take a back seat while the conservative camp pushed forth a series of retrenchment policies that threatened to reverse China's promarket trajectory. At this critical juncture, China's path could have taken a wholly different turn.

Fortunately, Deng's political will and ingenuity won the day. In 1992, Deng embarked on his famous Southern Tour, which was essentially a publicity campaign to rev up popular support for the continuation of capitalist reforms. On the pretext of a family vacation, the eighty-eight-year-old patriarch toured the southern provinces, where the stunning results of market reforms were widely broadcast on television. Along the way, Deng drummed up support from southern provincial leaders, the military, and the press. By the end of his tour, Deng had turned the tide of public opinion. The new CCP leadership assured that market reforms would not only continue but would deepen and expand.

Described as a "watershed," the year 1993 marked a structural break in China's reforms.[45] Deng officially retired from all his posts after the Southern Tour; Hu Yaobang had passed away; and Zhao Ziyang was placed under house arrest after Tiananmen. A new vanguard, led by Jiang Zemin, the general party secretary, and Zhu Rongji, the premier, took over the reins of power. Under Deng, the guiding tenet was to "cross the river by touching the stones," which implied that the destination that lay across the river was yet unknown. The reforms of the 1990s, however, would depart markedly from the 1980s. At the Third Plenum of the Fourteenth Party Congress in November of 1993, Jiang announced the decision to establish a "socialist market economy." The choice of words was deliberate and significant. The ultimate goal of the party was to achieve a market economy. The term "socialist" was an adjective appended to the market economy, rather than the objective of reform.[46] This time, the vision of what lay across the river was specified.

Whereas Deng and his team introduced market reforms only on the margins of a planned economy, the post-1993 reformers resolved to replace central planning with a market economy. To accomplish this structural overhaul, they recognized the need to construct a comprehensive institutional framework to support free-market activities. The 1993 decision was an extensive document that highlighted five pillars of reform: creation of modern enterprises, expansion of market mechanisms, enforcement of macroeconomic controls, redistribution of income, and construction of social safety nets. A commentary in *China Reform*, a leading Chinese business journal, raved, "These five pillars represent the finest of high-level designs and broad planning."[47] Evidently, the reforms of the post-1993 era were neither piecemeal nor narrowly targeted. Moreover, to enforce reforms in the economy, national policy makers also had to restructure public finance and the bureaucracy. Known for his authoritarian decision-making style, Premier Zhu Rongji was an ideal candidate to push through this massive restructuring program.

In the realm of public finance, Zhu's first order of business was to rein in the explosion of local revenue at the expense of central revenue. The particularistic fiscal bargains of the 1980s provided attractive incentives for local governments to generate revenue, spurring them to accelerate rural industrialization and growth. But the flip side of this arrangement was that local agents also tried to game the system by hiding revenue from their higher-level superiors. The lack of predictability and transparency in fiscal contracting exacerbated the difficulty of monitoring local tax collection. Hence, in 1994, the central government abolished fiscal contracting and replaced it with the tax-sharing system, which spelled out a uniform code of national, shared, and local taxes. The terms of sharing tilted sharply in favor of the center. To enforce the collection of central taxes, national tax collection agencies directly employed by the central government were established alongside local tax agencies. Through these measures, the 1994 fiscal reform effectively recentralized revenue, earning Zhu the reputation of "the great centralizer."[48]

Meanwhile, on the bureaucratic front, the central reformers simultaneously sought to revamp the bureaucracy into a modern regulatory organization capable of administering a market economy. To this end, Zhu advanced an ambitious program of reforms that spanned the areas of budgeting, auditing, accounts management, fiscal reclassification, extrabudgetary control, collection of fees and fines, licensing approvals, anticorruption, and more.[49] To be clear, these technical advancements did not and could not obliterate exchange-based corruption between powerful officials and businesses seeking privileges. Yet their effects in countering petty theft and extortion among low-level cadres were palpable, as I will further detail in chapters 4 and 5.[50]

Although China's reforms in the 1990s may seem to exemplify comprehensive, top-down institutional design, its distinction from the big-bang approach in the former Soviet Union must be sharply drawn. Essentially, the big-bang reforms tried to leap straight from socialism to capitalism. Quoting Leszek Balcerowicz, who was twice the prime minister of Poland, the reformers in Eastern Europe had decided from the beginning that it was "better to take proven models," namely, those found in the capitalist-democratic West.[51] On the other hand, the ambitious post-1993 reforms in China were only possible because Deng's team had *already taken the first few steps of partial market reforms*. In addition, thanks to Deng's skillful maneuvers, the CCP had reconsolidated power and rebounded from a major political crisis, giving the new vanguard the mandate to move forward.

Sequence matters. Transported back in time to the 1980s, the Jiang-Zhu leadership could not have accomplished what they aspired to do a decade later. For example, if the 1993 decision had been implemented in 1979, it would have meant that prices would suddenly have been liberalized across the board and that millions of SOE workers would have been laid off at a snap. Furthermore, even though the post-1993 leadership clearly spelled out the goal of building a "socialist market economy," it did not intend to copy wholesale models from

Western capitalist economies. The adjective "socialist" underscored the CCP's commitment to building a market economy tailored to China's social and political realities.

Even though the 1993 decision was planned by bureaucrats and experts at the central level, the implementation of the program was not immune from unexpected downstream consequences. Inadvertently, the reforms of the 1990s planted the seeds of new problems and crises that we read in news headlines today. Most notably, the 1994 fiscal reform recentralized tax revenue without adjusting expenditure assignments. Local governments retained less revenue but had to continue to spend; in fact, they were compelled to spend more than they did in the 1980s as social demands for public education, health, pension, and infrastructure surged over the years. Budgetary pressures escalated after 1994, as the "fiscal cliff" in figure 3.2 clearly shows. But unlike state governments in most federal systems, China's local governments had no authority to issue bonds or to enact local taxes. They were also constitutionally forbidden from incurring budget deficits. The central government did provide fiscal transfers, but they were far from sufficient to meet budgetary needs in most localities.[52] Moreover, reliance upon fiscal transfers put local authorities at the mercy of higher-level superiors who distributed the funds. Crushed by growing fiscal pressures, local authorities had to find a new source of revenue, and there was none more attractive than revenue from land.

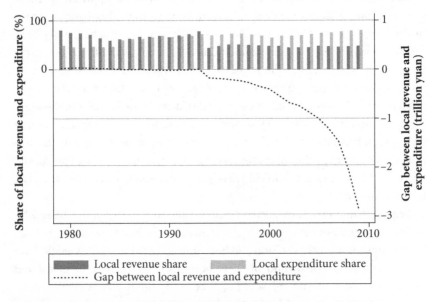

FIGURE 3.2 The post-1994 fiscal cliff of local governments. Author's calculation from *China Finance Yearbook* 2010.

The financial pressures wrought by the 1994 fiscal reform ushered in the rise of what came to be known as "land financing." As a compromise, in 1994, the same year the tax-sharing reform was implemented, the central government decided to allow subnational governments to retain all revenue obtained from the leasing of land, which was previously shared with the national government.[53] In principle, land in China is owned by the state. Developers and businesses may only "lease" parcels of land for a stipulated period of time. To lease land, they have to pay a one-time "land-leasing fee," which may amount to millions of dollars or more in a single transaction. Thus, for local governments, the land-leasing fee presents an irresistible revenue windfall.[54]

Land financing unintentionally spilled into the realms of state investment and the financial sector. As China's local governments are not legally allowed to sell bonds to raise revenue, they adapted land financing for public borrowing. Using land revenue as collateral, local governments throughout the country scrambled to set up shell companies, known amorphously as "financing platforms" or "investment vehicles,"[55] to borrow from state banks. These land-backed loans were then used to finance legions of mega-projects, which would otherwise be impossible to fund using tax revenue or land proceeds alone. Even a casual visitor to China will not fail to notice the scene of constant and rapid construction, as if Legoland has sprung to life on a supersized scale. Pointing to the gap in infrastructure development in China and India, Bardhan calls it "the dazzling difference."[56] Some mega-projects produced empty stadiums and half-finished parks that sit eerily abandoned. Yet other projects have increased public services provision and infrastructural amenities.[57] Especially for inland locales, land proceeds are indispensable for financing transportation projects that improve accessibility and thereby enable these locations to attract investment.[58]

Despite the benefits of an urban infrastructure boom fueled by land finance in the 2000s, both policy makers and experts agree that China's model of rapid economic growth has become "imbalanced," that is, too dependent on investments and prone to overcapacity.[59] Even more worrisome, the financing platforms established by local authorities are nontransparent and virtually unregulated.[60] As a result, hidden debts mounted as local states borrowed in disguise. This entire system came to be dubbed a "shadow banking" industry. Pessimistic reports abounded that banking defaults could threaten to wreck the Chinese economy.[61] At the time of writing this book, the current administration is still mulling ways to clean up the debt mess.

Before we jump to the conclusion that these are problems unique to authoritarian China, though, it is worth noting that this system of public finance bears some striking similarities to that of "taxless financing" in postindependence

America (which I will discuss more in chapter 7). American state governments were reluctant to impose taxes on local populations for a different reason—they did not want to lose voters—but as a result, they too resorted to taxless sources of public finance to sponsor landmark infrastructure projects like the Erie Canal.[62]

We have seen how national reforms in China were formulated and evolved over time. The reform package of the 1980s and later after 1993 pursued different objectives of reforms and used different approaches. The former was more experimental and bottom-up, whereas the latter was more designed and top-down. And whereas the reforms of the 1980s served to *build* markets, those of the 1990s aimed to *expand* and *preserve* emerging markets. Yet despite these differences, both periods of reform share the characteristic of building upon preceding systems and steps instead of skipping straight from one starting point to another idealized destination. This feature of making changes step by step is what qualifies Chinese reforms as incremental. Incremental reforms, however, need not be piecemeal, narrow, or slow. In fact, a review of China's reform history suggests that incremental reforms are likely to work better when they are wide in scope and when complementarities across various policy domains are taken into account.

Going back to the analogy of a local official I earlier quoted, the national reform package determines the structure of the "briquette," how many holes and where the holes should be punched in the combustible block of the command hierarchy. Once the central authorities announce the configuration of reforms to be carried out across the country, this ideological framework will empower local officials to improvise within the authorized structure.

Yet activating local action is only the first step. After deciding the structure of the briquette, the next step is to signal to local authorities which holes are firm and which ones could be stretched. In other words, in any given national policy package, some policies must be strictly enforced but others may be flexibly implemented. How can central authorities calibrate and signal the amount of local discretion in various policy realms? This takes me to the art of giving commands in a decentralized authoritarian regime.

Issuing Variant Signals to Guide Variation

In the United States, state legislation is clearly inked in parchment and sometimes exhaustively detailed, even running into thousands of pages. State laws and regulations are then posted in the U.S. *Federal Register* for public viewing. By contrast, in the Chinese political system, the leadership is well-known for pronouncing broad and even enigmatic guidelines. Vogel describes Deng's slogan of "socialism with Chinese characteristics" as a "grand but marvelously vague expression."[63] Brandt and Rawski elaborate:

> Functionaries at all levels must study and discuss the speeches and writings of top leaders. . . . These guidelines become encapsulated in catchy slogans that gain wide currency in official circles and also among the Chinese public. These slogans, and the policy guidelines that inform them, direct the flow of policy implementation at all levels.[64]

Although it is widely recognized that Chinese leaders rely on speeches and slogans to express their policy goals and preferences, how this system *really* works remains an underappreciated mystery. How can a vast developing country, facing daunting challenges, be governed and transformed through catchy slogans and vague expressions from the authoritarian leadership? Since China's top leaders exercise supreme power, why do they not just dictate exactly what local officials are expected to do?

In this section, I propose an adaptive logic behind policy articulation in the Chinese command hierarchy. I will first argue that instructions from the higher levels are in fact not always vague; rather, they come in varying degrees of clarity. Then I further argue that by adjusting the degree of clarity in its dictates, the leadership can influence the amount of discretion that local agents exercise when implementing different policy goals.

Understood in a stylized manner, the directives issued by the Chinese leadership may be grouped into three colored signals: red, black, and gray. Directives that make clear what cannot be done by local agents are known in Chinese policy discourse as "red lines." Red policies permit no variation. For local governments, red lines constitute binding constraints.

A second, "gray" variety comprises policy statements where the leadership is deliberately ambiguous about what can and cannot be done. These policies permit local experimentation and variation because restrictions are not explicitly stated. Adaptive responses to ambiguous directives produce feedback that then informs the central authorities about how policies should be adjusted.

The final category is what I call "black" policies: written and publicized instructions that clearly sanction a particular course of action. This form of directive empowers local agents to take bold action. Because of the potency of clear-cut mandates, a prudent leader like Deng would only issue them after careful deliberation. Hence, as I will show, black policies typically evolve from gray policies. The former serve to officially endorse informal practices or bottom-up coping strategies that had emerged under ambiguous gray directives. These three varieties of policy directives are summarized in table 3.1. Below I translate and quote from selected central documents to illustrate each variety.

TABLE 3.1 Three varieties of policy directives

SIGNAL OF GUIDELINE	FUNCTION	EXAMPLE
Red	Clearly forbids a particular course of action	"A Summary of Plans for National Land Use" [2008]: Specifies concrete quotas that limit the conversion of arable land for urban use
Gray	Permits bounded experimentation and generates bottom-up policy feedback	"Guidelines on the Development of Commune and Brigade Enterprises" [1979]: Encourages commune and brigade enterprises to "make big progress" and to "adapt to local conditions"
Black	Clearly sanctions a particular course of action	Amendment to Article 11 of the Constitution [2004]: Announces that the state "encourages and supports" the private sector

Signaling What Cannot Be Done

Policy guidelines that are coded red usually relate to matters of national security or collective action problems that require central intervention. Land is one example of a common pool resource. In their myopic eagerness to sell land for revenue, local officials have been depleting the national pool of arable land. Hence the central government drew a bright red line to restrict the conversion of agricultural land to urban and construction purposes. According to central policy, encapsulated in a document issued by the Ministry of Land and Resources in 2008 titled "A Summary of Plans for National Land Use," the country must preserve a minimum of two hundred million hectares of farmland nationwide.[65] This quota is distributed across the provinces and then level by level down to the grassroots. Each locality is assigned a concrete numerical target in terms of the amount of farmland that must be retained within its jurisdiction at any given point in time. Local officials refer to this binding restriction that is imposed by the central government as the "1.8 billion *mu* (200 million hectares) red line."

The genesis of this red line can be traced back to the 1994 fiscal reform. As recounted earlier, the 1994 reform dramatically reduced the share of tax revenue that could be retained by subnational governments. To compensate for the shortfall in local revenue, the central government allowed local governments to convert agricultural land into land for urban use, which could then be leased to developers for lucrative land transfer fees. In a mad rush for revenue, local governments turned more and more arable land over to commercial hands for urban use. From

1997 to 2009, China lost about 123 million *mu* of arable land.[66] For central authorities, the rapid loss of arable land posed a grave threat to China's grain security.
It also endangered social stability in the countryside,[67] as evidenced by numerous
media reports about mass protests against alleged land grabs by local officials. In
response, the central authorities imposed tougher and more concrete restrictions
on the conversion of arable land. The central document, titled "A Summary of
Plans for National Land Use," not only declared the aggregate amount of farmland
that had to be maintained at any point in time, but it also went further to detail the
allocation of quotas for varying land-use purposes in each province.

Yet another example of a common pool resource is water. During the past
decades, the feverish growth of China's economy has rapidly depleted its natural
resources, including water. Eleven of thirty-one provinces have less water per
resident than the World Bank's benchmark for water shortage.[68] To address this
looming crisis, the State Council issued Directive No. 1 in 2011: "Decision on
Accelerating the Regulation of Water Consumption."[69] The document opens by
declaring the urgency of controlling water usage: "In the face of rapid industrialization and urbanization and the growing impact of global climate changes, the
problems of water management and use have become more severe than ever." As
in the case of the land-use restrictions, the State Council drew a bright red line in
this document of 670 billion cubic meters for the total annual consumption of
water. Quotas on water consumption were then distributed by region, industry,
and product. On the heels of the State Council's orders, the Ministry of Water
Resources vowed to "formulate a string of regulations to implement the strictest
management system."[70]

The Ministry of Water Resources was not trumpeting an empty promise.
After the central government draws a red line, the policy is followed by a host of
enforcement mechanisms to ensure that the restriction has bite. One of the first
steps is to specify a national quota, which is then disaggregated and allocated to
the subnational units. The quotas are integrated into the cadre evaluation system (more in chapter 4). For example, in terms of water conservation, the State
Council's decision required that all localities name specific departments and
officials to be held accountable for implementing water-management policies.[71]
Also, the directives state that individual violations against red-line policies are
criminal offenses.[72] This implies that local leaders who violate red-line policies,
such as by ignoring land and water quotas or by misappropriating land revenue
for nonconstruction purposes, will not only risk their careers but could even land
in jail on criminal charges.

Personnel management mechanisms are further strengthened by efforts to
construct a comprehensive infrastructure for data collection and audits. For
instance, in order to enforce land quotas, China has developed a sophisticated

monitoring and information system, including the use of GPS (global position-ing system) technologies, to track land use across the country.[73] A local land bureau officer admonished, "Even if the local government can attract investors, it is no use if there is no excess quota for land. No one dares to mess around. Nowadays there is a GPS system watching from above."[74] Another officer even hummed a rhyme that describes the enforcement of land quotas: "GPS runs in the sky, the city runs on the web [city-level inspectors monitor electronic records], and we run on the ground [county-level officers carry out on-site inspections]."[75] Echoing the views of other local officials, the party secretary of a wealthy county lamented, "Industrial growth requires a large amount of land, but the national policy of '1.8 billion *mu*' restricts our locale."[76] In short, when it comes to red policies, the instructions are clear and firm; there is little leeway to "mess around."

But, skeptics may counter, media reports about land grabs give the impres-sion that China's local officials blatantly violate central restrictions against land conversions and sales. In fact, what lies behind the headlines is a complex story of local adaptation to centrally imposed constraints that the media rarely notices or understands.[77] Local governments are caught in a double whammy: on the one hand, they need to convert land to urban use in order to build fac-tories, attract investors, and generate revenue; on the other hand, they must abide by the centrally imposed land quotas lest they risk personal liability for violating a red-line policy.[78] Local officials discovered that one way of coping with this dilemma is to compact dispersed villages into apartments and then turn previously unused rural land into active farmland.[79] This exercise increases the amount of farmland within a local jurisdiction, thus giving local govern-ments extra room to legally convert more valuable parcels of land for urban use. Developers then bid to purchase these freed-up quotas. This has generated an unusual market for land quotas rather than for actual parcels of land. Chengdu was among the first cities to establish such a market; between 2008 and 2011, more than sixteen thousand transactions were made at an accumulated value of more than 11.5 billion yuan (US$1.9 billion).[80] Through these strategies, each locality keeps within its quota, and the country on aggregate maintains the "1.8 billion *mu* red line."

The unintended consequence of such coping strategies, though, is that tens of millions of farmers have been and continue to be abruptly urbanized. Once farmers trade their farmland for apartments in suburban high-rises, they lose their traditional occupations and ways of life. During a field trip arranged by local governments, we visited several model residential communities that were truly impressive and equipped with centers dedicated to helping relocated farm-ers secure urban jobs. But beyond these models, I have witnessed other suburban high-rises that were shoddily built, looked like jails, and lacked social amenities.

Compacted suburban communities for relocated farmers in a model site. Chengdu City, Sichuan.

Other suburban high-rises are less attractive and look almost like jails. Nanning City, Guangxi.

Social tensions triggered by this state-led wave of urbanization in the countryside will trouble China for years to come.

From Signaling What Might Be Done to What Can Be Done

In contrast to restrictive red policies, permissive black policies officially approve particular actions. Black policies are typically preceded by gray directives that are vaguely worded and deliberately ambiguous. In effect, gray policies give local agents room to experiment as long as they do not breach the red lines. As Kellee Tsai observed, such bottom-up adaptive efforts "may take on an institutional reality of their own."[81] When adaptive strategies are widely adopted and proven to work, central reformers are then motivated to turn previously gray signals into black signals, in other words, to shift from ambiguity to clear endorsements.

For an illustration of a gray-to-black policy stance during the pre-1993 period, Deng's handling of bottom-up experiments in private farming provides a useful illustration. As earlier discussed, the reformist leaders did not come up with the idea of decollectivizing communes and contracting production down to households. Instead, this was a desperate experiment initiated by starving farmers in the poorest parts of China. In the realm of agricultural reform, Deng had given Wan Li, who was then the provincial party secretary of Anhui, the autonomy to deal with the problems in his domain. Deng listened keenly to Wan's feedback on the experiments carried out by farmers in Anhui, but he was careful not to publicly support decollectivization prematurely.

Deng was cautious for several reasons. First, as Vogel acutely notes, Deng knew from experience that "signals from the top were studied very carefully by those below."[82] If the leadership sends a clear signal that a particular policy should and can be adopted, the entire country will march along. For a dictator, the power of central mandates to "turn heaven and earth upside down," as it is said in Chinese, may seem enviable. But for the people, if the mandate is poorly formulated, the results will be widespread and disastrous, as witnessed in Mao's campaign of the Great Leap Forward, which led to mass starvation. Hence, Deng "was careful about what he said."[83] He wanted to make sure that a local experiment or proposed policy worked before he officially supported it.

Second, in order to overcome political resistance to change, central leaders must first build up public support for new policies. To this end, even before he formally endorsed Wan's push for decollectivization, Deng "shaped the atmosphere" by widely publicizing the success of the proposal through high-profile party meetings and the media.[84] Notably, this was an exercise in political influence rather than control. By the fall of 1978, Anhui reported bountiful harvests in places where private farming was practiced. At national conventions, other local officials chimed in to support the experiment.

Once Deng assessed that political conditions were ripe, he made his position clear. In May of 1980, he publicly expressed his approval of the experiment in Anhui: "[It] has proved quite effective and changed things rapidly for the better. . . . It is extremely important for us to proceed from concrete local conditions and take into account the wishes of the people."[85] Shortly after, Wan Li was promoted to vice premier and a member of the party secretariat responsible for agriculture. In September of 1980, the central party issued Directive No. 75, officially permitting the assignment of rural production to individual households.

Following this resounding endorsement, a wave of decollectivization swept across the country. Even collective farms that worked in some areas were pressured to close,[86] validating Deng's apprehension about overly eager local enforcement of clear central mandates. By 1982, communes were abolished. Five years later, the constitution was revised to guarantee household contracting rights. And by 1989, nearly half a century since the CCP took power, China finally produced enough grain to abolish grain rationing altogether.[87]

Next, I turn to the important case of collective or township and village enterprises (TVEs). As in the case of rural household contracting, Deng and his colleagues had neither conceived nor approved of TVEs at the beginning of reform. A local official who formerly headed the Office of TVE Management in a county of Shandong recalled:

> The institutional precedent to the TVEs was the people's communes. Each year from 1979 to 1984, the central government issued a Document No. 1 concerning rural economic development. These documents were called No. 1 because they signaled that they had crucial implications for all aspects of rural development. From 1979 to 1984, the TVEs were not completely politically permitted because it was not part of the plan. Nor were they politically acceptable because townships and villages were supposed to engage in agriculture. Back then, there was no plan for industrialization [at these two lowest levels of government].[88]

Consistent with the above recollection, the central government's ambiguous stance toward TVEs was evident in its policy statements. In Directive No. 1 issued by the State Council in 1979, titled "Guidelines on the Development of Commune and Brigade Enterprises,"[89] the phrase "township and village enterprises" did not appear even once. Instead, the document referred to "commune and brigade enterprises." The document urged local authorities to be entrepreneurial, but it did not say whether or not township and village governments could establish their own enterprises. The first section opens with a vague declaration: "Following the Party's decision at the Third Plenum to accelerate rural develop-ment, commune and brigade enterprises are urged to make great progress."[90] But exactly what form of "great progress" the leadership expected was nowhere specified in the guideline. It merely listed some commonsense reasons for why making "great progress" would benefit rural development.

The second section then emphasized that the collective enterprises must abide by socialist principles. But, again, how this was to be done was left blank. Instead, the guideline stressed two broad points. First, the formation of collective enterprises should "adapt to local conditions," namely "the availability of local resources and demand." Second, such efforts must be "self-independent," that is, local governments should not expect to receive handouts from the central state. Throughout the guidelines, the terms "according to local conditions," "for those localities that have the right conditions," and "based on need and feasibility" were prefixed to the broad policy prescriptions.[91] At the local levels, each of these terms for an action plan could be interpreted in multiple ways.

In equally ambiguous language, the directive glossed over the potential for competition between the existing and notoriously inefficient state-owned enter-prises and upstart collective enterprises.

> In places where the government has already established state-owned [agricultural goods] processing firms, the question of whether com-munes and brigades can also set up processing firms should be decided by the relevant departments in the respective provinces, cities, and regions, whose decisions will be based on their assessments of the pros and cons.

The central state essentially deflected the thorny political problem of how to handle competition between collective and state-owned enterprises back to the local authorities. Additionally, note that the guidelines did not even specify who the local authorities were; instead it invoked the amorphous phrase "the relevant departments" (a term that, until this day, commonly appears in official Chinese documents). These "relevant departments" were advised to decide whether or not to set up nonstate firms "based on their assessments of the pros and cons."[92] In colloquial terms, the document essentially says: you (whoever you are) decide for yourself whether this works for you.

Nevertheless, although much of the document was vague, it named a few red lines that could not be crossed. One major restriction was related to private ownership. It was emphasized that "commune and brigade enterprises" are "an economic institution under the socialist system of collective ownership, owned by the communes and brigades who run them."[93] It also stressed that commune and brigade enterprises were required to comply with national price controls.

They were not allowed to charge prices beyond those ceilings set at the central levels.[94] Hence, in the first few years of reform, local officials experimented cautiously with collective entrepreneurship. The earlier quoted official from Shandong recounted, "We tried to find whatever loopholes that existed at that time. If we were explicitly barred from doing something, then we would try something else that was not restricted."[95]

To the surprise of the central leaders, collective enterprises became hugely successful in parts of the country. This success emboldened the leadership to officially embrace this experiment. In 1984, the State Council issued Directive No. 1, titled "Guidelines on Rural Work in 1984."[96] Compared to the directive of 1979, this directive expressed greater optimism about the growth of collective enterprises. Sanctioning these institutions in stronger language, it specifically allayed political concerns as to whether collective enterprises constituted private capitalism.

> Currently, among enterprises that hire more employees than approved by the previous regulations, some have instituted practices that are different from those of private enterprises. For example, they retain a portion of the after-tax profits and use it as collectively owned capital. . . . This constitutes elements of a collective economy. So we should help refine and improve them. We can choose not to regard them as a capitalist form of enterprise that hires labor.[97]

Indeed, when the central state's ambiguity toward collective enterprises was expressed in starker, more approving language, local agents responded with enthusiastic initiative. As figure 3.3 shows, the number of industrial collective enterprises jumped dramatically after 1984.[98] The absolute value of gross industrial output produced by collective enterprises took off in the 1990s, reflecting the deepening of market reforms. From the 1980s up until the early 1990s, the collective sector unexpectedly became the driver of China's rural industrial boom.

A third illustration of a shift in the central policy stance from gray to black is found in the development of the private sector. Throughout the 1980s and even well into the 1990s, the terms "private" and "capitalist" were taboo. After all, during the Maoist period, bourgeois capitalists were the prime targets of political persecutions. A major innovation of the Deng period was the revival of small private businesses, defined as businesses that employed fewer than eight employees. (The numerical stipulation was based on a literal interpretation of Marx, who described an exploitive capitalist with eight employees in *Das Kapital*.)[99] Although small private businesses were at last allowed to operate, the owners continued to fear political reprisals and faced myriad restrictions. One way of circumventing these restrictions was for private entrepreneurs to

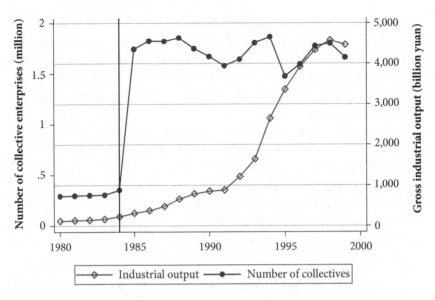

FIGURE 3.3   Change in industrial collective enterprises, 1980–2000. *China Statistical Yearbook* (1991, 1996, 2000), section on industrial sectors. "Collective enterprises" include township enterprises (*xiangban qiye*), village enterprises (*cunban qiye*), and urban-rural joint enterprises (*chengxiang hezuo jingying qiye*).

obtain permission from township and village governments to register their firms as TVEs. This informal coping strategy came to be known as "wearing a red hat."[100]

Central leaders, it seemed, knew of such disguises on the ground,[101] but they did nothing to forbid the trend. Nor did they approve of it with a single policy stroke. Instead, from the 1980s through the 1990s, the leadership kept its position ambiguous as it incrementally sharpened its endorsement of the private sector. Following accounts by Tsai and others, one of the first pivotal pronouncements on private entrepreneurship was made in 1987.[102] Premier Zhao Ziyang announced at the Thirteenth National Congress of the CCP that the "cooperative, individual and private sectors of the economy in both urban and rural areas should all be encouraged to expand." Then, in 1988, the State Council issued official regulations governing "private enterprises" with more than eight employees, essentially acknowledging the existence of these firms. The PRC Constitution was also amended to include an additional line in Article 11: "The private sector [can] exist and develop within the limits prescribed by law."

After the interlude of the Tiananmen incident in 1989 and Deng's Southern Tour, the CCP stepped up its approval of private entrepreneurship. As part of the November 1993 decision to build a socialist market economy, the central leadership announced that state ownership is the "principal component of the economy," while the private sector is only "supplementary." Four years later, at the Fifteenth Party Congress in 1997, private ownership was labeled "an important component of the economy," whereas the state sector was downgraded from a "principal component" to "a pillar of the economy." Then, in 1999, the paragraph in Article 11 of the Constitution was revised to read, "Individual, private, and other non-public economies . . . are major components of the socialist market economy." By 2004, Article 11 was amended again, and this time the private sector was endorsed in resoundingly black language: "The state encourages, supports, and guides the development of the private sector."[103]

As Qian and Wu incisively observe, "In Chinese politics, subtle changes in rhetoric reflect a big change in ideology."[104] Slight modifications in wording send powerful signals that will trigger seismic changes nationwide. As the private sector became less politically taboo, the relative share of TVEs in the economy declined. From the mid-1990s onward, many TVEs were either privatized or turned into shareholding companies. The private sector registered steady expansion, as seen in figure 3.4. Prior to 1989, only household businesses that hired

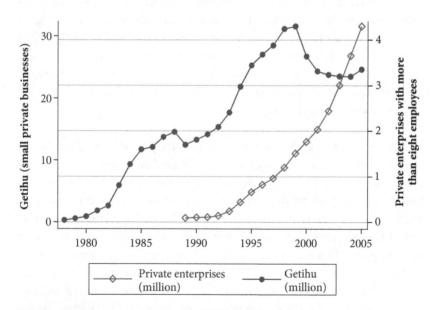

FIGURE 3.4   Change in number of private enterprises, 1980–2005. Zhang, Ming, and Liang, eds., *Blue Book of Private Enterprise*, cited in Tsai, *Capitalism Without Democracy*, 55. *Geithu* refers to small businesses that hired fewer than eight employees, while private enterprises are those that hired eight or more employees.

fewer than eight employees, known in Chinese as *getihu*, were recorded. The category of "private enterprises" did not appear on file until the central provision of 1988 permitted businesses with eight or more employees to register. In 1989, hurt by the Tiananmen crisis, the number of *getihu* dipped, but it rebounded after Deng's Southern Tour in 1992. The number of private enterprises grew even faster than *getihu*, peaking at an annual growth rate of 82 percent in 1994. From 2000 onward, although *getihu* (small household businesses) declined, the number of private enterprises with eight or more employees (larger private firms) continued to rise, reaching 4.3 million by 2005.[105] By 2012 private firms accounted for more than 60 percent of GDP, making China a predominantly private-sector economy.[106] A recent study by Lardy affirms that the private sector is the main contributor of China's growth.[107]

The preceding narrative suggests that guidelines from the Chinese leadership are only sometimes—rather than always—broad and vague. By issuing instructions with varying degrees of clarity, the center signals which policies demand strict compliance and which policies offer room for experimentation and adaptation to local conditions. My account also helps us to understand the apparent obsession among party-state functionaries at all levels with reading signals from the top, or as one official puts it, "to completely digest documents issued by the higher levels."[108] The numerous study sessions organized to examine the slogans, speeches, and reports that flow from policy makers in Beijing cannot be entirely dismissed as an exercise in propaganda and pretension. Just as an astute stockbroker must learn to read between the lines of what the Fed chairman says, a shrewd bureaucrat must decipher the subtleties of central directives in order to "get along and get ahead" in the communist hierarchy.[109]

This chapter focuses on the theme of variation—the generation of alternatives— the first of three adaptive dynamics I examine in this book. Generically stated, the core problem of variation is to "balance variety and uniformity."[110] Having too few or too many alternatives both impedes adaptation; effective adaptation requires a right balance of consistency and flexibility. Translated into the context of China's political system, this brings attention to the role of the central leadership in setting a national agenda of change and in signaling the amount of discretion that may be exercised in different policy realms. My focus on the central leadership's exercise of *influence* departs from the traditional focus on *control*, which presumes that principals have certain precise fixed preferences and want local agents to fall strictly in line. There are no doubt instances, as discussed, when the central authorities demand conformity. Yet the story of China's reforms has largely revolved around those policy areas where flexibility was deliberately assigned.

My interpretation of China's national reforms yields broad lessons for tailoring reforms to local contexts. Again, I must reiterate that efforts to move away from best-practices toward best-fit and localized approaches in the development field are highly promising. One of my goals is to advance this agenda by unpacking the problems of localization and carefully revisiting China's important experience for new insights.

First, it is worth highlighting that "good-enough governance" may not actually be good enough to promote early development. As Grindle defines, good-enough governance "directs attention to considerations of the *minimal* conditions of governance necessary to allow political and economic development to occur."[111] Aligned with this minimalist view are others who advocate targeting reforms at "the most binding constraints" or "strategic bottlenecks."[112] To be clear, I do not think these recommendations are wrong. Instead, my point is that such strategies are not likely to produce systemic political-economic changes of the type witnessed in China. Being pragmatic and realistic does not mean to *do less*. Rather it means to *do things differently*.

Second, in order for localization and experimentation to work, it is important to place limits on the amount of variation. This chapter is essentially a study of the adaptive function of political communication in a hierarchical context. I have illustrated this dynamic through central-local state relations in China's case. But similar situations of delimiting flexibility may also be found in other hierarchical relationships, for example, between aid agencies and aid recipients, American policy makers and officials in Afghanistan, even Cosimo (the powerful patriarch of the Medici family in Renaissance Florence) and his clients.[113] Instead of always dictating instructions in black and white, which is the norm in formal legal settings, the Chinese experience suggests that variegated signals and deliberate ambiguity can be useful for balancing variety and uniformity.

Deliberate ambiguity can also be found in other countries, but the explanation for it is very different from what I propose. As Huber and Shipan relate in *Deliberate Discretion*,[114] there is variation in the amount of procedural details specified in legislation among developed democracies. They advance a theory of political control to account for such variation: legislators who believe that the preferences of state agencies diverge from theirs are more likely to write detailed laws in order to restrain the bureaucracy. I agree that control is always a salient problem in hierarchical organizations, including in China's political system. But I choose to look beyond control because, especially in developing and transitional contexts, fostering adaptation is just as important as—if not more important than—exerting control. Ambiguous directives allowed the Chinese leadership to "wait and see," to incorporate feedback from the ground to adjust its policy positions in a highly *uncertain* environment, where they could not foresee the range of problems and possible solutions that may arise.[115] The greater the degree of uncertainty, the more salient it is to study the exercise of influence than that of control.

Authorizing and delimiting localized policy implementation is one major step toward effective adaptation. The next step concerns the definition of successful adaptation and its associated rewards. Why might local bureaucratic agents care to actively tailor central goals to local and changing conditions? And what shapes the particular choices they make in the process of adaptation? Chapter 4 answers these questions.

4

FRANCHISING THE BUREAUCRACY

> Bureaucrats don't have as much control over their own salaries,
> offices, and budgets as do business people. For these reasons,
> or others yet to be discovered, it should not be surprising to find
> government agencies that actually refuse to take on new tasks
> or try to give up tasks they now perform.
>
> —James Q. Wilson, *Bureaucracy*

Public schools are not a place where you would expect to find entrepreneurial bureaucrats. After all, these organizations rely on the government for funding, and there are legal and ethical limits on methods of fundraising. This is unless, of course, if you're in China.

Principal Zhou swelled with pride as he introduced me to the state-of-the-art amenities at the public elementary school he ran: a newly constructed multifloor campus extension, a rubberized running track, and projectors installed in every classroom. This was only the beginning of Zhou's grand vision of refurbishment, captured in an architectural blueprint that he framed and displayed in his office like a prized work of art. To date, Zhou estimated, the school had spent eight million yuan (about US$1.3 million) on upgrading, for which the county government provided only partial budgetary support. He had already asked the county for authorization to spend another ten million yuan, bringing the total expected costs to a whopping eighteen million yuan.

How was the school able to raise millions of dollars for refurbishment, a significant sum even by American standards?

Zhou's eyes lit up. "First, I appealed to the teachers to hand me their savings, and I promised to pay them back with interest."

In my head, I thought this was problematic. But, in good fieldwork manners, I made no expression and continued to ask, "What else did you do?"

"I also borrowed from banks."

"But why would the banks lend to your school? What could you use as collateral?"

"Ah ha, I came up with an idea!" Zhou replied, this time looking even more pleased with himself. "I asked our teachers for their property as collateral."

My encounter with Principal Zhou illustrates an abiding puzzle about the entrepreneurial behavior of public bureaucrats in reform-era China. Quoting Wilson, a guru of American bureaucracy, the stereotypical image of bureaucrats is that of "lethargic, incompetent hacks who . . . [go] to great lengths to avoid the jobs they were hired to do."[1]

In developing countries, signs of bureaucratic laziness and apathy are even more common. Take India for example. For Modi, the newly elected prime minister, the first order of business was to require bureaucrats to show up for work. The newly appointed minister of information and broadcasting lamented after making a spot check on his subordinates in the morning: "There were no people in their offices. They must come on time and they must work. This whole government mindset needs to be changed."[2]

China certainly has its share of lazy bureaucrats. Yet many of these bureaucrats are also widely observed displaying initiative, even audacity, especially when it comes to making money. Notably, such behavioral norms are not exclusive to top leaders in the political hierarchy like party secretaries and mayors. Entrepreneurial vibes infect even rank-and-file agents in the bureaucracy, from school principals (like Mr. Zhou), party propagandists, and state administrators, to street-level regulatory officers. Also surprising is the general lack of qualms with which these agents pursue financing strategies. Whether it is to generate income for local state treasuries, agencies, or public service providers, Chinese bureaucrats seldom balk at doing whatever it takes, even if controversial, to fill and enlarge organizational coffers. They behave *literally* like entrepreneurs.

While many have previously noted the entrepreneurial and corporate-like features of the Chinese bureaucracy,[3] this chapter seeks to go further to lay out the microfoundation of these behavioral traits. More importantly, I situate this inquiry in the broader quest of the book, which, to use North's terms, is to uncover the underlying conditions of "adaptive efficiency" in China's political economy.[4] The preceding chapter explored the first of such conditions, namely, the ways by which the central leadership authorized yet delimited the boundaries of local adaptation. This chapter turns to a second theme: how to clearly define and reward successful actions.[5] This condition is especially hard to attain in public organizations, where the criteria of success is typically vague and inconsistent and where incentives are weak. How did China tackle this problem?

My answer is stark. China runs the party-state bureaucracy like a franchised corporation, dedicated to the financial bottom line. Franchised corporations (e.g., McDonald's), different from directly owned companies (e.g., Comet Coffee in Ann Arbor, Michigan), are organizations that merge hierarchical structures with high-powered incentives. Franchisees own a share of profits generated by their stores; thus their incentives are high-powered (meaning they are strongly motivated to earn profits).[6] The Chinese bureaucracy is a hierarchical organization in which cadres are appointed by higher-level superiors, but, as I will show, their incentives are also high-powered. Such an arrangement renders these agents more like franchisees than salaried public employees.

This manner of public organization produces certain benefits: it powerfully motivates bureaucratic entrepreneurism and initiative. But it also has clear downsides. Public agencies are supposed to serve goals other—or more important—than making money. This chapter unpacks the Chinese bureaucracy into its elite and nonelite tiers and chronicles the evolving methods by which these agents are evaluated and compensated.

Who Exactly Are Local Officials?

The first step in studying any bureaucracy is to specify the bureaucrats who make up the organization. This is hard to do for the Chinese bureaucracy because to foreign observers it is an opaque, single-party autocracy. Indeed, the popular and scholarly literature typically refers to agents of the party-state using the blanket term "local officials." This phrase is so broad that it captures nearly everyone in the public sector.

To illustrate, consider a sampling of articles from the *New York Times* that contain references to "local officials." This list of actors spans provincial party secretaries and governors,[7] city mayors,[8] economic planners in a city,[9] family planning officers in a county,[10] and leaders of a village.[11] Translated into an American context, this is equivalent to a list of state governors, county commissioners, city planners, public service workers in a city department, and elected members of a township. No serious study of American bureaucracy would attempt to make generalizations about bureaucratic behavior without first distinguishing between elected governors and welfare workers in a city agency.[12] Likewise, no serious study of the Chinese bureaucracy can advance theories of bureaucratic behavior and incentives without first unbundling the category of "local officials" into its vastly different components.

China scholars are surely well aware of the distinctions among different levels of bureaucratic actors; my point is that we can benefit from making these distinctions more explicit. Baum and Shevchenko's observations are instructive. Comparing the state of the literature to the parable of the blind men and the elephant, they ascribe the proliferation of conflicting labels about the Chinese state—from developmental, clientelist, entrepreneurial, to predatory—to observers taking different snapshots of the same massive entity. In their words, "Analysts probing different parts of China's reforming political anatomy often produce substantially dissimilar sketches of the body politic."[13] To avoid such confusion, clarifying the anatomy of the party-state is a necessary first step.

Three facts are pertinent. First, the Chinese bureaucracy is a giant matrix structure, composed of five horizontal levels of government (center, province, city, county, and township), and each level replicates the entire suite of party and state offices established at the central level. Second, unlike in a democracy, political party and public administration are fused. In principle, the bureaucracy is composed of two parallel hierarchies—party and state—but in practice many officials hold concurrent party and state positions and are transferred seamlessly between the two hierarchies. Within each level of government, the highest decision-making body is the party committee, led by the party secretary, who is also known in Chinese as the "first in command." The chief of the state hierarchy is the "second in command." Hence most analyses of bureaucratic incentives focus only on the party secretaries and state chiefs and ignore the remaining actors in the bureaucracy.[14] Third, China's bureaucracy comprises not only the party and state organs but also a sprawling extra-bureaucracy, which provides administrative support and delivers both public and charge-based commercial services. About 80 percent of China's public employment is in the extra-bureaucratic segment.[15] This basic anatomy is illustrated in the organizational chart of Liaocheng City in Shandong (figure 4.1).

With five levels of government, a panoply of party and state organs, and a sprawling extra-bureaucratic extension, the Chinese bureaucracy is a massive organization. In total, this party-state apparatus is staffed by about fifty million public employees,[16] as large as the entire population of South Korea. Given a bureaucracy that is as populous as a mid-sized country, we should take pause and ask: *Who exactly are local officials?*

The terms "official/bureaucrat/cadre" are blanket labels for drastically different actors.[17] One way to distinguish among elite and nonelite cadres is by administrative rank. Walder defines China's "political elites" as "all cadres at the rank of county magistrate or division chief and above" or the directorate (*chu*) rank.[18] Nationwide, there are roughly 500,000 political elites, making up roughly 1 percent of the entire bureaucracy. These officials at elite ranks are appointed by the next higher level,[19] forming a national pool of appointees for lateral transfer and upward promotion.[20] The remaining 99 percent of the bureaucracy are civil servants and public employees stationed permanently in one location. For an even more fine-grained disaggregation, I slice the bureaucracy at the local (provincial and below) levels into three layers: (i) rotated top leaders, (ii) quasi-stationary vice leaders, and (ii) stationary street-level bureaucrats.

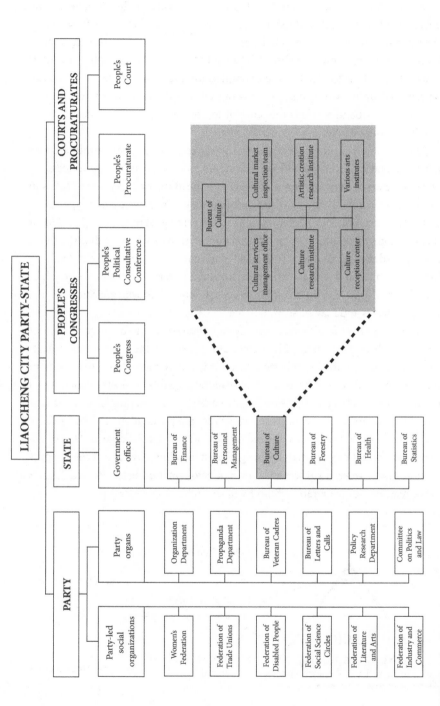

FIGURE 4.1   Formal organizational chart of a city government. Only a sample of offices is listed.

Rotated top leaders. As stated on the official website of the Chinese central government, the "local leadership" comprises four members:[21] party secretary (party), chief of state (state), chairperson of the People's Congress (legislative body), and chairperson of the People's Consultative Conference (policy consultative body).[22] These top leaders are appointed for a term of five years, which can be renewed up to two terms.[23] Borrowing Olson's distinction between roving and stationary bandits,[24] this tiny core of top leadership may be categorized as "roving" insofar as they are frequently rotated.

Quasi-stationary vice leaders. Below the ranks of the top leadership are vice party secretaries, vice state chiefs, and members of the Party Committees and State Secretariat, most of whom concurrently head major party-state organs in the local government. This mid-tier group, usually ranked vice *chu*, is appointed by the Organization Department at the same level of government, rather than at the next higher level, through an internal nomination process.[25] Unlike the rotating top leadership, the mid-tier is quasi-stationary. Vice leaders are not subject to term limits, and it is not uncommon for them to serve in one locale for a lifetime.[26] Term limits also do not apply to department chiefs, who are rarely rotated to other locales and may be served by natives.[27]

Stationary street-level bureaucrats. Lastly, the rest of the bureaucracy is not appointed through the party hierarchy but managed by local personnel departments as regular public employees. To use Lipsky's famous term, this segment may be referred to as "street-level bureaucrats," public officers who interact directly with citizens and firms on a daily basis.[28] Unlike leading officials, street-level bureaucrats are not rotated but serve lifetime posts in one locale.[29] In fact, many are native to the locales in which they work.[30] This is a large and heterogeneous group that can be further disaggregated into finer layers. But for the purpose of this chapter, it suffices to draw a basic distinction between local leaders and street-level bureaucrats (whom I will also refer to as cadres).

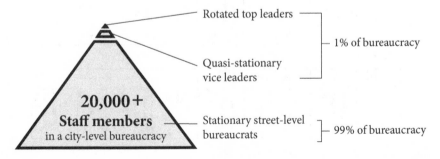

FIGURE 4.2 Three layers of bureaucratic actors

Once the distinction between local leaders and street-level bureaucrats is sharply drawn, it is apparent that many studies feature only the top 1 percent of the bureaucracy. For example, Lieberthal and Oksenberg's classic book, *Policy Making in China*, is an account of bargaining between provincial leaders and elite officials in the central ministries.[31] The flourish of statistical studies on the promotion and tenure patterns of local officials in the past decade feature exclusively party secretaries and state chiefs at the provincial,[32] city,[33] and county levels.[34] These studies exclude local vice leaders, department chiefs, and everyone else in the bureaucracy. Media reports expose grand corruption among top political elites who wield immense power. One notorious instance is Bo Xilai, the former party secretary of Chongqing, who fell from grace in 2012 and has since been imprisoned on corruption charges. Petty corruption happens at middle and low levels too, but, as I will later elaborate, it is not of the same type and scale as Bo's saga.

Local leaders and regular bureaucrats exercise different powers, perform different functions, and are motivated by different goals. Their behavior impacts development in vastly different ways too. Local leaders are the ones who make macro-decisions: for example, should our locale give tax breaks to this industry? Should we build a commercial park? Should we relocate companies into designated zones? Meanwhile, even though street-level bureaucrats do not make macro-decisions, the cumulative effects of their actions cannot be ignored. Those in administrative roles provide counsel and policy suggestions and execute decisions made by leaders. Others enforce regulations, conduct inspections, collect taxes, and directly deliver public services to society. The perception of governance among citizens and enterprises is shaped jointly by the decisions of elite officials and the execution of these decisions at the street level.

To clarify the incentives that drive local leaders and regular bureaucrats respectively, as well as their economic implications, I will divide my remaining discussion into two parts: (1) how the success of local leaders is defined and evaluated; and (2) how street-level cadres are compensated for their work and performance.

Evaluating Local Leaders like CEOs

To underscore the distinctive ways by which leadership is evaluated in China, consider the norms of bureaucracy elsewhere. As Wilson states in *Bureaucracy*, "Often we do not know whether a manager or an agency has achieved the goals we want because either the goals are vague or inconsistent, or their attainment cannot be observed, or both."[35] Corporations can measure performance concretely and noncontroversially in terms of profits, sales, and stock value. Governments and public agencies, however, have to juggle multiple and even contradictory demands, especially in democracies.[36] Wilson illustrates this dilemma through the case of the welfare department: one senator may blame the agency for processing welfare payments too slowly, but another may chastise it for not double-checking applications. Even if the goals of bureaucracy may be agreed upon, the measurement of public-sector performance is notoriously elusive.[37] In short, the evaluation of bureaucratic success hinges upon value judgments about the proper role of government, which is a political problem, not a technical one.

Turning to China, the method of evaluating local leaders is starkly mechanical. Through the "cadre evaluation system,"[38] each level of government designs a report card for leaders (party secretaries and state chiefs) at the next lower level. Each year, the higher level issues an internal formal document, typically restricted from public view,[39] which specifies a list of targets that subordinated leaders are expected to deliver in that particular year. Points are assigned to each target, usually totaling one hundred points. To step up competitive pressures, local leaders are ranked relative to their peers annually.

Surprisingly, despite abundant references to the importance of the cadre evaluation system,[40] only a handful of studies have shown what such evaluation criteria actually look like.[41] Filling in this gap, I will reproduce several evaluation documents that I collected in recent years, which will reveal the actual content of cadre evaluation, as well as the evolution of leadership evaluation criteria from the 1980s to the present day.

Leadership Evaluation in the First Two Decades

In the Chinese political system, the design of evaluation targets originated at the helm of power and then percolated layer by layer down to the grassroots. Breaking radically from Mao's fixation on class background and ideological radicalism, the reformist patriarch Deng advanced an economic- and results-oriented criterion of cadre evaluation. At the launch of market reforms, Deng announced that officials would henceforth be evaluated on the criteria of "advanced management, technical innovations, productivity, profits, and income."[42] His own selection of new talent to the core of the central leadership, including entrepreneurial and reform-minded leaders like Zhao Ziyang and Wan Li, proved his commitment to the revised standards and set a new and compelling exemplar of cadre evaluation for the communist hierarchy.

Going forward, the performance evaluation of local leaders was based on three targets: hard, soft, and veto. As Edin reports, "Hard targets tend to be economic in nature ... [and] completion of hard targets is important both for bonus and for political rewards."[43] Similarly, Whiting finds that economic targets constituted the bulk of scores in the evaluation of local leaders. Based on a township-level document she collected in 1989, Whiting reports that economic tasks, including the management of TVEs and agricultural sales, constituted sixty-three out of one hundred points (see table 4.1).[44] In addition, township leaders were sometimes required to sign "performance contracts," that is, written pledges to deliver concrete, quantifiable results in industrial growth and tax collection. Soft targets were lower-priority and mostly noneconomic tasks, such as implementing village elections and political education campaigns. Veto targets were goals that must be satisfied; in principle, failure to meet these targets could negate all other targets. A classic veto target was maintaining social stability. If a mass protest erupted, this could cancel out a local leader's achievements in that particular year and even provoke dismissal.[45]

Throughout the 1980s and 1990s, evaluation directives specified results in concrete terms that local leaders were expected to deliver. This is evident from the township document, issued in 1989 and shown in table 4.1. Economic targets were expressed as quantifiable ends (e.g., gross value of industrial output, total value of exports). Even among noneconomic tasks, performance was assessed in terms of numerical output. For instance, success in delivering education services was measured as "scale of funds dedicated to education" and "completion rate for compulsory education." Equally important, the allocation of points for each target unambiguously signaled the priority of tasks.

In short, during this period, it was clear to local leaders what they had to prioritize and accomplish. It was equally clear which outcomes they need not deliver. Conspicuously absent from leadership evaluation were targets for environmental protection, energy conservation, cultural preservation, and other soft goals that were nonessential for—and even antithetical to—achieving rapid economic growth.

Another advantage of defining success in terms of economic results was that they were easier to quantify than social outcomes. Local officials could of course falsify GDP statistics (after all, GDP is a concept), which continues till the present day. This is an open secret, and local cadres sometimes even joke about it. Partly to mitigate falsification, economic performance is measured not only as GDP, but also as tax revenue, actualized investments, and other monetary outcomes. Unlike GDP, tax revenue is actual funds deposited in banks. It was still possible to game the system, such as by "borrowing taxes" from local enterprises or other locales to decorate one's record;[46] but borrowed taxes would still have to be returned, and lending was not guaranteed. Moreover, excessive falsification of economic results came at a price. Each year's targets and spending responsibilities were based on the preceding year's reported statistics. If local leaders exaggerated too much, they would confront higher targets the next year. Thus I have encountered instances where high-performing locales deliberately *under*reported economic statistics in order to keep their targets from ratcheting up too much.[47]

The specification of bureaucratic success in unambiguous and measurable economic terms was reinforced by career, financial, and reputational rewards. High evaluation scores improved the prospects of promotion, as evidenced by several statistical studies that report a tight correlation between economic performance and promotion.[48] In addition, local governments were entitled to dispense bonuses using retained tax revenue. Leaders of top-performing locales were also crowned with honorary titles.[49] In each locality, the ranking of subordinated units based on their evaluation scores were publicly announced. Competitive rankings bestowed prestige or what might be termed "face" in Chinese, which was valued not only by local leaders but also by local cadres and residents. This cadre from a township in Sichuan recounted:[50]

> Affectively speaking, the people of our township cannot accept being ranked number 2 [vis-à-vis other townships in the county]. Our cadres and villagers care deeply about ranking. For all our hard work, there should be a concrete result. I remember one day our party secretary asked me if I thought our township could be ranked number 1 that year. I told him it would not be easy. We were ranked number 2 last year. But we are determined to rank number 1 this year.

When bureaucratic success was unambiguously defined and reinforced by powerful rewards, the behavioral and economic effects were tsunamic. Local leaders dove headlong into promoting industrialization and growth, primarily by setting up township and village enterprises (TVEs). Paired with central policy guidelines that firmly endorsed the creation of TVEs (as recounted in chapter 3), these enterprises flourished. But because the success of TVEs was evaluated primarily in terms of gross output, rather than innovation or productivity, TVEs were incentivized more to produce than to perform. Over the long term, the profitability of TVEs declined.[51] Some even incurred heavy debts. This and many other unintended problems pushed the leadership toward the watershed decision in 1993 to shift gears from partial to comprehensive market reforms.

Cadre Evaluation from the 2000s Onward

The era after the 1990s presented a new policy environment that demands an update of earlier conclusions regarding the operation of leadership evaluation and incentives. In particular, I highlight two key changes. First, I argue that for local leaders (though not for street-level cadres), the appeal of performance-based bonuses to local leaders, as earlier described by Whiting, Oi, and Edin,[52] has been vastly overshadowed by the potential gains from high-stakes graft.[53] During the early decades of reform, bonuses that amounted to thousands or tens of thousands of dollars were attractive rewards, especially in rural townships and villages,[54] where income was low. But since then, the situation has changed dramatically. After 1993, further market liberalization accelerated economic growth and also stimulated the exchange of money for preferential access to emerging markets, generating new avenues of grand corruption.[55] These avenues were further inflamed by a housing boom and the rise of land-based public finance. In this context of accelerated capitalism, powerful leaders could exchange lucrative deals and prime land for colossal kickbacks. One officer related an instance wherein an enterprise had bought a piece of land for industrial use at thirty-five thousand yuan per *mu* but was later able to convert the land to commercial use, increasing its value nearly thirty times. "You can easily imagine the amount of grease involved in this transaction," he said rhetorically.[56]

Hence, in the twenty-first century, *commanding power over thriving economies* will probably be the primary incentive for political elites. This incentive overlaps with promotion, but being promoted to a higher rank in a "dry" office may not necessarily endow one with more power or rents. This calls into question the widely held assumption in statistical studies that all local leaders desire to be promoted. Nonetheless, this condition only applies to high-ranking officials who are positioned to dispense valuable favors. For the vast majority of the bureaucracy, which does not wield immense power individually, compensation is still the main source of rewards, as I will later discuss.

Second, the growing list of demands on local leadership has spawned a new problem that Americans may term "mission creep." In particular, during the past decade, environmental protection has been elevated in cadre evaluation. Previously, degradation of the environment and depletion of natural resources and energy were absent from the national agenda. By the 2000s, however, it became clear to the leadership that environmental damage not only threatened long-term economic growth but also provoked social unrest, as seen in the spread of mass environmental protests.[57] Hence, following the eleventh five-year plan, carbon reduction and energy conservation targets were added to cadre evaluation, including in some regions as veto targets.[58] In addition, adapting from the earlier practice of issuing performance contracts for economic growth, I found that some locales now also require local leaders to sign similar contracts for environmental targets.[59]

Another area of growing emphasis is social stability. Since the 2000s, new sources of political tensions have arisen, including widening class inequality and searing conflicts between farmers and local officials over land. More generally, with a rising middle class that commands greater exposure to information and freedom of expression on the Internet, Chinese citizens are better armed than before in contesting the state. These rising tensions set the stage for the Hu-Wen administration's emphasis on "building a harmonious society." This stability-centered governance fed and was fed by the escalation of police forces under the charge of Zhou Yongkang, the power-grabbing security czar who has since been convicted for corruption and expelled from the party. In an increasingly paranoid political environment, higher-level authorities responded by demanding that their subordinates deal with *all* the tensions. As a result, more and more items were added to the criteria of cadre evaluation, a problem that surprisingly few have documented in the literature.[60]

To illuminate the sprawl of cadre evaluation targets over time, I compare the national guidelines on the evaluation of local party and state leaders in 1991, as reported by Whiting, and in 2009, following a circular issued by the Central Organization Department (see table 4.1 and table 4.2 respectively). In 1991, eighteen items were listed for evaluation. By 2009, there were twenty-six items. In 1991, fourteen of the eighteen items listed were economic tasks, and the measurements

TABLE 4.1   National guidelines on evaluation of local leaders, 1991

CATEGORY
Gross national product
Gross value of industrial output
Gross value of agricultural output
Gross value of output of township- and village-run enterprises
National income per capita
Rural income per capita
Taxes and profits remitted
Fiscal income
Labor productivity of state and collective enterprises
Procurement of agricultural and subsidiary products
Retail sales
Infrastructure investment realized
Natural population growth rate
Grain output
Local budgetary income
Local budgetary expenditure
Forested area
Nine-year compulsory education completion rate

Source: Reproduced from Whiting, *Power and Wealth in Rural China*, 103. The original source was Central Organization Department, "Notice Regarding Implementation of the Annual Job Evaluation System for Leading Cadres of Local Party and Government Organs," in China Personnel Management Yearbook (1991).

TABLE 4.2   National guidelines on evaluation of local leaders, 2009

CATEGORY

I. Economic development

       Level of economic development

       Overall economic efficiency

       Income of urban and rural residents

       Economic disparity

       Development costs

II. Social development

       Compulsory education

       Urban employment

       Medical system and hygiene

       Cultural life of urban and rural residents

       Crime control and community safety

III. Sustainable development

       Energy conservation, emissions control, and environmental protection

       Ecological protection and conservation of arable land

       Family planning and birth control

       Technological input and innovation

IV. Livelihood

       Income and living standards of residents

       Social security net expansion (*dibao*)

       Access to health care, education, and transportation

       Cultural infrastructure and activities

V. Social harmony

       Public security

       Grievance procedure and conflict resolution (e.g., petitions)

       Civic and moral education

       Civil rights protection and grassroots democracy

VI. Party and cadre discipline

       Legal compliance and transparency

       Quality of administrative services

       Party organization at the grassroots

       Anticorruption and clean governance

Source: Translated from Central Organization Department, Document No. 13, "Criteria of Comprehensive Evaluation of Local Party and State Leadership," 2009.

were fairly straightforward (e.g., gross national product, gross value of industrial output, taxes and profits remitted). By 2009, we find twenty-six items grouped into six broad categories. Even in the category of "economic development," economic performance was no longer measured in unambiguous quantifiable terms. Rather, it included conceptually vague items like "overall economic efficiency" and "development costs," which are difficult to assess objectively.[61]

Whereas in the past local leaders were instructed to focus primarily if not only on the economy, by 2009 they were told that nearly every target is a priority. Leaders were expected to advance "social development" (encompassing education, employment, health care, culture, and community safety), promote "sustainable development," support "livelihoods," maintain "social harmony," and enforce "party and cadre discipline." Worse still, several of these targets are in tension with one another. For example, promoting economic growth—still the number 1 item on the evaluation circular—is in conflict with the goals of conserving energy and protecting the environment, at least in the short term. Within the category of "social harmony," the tasks of according "civil rights protection" and facilitating "grassroots democracy" could undermine "public security" by emboldening civic protests.[62]

When national guidelines percolate down to the grassroots level—that is, townships—the list of evaluation criteria grows even longer and incredibly fine-grained. Again, I compare a document on the evaluation of township leaders in 1989, from Whiting, and a recent document issued in 2009 that I collected, shown in tables 4.3 and 4.4 respectively. Although the documents are issued by two different townships (the former in Shanghai and the latter in Zhejiang), both townships are in prosperous parts of coastal China and hence comparable. In order to illuminate the extent of cadre evaluation sprawl, I reproduce the entire list of targets.

Several differences between the targets in 1989 and 2009 stand out. In 1989, townships were evaluated based on one page of targets, in six categories, totaling 100 points. By 2009, the targets ran several pages long, in five main categories, which were further subdivided into sixty-six categories totaling 400 points. Some items were even graded in decimal points. For example, auditing village accounts was worth 0.5 points; upholding "civil service morality and ethics" was 5.6 points; and addressing "the root causes of corruption" (a task that even central leaders can scarcely claim to handle) was assigned another 8.1 points. What began as the evaluation of local leaders as CEOs, based on economic performance and in clear measurable targets, had by 2009 evolved into the evaluation of super-leaders who were expected to deliver nearly everything.

What are the implications of these changes in leadership evaluation? First, as targets snowball over time, the ability of local leaders to effectively prioritize among multiple targets is compromised. In an earlier work, O'Brien and Li argued that local officials could resolve contradictions among various targets by prioritizing hard targets and exerting less effort to implement soft targets, a strategy they term "selective policy implementation."[63] Indeed, when there were only six main targets, as was the case in 1989, developing an internal ranking of priorities from most to least important was manageable. But when the list grows

TABLE 4.3 Performance evaluation criteria for township leaders, Shanghai, 1989

CATEGORY	POINTS
Township- and village-run industry	**33**
Increase in gross value of industrial output	10
Increase in industrial profits	10
Increase in profit rate on gross value of output	5
Township ranking by profit rate on total capital	4
Increase in total value of exports	4
Agriculture	**30**
Sales to the state of grain and vegetables	15
Sales to the urban market of pigs	10
Sales to the state of oil-bearing crops	3
Sales to the state of leather and cotton	2
Party building	**21**
Building of party organizations	7
Building of party spirit and discipline	7
Education of party members	7
Education	**9**
Completion rate for compulsory education	3
Participation rate for worker training	3
Scale of funds dedicated to education	3
Family planning	**7**
Family planning compliance rate	7
Public order	
Total	**100**

Source: Reproduced from Whiting, *Power and Wealth in Rural China*, 106. The original source was Jiading Party Document, Issued in 1989, Jiading County Yearbook 1988–1990.

to five main categories and sixty-six subcategories, the "fine-tuning" and juggling ability of local leaders, or any agent for that matter, starts to flag.[64]

Second, with a creeping list of evaluation criteria, we can no longer assume that linking promotion to particular targets would incentivize local leaders to pursue these goals. Some believe that the solution to China's environmental problems is to include environmental targets in cadre evaluation and to promote leaders for measurable improvements in the environment. One corporate report concludes that "China's pollution problem can be solved only if measurable environmental targets are prioritized."[65] Another study focusing on air quality asserts that "explicitly rewarding cadres with promotions for improving environmental conditions in their cities and explicitly punishing cadres who oversee

TABLE 4.4 Performance evaluation criteria for township leaders, Zhejiang, 2009

CATEGORY I: ECONOMIC PERFORMANCE

CRITERIA	MAXIMUM POINTS
1 Speed of development	
Gross industrial output value of enterprises above designated size	4
Gross agricultural output value	6
Fiscal Revenue: national tax	5
Fiscal Revenue: local tax	5
2 Quality of development	
Development of efficient agriculture	10
Building of agricultural produce hubs: beyond city	2
Building of agricultural produce hubs: for branded produce	8
Per capita income of the rural population	2
Income growth of low-earning farming households	3
Shifting agricultural workforce to other sectors	4
Development of rural tourism	4
Brand name building	bonus
Development of the animal husbandry industry	bonus
Pest control and management	bonus
Abandonment of farmland	penalty
3 Development potential	
Investment attraction: foreign/outside investment	bonus
Investment attraction: local investment	5
Industrial investment	5
Cultivation of market economy	bonus
Request for funding from higher levels of administration	bonus
4 Development of environment	
New infrastructure in villages	10
Safe drinking water	3
Ecological conservation	bonus
5 Development of special characteristics	
Special services projects	4
Outstanding work/projects	20
Work innovation	bonus

CATEGORY II: BUILDING A HARMONIOUS MIDDLE-CLASS SOCIETY (XIAOKANG SHEHUI)

CRITERIA	POINTS
1 Land management	
Farmland preservation	1
Supply of land converted from agricultural use	2
Requisition and revitalization of land reserve	3

TABLE 4.4 (Continued)

CRITERIA	POINTS
2 Agricultural development and construction of new countryside	
Training of the agricultural workforce	0.5
Area of early-season rice paddies	0.5
Area of food crops grown	0.5
Management and control of agricultural pollution	0.5
Training on use of service website for farmers	0.5
Provision of relocation assistance to residents in mountainous areas	bonus
Public sanitation	bonus
Audit village accounts	0.5
Agricultural insurance	0.5
Home insurance for farmers	0.5
Cultivation of noncommercial forests; prevention and eradication of major forest pests	0.5
3 Education-related indicators	3
4 Culture- and sports-related indicators	2
5 Hygiene-related indicators	2
6 Social welfare-related indicators	2.5
7 Environment-related indicators	1
8 Talent management and labor-related indicators	1.5
9 Disaster and flood prevention	1
10 Creation of democracy and the rule of law in villages	1
11 Maintenance of social stability and public order	3
12 Town planning and management	2
13 Birth control	4
14 Handling of petitions (letters and visits)	3
15 Production safety	2
16 Food and drug safety	1

CATEGORY III: PARTY BUILDING AND POLITICAL WORK

CRITERIA	POINTS
1 Ideological, political and spiritual education	
Ethics	3
Promotion work	3
Dissemination of directives from higher-level units to the public	3
Culture	3
Spirituality and civility	3
Promotion of antipornography messages and related survey work	1
Special projects	2
2 Research	3

(Continued)

TABLE 4.4 (Continued)

CRITERIA	POINTS
3 Technician appointment scheme	
Assignment of technicians to villages	2
4 Organization building	
Learning and implementation of the scientific development concept	3
Intraparty democracy	3
Cadre team building	3
Cadre education and reserve cadre team building	1.5
Talent management	5.5
Grassroots organization building	13
Distance education	4
Survey research and information dissemination	2
5 Old cadres	
Work related to old cadres	2
Works related to the sports association for the elderly	0.5
6 Party building within core organs	
Party building within core party-state organs	1
7 Building a clean party	
Civil service morality and ethics	5.6
Anticorruption leadership responsibility scheme	4
Punishment and prevention system	3
Establishment of a disciplinary board	2.3
Address root causes of corruption	8.1
Address petitioners' complaints	9
8 Creating a united front	
Non-Communist Party (Democratic Party) members	0.5
Ethnic and religious groups	3
New social class (entrepreneurial class)	2
United front work in Hong Kong, Macau, Taiwan, and overseas	2
Publicize research findings	0.7
Integrated tasks	1.8
Special projects	2
9 Party leadership on work related to the NPC and PCC	
Party leadership on work related to the National People's Congress (NPC)	3
Party leadership on work related to the People's Political Consultative Conference (PCC)	3
10 Work related to armed forces	
Party control over the military	1.4
Recruitment	2

TABLE 4.4 (Continued)

CRITERIA	POINTS
Organization and training of militia units	2.6
Political construction	0.8
National defense education	0.8
Military family support services	1.4
11 Work related to mass organizations and groups	
Trade union	2
Communist Youth League	2
Women's Federation	2
Association for science and technology	2
Old age	1.5
Disabled persons' federation	1.5
Working committee for care of the next generation	1.5
Charity work	1
12 Responsibility system for party building	
Implementation of the party-building responsibility system	2
Creation of a rating system for party and government organizations	2
13 Innovative party-building initiatives	12

CATEGORY IV: PROMOTING SPECIAL CHARACTERISTICS OF TOWN

CRITERIA	POINTS
1 Technological collaboration	1
2 New products	0.5
3 Major technological innovation projects (including agricultural technologies)	1.5
4 Ratio of research and development (R&D) spending to sales revenue of enterprises above designated size	0.5
5 Number of patent applications	0.5

CATEGORY V: BONUS AND PENALTY ITEMS

1   Support for infrastructure projects
2   Promotion of efficient agriculture and culture in villages
3   Intervillage competition
4   Building standardized factories
5   Technology and innovation hubs for small and medium-sized enterprises
6   Service sector development
7   Commercial flow
8   Promotion of headquarters economy (attracting corporations to set up headquarters in locale)
9   Tourism promotion
10 Handling of land-related petitions

(Continued)

TABLE 4.4 (Continued)

CATEGORY V: BONUS AND PENALTY ITEMS

11	Separation of secondary and tertiary activities
12	Matching technologies between military and civilian sectors
13	Creation of a harmonious community
14	Raising living standards of rural households
15	Information management
16	Management of records and statistics
17	Law-abiding administration
	Transparency of government administration
	E-government
	Website/online portal for farmers
18	Fire safety
	Rate of damage of forest fires
	Management of mixed-use (residential, production, storage) properties
19	Prevention and control of pests and diseases
20	Funeral and interment management
21	Proposals and suggestions
22	Emergency management
23	Management of floating population (migrants)
24	Monitoring pollution from small-scale industries
25	Notable entrepreneurial efforts
26	Giving recognition
27	Circulation of critiques from supervisory bodies

environmental catastrophes might lead to visible ameliorations of China's environmental problems."[66] This recommendation ignores the fact that air quality is not within the direct control of government officials; pollution may flow in from surrounding regions even if a locale restricts air pollution within its jurisdiction. Assessing environmental outcomes is much trickier than measuring tax revenue and investments.[67] Moreover, we must keep the *full* picture of cadre evaluation in mind, which is clear only if we view the actual sprawling contents of evaluation guidelines. Linking promotion to environmental outcomes might work if there are only a few items by which leaders are assessed, but it will not when so much else has also been included.

Third and most important of all, the sprawl of cadre evaluation criteria implies that local leaders will continue to rank economic and fiscal growth as the highest priority, despite a growing number of additional mandates. This not only because growth promotion is still listed as the first item on the guidelines and constitutes the largest share of total scores, but also because economic outputs, compared to other soft targets like environmental protection, are more measurable and visible. More importantly, regardless of the points they contribute to evaluation and promotion, thriving economies bring numerous personal benefits to local leaders, including opportunities to exert power, command prestige, distribute patronage, and collect personal rents. Hence, even though local leaders are compelled to cater to more and more demands, they will behave first and foremost as CEOs and only secondarily as populists.

My interview with the party secretary of a subdistrict government (administratively equivalent to a township) is illustrative.[68] On the one hand, the party secretary bemoaned an "infinite" scope of responsibilities that is imposed on subdistricts:[69]

> The subdistrict government has to be responsible for everything: for example, traffic accidents, local crime rates, and mass incidents. And yet we do not have enforcement power; we cannot perform the work of the police or regulatory agencies [at the higher levels]. But as soon as something happens, we are held accountable for it. That is why I say we have infinite responsibilities!

On the other hand, there was little doubt that his first and foremost concern was to promote the economy and grow the tax base.[70]

> In 2010 we generated 159 million in tax revenue, ranking first in the entire county. Next year, I expect they will raise our target to 200 million. The other day I was calculating in my head that we are still 6 to 7 million short of hitting the target. My pressures are intense! All the subdistricts and townships are competing hard. We have to think about creating attractive business conditions, and only then will investors consider coming to our locale.

Taking office in 2006, this party secretary had replaced a low-performing predecessor and had turned the financial situation around. In 2006, the subdistrict was ranked last in the county in terms of tax revenue. Four years later, it rose to the top of the list. Despite this impressive turnaround, the party secretary had not been promoted, mostly because spots rarely open up for promotion, even when there are high performers.[71]

Nevertheless, the benefits of a revived economy are obvious, even to an outside observer. At the time of my visit, the subdistrict had been newly renovated, equipped with a modern boardroom and computers for all the employees, a fresh break from the earlier "paltry work environment with bare offices and unpainted walls." This remodeling was financed by an entrepreneur, who donated a hundred thousand yuan as an "affective reciprocation of our services," the party secretary stressed. Further, armed with a larger tax base, the subdistrict leader could afford

The newly renovated façade and boardroom of the subdistrict government,
following a financial turnaround

to pay his staff members more. Whether there were private benefits beyond these organizational benefits, nobody knows. What is clear, however, from the perspective of local leaders is that economic prosperity yields concrete rewards, including more resources at their disposal, respect from their colleagues, and friendly relations with the business community.

During the initial period of reform, when China was transitioning away from a Maoist system that had punished cadres for capitalist leanings, local leaders needed clear-cut directions from the higher levels that economic results were the new yardstick of success. Today, however, local leaders need not check their report cards to know what capitalism can bring for their people, their organizations, and for themselves.

Paying Street-Level Bureaucrats like Corporate Employees

The preceding section traced the evolution of the evaluation criteria and incentives of local leaders. In this section I move to the remainder of the bureaucracy: public administrative employees who are not party secretaries, state chiefs, or members of party-state committees. What motivates the remaining 99 percent of China's bureaucracy?

The incentives of street-level bureaucracy are distinguished from officials in leadership positions in two main ways. First, for regular cadres, promotion is *not* a relevant incentive. As most public employees have lifetime tenure, spots rarely free up for promotion, even among elite officials.[72] For instance, two officers at a county-level Environmental Protection Bureau grumbled that they had worked in the same office and at the same rank for ten years. They acknowledged that their presence blocked the promotion of newcomers.[73] Second, lacking the immense power of local leaders, street-level cadres do not expect to be handed huge bribes. Instead, for them, salary and benefits is of practical and pressing concern. As one civil servant stated, "Incentives for regular people [like me] are quite simply incentives supplied by compensation."[74]

Yet in China, like in many other developing countries, official salaries for public employees are low. Figure 4.3 provides an estimation of the formal basic wages for civil servants, which are set by the central government, compared to the average income of urban and rural residents.[75] Rural residents, not surprisingly, fare the worst among the three groups, but formal civil service pay actually fell below average urban income after 1995.

Consider a more concrete illustration. In a county of Sichuan that I studied in 2011, entry-level civil servants were entitled to formal basic wages of only 830 yuan a month (US$138), less than the county's minimum monthly wage for

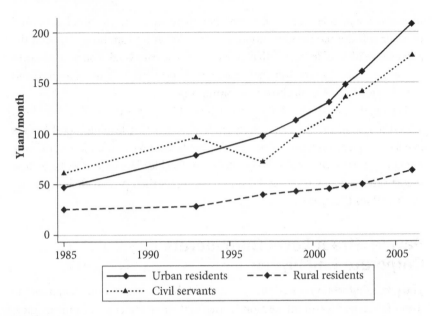

FIGURE 4.3   Formal civil service wages vs. average rural and urban income.
Author's calculations from *China Statistical Yearbooks* and *Organizational History
Statistics*.

workers, 850 yuan.[76] To put this sum in context, it costs about 500 yuan a month
to rent a room in an urban slum, which implies that in the absence of additional
income sources, a college-educated civil servant would live no better than an
unskilled migrant worker. Such a scenario fits Besley and McLaren's description
of "capitulation wages," wherein governments "abandon any attempt to solve
either the moral hazard or adverse selection problem via wage incentives."[77] More
simply put, when formal public wages are that low, civil servants are expected to
steal, extort, or take petty bribes to finance themselves.

Although capitulation wages are commonly perceived as a problem unique
to contemporary low-income countries, they were in fact the *norm* of public
administration throughout much of human history, including in the West. As
Weber observed, all premodern governments were characteristically prebendal.
This means that public officials received little or no salary at all from governments. Instead, rulers assigned officials the right to extract prebends (or rents)
from office, such as by extracting fees from local residents, conducting monopoly
trades, or accepting gifts in exchange for services.[78] Even in the United States,
prebendal practices persisted well into the early twentieth century, as Parrillo
described: "Judges charged fees for transactions in the cases they heard. . . . Tax
investigators received a percentage of the evasions they discovered. . . . Clerks deciding immigrants' applications for citizenship took a fee for every application."[79]

Prebendal practices of compensation, when understood in modern economic terms, are essentially *profit-sharing* schemes. Public agents took a cut, directly or indirectly, of income earned through the exercise of power, from adjudicating disputes, collecting taxes, to processing permits (in the Chinese context, we may add, attracting investments, promoting growth, and enforcing regulations). Weber calls such practices "owning the means of administration." In the past, instead of directly collecting taxes from the populace, feudal kings and lords assigned local officials the right to harvest taxes from subjects in their jurisdictions. After surrendering a portion of taxes to the royal treasury, tax farmers were allowed to retain the surplus for their own profit. Hence, Weber sums up in entrepreneurial terms, "The tax farmer was a private capitalist."[80]

Tax farming and prebendal practices posed distinct advantages given the constraints of premodern environments. In the absence of fully monetized economies and stable tax collection systems, royal treasuries were "exposed to the vicissitudes of income fluctuation," Weber wrote. In this context, it was a crushing burden for rulers to pay administrators regular wages in money. Instead, by allowing administrators to finance themselves by collecting fees or rents from office, "the lord can transfer the trouble of transforming his income-in-kind into money-income to the officer-farmer."[81] In modern language, it means that instead of running an in-house bureaucracy, rulers chose to outsource administration, allowing individual officials to collect rents from running their offices, akin to the way McDonald's franchises its stores to individual entrepreneurs.[82]

Yet although tax farming and prebendal arrangements presented certain advantages, they posed obvious risks. Granted the license to extract rents, public officials were inclined to overextract by applying coercive force.[83] With weak monitoring mechanisms in place, it was extremely difficult for rulers to keep bureaucratic agents in check. They frequently did not know about the extent of extraction and abuses of power until revolts from overtaxed populations erupted. Facing the risk of predatory agents, as Weber observes, "The lord seeks to safeguard himself against this loss of control by regulations." And ultimately, he adds, the modern bureaucracy has to eradicate prebendalism altogether and instead provide agents "fixed salaries paid in money."[84]

In other words, the process of modernization requires the transition of bureaucracy from prebendal and profit-oriented to fully state-funded and service-oriented. We know astonishingly little about how this transition occurs, despite its theoretical and practical significance. Tracing the coevolution of bureaucratic compensation practices and the economy in reform-era China helps to fill this gap. I will identify how the emergence of a dual-track compensation structure (fixed formal salaries alongside variable perks pegged to economic performance) provided an intermediate step between prebendalism and modernized administration. Figure 4.4 summarizes my account.

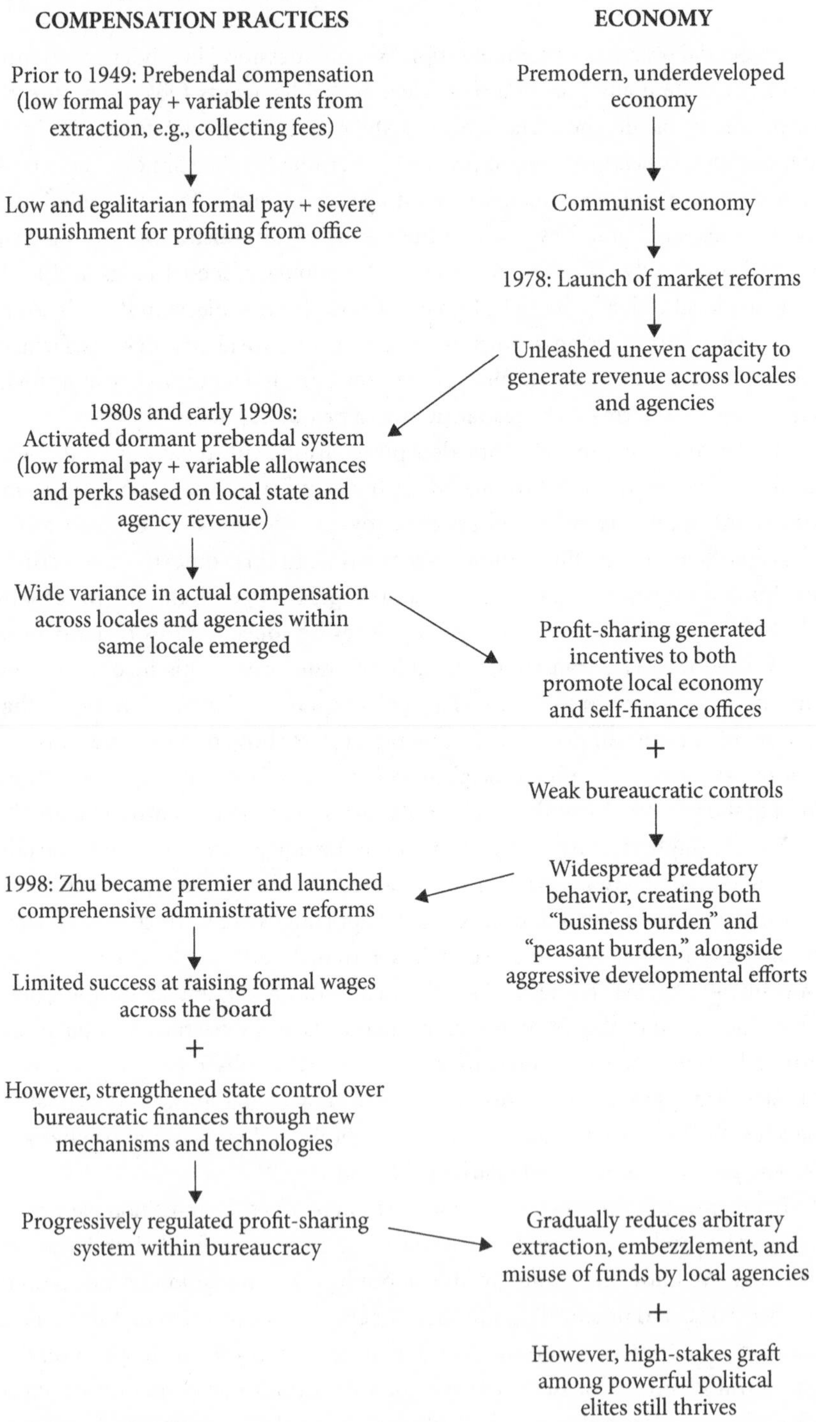

COMPENSATION PRACTICES   ECONOMY

Prior to 1949: Prebendal compensation
(low formal pay + variable rents from
extraction, e.g., collecting fees)

↓

Low and egalitarian formal pay + severe
punishment for profiting from office

Premodern, underdeveloped
economy

↓

Communist economy

↓

1978: Launch of market reforms

↓

Unleashed uneven capacity to
generate revenue across locales
and agencies

1980s and early 1990s:
Activated dormant prebendal system
(low formal pay + variable allowances
and perks based on local state and
agency revenue)

↓

Wide variance in actual compensation
across locales and agencies within
same locale emerged

Profit-sharing generated
incentives to both
promote local economy
and self-finance offices

+

Weak bureaucratic controls

↓

1998: Zhu became premier and launched
comprehensive administrative reforms

↓

Limited success at raising formal wages
across the board

+

However, strengthened state control over
bureaucratic finances through new
mechanisms and technologies

↓

Progressively regulated profit-sharing
system within bureaucracy

Widespread predatory
behavior, creating both
"business burden" and
"peasant burden," alongside
aggressive developmental efforts

Gradually reduces arbitrary
extraction, embezzlement, and
misuse of funds by local agencies

+

However, high-stakes graft
among powerful political
elites still thrives

FIGURE 4.4   Coevolution of economy and bureaucratic compensation practices

Bureaucratic Compensation in the 1980s and 1990s

In China, prebendal practices were the norm for centuries throughout the dynastic periods. Hickey's description of the Qing administration, which still bears uncanny similarities to contemporary China, is worth quoting at length:

> The inadequacy of salaries for government officials was one of the defining characteristics of the bureaucratic system of late imperial times. Because salaries failed to cover the real costs of obtaining and holding office, officials, as a matter of fact, resorted to collecting fees from their subordinates or the people in their jurisdictions."[85]

When the CCP took power in 1949, it did not root out prebendal practices. Cadre wages were centralized by the state and kept low and compressed, aligned with the party's egalitarian ideology. The Maoist state meted out severe punishments against anyone who dared to profit from their positions. As one cadre recounted, "During the days following state establishment, people were summarily executed for even a bit of corruption. Nobody dared to be corrupt."[86] Mao temporarily deterred corruption through harsh punishments, and his suppression of markets also kept cadres and citizens equally poor.

When Deng announced "reform and opening" in 1978, market reforms in effect reactivated a dormant legacy of prebendal bureaucracy. On the one hand, the central government maintained centralized control over formal wage setting, which it still does today. Official public salaries, termed "basic wages" in Chinese, are set by the Ministry of Personnel Management. Formal public wages are standardized by rank and length of service. As Xu Songtao, a former vice minister of personnel management, acknowledged, throughout the reform period, formal wages were highly compressed and fell woefully behind China's rapid inflation.[87] In addition, the nationally standardized wage scale failed to reflect widening economic disparities among regions and departments within regions.

On the other hand, the provision of extra allowances and perks to public employees—over and above basic wages—was de facto decentralized. Market liberalization unleashed the inherently uneven capacity for revenue generation among different regions and departments within each region. Among local governments, fiscal inequality widened following the central policy of fiscal contracting, under which localities were allowed to keep surplus revenue after remitting prenegotiated quotas to the higher levels. Favorably located coastal regions raced ahead economically, generating and amassing more tax income than the interior regions. Meanwhile, within each locale, fiscal disparities also surfaced across agencies. Depending on their functions and targets of regulation, some agencies were better poised than others to generate revenue by collecting fees or charging for the provision of services through extra-bureaucratic subsidiaries.

Wealthier local governments and agencies had more income at their disposal to dispense supplementary items of compensation. These items included bonuses, allowances, overtime pay, and a sprawling array of in-kind (nonmonetized) benefits, such as "daily necessities like rice and eggs, electricity, and gas,"[88] "housing at greatly subsidized prices,"[89] and "luxurious office buildings."[90] In one county I visited, cadres regularly took home gifts from their departments, such as seafood, skin care products, visits to salons, and even shopping certificates. Importantly, such supplemental compensation must be distinguished from corrupt monies, such as bribes, extorted payments, and embezzled funds.[91] Whereas corrupt monies are illegal sources of income extracted by individual bureaucrats, supplemental compensation comprises pay and perks supplied by local governments and agencies to top up meager formal wages. Different from corrupt monies, supplemental compensation may or may not be illegal, depending on the context, and it is dispensed organizationally. Expressed visually, if centrally fixed formal wages are explicitly "white" (legal) and corrupt monies like bribes are "black" (illegal), then supplemental compensation occupies an intermediate gray category.

As local states and agencies supplied extra pay and perks based on their revenue capacity, gaps in *actual* compensation widened progressively, even as formal wages scarcely budged. This impact was personally felt by all local cadres. For example, one cadre from a county in Tianjin complained about the inferiority of his pay compared to equally ranked cadres in a wealthier neighboring county: "Our compensation is only about half of cadres in County Y. Our formal wages are the same. The difference lies in the [locally paid] subsidies and allowances, which is a function of local tax finances."[92]

Within each locale, disparities in staff benefits across departments also sharpened. Offices that were empowered to extract lucrative fees, fines, and charges were nicknamed "greasy agencies," whereas those lacking such income streams fell into the unenviable class of "distilled water agencies."[93] The Construction Bureau is a quintessential greasy agency that profits from its exercise of regulatory power over a booming construction industry. A finance officer described it: "The Construction Bureau collects so many fees! Inspection fees, construction fees, proxy fees, bidding fees, monitoring fees. Whenever a state agency can issue approvals, it is greased."[94] As the Construction Bureau had access to lucrative income, it could afford generous staff benefits that other agencies could not. Thus, as one officer remarked caustically, "Between the Construction Bureau and the Archive Office, even an idiot knows their gap in benefits!"[95]

Stated in neo-institutional terms, the marriage of rigid formal wages and market liberalization spawned a hybrid product: a dual-track profit-sharing scheme within the bureaucracy. Essentially, regular cadres took a share of income generated by local governments *and* by agencies within local governments. One part of cadre compensation came from centrally fixed formal wages and another portion was variably dispensed based on financial performance. Minister Xu openly acknowledged the existence of this "dual-track" compensation structure,[96] a term that also described the pre-1993 pricing system, wherein some prices were fixed by central planners and the remainder by market forces.

This dual-track incentive structure stimulated rather odd and contradictory economic behavior among street-level bureaucrats. On the one hand, all the cadres had high-powered incentives to contribute to local business growth, such as by recruiting investors into their locales, because the wealthier their locales the higher their allowances. On the other hand, the same agents also had high-powered incentives to generate revenue for their departments, because the more income their departments earned the more benefits they received. Even Chinese journalists were puzzled by the contradictory behavior they witnessed, as the *Southern Daily* reported, "There exists a paradox: on the one hand, local governments devise a variety of preferential policies to attract capital and investments; on the other hand, high barriers to entry, a labyrinth of licensing rules and approval procedures make things difficult for firms."[97] This seeming paradox becomes sensible once the dual incentives of street-level bureaucracy are specified.

Although its behavioral effects were not ideal compared to a purely business-promoting bureaucracy, dual-track compensation brought certain advantages in an environment of partial market liberalization and early growth. The central government retained control over formal wage setting, giving the entire bureaucracy a semblance of cohesion. Local governments and agencies could top up formal pay based on their revenue capacity, giving them the ability to reward entrepreneurial efforts. Also, by linking staff benefits to income, local agencies were motivated to be financially self-independent, which relieved the formal budgetary burden of local states. Despite vastly different settings, the essential logic is still aptly captured by Weber's description of prebendalism in a feudal context: "the lord can transfer the trouble of transforming his income-in-kind into money-income to the officer-farmer."[98] In the context of post-Mao China, feudal lords and officer-farmers were replaced by local governments and agency-farmers.

Yet the disadvantages of this compensation and incentive structure were just as clear. During the 1980s and through the 1990s, state control over the bureaucracy was weak. Even the most basic instruments of fiscal management were absent.

For instance, China did not yet have a centralized system of state bank accounts. Instead, the norm was that agencies opened multiple bank accounts on their own to deposit collected monies.[99] Weak institutional controls paired with the right to dispense staff allowances and perks from earned income naturally bred arbitrary and excessive extraction in cities and the countryside, triggering the problems of "business burden" and "peasant burden." In the urban areas, local agencies frequently inspected and regulated firms for the purpose of extracting fees and fines, coerced businesses to pay for mandatory services, and even required them to attend fee-charging conventions and subscribe to magazines published by the agencies. Thus it is no surprise that many observers, including the Chinese public, instinctively equated supplemental compensation with "organizational corruption" and "small treasuries" (allegedly illegal bureaucratic accounts).[100]

At an early growth stage, prebendal practices supplied high-powered incentives for local offices to self-finance. Long-term capitalist development, however, requires the "rational, predictable functioning of legal and administrative organs," as Weber stresses.[101] The predatory risks of a partially prebendal bureaucracy sharpened the central reformers' resolve to advance comprehensive market and institutional reforms.

Bureaucratic Compensation from the 2000s Onward

After Zhu Rongji assumed the role of premier in 1998, he launched an ambitious and forceful program aimed at rationalizing the administration.[102] From the 2000s onward, China's bureaucracy entered a new era of institution building. Zhu and his team knew well that paying adequate salaries to public employees is one prerequisite—necessary but insufficient—for eradicating petty predation. Hence the central government raised the formal pay scale throughout the country five times between 1997 and 2006.

The practical effects of these formal pay raises, however, were limited. For descriptive evidence, I draw upon an original dataset I created using the line-item budgets of county governments in Shandong Province, which provides a rare estimation of formal wages and the elusive category of supplemental compensation.[103] Figure 4.5 tracks the rate of formal salary and supplemental compensation among these counties from 1979 to 2005. We can see that in 1979, when market reforms had just started, the majority of cadre compensation already came in supplemental forms, although in absolute terms the amount was meager. From 1979 to 1993, the early phase of reform, formal wages barely increased while supplemental compensation nearly doubled in absolute size. Then, from 1994 onward, the formal wage rate began to climb, reflecting nationwide pay raises made by the central government. Even by 2005, though, these raises were modest compared to the rapid growth rate and surging costs of living. Figure 4.5 makes it clear that it was the expansion of supplemental benefits that compensated for the growing gap between formal public wages and China's phenomenal economic boom.

The central government was politically and economically constrained when it came to raising formal wages. Public wage raises are contentious because of deeply ingrained perceptions among the Chinese public that public employees are already excessively privileged. This is a vicious cycle. Low formal pay and weak controls in the past spawned predatory bureaucracies, which entrenched public distrust of the government and in turn obstructed formal wage raises. Economically speaking, China is so large and heterogeneous that no single wage scale could accommodate such vast differences and fluctuations. If the national wage scale was too low, civil servants in prosperous locales would be underpaid; conversely, if the scale was too high, poor locales could not afford to pay even basic public wages. Thus, as figure 4.5 clearly shows, the bulk of compensation still came from supplemental components financed by the income of local governments and of local agencies. More precisely, my dataset of the Shandong counties estimates that only 26 percent of actual cadre compensation comes from formal salaries; the remaining 72 percent are allowances, bonuses, and various other in-kind benefits.

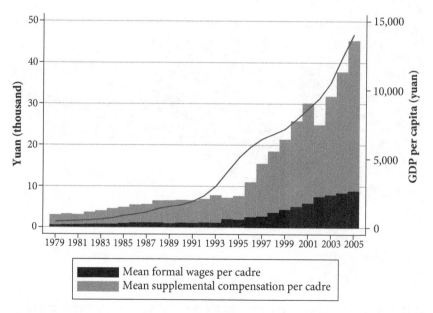

FIGURE 4.5 Formal wages vs. supplemental compensation, 1979–2005. From author's dataset of line item spending among counties of Shandong Province.

Nevertheless, even though supplemental compensation has not been eliminated even today, the processes by which agencies collect and spent revenue underwent a quiet revolution starting in the 2000s. This revolution becomes apparent when we disaggregate the life cycle of fee collection. During the 1980s and 1990s, fees and fines were simply "collected and then spent."[104] For example, an inspecting agency could accuse a producer of violating regulations and demand a fine; the inspector could privately pocket a bribe, collect the fine in cash and turn it over to departmental coffers, or do both.

Today, however, the processes by which fees are collected, deposited, and spent are different. One major institutional reform undertaken by the Ministry of Finance in the 2000s was to replace the previously fragmented system of independent bank accounts with a centralized network of accounts, connected between and within levels of government, in collaboration with the banks.[105] This reform vastly improved the ability of finance and audit offices to track the transactions of all the departments. The centralization of accounts was paired with the introduction of cashless payments of fees and fines. In order to collect a fee, regulatory officers are required to issue a "non-tax revenue collection certificates,"

A one-stop administrative services center, with representatives from various agencies stationed at booths to issue licenses and fee collection certificates. Chengdu City, Sichuan Province.

After collecting payment certificates from the agency representatives, fees can then be paid at an on-site bank that remits funds directly into state bank accounts.

instead of collecting payments in cash, as was done in the past.[106] Like official receipts, these certificates are issued at the provincial level and each is coded with a unique number,[107] so that local agents cannot arbitrarily print a certificate and that every payment can be electronically traced. To pay the fee, a business then takes the payment certificate to a bank stationed at a one-stop administrative services center, established in cities and counties nationwide. Then the payer is issued an official receipt. The bank directly deposits the fee into a centralized system of public accounts.

Now to be clear, local offices may still break rules and set up independent accounts without authorization, but compared to the past, such actions now count unambiguously as corruption, and agency chiefs who break the rules will personally risk criminal charges. In addition, with the centralization of accounts and digitization of transactions, it is much easier to detect hidden funds than in the past.

These new institutional controls and technologies strengthened state control over bureaucratic finances on an unprecedented level. And yet, interestingly, I found that, in practice, local agencies still exercise rights to spend the revenue they earn. Indeed, in my interviews with local cadres, including with finance officers, they frequently use the term "spending rights."[108] In practice, during the internal budgeting process, the finance bureaucrats continue to allocate budgets based on each department's revenue. Why? One budgeting officer explained that it was a simple incentive problem: "The financial burden of our county would be too large otherwise. If we agreed to fund all the departments fully, then they would have no motivation to generate revenue for themselves."[109] My fieldwork showed that some of the richest locales could currently afford to fully finance bureaucracy and supplement formal wages using local tax revenue, thereby obviating the need for individual offices to self-finance. But in vast areas of China, most local governments have not yet amassed sufficient wealth to afford adequate and stable salaries. In these places, prebendal practices persist, albeit in a more regulated fashion than before.

In sum, over three decades, compensation practices in China evolved from a dormant prebendal system into a progressively regulated profit-sharing scheme. Thus understood, the present-day Chinese bureaucracy is neither purely Weberian nor recklessly predatory. This evolution of bureaucratic structure underlies the changing patterns of corruption. As Ko and Weng found in a recent study, the number of corruption cases related to embezzlement and misappropriation of public funds has steadily fallen, which reflects the sweep of administrative reforms implemented since the late 1990s.[110] At the same time, bribery has grown in scale over time, involving grander sums, larger transactions, and higher-ranked officials. This particular combination of corruption trends approximates the Gilded Age in America, a time when high-stakes graft between politicians and businesses raged but petty corruption was gradually being brought under control.[111]

The thesis of this chapter can be summed up in one line: Adaptive and entrepreneurial public bureaucracy is something we all love to have, but it comes at a price. So when we exhort bureaucracy to behave adaptively, as Andrews recommends, to "[respond] to locally defined problems" and use "step-by-step experimentation to solve such problems,"[112] we must not neglect the deeper problem of actualizing such desirable behavior—namely, how can success be clearly defined and powerfully rewarded in the public sector?

Underlying the unusually entrepreneurial and even audacious behavior so commonly seen in the Chinese bureaucracy is a franchised mode of operation. This franchised mode, as I have shown, operates in two different ways for two broadly distinguished sets of bureaucratic actors: a thin sliver of elite local leaders versus an enormous mass of street-level cadres. Local leaders, numbering about 500,000 individuals, were evaluated like CEOs for most of the reform period, based on quantifiable economic targets that were unambiguously spelled out in writing. Even though I show evidence of mission creep over time, which makes it increasingly hard for local leaders to prioritize among multiple tasks, pursuing economic growth is still the number one target that is most aligned with the personal interests of the elites.

Then, turning to the forty-nine million remaining street-level cadres, I emphasize that the incentives most relevant to this group come in the form of compensation, not promotion. Street-level cadres are paid partially like corporate employees, in a profit-sharing manner. Even though their formal salaries are fixed, they also receive a share of income earned by local states and by local agencies through supplemental allowances and perks. In this way, their incentives were divided between promoting local business growth and generating revenue for their particular agencies. Over time, this contemporary adaptation of prebendal practices was not eliminated but institutionalized through the incorporation of new technologies of bureaucratic control. The wealthiest locales in the country were among the first to be able to finance local agencies adequately through tax income (more in chapters 5 and 6) and thereby diminish prebendal practices.

Running a public bureaucracy like a franchised corporation has its benefits and drawbacks. On the positive side, this mode of operation generates a pervasive organizational culture that almost worships money making. On the negative side, however, the very same corporate qualities that drove rapid growth and boldness are also a source of corruption and public discontent against the bureaucracy. As China grows wealthier and its citizenry expects more from government than just economic results, the bureaucracy faces the strenuous test of transforming from a profit-oriented to a service-oriented organization.[113]

In combination, the previous chapter and this chapter have identified two meta-institutions that steer and motivate local improvisation within a national framework of reforms: first, measures that authorize and delimit local adaptation, and second, measures that define and reward bureaucratic success. With these in mind, we are now ready to move from the national perspective to the local levels. How do local officials adapt central goals of development to varied conditions in different parts of China and over time? In the next chapter, we will unpack the coevolutionary path of a city in Fujian Province to see how states and markets mutually adapted and transformed since reforms began.

Part 3
IMPROVISATION

5

FROM BUILDING TO PRESERVING MARKETS

Needless to say, even within the same country the focus of [growth] promotion can—indeed has to—evolve over time with changing domestic and international conditions. Typically, the successful countries have been those that were able skillfully to adapt their policy focus to changing conditions.

—Ha-Joon Chang, *Kicking Away the Ladder*

The preceding two chapters have examined two ways by which the central party-state directed local improvisation. First, it authorized and at the same time delimited the boundaries of local adaptation in policy implementation (chapter 3). Second, central authorities defined bureaucratic success and structured rewards in the style of a franchise corporation, spurring entrepreneurial behavior from the highest to lowest levels of the hierarchy (chapter 4). Taken together, these meta-institutions empowered, guided, and incentivized local agents to adaptively pursue development.

Part 2 of the book, comprising this and the next chapter, shifts from the top-down to the bottom-up perspective. We turn to how processes of local improvisation progressed within shared national parameters and the consequences produced by these processes across a variety of local settings facing vastly different opportunities and constraints.

In this chapter, we unpack the coevolutionary path of one particular locale: Forest Hill, a city of about two million residents (about twice the population of San Jose, California, or a quarter of Hong Kong's), tucked in the interior of the coastal province of Fujian. Like many other parts of China, Forest Hill has undergone dramatic economic and institutional transformation. Such development should not be taken for granted. Although this city is in a coastal province, it is hill-locked, surrounded by forests and hills, hence its pseudonym: Forest Hill.[1] Without concerted and sustained efforts by local state authorities to bring industry and commerce into this hilly area, Forest Hill would have remained an idyllic—but ultimately poor and rural—political economy.

How did development *actually* happen in Forest Hill? Did the city's leaders heed the advice of international experts to establish good governance as a first step of development, namely, by furnishing secure property rights to private entrepreneurs and resolutely eradicating corruption?[2] Or did it model itself after the developmental states of East Asia, by establishing technocratic state agencies and channeling resources toward targeted industries?[3] Alternatively, did the city make do with "good enough governance," delivering only minimal government performance and waiting until it had become sufficiently wealthy before improving governance?[4] The answer to all three hypotheticals is no.

To understand how development actually occurred in this locale, I map the steps of state-and-market coevolution, starting with the central decision to open markets in 1978. My analysis yields a simple but powerful conclusion: the institutions, policies, and state capabilities that promote growth evolve *over the course of development*, even within a single locale.

More specifically, I distinguish between the tasks of *building* markets and *preserving* markets. Dominant theories in political economy are theories about good or strong institutions (such as professional bureaucracies, rule of law, private property rights protection) that are necessary to *preserve* markets that have already been built. But where markets *barely exist*, which is the situation facing most low-income, preindustrialized, and premodernized societies, building markets from the ground up demands drastically different institutions and strategies. Why is that? My answer is that the *goals*, *constraints*, and *resources* for development vary at low and middle levels of income; therefore, the selections that *fit* these different contexts must also be different.

Institutions for Building vs. Preserving Markets

The idea that early and late stages of development demand different institutions is not new. In the beginning of this chapter, I quoted Chang, who observes that "even within the same country the focus of [growth] promotion can—indeed has to—evolve over time with changing domestic and international conditions."[5] Taking a historical approach, Chang contends that Western developed nations, when they were developing, did not in fact use the "good" policies (such as limited government, deregulation, and labor laws) that they recommend to developing countries today. Instead, the West had deployed interventionist and protectionist measures to help their domestic industries take off. Similarly, Rodrik states that "igniting economic growth and sustaining it are somewhat different enterprises."[6] This opinion has been echoed by several others,[7] who argue that reforms in developing countries should take into account "local context" and that "good government means different things in different countries."[8]

Borrowing Rodrik's terms, how exactly is igniting economic growth different from sustaining it? The answers we give to this question will fundamentally affect our inferences about the particular institutional forms that fit different stages of development. One common response is that sparking growth is "easier" than maintaining it. As Rodrik asserts, "Instigating growth is a lot *easier* in practice than the standard recipe, with its long list of action items, would lead us to believe."[9] One policy implication of this perspective is that developing countries should not aim unrealistically to replicate the whole panoply of good governance at once. "Countries do not need an extensive set of institutional reforms in order to start growing," Rodrik states.[10] Instead, as others agree, they should take the more pragmatic route of settling for "good enough governance" or "second-best institutions" and "target fewer changes."[11]

The theoretical and practical question that follows is: How good must good enough be? And what should good enough (or second-best) governance look like in practice? Although the above literature points correctly to the unrealistic expectation of getting governance right in one step, it falters at spelling out concrete guidelines on alternative steps. For instance, let's examine the response of Rodrik's seminal work. In a section titled "An Investment Strategy to Kick-Start Growth,"[12] he emphasizes the importance of measures that correct "government failures" and "market failures." On the former, he lists these problems that must be tackled: "macro-economic instability and high inflation, high government wages, a large tax burden, arbitrary regulations, burdensome licensing requirements, corruption, and so on." Then, on correcting market failures, Rodrik suggests some of the following measures: "crowding in of private investment through subsidization, jawboning, public enterprises, and the like." Further, he adds that "the implementation of the market failure approach requires a reasonably competent and noncorrupt government."

In other words, according to Rodrik, what does it take to kick-start growth? *Almost everything.* And yet he maintains that "the requisite policies need not be wide-ranging" and furthermore, that "the most effective point of leverage for stimulating growth obviously depends on local circumstances." He does not specify, however, what these "local circumstances" are or what institutions could evolve given these circumstances. So now his answer seems to be: *it all depends.*

Clearly, we need a theory of differential institutions for early and late growth stages that is more than just a watered-down version of good governance or that it all depends. To build such a theory, we must first revisit the question of *why* building and preserving markets might require different institutions and methods. For a start, what are the goals and concerns of development at a start-up stage? Are they different compared to mature stages? Many theories in political economy do not make a distinction among the imperatives of development at low, middle, and high levels of income. Instead, the problems *unique to* already developed economies are posited as *universal* problems of all economies, whether developed, developing, or not developed at all.[13]

Consider the argument, advanced by leading political economists, that the norms of limited government and private property rights protection are essential for economic growth. As North and Weingast propose in a seminal article,[14] the central problem of development is how to constrain a powerful government from preying upon the private wealth of citizens. Using the case of the Glorious Revolution in England in 1688, they argue that once the power of the monarchy was constrained through the establishment of parliamentary institutions and an independent judiciary, bonds and stock markets flourished, and England was catapulted into modern prosperity.[15] This is indeed a compelling argument and an illustrative case.

But was the context of England in 1688 universal to all economies? Were English markets completely barren prior to the seventeenth century? According to Greif's historical account, as early as 1275, centuries before 1688, England had already promulgated the Statute of Westminster I, which replaced a previous communal system of contract enforcement with institutions of "individual responsibility, territorial law, the central administration of justice, and personal collateral."[16] The Royal Exchange (the precursor of the London Stock Exchange) opened in 1571, and the East India Company was officially founded in 1600, eighty-eight years before the Glorious Revolution. By the seventeenth century, England had a sizable propertied class, large enough to press for political reforms, which led up to the events of 1688.

Even on a superficial level, the conditions that prevailed in seventeenth-century England do not comport with what is generally found among Third World countries today and certainly not in China after 1978. Countries like Afghanistan and Malawi are nowhere close to having stock exchanges, a vibrant middle class, and centralized justice systems, much less their own versions of the East India Company. When the post-Mao leadership first launched reforms, markets and their associated institutions barely existed. The starting point was an autarkic, centrally planned economy, a bureaucracy devastated by the anarchy of the Cultural Revolution, and a society scarred by more than a century of foreign invasion and civil wars, followed by three decades of tumult under Mao. In these contexts, *building* (or rebuilding) markets is the first order of development. Indeed, Weingast's famous term "market-preserving" institutions is revealing;[17] institutions like secure private property rights, rule of law, and limits on government are ones that *preserve* markets. *When markets have not yet been built, there is nothing to preserve.*

What are the imperatives of development when markets are being built from the ground up? While secure protection of private property rights is certainly desirable, it may not be the foremost concern of market actors in these situations. This is because *some* assurances of property rights may be worth taking risks and making initial investments,[18] especially since the gains one can potentially reap in uncertain, emerging markets are potentially phenomenal (the biographies of present-day billionaires in China can attest to the axiom of "no risk, no gain.").[19] Moreover, at an early stage, there can be informal substitutes for formal property rights protection; for socially connected individuals, an uneven playing field actually benefits them. Hence, the first-order problem of kick-starting markets is not the provision of absolutely secure property rights, but rather, as a provincial economic bureaucrat from Jiangsu once told me, "to take care of the basics."[20] By which, he means providing the necessary hard (physical) infrastructure for operating businesses. For instance: Are there roads? Does electricity run? Are there banks?[21] It is difficult—but not impossible—to set up factories in the absence of secure property rights. But it is impossible if there are no roads or electricity or even a basic financial apparatus to deposit funds.

For governments in start-up economies, the primary concern is less to assure citizens of their individual rights than to attract an initial wave of investments, jobs, and growth opportunities. Chinese bureaucrats use a figurative phrase to describe this problem: how to earn "the first pot of gold"[22] or, stated in Western terms, "start-up capital." Also, before such governments can attempt to improve the status quo, they must first cope with various constraints common to impoverished environments, including financial constraints (scarce revenue to pay bureaucracy and finance essential infrastructure), institutional constraints (scarce capacity to enforce decisions, gather information, and monitor bureaucratic behavior), knowledge constraints (lack of basic knowledge about economic production and management), and human capital constraints (lack of public and corporate professionals). It makes little sense to constrain the power of governments before they have even acquired the capacity to perform basic tasks.

Importantly, poor, rural, and premodernized societies do not only face constraints; they also possess certain unique advantages that wealthy capitalist ones may lack. This tends to be overlooked in the existing literature, which highlights the constraints but less the resources of developing countries. For instance, Grindle states that "well-institutionalized states" have more to build on, but among "some collapsed states and ones dominated by personal rule, there may be *little* to build on for improved governance."[23] In fact, I argue, even personalist societies have *something* to build on for development.[24] In particular, this chapter will highlight the reconfiguration of pre-existing personal and informal networks

and communist modes of political organization to stimulate capitalist investments. Chapter 4 recounted the harnessing of high-powered incentives embedded in prebendal practices (i.e., allowing public agents to collect a share of public
revenue generated rather than paying them fixed formal salaries) to motivate
bureaucratic self-financing and entrepreneurism. Chapter 7 will explore the role
of communal affiliations, noncodified public financing, and rampant piracy in
market building in other national and temporal contexts. Together these cases
will provide concrete illustrations that start-up economies have *something* to
build on; it is just that standard accounts have not registered these occurrences
and possibilities.

Once the defining imperatives, constraints, and resources in start-up economies are taken seriously into account, it becomes clear that the particular institutions, both economic and political, that would *fit* these contexts could not
be identical to those that *fit* middle- and high-income economies. When we
place *goodness of fit* at the heart of analyses, it is *not* even apt to think about
market-building institutions as merely "second-best" or "good enough" variants of market-preserving institutions. This is because each bundle of institutions fits different functions. For example, would we think about hammers as
second-best screwdrivers? We need hammers to hit nails and screwdrivers to
loosen and tighten screws. Switch their uses around and these instruments cease
to be useful. In the context of development, the methods that spark early growth
may be supremely ill-suited to the tasks of economic restructuring and upgrading. Likewise, market-preserving institutions may do little good for start-up
economies.

As I have examined in chapters 3 and 4, central reformers in China crafted
a set of meta-conditions that empowered local agents to improvise solutions to
particular contingences specific to their locales and that evolved over time. Turning to the case of Forest Hill, our next step is to examine which particular solutions were improvised at various points of development in a location endowed
with certain environmental features.

Introducing the Protagonist: Forest Hill City

Two pieces of background information are useful before I proceed to the case.
First, it is worth reiterating that China is a highly decentralized state, both economically and administratively, even though it is a single-party authoritarian
regime. Some economists characterize China as an "M-form" hierarchy, wherein
each locale operates as a self-sufficient and autonomous unit.[25] According to
the World Bank's *China 2030* Report, subprovincial governments in China

shoulder 59 percent of government expenditures, compared to 14 percent in other developing countries and 32 percent in high-income countries.[26] Cities are a level of government below the central government and the provinces. I focus on a city in this chapter because this is a level of government responsible for the provision of important public goods like urban infrastructure and pensions. This is also a level of administration that features a mixture of macro planning and micro policy implementation, as this city mayor and former county chief described:[27]

> My work at the city level is a mixture of macro and micro. The center is super macro, at the level of grand strategy and direction. At the province, it's still macro. Micro policy execution happens at the county level. Townships lack autonomy and power to solve problems entirely on their own.

Each city is made up of several urban districts at the geographic core and suburban or rural counties that fan out into the periphery. My later discussion of developments in the city of Forest Hill applies mainly to the urban districts. Policies made by the city and usually implemented first among the districts guide the formulation of policies at the county level. But even among these counties, their speeds and outcomes of development vary.

Second, since the party-state plays an oversized role in China's adaptive and development process, the issue of agency—who decides and does what— deserves some elaboration. Agency is a deceptively simple issue; to avoid digressing, I clarify the relationship between the party and the state and the economic roles of various bureaucratic actors in a separate essay.[28] To follow my narratives in this and the next chapter, it suffices to know a few organizational features. In any local government, the top decision makers are usually the party secretary (head of party), the state chief (head of state), and members of the party committee (comprising the party secretary, the state chief, and the leaders of several key departments within the locale, who are appointed by the party secretary).[29]

Once decisions are made, they are implemented by the rest of the bureaucracy, which comprises an administrative civil service and subsidiary extra-bureaucracies that provide administrative support, public services, and charge-based services.[30] The civil service is divided into tiers; officers on the higher tiers (such as department chiefs, deputy department chiefs, and section chiefs) are deeply involved in policy deliberations with the leadership body and craft the details of policies. On average, a city (excluding the districts and counties below it) and county party-state apparatus is made up of about twenty thousand public employees, with 20 percent in the core civil service.

As outlined in chapter 4, while the top leaders are rotated on fixed terms, the remaining cadres are stationed in one locale and many are natives. Despite their limited tenure, party secretaries and state chiefs can and do exert strong influence on the focus and direction of development in their locales, as we'll see in the case of Forest Hill (and also later in chapter 6). To distinguish their legacies, many of these leaders advanced their own signature programs and slogans. To avoid identifying my respondents, I assign pseudonyms to local leaders and a few officials who are frequently quoted.

Like a person, every locale has a distinct story, shaped by its inherited conditions and past experiences. The life path of the protagonist in this chapter, Forest Hill City, is molded by three main factors. First, this is a city in Fujian, a coastal province that lies across the straits from Taiwan. In that sense, Forest Hill enjoys the privilege of being in a relatively prosperous region of China.[31] Fujian and Guangdong were among the first provinces granted permission by the central leadership to welcome foreign investments.[32] Second, although Forest Hill is in a coastal province, it lies deep in the interior of Fujian, lush with trees and flanked by hills. Third, also as a result of its geography, the city is endowed with natural resources, including wood, metals, and minerals.

I refer to Forest Hill as my Goldilocks case. Because of its mixture of growth advantages and constraints, the pace of change in this city is neither too fast nor too slow, but just right, making it an especially apt case for mapping the steps of state-and-market coevolution.

Although Forest Hill is not the most prosperous city in Fujian Province, the city has nonetheless undergone dramatic economic, infrastructural, and social transformation since the launch of market reforms. In 1979 Forest Hill's GDP per capita was less than three hundred yuan (about US$60 by current-day exchange rates), only 0.5 percent of the income level in the United States.[33] Thirty-five years ago, Forest Hill was a predominantly agrarian society. Today its downtown area is congested with mega-malls, bustling crowds, and heavy traffic. Recently, a large suburban area was cleared of farmland to make way for the construction of a new central business district. A skyline dotted by international hotels, condominiums, and office towers heralds the city's future look.

One of the leadership's greatest sources of pride is that the city's GDP had exceeded the benchmark of one hundred million yuan. Some officers were not afraid to admit that growth statistics could be manipulated, like everywhere else in China. "There's water in the numbers," said an officer from the Statistical Bureau. Nevertheless, he added, "the overall trend indicates real change," and the surge of taxes and investments over the decades are also solid measures of economic growth.[34] Moreover, another officer pointed out, "Development is most

The bustling downtown in Forest Hill

visible in the construction. In the past, a six-story building would be considered tall, but today, there are many skyscrapers."[35]

Beneath the veneer of heady growth, the city has experienced—and is still experiencing—growing pains. The brutal costs of rapid industrialization were as conspicuous as the signs of emerging wealth. One of the oldest preserved villages in Forest Hill provided a peek into what the city might have looked like had it not industrialized. The village's environment was pristine and its scenery absolutely breathtaking. A farming family welcomed me with utmost generosity in their home, serving rice they had cultivated in their fields. But as soon as I stepped away from the village, the scene turned uniform, drab, and gray. Mining and heavy industries ravaged the rivers and choked the air with smog. The level of PM 2.5 (small airborne pollutants) exceeded national safety standards. According to a recent pollution scandal, a mining company had allegedly spilled pollutants into a lake, killing fish and sickening residents.[36]

Beyond the physical degradation of the environment, rapid urbanization has also disrupted rural traditions and family lives. Even young children were not spared from anguish. As part of an urbanization drive in the past decade, many village schools were forcibly closed, and children as young as five were made to attend boarding schools in the suburban towns. One of my students from the area recalled that she and her classmates were only allowed to take a bath and to eat something other than rice and pickled vegetables once a week,

The idyllic countryside in Forest Hill

when they returned home, but only briefly. Yet this student was fortunate compared to her peers because her parents, who chose to remain in the farms, were home. Many other rural children were "left behind" with only the old and feeble and sometimes no one when all the adults left the countryside to labor in the cities.[37]

When we speak about development in Forest Hill, these are the concrete outcomes experienced and witnessed. I wish to paint the picture as fully as I can because development is not just growth, a bloodless statistic of rising income.[38] Rather, development—which we have come to regard as the attainment of factories, cities, automobiles, mass consumption, and all things modern—is an all-round transformation and a painful process, especially when this process is as hurried and as compressed as it is in China.

How did Forest Hill make the Great Leap from a poor, agrarian, and socialist political economy to its current middle-income, heavily industrialized, and capitalist status? To illuminate the multifaceted process of development, I will divide my discussion into two overlapping sections: (1) the coevolution of property rights and markets; (2) the coevolution of development strategy and markets. While property rights provided an essential and basic foundation for entrepreneurial activities, it was the party-state's development strategies that accelerated the building and subsequent preserving of markets. Hence the two dynamics proceed together and spill into each other. Table 5.1 summarizes the major political-economic changes from market opening to 2014.

TABLE 5.1 Summary of state and market changes in Forest Hill

| | | | MARKET | | STATE | |
TIME PERIOD	CHARACTERISTICS OF PERIOD	SLOGANS AND CAMPAIGNS	GDP PER CAPITA	ECONOMIC FEATURES AND REFORMS	PROTECTION OF PROPERTY RIGHTS	DEVELOPMENT STRATEGY
Stage 1: 1980s	Mini growth spurt through partial liberalization	"Finish your meals and hurry off to the factories."	1979: Less than 300 yuan	Started as predominantly agrarian economy; rudimentary industrialization via township and village enterprises (TVEs)	Partial property rights assigned to collective enterprises Some privately managed enterprises disguised as TVEs	Generally adopted crude methods of growth promotion Local cadres mobilized personal networks to source capital, raw materials, and customers for TVEs
Stage 2: 1990s	Creative destruction	"Emancipate your minds and embrace openness."	1996: More than 5,000 yuan	Privatized TVEs; restructured SOEs; launched efforts to attract investments	Spread of private ownership following 1993 central decision Informal property rights protection via personal connections with individual officials From 1998 onward, pronounced formal commitments to protecting private property rights Launched institutional reforms to strengthen bureaucratic control and fight petty corruption	Began construction of transportation infrastructure to overcome geographic barriers, primarily using land proceeds Beehive campaign: all agencies courted investors Gave away generous attractions indiscriminately

(Continued)

TABLE 5.1 (Continued)

TIME PERIOD	CHARACTERISTICS OF PERIOD	SLOGANS AND CAMPAIGNS	GDP PER CAPITA	ECONOMIC FEATURES AND REFORMS	PROTECTION OF PROPERTY RIGHTS	DEVELOPMENT STRATEGY
			MARKET		STATE	
Stage 3: 2001–2005	Big growth spurt but without regard to quality of growth	"3-100s"	2001: More than 8,000 yuan	Peak of investment growth; emphasis on quantity of growth only; jack-of-all-industries	Continued to expand and refine institutional reforms Visible signs of reduced petty corruption and predatory practices among local agencies	Continued expansion of transportation infrastructure Beehive campaign peaked to feverish mode
Stage 4: 2006–2010	Simultaneous pursuit of quantity and quality growth	"10+3"	2006: More than 16,000 yuan	Shifted focus to simultaneously pursuing quantity and quality growth	Expanded room for high-stakes transactional corruption among political elites; recent exposes of corruption scandals involving local leaders	Toward provision of soft infrastructure through business-friendly services Toward specialized and regularized investment promotion Toward selective privileges for lead enterprises and targeted industries
Stage 5: 2011 onward	Pursuit of quality growth and sustainability	"1+2"	2011: More than 40,000 yuan	Industrial restructuring with emphasis on technological upgrading and cultivating comparative advantages	In 2014 the city was selected by the central government as a pilot case for strengthening intellectual property rights	As part of sustainability drive, encouraged major mining companies to invest outward, extract resources from elsewhere and refine them at home

The Coevolution of Property Rights and Markets

The protection of property rights is a fitting place to launch an examination of the coevolutionary path of Forest Hill City. As standard economic theories tell us, economic growth requires the provision of secure private property rights and eradication of predatory state behavior. Defying expectations, China's economy took off in the 1980s despite the absence of private property rights and rule of law and in the presence of widespread petty corruption. As richly documented in earlier literature, during the initial period of partial market reforms, China's economy was stimulated by the assignment of partial property rights to collectively owned enterprises.[39] But how did property rights structure continue to evolve from the early 1990s up until the present day?

Extending earlier accounts, I will trace the coevolution of the structure of property rights and markets over three phases: (1) prior to 1993, the assignment of partial property rights to collective enterprises; (2) after 1993, informal property rights protection through personal relationships between bureaucracy and businesses; (3) from 1998 onward, state efforts to formally protect private property, promote the private sector, and rein in bureaucratic predation. Along the way, I will also outline the evolution of corruption patterns in Forest Hill since the 1980s, from decentralized petty corruption to the rise of grand corruption in a context of accelerated capitalism. Figure 5.1 summarizes my discussion in this section.

Assignment of Partial Property Rights

At the start of market reform, the priorities of the leadership were clear: feed the population and increase industrial production. Huang, the party secretary who presided over the reforms of the 1980s, was single-mindedly focused on industrialization. He coined a catchy slogan that conveyed the urgency of the task: "Finish your meals and hurry off to the factories." Even though the objectives of development were clear, however, the menu of choices in the 1980s was constrained by two political imperatives. First, private ownership was still taboo and not endorsed by the central party. Second, the implementation of market reform required the political support and even enthusiasm of local communist cadres. Many of these cadres had monopolized the allocation of resources under central planning. If the introduction of markets eroded their traditional base of power and gave them no benefit in return, they would resist reforms.[40] What structure of property rights would fit within these constraints, that is, is not private, could incentivize production, and would enlist local communist cadres in the process of industrialization?

The answer is township and village enterprises (TVEs), collectively owned and managed by township and village governments rather than by private

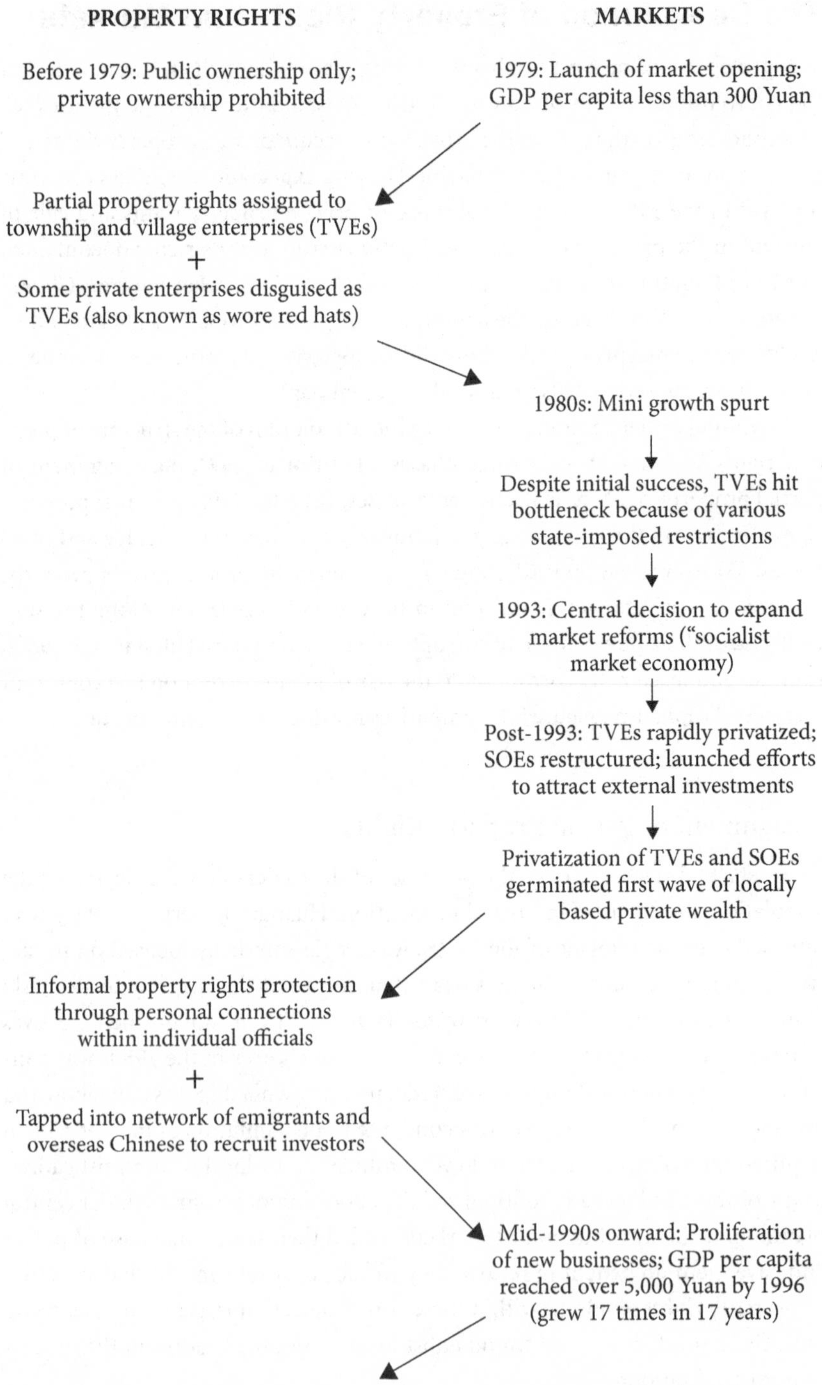

PROPERTY RIGHTS

Before 1979: Public ownership only;
private ownership prohibited

Partial property rights assigned to
township and village enterprises (TVEs)
+
Some private enterprises disguised as
TVEs (also known as wore red hats)

MARKETS

1979: Launch of market opening;
GDP per capita less than 300 Yuan

1980s: Mini growth spurt

Despite initial success, TVEs hit
bottleneck because of various
state-imposed restrictions

1993: Central decision to expand
market reforms ("socialist
market economy)

Post-1993: TVEs rapidly privatized;
SOEs restructured; launched efforts
to attract external investments

Privatization of TVEs and SOEs
germinated first wave of locally
based private wealth

Informal property rights protection
through personal connections
within individual officials

+

Tapped into network of emigrants and
overseas Chinese to recruit investors

Mid-1990s onward: Proliferation
of new businesses; GDP per capita
reached over 5,000 Yuan by 1996
(grew 17 times in 17 years)

FIGURE 5.1 Coevolution of property rights and markets in Forest Hill

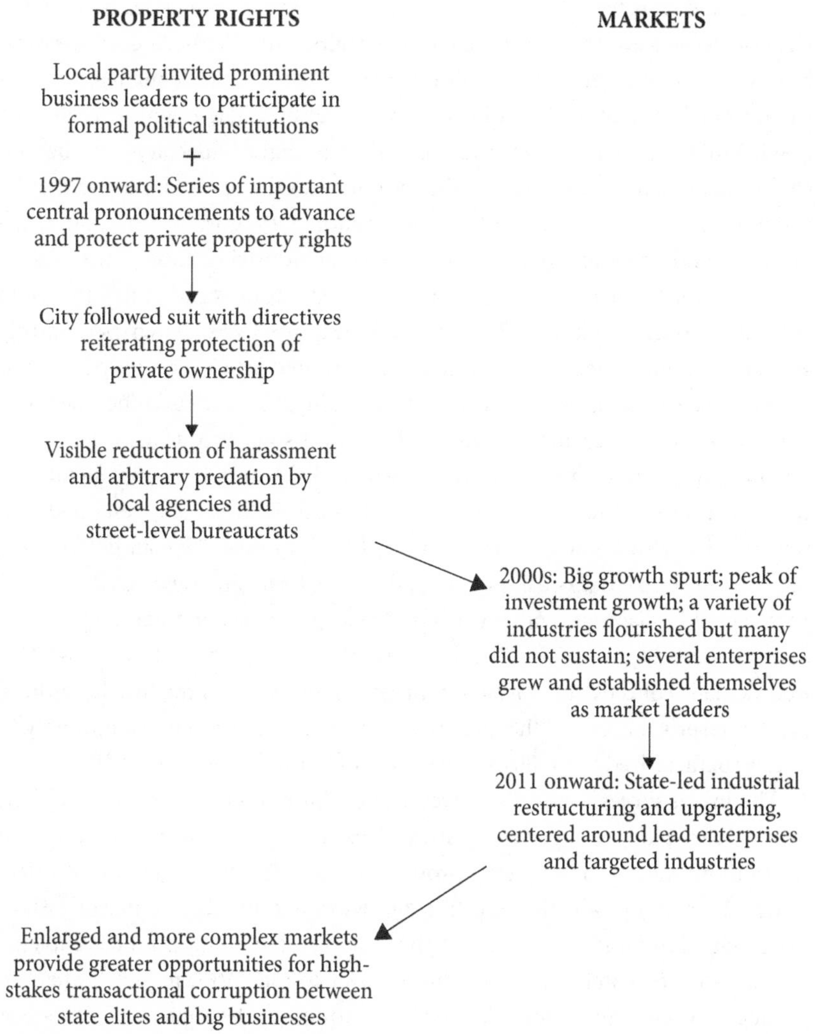

PROPERTY RIGHTS   MARKETS

Local party invited prominent
business leaders to participate in
formal political institutions
+
1997 onward: Series of important
central pronouncements to advance
and protect private property rights

↓

City followed suit with directives
reiterating protection of
private ownership

↓

Visible reduction of harassment
and arbitrary predation by
local agencies and
street-level bureaucrats

2000s: Big growth spurt; peak of
investment growth; a variety of
industries flourished but many
did not sustain; several enterprises
grew and established themselves
as market leaders

↓

2011 onward: State-led industrial
restructuring and upgrading,
centered around lead enterprises
and targeted industries

Enlarged and more complex markets
provide greater opportunities for high-
stakes transactional corruption between
state elites and big businesses

FIGURE 5.1 (Continued)

individuals. As discussed in chapter 3, central leaders had not anticipated the emergence of TVEs, much less dictated their specific forms. So why did these enterprises mushroom spontaneously across the country in the absence of central planning? Because TVEs *fit* the nationally defined priorities and parameters of the time: grow industries without going private.

TVEs operated on the basis of *partial* property rights. As Oi and Walder clarify, property rights are actually a bundle of rights, comprising rights over control, income, and transfer.[41] TVEs were aligned with socialist principles because the right of transfer was collectively held by townships and villages. At the same time, however, individual officials and TVE managers could exercise managerial control over daily operational decisions. They were also assigned rights over income flows. Profits earned by TVEs were classified as extra-budgetary revenue and could thus be retained entirely at the local levels. Oi and Walder argue that by assigning partial property rights to collective entities, the government created sufficient incentives for an impressive spurt of rural industrialization in the 1980s.

The national dynamic described above played out in Forest Hill.[42] Township and village officials played a lead role in setting up TVEs, which were mostly small paper and cement factories that later ventured into making plywood and alloys. Local cadres mobilized villagers to work in TVEs and used their personal contacts to scout for customers. During this period, some private managers seized the opportunity to operate in the disguise of TVEs. A long-time bureaucrat who worked in resource management, whom I will call Officer Tian, described how this practice, also known as "wearing a red hat," worked: "Say an enterprising individual wanted to do business, but at that time he or she could not do so. This person could collaborate with township and village officials and start a TVE in the name of the local government."[43] It is impossible to know for sure how many TVEs were actually collective or privately managed or a mixture of the two. Regardless, these enterprises became "the major driving force of our industrial economy."[44] Locals characterized the 1980s as the decade of "a mini growth spurt."[45]

The initial success of TVEs, however, soon hit bottlenecks. Because of their hybrid (part-plan, part-private) status, TVEs were burdened by state-imposed restrictions, such as mandatory production targets. Officer Tian recounted, "I was there at a production meeting and witnessed the deputy mayor assigning production targets. During that time, targets that could not be completed [by state-owned enterprises] were turned over to the TVEs, requiring them to produce however much was planned."[46] In addition, the success of TVEs was defined by higher-level governments in terms of sales and output, rather than long-term profitability.[47] Such criterion was emblazoned on performance contracts and circulars on leadership evaluation.[48] In a revealing choice of words, a veteran economic planner, Officer Wu, noted that this overly narrow focus on output stimulated "industrial activities but not industries."[49] Elaborating on the TVEs' short-lived success, another veteran, Officer Han, pointed sharply to the limitations of partial property rights:[50]

> The development of TVEs did not last long because collective property rights were still not clear enough; they were incompatible with modern enterprise management and corporatization. On the other hand,

> private property rights are clear. Mine is mine, and yours is yours. Both restraints and incentives are much easier to establish [under a system of private property rights].

Yet despite knowing the limitations of collective ownership, local officials and enterprise managers had no authority to attempt outright privatization during the first decade of reform. Crossing the red line of privatization risked persecution and grave personal casualties. The decision to transform collective into private property had to come from the highest ranks of the party. This momentous shift finally came in 1993, when the post-Deng leadership led by Jiang Zemin announced the groundbreaking decision to establish "a socialist market economy," that is, to pursue full-fledged market reforms.[51]

Informal Property Rights Protection

Referring to the 1993 decision, a former city bureaucrat and county leader, Chief Ma, remarked, "When the central government makes a firm decision, this decision will trigger seismic changes across the country."[52] The impact of ideological shifts at the center was felt deeply at the local levels, but each locale's response to the opportunities provided by central-level changes was different, as Ma further explained:

> At the grassroots, our actions are broadly guided by central decisions, but not in a precise way ... because work at the grassroots must be tailored to local conditions. Development succeeds only if we take advantage of the unique features of each locality. This is different from policy making at the central level."

The leaders of Forest Hill took the first step of observing how other economically advanced cities in Fujian Province responded to central calls for bolder reforms. "Our leaders took study trips to the coastal cities of Ocean View and Long Beach [both in Fujian], learned from their experiences and brought them back to Forest Hill," Officer Tian recounted. The study trips emboldened the city's leadership to go ahead with privatizing TVEs, even though they were still careful not to use the word "privatize." Instead, he said, "We coined a nicer term: restructure."[53] Within a few years after 1993, scores of TVEs were restructured. Through this process of ownership transfer, "the individuals who started the TVEs earned their first pot of gold."[54]

Next, Forest Hill embarked on "state owned enterprise (SOEs) restructuring," a code phrase for bankruptcy and closures. Many SOEs had long been inefficient and saddled with losses. The city government retained the large SOEs in the profitable sectors, primarily mining and tobacco, and proceeded to shut down the rest. Officer Tian also recalled the closure of a state-owned timber factory through the policy of "two transfers." The status of thousands of employees was transferred from "state workers" to "free social agents" (a euphemism for unemployed) during massive layoffs. Property was then transferred from public to private hands. The city used the land occupied by the factory to pay its debts and workers' severance. The remaining assets were sold at a fraction of their value to "budding private bosses," who profited handsomely.[55]

Importantly, the restructuring TVEs and SOEs germinated the first batch of local private wealth holders. "One part of our private economy sprang from TVEs, benefiting from the collective, and the other from SOEs, benefiting from the state," Tian summed up. Bear in mind that only about a decade before, Forest Hill had no private economy and was a hill-locked location. Left to their own means, enterprising individuals could not easily accumulate the necessary capital, assets, networks, and experience to start factories. Nor might they have been willing to bear the risks of failure. Collective and public ownership provided a springboard and preparatory ground for private entrepreneurship.

Along with the birth of a local private sector, another major shift after 1993 was the city's enthusiastic embrace of foreign investments. A distinctive feature of China's FDI (foreign direct investment) inflows were that they came predominantly from a Chinese business diaspora spread throughout East Asia, especially in neighboring Hong Kong and Taiwan.[56] Fujian Province was among the first to welcome foreign investors; one of the first special economic zones (SEZs) was established in the city of Xiamen. But because Forest Hill is located in the interior of Fujian, it lagged behind its coastal peers and only began to court foreign investors aggressively from the 1990s onward. (In the next section, I'll discuss in more detail its strategy of wooing investments.)

Despite the central's expressed commitment to full-fledged capitalist reforms, local business environments during the 1990s were far from predictable, much less friendly. Private and foreign businesses alike were prey to excessive red tape and widespread extraction by myriad local agencies, a problem known throughout China as "the three arbitraries" (arbitrary extractions, arbitrary fees, and arbitrary fines). Also, companies could not rely on the legal system to resolve disputes, as courts were in their infancy and patently not independent. In fact, prior to 1998 Forest Hill authorities made no formal commitments to protect private property rights. On top of these burdens, businesses were frequently compelled to entertain party-state functionaries at their expense:[57]

> Personnel from various party-state offices chose to hold meetings not at the government buildings but at the enterprises. Their pretext was

to show concern for businesses. In reality, they went there to eat, drink, and stay, and the companies had to host them. . . . Throughout the 1980s and 1990s, this was a common practice. I once attended such a meeting at a major enterprise. Not only did it have to serve meals and beverages, it also had to prepare little gifts [like briefcases] for every bureaucrat at the end of each meeting. Every expense, big and small, was delegated to these enterprises, so for them, it was a significant burden.

Bothersome hosting requests and arbitrary extractions made by local agencies, which Lu describes as "organizational corruption," were not the only scourge in the 1990s.[58] Petty corruption was equally common. In an environment of extensive regulatory controls and discretion, individual low-level officers could demand petty bribes in exchange for speeding up administrative approvals. Social scientists refer to such petty corruption as "speed money,"[59] while Officer Tian termed it euphemistically as "lubricant."

Some licensing procedures were of course necessary, but it depended on how the bureaucrat chose to process them. Some take only two or three days to be completed. That would require some "lubricant." You'll have to prepare an envelope. Otherwise the process would be slow.[60]

In short, throughout the 1980s and 1990s, which were two decades of impressive growth, apparent in figure 5.2, Forest Hill experienced all the problems of petty corruption and excessive red tape that debilitate poor and weak states elsewhere. So why did problems of weak property rights and predatory bureaucracy not suffocate growth here?

The theory of "market-preserving federalism," famously advanced by Qian, Montinola, and Weingast, provides only a partial and overly optimistic explanation of this puzzle. According to them, intense regional competition should deter local governments from engaging in harassing and extractive practices. In their words, "When a particular jurisdiction imposes an onerous restriction on its firms, the latter face a competitive disadvantage relative to competing firms from other jurisdictions that are not bound by the restriction. . . . Jurisdictions are thus induced to provide a hospitable environment."[61] While the idea that free competition deters predatory practices may have appeal, their theory rests on an unrealistic assumption: that firms can move freely. In reality, corporate mobility is constrained. When businesses are still deciding where to invest, they do enjoy plenty of choice and may even play local governments off against one another to extract favorable deals. But once businesses invest in a location and factories are built, it is costly to relocate. This is especially true in China

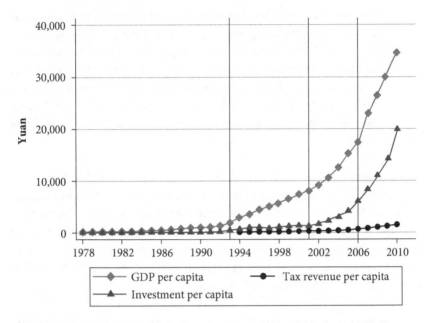

FIGURE 5.2   Forest Hill's economic statistics, 1978–2010. Forest Hill City Yearbooks.

given that the vast majority of investments are in manufacturing, not services.[62] The costs of relocation are even higher in resource-oriented economies like Forest Hill.[63]

Therefore investors could not pin their hopes on local governments to self-restrain due to competitive pressures. Instead, to adapt to a less-than-hospitable environment, the more effective means of protecting property rights was to cultivate close personal relationships with individual officials, who could help investors mediate disputes, navigate complicated regulations, obtain necessary approvals, and avoid onerous charges. This is why investment courtship during the 1990s was highly personalized (more in the next section); clientelist relationships between bureaucrats and investors substituted for formal property rights protection.[64] The more highly ranked and influential the official to whom an investor was connected, the stronger the protection accorded. In some extreme instances, which are still seen in parts of China today, companies would prominently display state-awarded "protection plaques" at their factory gates to ward off inspecting and potentially predatory agencies.

Tapping on ethnic ties provides yet another layer of informal property rights protection. Compared to business executives in Western multinational corporations (MNCs), returning émigrés and overseas Chinese entrepreneurs speak local dialects and know informal norms; many are related to the native populace by kinship or friendship. Owing to its coastal location and long emigration history, the facilitating role of ethnic ties to local communities is especially pronounced in Zhejiang Province (later illustrated in chapter 6, through the case of Blessed County). As a business owner in Zhejiang related, "Here in my hometown, I know many people. So if there's any problem, I can find someone on the higher or lower levels to help. There's bound to be someone who can help."[65] Forest Hill too benefited from returning émigrés. One of the city's industrial titans, Phoenix Corporation, was founded by a native who migrated to Hong Kong in the 1980s and returned to Forest Hill in 1993 to set up a machinery factory. This founder is famously quoted as saying, "Love for one's hometown is an essential virtue of entrepreneurship."[66] The diasporic business community played a significant role in stimulating early growth because of its unique advantage in navigating an environment of weak formal property rights.

To sum up the developments thus far, if the 1980s was a decade of a "mini growth spurt" accomplished through partial market reform, then the 1990s was a Schumpeterian era of creative destruction. Collective ownership and mechanisms of central planning were dismantled and replaced by an influx of new business forms. GDP per capita grew from less than three hundred yuan in 1979 to five thousand yuan by 1996; the size of the economy grew seventeen-fold in seventeen years. As the seeds of capitalism were laid, these changes spawned new patterns of state-business relations in the latter half of the 1990s.

Toward Formal Property Rights

Forest Hill's founding class of capitalists sprang out of the privatization of state-owned and collectively owned enterprises after 1993, as well as out of the inflow of Chinese diasporic investors. Seeing the rise of this promising class, city leaders responded by co-opting it.[67] Party bosses invited entrepreneurial stars and the managers of local state-owned companies to participate in formal political institutions, most notably the city's people's congress (equivalent to the legislature) and consultative conference (a policy discussion forum).[68] Participation in formal political institutions gave business leaders the opportunity to voice their concerns to the government and potentially influence policy making. Even more importantly, behind the scenes, political participation helped capitalist delegates strengthen connections with state bureaucrats and thereby enhance their own business interests.[69] For state and business alike, it was a win-win arrangement.

Such on-the-ground developments throughout the country quickly fed back to decision making at the central level. As Tsai observes, "The economic success of private businesses ... offered reformers evidence (against 'leftists' or conservative leaders) that enhancing the scope of the private sector would be in the country's political and economic interest."[70] To enhance the private sector, central reformers had to assuage private owners about their fears of political reprisals and widespread bureaucratic predation. In response, the central party took steps to progressively affirm the political status of private ownership. At the Fifteenth Party Congress in 1997, private ownership was elevated in a nationally broadcast speech to "an important component of the economy."

These central signals percolated powerfully back to the localities. In Forest Hill, Chen, the party secretary who took office in 1998, made "emancipating our minds and embracing openness" his governing motto. Under his charge, the city promulgated a series of directives that formally and concretely ratified its commitment to protecting private property rights. Issued in 1998, the first of these documents was titled "Implementation of the Decision to Promote the Private Economy's Rapid Development." The year after, the city government issued a more detailed directive that pronounced, "In accordance with the Constitution, all levels of government must seriously incorporate the private economy into local development plans." The directive spelled out concrete measures to "protect the rights of private enterprises according to the law," including prohibitions against "extortion, indirect extortion, forced purchases of services [by local agencies] ... forced subscriptions of publications [published by local agencies], demands for free meals, and monopolies in services provision."

Such formal pronouncements were encouraging but would have little bite if they were not backed up by institutional reforms. The year 1998 coincided with Zhu Rongji's arrival in office as premier. He forcefully advanced a nationwide program of administrative reforms to overhaul the practices of accounting, budgeting, fee collection, and more.[71] The advent of administrative controls was accompanied by the adjustment of local public compensation. Recalling my discussion in chapter 4, nationally standardized salaries set by the central government were abysmally low. A civil servant in the Trade Bureau recalled that his formal wages during the early 1990s was only 117 yuan (less than US$20) per month.[72] To top up formal wages, the Forest Hill government provided staff allowances and benefits by drawing on local tax income. In this way, operating like dividend payments, all cadres from the highest to the lowest ranks benefited from the city's wealth. Reminding all the agencies of their personal stake in local prosperity, a deputy mayor once declared at a meeting, "Do not forget that taxes paid by our enterprises are closely and personally connected to your benefits. Taxes collected go toward paying your allowances. So serve our enterprises well!"[73] As the tax base grew, the city government could better afford to pay the bureaucracy higher budgets and salaries and thereby reduce their reliance on extracting fees and fines.

Reforms within the bureaucracy were reinforced by corporate demands for political change, not in the form of democratization but in the manner of what the businesses termed "release";[74] that is, the removal of administrative red tape and harassment. As businesses swelled and contributed to the political achievements of leaders and the material welfare of bureaucracy, they were emboldened to voice their grievances. As Officer Tian recounted, "Businesses were unhappy about the situation, so they complained, saying 'Why should we pay for the government's expenses?' Once the top leaders took serious notice, those on the ground didn't dare to mess around."[75] In practice, predatory practices were not eliminated in a snap by top-down commands. Nevertheless, the movement toward administrative rationalization that started in the 1990s continued into the next decade, paving the way for a new phase of market building.

Petty Corruption Subsided, Grand Corruption Rose

Locals characterized the decade of the 2000s as a "big growth spurt," compared to a "mini growth spurt" of the 1980s. Indeed, if you look at the economic statistics in figure 5.2, income, investments, and tax revenue per capita inched upward during the 1980s, grew at a robust rate during the 1990s, and then galloped steeply in the 2000s. Underlying the impressive trajectory of the 2000s were several conditions laid down during the 1990s that provided a more predictable, rules-based environment for doing business. These conditions included formal commitments to property rights protection, a raft of administrative reforms, salary raises financed by a growing tax base, and an increasingly large and assertive capitalist class. Simultaneously, during the 1990s and into the 2000s, the city government aggressively courted investors and channeled significant efforts into improving the city's transportation links (more in the next section).

Whereas the decade of the 1990s was one of creative destruction, the 2000s was a time of economic coagulation around a few emerging industrial titans in the city. Such changes in the economy fed back to both the elite and nonelite tiers of bureaucracy. On the latter side, Forest Hill saw a steady reduction in individual-level petty corruption as well as agency-level predatory practices. Local businesses observed a discernible break in the behavior of street-level bureaucrats from the 2000s onward, as one manager related:[76]

> Before 2000, the business environment was not good. At that time, there were comparatively few enterprises. Bureaucratic personnel frequently came to patrol enterprises, dining and wining along the way. Nowadays, however, there are many enterprises, and the officers cannot eat so much. Moreover, people are more civilized today. I personally know some regulatory officers who really have no desire to harass businesses. Not to mention that there is so much food available these days. There are many occasions for dining and wining, and our society has become health conscious too, so local officers are not keen to "eat" anymore.

Notice, as described above, that the decline of low-level predation stemmed from an ongoing growth process, which created more enterprises, more food, and new social mores emphasizing "civilized values" and "health consciousness." At the same time, these economically motivated changes within the bureaucracy were buttressed by the introduction of new control mechanisms. For example, starting in the late 2000s, civil servants were required to make purchases using state-issued credit cards, so that transactions could be precisely tracked electronically. The city also created a one-step administrative center for issuing licenses and collecting regulatory fees, where cameras were installed to deter individual administrators from taking petty bribes or gifts.[77]

Although accurate data on bureaucratic extractive practices are sparse, official reports about the collection of "unauthorized fees" in the education sector provide some clues about malfeasance trends over time. Nationwide, the problem of unauthorized school fees was a source of public outrage. Although Chinese citizens are entitled by law to ten years of free education, many public schools burdened families by charging additional fees. Figure 5.3 shows the trend of unauthorized fee collection in Forest Hill, based on my coding of reports in the city yearbooks. We can see that the number of penalized cases peaked around 2000 but steadily declined afterward. The reported amount of illegal fees also surged in the early 2000s but fell precipitously after 2007. From the descriptive statistics alone, we cannot tell for sure whether the spikes around 2000 reflect an actual increase in extraction or stronger state enforcement against such behavior. The onset of administrative reforms in the late 1990s, however, followed by a dramatic fall in the incidence and amount of unauthorized fees suggest that stronger institutional checks are more likely the reason for the trends observed in the 2000s.

This snapshot in Forest Hill's transition to a market economy suggests a major lesson: growth itself is a strong antidote to petty corruption;[78] it enables

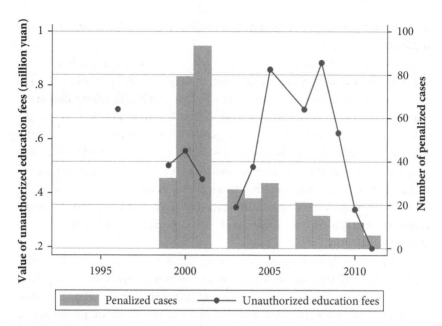

FIGURE 5.3　Trend of unauthorized fee collection in education. Forest Hill City Yearbooks.

the meaningful implementation of administrative reforms. The institution that spurred early growth, however, was *not* formal protection of private property rights, but rather a system of partial followed by informal property rights protection, paired with an unorthodox bundle of market-building strategies (more details later). Once markets took off, diminished economic scarcity and strengthened mechanisms of control worked together to extricate predatory practices at their roots. Seen in this light, recommendations that poor and weak states eradicate petty corruption as a necessary first step toward building markets have confused the causal order of corruption and growth.

The administrative improvements that started in the late 1990s and continued well into the 2000s laid a foundation for the next lap of Forest Hill's development. From 2011 onward, the city's leaders shifted the focus of development decisively from growing the size of the economy to industrial restructuring and upgrading. In 2014, Forest Hill was selected by the central government as a test point for strengthening intellectual property rights. The city incorporated the number of patents into its cadre evaluation targets, established a specialized legal aid center for intellectual property rights, and provided training programs to agencies and companies.[79] As Weber-inspired scholarship correctly observes, for states to preserve and upgrade markets, a nonpredatory, rules-based administration is a minimum requirement.

But even though petty corruption and agency-level malfeasance subsided over the 2000s, we would be seriously mistaken to think that all forms of corruption had diminished. Indeed, this is what Weber's theory critically fails to notice: the march of capitalism is accompanied by administrative rationalization *and* the emergence of grand corruption in new guises. What are these guises? Examples abound in advanced capitalist economies, including in the United States: campaign support from super wealthy donors; ever-revolving doors between public and private sectors; companies that lavish perks on legislators in exchange for favorable laws and exemptions from taxes and regulations; and, not to forget, collusion among banks, regulators, and corporations that led recklessly to the 2008 financial crisis.[80]

As it is still a developing economy, Forest Hill has yet to evolve the highly sophisticated and legalized guises of corruption commonly found in the most advanced capitalist markets. Nevertheless, as its economy boomed, instances of grand transactional corruption between political elites and influence-buying capitalists rose conspicuously to the surface. In the wake of Xi's anticorruption campaign, several of Former Hill's top officials "fell off the horse," that is, were arrested for corruption. These toppled officials include a former city party secretary (the number one leader in the city), a deputy mayor, a chief of the city assets-management committee, and a county party secretary.

Official reports shied from revealing the details of their crimes, perhaps because the central party feared that such information would stir public ire. Nevertheless, we know from available procuratorial and press reports that the crimes of these former top guns included taking bribes, engaging in profit-making activities, and keeping mistresses. Notably, different from Zairian-style predatory states, their crimes did *not* include extortion (demanding payments without providing benefits in return) and embezzlement (outright stealing of public funds). To be clear, theirs was corruption that greased access to markets for a small number of players who desired and could afford to pay for privileges.

Available exposes of these fallen leaders reveal another important pattern of corruption: their crimes were inextricably intertwined with their economic accomplishments. A former party secretary, who has been sacked on charges of "illegally accepting huge bribes in exchange for favors," provides a sharp illustration. During his reign, this party secretary oversaw a period of impressive growth, including an ambitious program of state-led urbanization. This scheme involved resettling thousands of rural families into newly constructed and densely packed suburban towns, thereby freeing up farmland for industrial and commercial uses.[81] Before his arrest, this leader was praised for attracting multibillion-dollar investment projects. Locals remember him especially well for presiding over the construction of a high-end mall. Although official reports do not indicate who gave him bribes and for what, rumors swirling on online forums alleged that the party secretary's family members had monopolized road construction projects. It was also rumored that developers bribed their way to constructing the many suburban towns that decorated his career. His developmental dazzle lasted until he fell from the horse.

The Coevolution of Development Strategies and Markets

Property rights are a necessary ingredient of development, but they are not the only ingredient. Especially for late developers, which do not have the luxury of time to build markets over centuries, state interventions are necessary to accelerate the process of economic catch-up. As the developmental state literature tells us, the East Asian economies succeeded through the formula of "market-conforming methods of state intervention," the establishment of elite Weberian agencies, and the targeting of preferential policies and subsidies at industries of comparative advantage.[82] Although some observers have characterized China's local states as developmental,[83] the city of Forest Hill did not in fact follow the standard developmental formula, at least not in the beginning. Figure 5.4 summarizes my account in this section.

Capitalizing on Market Opening

Rewind the timeline back to 1979, when central authorities had just announced the decision to reform and open. Given the green light to increase production but the red light against private ownership, the predominant mode of development in the 1980s was rural industrialization through TVEs. As earlier described, cadres in township and village governments led the drive to start up TVEs. In general, the methods used to spur production during this period were "coarse," as termed in Chinese.[84] Officer Tian described, "During the 1980s, the motto was 'go wherever the water flows.' This means if you can find any way to make money, do it. Dig up metals in the hills; disregard pollution."[85] This first decade produced a mini growth spurt, but he lamented in hindsight that "it also resulted in tremendous waste of human capital, assets, and natural resources."

Meanwhile, at the city level, the priority of development was stark and pressing: build railways and roads. Without basic transportation links, Forest Hill was a hill-locked city. No amount of strategizing or business-friendly services could

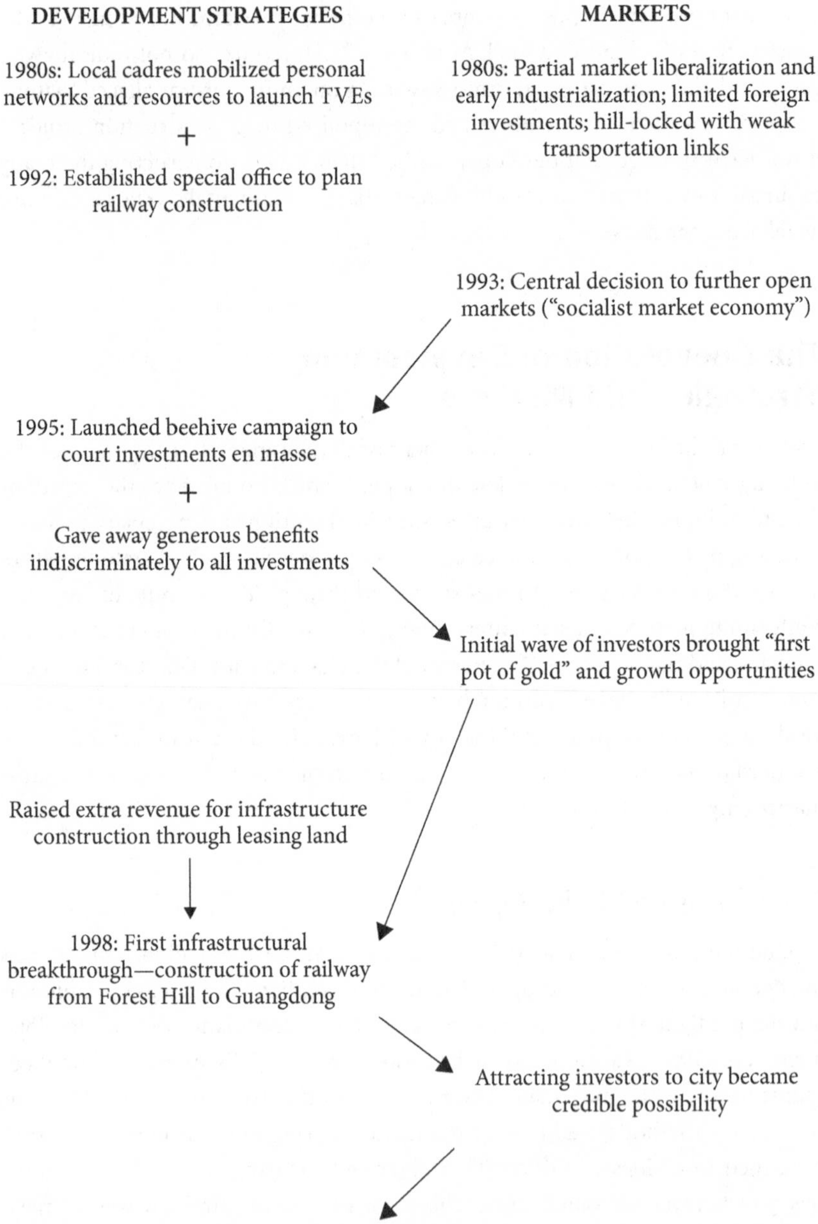

DEVELOPMENT STRATEGIES	MARKETS
1980s: Local cadres mobilized personal networks and resources to launch TVEs	1980s: Partial market liberalization and early industrialization; limited foreign investments; hill-locked with weak transportation links
+	
1992: Established special office to plan railway construction	
	1993: Central decision to further open markets ("socialist market economy")
1995: Launched beehive campaign to court investments en masse	
+	
Gave away generous benefits indiscriminately to all investments	
	Initial wave of investors brought "first pot of gold" and growth opportunities
Raised extra revenue for infrastructure construction through leasing land	
1998: First infrastructural breakthrough—construction of railway from Forest Hill to Guangdong	
	Attracting investors to city became credible possibility

FIGURE 5.4 Coevolution of development strategies and markets in Forest Hill

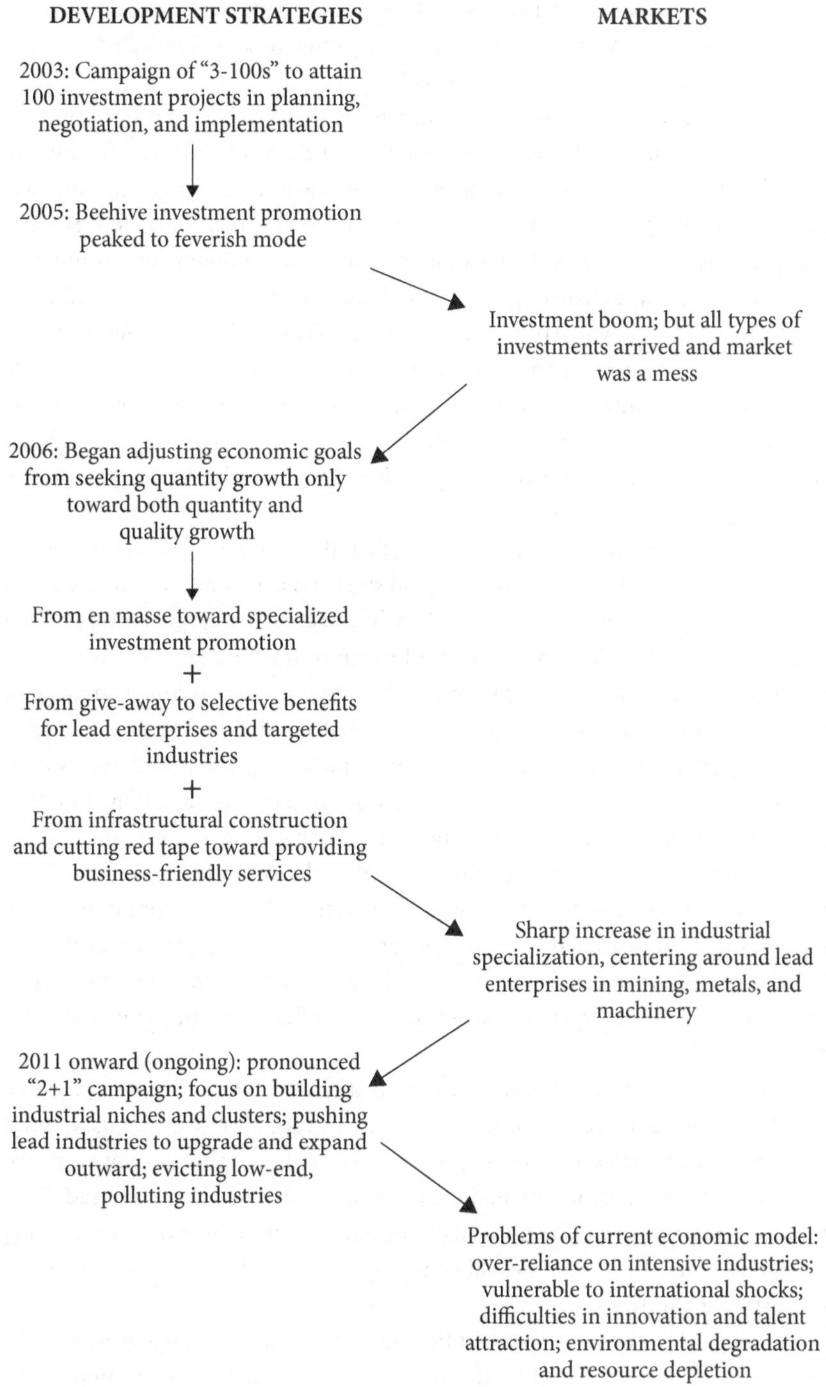

DEVELOPMENT STRATEGIES   MARKETS

2003: Campaign of "3-100s" to attain
100 investment projects in planning,
negotiation, and implementation

2005: Beehive investment promotion
peaked to feverish mode

Investment boom; but all types of
investments arrived and market
was a mess

2006: Began adjusting economic goals
from seeking quantity growth only
toward both quantity and
quality growth

From en masse toward specialized
investment promotion
+
From give-away to selective benefits
for lead enterprises and targeted
industries
+
From infrastructural construction
and cutting red tape toward providing
business-friendly services

Sharp increase in industrial
specialization, centering around lead
enterprises in mining, metals, and
machinery

2011 onward (ongoing): pronounced
"2+1" campaign; focus on building
industrial niches and clusters; pushing
lead industries to upgrade and expand
outward; evicting low-end,
polluting industries

Problems of current economic model:
over-reliance on intensive industries;
vulnerable to international shocks;
difficulties in innovation and talent
attraction; environmental degradation
and resource depletion

FIGURE 5.4   (Continued)

lure investors to Forest Hill if goods could not be conveniently transported to the coast for sale and export. Thus in 1992 the city government established a special office to plan the construction of railroads.

Deng's revival of capitalist reforms in 1993 emboldened local officials in Forest Hill to pursue growth opportunities beyond domestic borders. "Attracting capital and investments" became the hottest buzzword. Within Fujian Province, coastal cities like Xiamen had opened their doors to FDI as early as the 1980s and had prospered. Now Forest Hill wanted a share of these opportunities too. But how was it to stand a chance against formidable coastal competitors like Xiamen and Shenzhen? Following conventional wisdom, Forest Hill should follow in the footsteps of the East Asian tigers, that is, it must first create a corps of technocrats to design and execute investment promotion policies citywide. Additionally, as the theory of market-preserving federalism predicts, the way to beat regional competition is to eradicate corrupt practices and to entice investors with the most hospitable business environment.

These ideal measures could have been taken if Forest Hill were already developed or had enjoyed an exceptionally good start. Alas, its conditions in the 1990s were far from favorable. Unlike Japan, South Korea, or Singapore, Forest Hill did not inherit a technically competent and foreign trained bureaucracy from colonial legacies.[86] Instead, it had a communist bureaucracy barred from contact with the outside world and from engaging in capitalist activities for three decades. Attracting FDI was entirely new to the city. Eradicating petty predation would also have been ideal, except, prior to an economic takeoff, the city had neither an ample tax base to adequately finance its bureaucrats nor sufficient capacity to discipline them. Moreover, during the 1990s, the very idea of "serving businesses" had not occurred to the bureaucracy. Bear in mind that communist state planners were accustomed only to exerting control. As one planner explained, "Under the command economy, there was no private sector, only state-owned enterprises. These enterprises were all state controlled, and our job was to command them."[87]

The conditions facing Forest Hill shortly after 1993 added up to a paradox: Use the existing communist bureaucracy to court capitalist investments. Central reformers had signaled the green light to court foreign capital and investments, but they gave no specific instructions on how it was to be done. Instead, local leaders were left to capitalize on available opportunities on their own. In selecting a response, their first and practical consideration was: How might we make use of existing institutions?

Although the existing communist bureaucracy was flawed in many ways (petty predation was common and local cadres were utterly lacking in cosmopolitanism and market savvy), it possessed certain advantages. The first was networks.

In poor and agrarian political economies, people are deeply embedded in affective personal relationships, known in Chinese as *renqing* and *guanxi*. Whereas relationships in urban, industrialized societies are distant and impersonal, those in rural settings are rooted in familiarity and trust. On this important point, Fei Xiaotong's incisive observations deserve to be quoted at length:[88]

> Modern society is composed of strangers. We do not know each other's pasts. When we talk, we must explain things clearly. Even then, we fear that oral agreements are not binding; therefore, we draw up written contracts to which we sign our names. Laws arise in just this fashion. But there is no way for laws like this to develop in a rural society. "Isn't that what outsiders do?" rural people would say. In rural society, trust derives from familiarity. This kind of trust has very solid foundations.

As Fei's quote underscores, the "market-preserving" institutions advocated in the dominant literature (e.g., rule of law, written contracts, and impartial administration) are institutions that undergird modern societies, which are "composed of strangers." But pre-urbanized locales like Forest Hill—as well as many communities throughout the developing world—are distinctly societies *without* strangers. Indeed, the term "a society of familiars" continues to be used in China today.[89] When I conduct fieldwork in townships and villages, even in counties, it is apparent that *everyone knows everyone*. Fei, an astute observer of Chinese society (and of rural societies in general), does not view personal connections through a rosy lens. He admonishes, "China is undergoing a rapid transformation that is changing a fundamentally rural society into a modern one. The way of life that has been cultivated in rural society is now giving rise to abuses."[90] In other words, we normally view personal ties and patronage as negative not because they are inherently bad, but because they present a poor fit with urbanized societies peopled by strangers. *Prior to* urbanization, however, personal relations were a vital social resource for building markets. And this is a resource into which Forest Hill tapped.

A second advantage of communist bureaucracy is the power of mobilization. Mao's revolutionary style of governance featured the use of campaigns, during which the entire society and bureaucracy was mobilized to channel their efforts and resources single-mindedly toward narrow state goals. Campaigns can be dangerous, as evident during the terrible famine of the Great Leap Forward. The application of extremely forceful methods like intensive propaganda and top-down targets could lead, in Perry's words, to "coercive enforcement by over-eager cadres." Yet, Perry adds, when directed toward development, campaigns are "capable of impressive achievements."[91] Indeed, a cadre from Forest Hill made a similar observation: "I feel that our system has its unique advantage, namely, that we can get things done quickly and achieve great results."[92]

Given the patent lack of technocratic personnel and the strengths of personal networks and mobilization, how could the existing bureaucracy be adapted to the current goal of "attracting capital and investments"? The method adopted was unorthodox but sensible in light of Forest Hill's particular circumstances. Instead of a technocratic mode of investment promotion, all the city's agencies, regardless of formal functions, were mobilized in campaign style to recruit investors. Locally, this was known as "the beehive campaign." An official who worked in the commerce office recounted the situation:[93]

> The beehive campaign started around 1995. . . . First, the province set the investment targets, which were then distributed to the cities, and finally down to the counties and townships. The city ordered the assignment of investment promotion targets to all the agencies. These targets were included in bureaucratic evaluation. In some cases, such targets were even assigned to individual officials.

Along with the assignment of investment targets to all agencies, bonuses were assigned collectively to high-performing departments as well as individually to department chiefs. Each agency activated the personal contacts of its chiefs and staff members to scout for business opportunities. Returning émigrés and overseas family members were an especially promising source of investors. To supplement individual recruitment efforts, the Investment Bureau stepped in by organizing investment conventions and speaking tours.

En masse investment courtship went hand-in-hand with generous giveaways of tax breaks, electricity subsidies, discounted land, and other attractions to investment projects of all shapes and sizes. As the system of courtship was highly individualized, promises made and freebies given to investors were haphazard and uncoordinated. In one instance, the Forestry Agency, which was "assigned targets to recruit wood refinery companies," attracted investors by "ensuring that they had ample access to raw materials." This was done by "excluding our refineries' extraction [of timber] from the official quota on deforestation."[94] In another instance, an investor was given land rebates, described as follows by Officer Wu, the industrial planner: "Say the enterprise auctioned a parcel of land for an official price of 200,000 yuan. In practice, the government took only half the price and refunded the remainder back to the enterprise in the form of bonuses."[95]

The beehive strategy was not so much a "policy" strategically hammered out by elite decision makers in boardroom meetings as it was a common-sense response to prevailing pressures, or what an investment officer termed "a widespread emergent phenomenon."[96] As he explained, "After Deng's Southern Tour in 1992, markets opened and regional differences widened. At the same time, the 1994 fiscal reform spearheaded by Zhu Rongji heightened local fiscal pressures. If we wanted to eat, we had to expand the tax base by attracting new investments. This was the context that gave rise to the beehive campaign."[97] In Forest Hill, such aggressive efforts were not made in vain (though this was not the case throughout China, as we'll later see in chapter 6). Within only two years from 1993 to 1995, investments doubled from about 700 to over 1,400 yuan per capita. Stated in the terms of the locals, the city earned its "first pot of gold" since the 1993 decision.

This initial inflow of capital and growth opportunities fed back to development strategy by giving city authorities stronger impetus and more financial resources to realize an abiding goal: improve transportation links. Owing to a combination of familial ties and natural resource availability, Forest Hill was able to attract some investors shortly after 1993, but these initial gains were modest. A sustained economic takeoff would not be possible unless Forest Hill overcame its geographical barriers. To that end, Party Secretary Chen—aka "the Builder"—who took office in 1998, made infrastructure expansion the keystone of his administration. The year he arrived, the city achieved its first infrastructural breakthrough. After years of appealing to central authorities, they finally approved the construction of a railway from a county in Forest Hill to Guangdong Province. The project was slated for completion in 2001.

A railway network dramatically shortened travel time to Forest Hill and stimulated growth opportunities.

Land finance provided a vital source of start-up funds for major infrastructure projects, such as the railway to Guangdong, which could not feasibly be financed through tax revenue alone. As a finance bureaucrat explained, "Our within-budget revenue [primarily taxes] is used to finance all the necessary public services, whereas land transfer fees are earmarked for urban and infrastructure construction. Fiscal transfers from the higher levels are definitely insufficient to meet our financial needs. Without land finance, it would be impossible to build up a city."[98] One of the earliest land sales in Forest Hill took place in 1993 for a parcel of land that was previously occupied by a farm equipment factory.[99] A flurry of infrastructure construction continued from the 1990s to the 2000s, including highways, additional railroads, a county airport, and industrial parks.

The prospects of improved transportation links fueled the beehive practices that started around 1995. This was because "once the basic infrastructure was in place, we had a solid basis to attract investors."[100] Forest Hill now became a credible attraction to a wide range of investors, not merely to overseas relatives or opportunists seeking to extract natural resources. Against this backdrop of infrastructure expansion under the charge of Party Secretary Chen, an ambitious mayor, Yang—aka "the Recruiter"—who took office in 2002 as the city's second-in-command, launched an investment campaign that he labeled "3 100s." Whipping the beehive campaign into turbo mode, he set a goal of attracting one hundred investment projects every year at each of the three stages of planning, negotiation, and execution. "Investment fever reached a peak under Yang," Officer Wu said, "producing a big growth spurt."[101] This growth spurt was accompanied by some "early efforts at industrial adjustment," focusing on scale but not structure. Small paper and fiberboard makers were closed, and cement factories were urged to step up production.

Evidently, the aim of development from the 1990s to the early 2000s was to grow the *size* of the economy as quickly as possible. And city officials selected a market-building bundle of strategies geared toward this particular objective: en masse and personalized investment courtship, across-the-board giveaways, and physical infrastructural expansion. GDP per capita doubled within this five-year period. Yet the economic changes that occurred during this period were more than just rapid growth. As the city's emphasis had been on achieving quantity—rather than quality—of growth, all types of investments arrived, leaving the market a miserable mess:[102]

> Back then, our commercial parks had no plan. A tofu factory sat beside another factory making fiberboards. How is that going to work? Previously, we had some toy factories. The production of toys demands a whole line of parts, like plastic molds, electroplates, and

so on. But the toy industry failed to create an industrial cluster, so it was not sustainable.

Up until this point, the development strategies we've seen in Forest Hill bore little resemblance to the East Asian newly industrialized economies, featuring technocratic agencies and coordinated policies that "picked winners" (i.e., targeted state support of valuable industries).[103] In Forest Hill, there were few signs of selectivity or macro-industrial planning. Instead, County Chief Ma said, "In order to grow the economy, we welcomed all investors."[104] Thus far, the city seemed intent only on pursuing quantity of growth and paid scant regard to issues of quality of growth and sustainability. But this would soon change.

No Longer Hungry

By 2005, Forest Hill had evolved from a crude start-up economy, featuring mostly small factories in low-end manufacturing, into a booming but messy bazaar. The size and sophistication of its economy still trailed far behind those of Xiamen and Shenzhen, and despite robust growth, financial pressures were ever palpable because public expenditures rose in tandem with the economy. But at least Forest Hill was no longer hungry. With an expanding tax base and rising income, even street-level regulatory officers "were not keen to 'eat' [i.e., harass businesses for free meals] anymore."[105]

The condition of not being hungry feeds back to development strategy in a powerful way. Initial growth, even if modest, modifies elite and social *preferences* for the type of development. It also changes the mix of *resources* available to execute change. In the words of a forestry officer, "Once basic issues of food and shelter are resolved, people start to pay attention to other needs, such as environmental protection."[106] Furthermore, once the economy has reached sufficient size and stability, both residents and officials are no longer desperate for any investment. Instead, "As the economy grows and people are more environmentally conscious, we no longer welcome high-polluting and resource-consuming industries."[107] These evolving preferences drove a subtle yet unmistakable shift in the city's development focus from 2006 onward, from the pursuit of *quantity of growth only* toward the simultaneous pursuit of *quantity and quality of growth*.

This shift in gears was reflected in the language of the annual government work reports, delivered at the start of each year by the mayor, which reviewed the past and outlined current priorities. The word "quality" first cameoed in the 2003 work report, under the charge of Mayor Yang, the Recruiter.[108] Yang mentioned "quality" in passing as he urged his comrades to "open and expand markets" and recruit more large-scale investment projects. Then, in 2005, "quality" appeared again, but this time noted for its *absence*. The work report openly acknowledged that "the quality of investments in the past years has not been high." The following year, Mayor Yang was promoted to party secretary—the first-in-command of the city—and replaced by a new mayor named Lin.

The address of 2006 was significant because it underlined a turning point: the need to pursue quantity and quality of growth at the same time. On the one hand, Mayor Lin declared a post-2006 economic policy that still aimed at developing everything. This policy, known as "10+3," pledged to grow ten manufacturing industries (tobacco, machinery, steel, copper, construction materials, textiles, food processing, electricity, coal, tourism) and three new services sectors (pharmaceuticals, telecommunications, and logistics). On the other hand, he added an important qualifier: "Even as we aggressively pursue the policy of '10+3,' we must also step up efforts to refine and upgrade our industries, and thereby improve the quality and efficiency of economic growth on a solid foundation." The term "quality" was mentioned five more times. In addition, the report introduced a new phrase and idea: "the *method* of economic growth." The word "growth" had always been sprinkled throughout official reports and speeches, but "method" debuted in the 2006 address. Among the methods of growth promotion discussed, the mayor highlighted the important of "channeling our resources toward leading enterprises and high-value industries" and "supporting our local corporate titans in implementing shareholding reforms and becoming listed on stock markets."

Then in 2007, the elevated significance of "quality" was signaled through its placement: The word appeared in the first paragraph that summarized the city's principal economic achievements. "We have continued to strengthen our economic foundation and steadily improved the quality of development," the report read. Repeating the previous year's terminology, the phrase "method of economic growth" appeared again, this time twice. Shortly after in 2008, we see another subtle yet profound change of language. The phrase "method of economic *growth*" was replaced by "method of economic *development*."[109] The former term, a short-lived semantic innovation, never appeared again. By 2010, "method of economic *development*" was mentioned in specific marriage to the term "quality." The report declared, "To upgrade the economy and speed up changes in our method of economic development, it is essential to alter the structure of our industries from dispersed to concentrated and their quality from weak to strong."

Although some observers may dismiss speeches as vacuous talk, these speeches heralded concrete policy changes, at least in Forest Hill. The period from 2006 onward was a time of intense deliberation, as the leadership, together with the administration, pondered new priorities for their development agendas, including the cultivation of comparative advantages, economic specialization, and technological upgrading. Officer Wu, who had served many years in the city planning commission, recounted valuable snapshots of the internal deliberation process. At one point, he urged his superiors and colleagues against developing every industry and instead to carve out niches that would exploit the city's natural resource endowments and existing successes:[110]

> During the "10+3" campaign, the city wanted to develop everything, for example, food processing. I laughed. Where else do you not find food processing industries? What's the point? I said, we should not think too wildly. Just focus on doing what we do best, like machinery parts.

The search for niches (or comparative advantages) was not without incident. Outcomes could have been ambushed by excessive ambition and potentially disastrous decisions. In one instance, the reigning mayor aspired to promote aircraft manufacturing; on the surface, importing this cutting-edge industry could put Forest Hill on par with other prosperous coastal cities. But again Officer Wu demurred:

> I told the mayor that first, we don't have the right talent. Second, the technologies of production are basically in the hands of foreign countries. Third, we are not on the coast. The wing of a plane is at least fifteen meters wide. How are we supposed to transport aircrafts if not by sea?[111]

Fortunately, this mayor dropped his idea of producing aircraft, which was a literal and metaphorical attempt to defy gravity. In the case of Forest Hill, even though the choice of targeted industries was briefly debated, the ultimate choice of industries for state promotion (including mining, energy production, metallurgy, and heavy machinery) was made obvious by the city's geographic limitations and its abundant supply of coal and metals.

Also, by the mid-2000s, several enterprises in these advantaged sectors had grown to titan status and came to be known locally as "lead dragons."[112] Building clusters and supply chains around them was another obvious development strategy. Unlike the East Asian path, wherein winners were preselected and nurtured with foresight by developmental bureaucrats, the lead dragons in Forest Hill ascended by capitalizing on early opportunities and political connections just as markets were being built. One example was Phoenix Corporation, the city's largest machinery maker. The founder was praised for his foresight in switching from cement to machinery production in 1993, at a time when few ventured into machinery. As his business prospered, the founder was invited not only to participate in formal political institutions at the city level, but also to become a delegate at the Fujian provincial consultative conference and the national People's Congress.[113] Small advantages at the point of market formation made huge differences later on because when the significance of selecting winners belatedly dawned on local authorities, they naturally gravitated toward the existing winners. The lead dragons were showered with generous support and attention that furthered their prominence.

The shift in development preferences motivated the adoption of new bureaucratic practices and investment policies. During the 1990s to early 2000s, when the goal of development was simply to attract an initial wave of capital and grow markets as rapidly as possible, en masse investment promotion and indiscriminate giveaways worked. But when the priority shifted from quantity toward quality of growth, previous strategies became a poor fit. As the city set ever-higher standards for investments, regular cadres could no longer satisfy these elevated targets with their limited personal contacts. Moreover, they complained about being thoroughly burned out by the beehive campaign. Equally important, as businesses matured they evolved too: "Nowadays, foreign enterprises know China well. If they come to invest, they will look for the expert departments. For example, in paper manufacturing, they will go to the Forestry Bureau, the Development Commission, but surely not the Women's Federation, right?"[114] Demand from the business sector for state professionals sharpened the impetus for bureaucratic change.

Thus, over the next few years, the bundle of development strategies was adapted in several ways. Campaign-style investment promotion resettled into a progressively technocratic mode. The assignment of investment targets evolved in several steps: every agency was initially evaluated by the absolute value of investments it recruited annually (regardless of scale or sector),[115] then by the number of projects that exceeded a certain scale, and subsequently by the number of projects in state-selected sectors, such as high-tech or green industries. In a final step, en masse investment targets along with high-powered bonuses of the past were abolished altogether. Instead, investment work was turned over to a team of specialized economic agencies. Chief Ma, who also previously worked as a city planner, said, "We still have to promote investments, except now it is a routine, not a statewide campaign like before." And instead of fixating on attracting investments, he added, "the focus is now to guide and regulate investments."[116]

Along with the specialization of investment promotion, indiscriminate giveaways were replaced by statewide policies of selective support for targeted industries, described as "a process from *attracting* to *selecting* capital and investments."[117] The selective allocation of state support was matched by a shift in emphasis from the provision of hard infrastructure like railroads and highways to soft infrastructure, namely, business-friendly services. During the 1990s and early 2000s, the focus of administrative reform was merely to reduce red tape and fight petty corruption, but now bureaucrats were expected to serve. The idea of a "service-oriented government" entered administrative discourse. "In the past, we stressed only regulation, but nowadays we care about services too," a regulatory officer said.[118] Examples of business-friendly services included the provision of research and development (R&D) grants, state-organized conventions to promote technological exchanges between local and foreign companies, and financial assistance for local businesses during the 2008 global financial crisis.

This multipronged adaptation of development strategies had a visible impact on the city's industrial makeup. Figure 5.5 shows a steady increase in industrial specialization from the 1980s to recent years. In 1987, four major sectors in Forest Hill (machinery, metallurgy, tobacco, and construction) made up 19.3 percent of GDP. Twenty years later, by 2009 their share jumped to 62.9 percent. The steep economic rise of the post-2006 era, seen in figure 5.2, does not merely indicate a *larger* economy; more importantly, it reflects a *restructured* economy.

These changes that took place within a five-year period led up to an official shift in the city's development stance in 2011. During the 2011 annual report, the mayor announced a new industrial strategy of "1+2." Instead of aiming for "10+3"

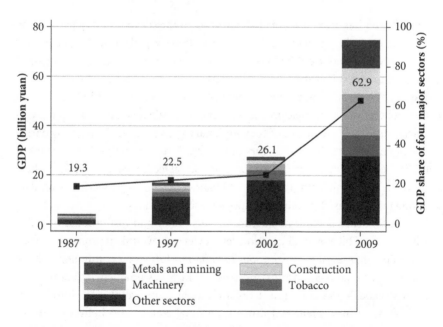

FIGURE 5.5 Change in industrial composition, 1987–2009. Compiled from Forest Hill City Annals, Regional Yearbooks, and Yearbooks.

(developing thirteen new industries), the leadership dramatically narrowed its targets to growing one primary (machinery) and two supporting (logistics and metal refinery) sectors. The choice and rearrangement of numbers in these slogans—from "3 100s" to "10+3" to "1+2"—signaled the city leadership's evolving priorities as markets grew and new aspirations and pressures arose.

My field research in Forest Hill concluded in 2014. From 1979 to 2014, this city experienced a radical economic and institutional makeover, everything from its income level, structure of property rights, prevalent mode of corruption, bureaucratic features, to the particular bundle of investment and industrial promotion strategies. Achieving such transformation is no easy feat. Yet the story does not end with happily ever after. *Building* markets is one challenge, *preserving* them is another. Officials in Forest Hill emphatically agreed that their city had only reached a "launching stage." Their list of worries about the future ran long: exhaustion of natural resources, severe environmental pollution, vulnerability to global economic shocks, low-tech products, an anemic services sector, difficulties in attracting talent to a third-tier city, and so on. This list is broadly symptomatic of the new challenges of development facing China in the next decades. Although many parts of China, as illustrated here by Forest Hill, have escaped the poverty trap, overcoming the particular obstacles of the "middle-income trap" will require adapting an altogether different set of institutions and policies.[119]

This chapter has provided a thick description of the coevolutionary path of one Chinese city. The particulars of any coevolutionary path will, of course, vary by context. Readers are urged not to fixate on whether the particular measures adopted in Forest Hill at particular periods may be replicated in other countries. Indeed, as we will see in the next chapter, even other locales within China could not replicate the same measures at the same time. What is useful and generalizable, instead, is the sequence of coevolutionary steps revealed through my narrative of Forest Hill's thirty-five years of history. If we line up the snapshots taken over time, we arrive at a causal sequence of mutual feedbacks that unfold in three steps: harness weak institutions to build markets → emerging markets stimulate strong institutions → strong institutions preserve markets.

This sequence is replicated across various policy and institutional domains within Forest Hill. For an illustration, let's review its investment promotion strategy. Step 1: *harness weak institutions to build markets* (pre-existing networks of affective personal relationships and trust—which has uniquely strong roots in rural societies—and communist organizational traits are blended into a beehive mode of investment recruitment; personal connections between bureaucracy and business also substituted for formal protection of property rights) → Step 2: *emerging markets stimulate strong institutions* (emergence of growing

TABLE 5.2   Bundle of strategies for building vs. preserving markets

INSTITUTIONS AND POLICIES	BUILDING MARKETS	PRESERVING MARKETS
Property rights protection	Partial and informal property rights through personal connections	Secure property rights supplied by formal institutions
Bureaucratic qualities	Nonspecialized and personalized	Specialized and impersonal (professional)
Bureaucratic incentives	High-powered but also high-risk incentives, providing all bureaucrats a personal stake in generating wealth	Low-powered but also low-risk incentives, through adequate and stable salaries paired with strong institutional controls against petty corruption
Policy implementation style	Campaign-style policy implementation	Technocratic mode of policy implementation
Investment promotion strategy	Indiscriminate giveaways; primary focus on hard infrastructural provision	Targeted giveaways; primary focus on soft services provision
Industrial strategy	Policies to grow quantity of industrial production as quickly as possible, with little regard to structure or quality	Policies to attract and cultivate only selected high-value industries, paired with coordinated macro-planning

but chaotic markets, along with capitalist demands for administrative improvements, spurred the leadership to shift its priorities from the pursuit of quantity of growth to quality of growth; correspondingly, it selected new bureaucratic traits and economic policies that better fit the evolved success criteria) → Step 3: *strong institutions preserve markets* (emergence of professional bureaucratic traits and replacement of decentralized petty corruption with grand elite corruption provide a predictable basis for markets and advantages for some connected and powerful capitalists).

The beehive campaign of investment recruitment presents one concrete instance of building markets with weak institutions, but it is not the only one. Table 5.2 summarizes other instances that were reviewed in my narrative. Different from previous arguments, these examples are not merely "good enough governance" that delivered "minimal government performance."[120] Rather these were innovations that harnessed the unique sociopolitical traits of premodernized and communist environments to ignite capitalist growth. In my account, features that *defy* expectations of good governance and that we normally think must be eradicated before markets can grow actually constituted the raw material of market-building institutions.

My conclusions thus go much further than earlier arguments that institutions should be stage-specific. For instance, Doner's excellent study of modern Thailand argues similarly that "different levels of development require *goodness of fit* between the tasks involved and the capacities of institutions."[121] Unlike my theory, however, he interprets the differences in early and advanced development to be "additive" in nature, that is, the latter entails "more difficult problems," which in turn "requires greater *degrees* of institutional capacity."[122] In his view, early development needs only good-enough institutions, while institutions at later stages become better.

My argument is different. This chapter shows in thick details that the developmental tasks of building and preserving markets vary by *type* (from goal A to goal B), rather than by *degree* (from easy to hard). Any reader with some parenting experience may relate to this analogy: it is not "easier" to care for an infant than it is to raise a toddler or a teenager; the challenges of each parenting stage are categorically different. By extension, the strategies that best fit early and late growth stages do not run along a straight line from less good to good to best; rather, they are different types of solutions for different types of problems. Moreover, as I have also stressed, start-up and mature environments do not only vary by the challenges faced, but also by the type of resources available. Unless one gets this point, one will miss the alternative—often wacky—arrangements that successfully kick-start markets even when they occur right in front of our eyes.

Aside from chronicling the coevolution of states and markets in one city, this chapter has also illuminated some underlying conditions, which I term meta-institutions (see chapter 2), that allowed the coevolutionary process to unfold the way it did. The political economy in Forest Hill was able to evolve from phase to phase because city officials selected particular institutions and strategies they thought fit their changing preferences and constraints. Reformers in many developing countries are often deprived of the autonomy to choose what fits, because they either must conform to international best practices or are bound by too many conflicting demands at home. State actors in Forest Hill, however, were not free to adopt any strategy or policy. Over the course of development, they selected responses to new opportunities and problems within broad parameters drawn by the higher levels. Bottom-up experimentation was bounded by top-down guidance. The trajectory of Forest Hill from 1978 is a microcosm of directed improvisation.

As we have seen, local officials in the city first prioritized the quantity of growth and then later on pursued quality of growth. Not everyone would agree with this sequence of priorities; some may contend that low-income countries should try to aim for all things good and modern at once. But this is an ideological disagreement over goals, not methods. The Kingdom of Bhutan has an admirable alternative model of development; its rulers choose to pursue what they call Gross Domestic Happiness. Instead of focusing on brute capital accumulation, Bhutan cherishes environmental conservation, social inclusion, and other soft goals. Bhutan's income, however, is among the lowest in the world; it was also one of the last countries to introduce television and the Internet to society. And in the event of foreign invasion, Bhutan probably lacks the capacity to defend itself against "guns, germs, and steel."[123] The CCP wants material wealth and power for China.[124] And, given this definition of success, it follows a certain path of coevolution.

Even in one modest local case, a city with only a quarter of the population of Hong Kong, we witness astounding complexity over thirty-five years of development, making it all the harder to believe that development among countries could really follow simple paths leading from good institutions to market success or the other way around. Forest Hill is a locale tucked in the interior of a coastal province and rich in metals and mineral resources. What would coevolutionary paths look like in other parts of China with *more* advantageous and *less* advantageous endowments than Forest Hill? And how might their paths connect? In the finale, we turn to a paired comparison of the development paths of two contrasting counties, one located on the coast of Zhejiang and another in the central province of Hubei.

6

CONNECTING FIRST MOVERS
AND LAGGARDS

**I was deeply inspired by Comrade Deng Xiaoping's statement to
"Let some get rich first." We should not be afraid of people getting
rich. There is a limit to the private consumption of wealth. The rest
of it will go toward society. We must be bold. We must take risks.**

—Bureaucrat, Blessed County, Zhejiang Province

**For us, the biggest challenges are that our industries are
weak and tax revenue is scarce. Inland regions do not have the
natural advantages of the coastal areas. Who doesn't want to be
a tax-contributing member? But currently, we have not reached
that level of development.**

—Bureaucrat, Humble County, Hubei Province

In the previous chapter, I mapped the coevolutionary path of Forest Hill, a hill-locked city in the coastal province of Fujian, focusing on the coevolution of markets, property rights, and development strategies. My analysis reveals that the institutions required to build markets were functionally and qualitatively different from conventionally good institutions (such as formal property rights and Weberian bureaucracies) that emerged only after markets had taken off. What patterns might we find in other parts of China with different starting points and geographical conditions?

In this chapter, I chronicle the coevolution of markets and development strategies in two contrasting locales.[1] My first protagonist, Blessed County in Zhejiang, sits directly on the coast and has a long entrepreneurial history stretching back to the Song dynasty. Thanks to Deng's bold vision of reform, Blessed County was among the privileged "some" to get rich first after China opened its markets to the world. My second protagonist is Humble County, located in the central province of Hubei. Like many of its peers in central and western China, Humble has benefited visibly less from the national drive toward capitalism. "We lag behind the coast by *at least* twenty years and in *every* respect," one official of the county said in exasperation.[2] "Moreover," he added, "although all of China is wealthier than in the past, our gap vis-à-vis the coast continues to widen. By now, the distance between us already exceeds twenty years."[3]

My paired comparison of the two contrasting paths reveals two surprising findings. The first surprise is that although the speed and outcomes of development in the two locales obviously diverge, they share many remarkable similarities in the process of state-and-market coevolution. Whether it is the most or least advantaged case, the path of development was never linear, that is, it was never either good institutions that led to markets or markets to good institutions. Nor did their experiences conform to the East Asian developmental model or standard accounts about the rise of the West. Both local cases took off through unorthodox measures, albeit of different varieties.

The second finding is even more surprising. Although Blessed County and Humble County are clearly unequal and variant cases, their paths of development were in fact inextricably connected. Humble County had been stuck in a poverty trap for the first twenty-five years since market opening; its economy only began to take off in the mid-2000s, triggered by the migration of low-end industries from the coast (including places like Blessed County and Forest Hill). Once its growth engine was jump-started by new opportunities flowing from its privileged cousins, the processes of state-and-market coevolution, witnessed one or two decades earlier on the coast, was jump-started in this part of China, albeit in an altered national environment. On the other hand, the early takeoff of coastal locales like Blessed County had also benefited from the flow of cheap labor and raw materials from their laggard peers in the interior. Regional inequality as a *consequence* of market opening is already well-known; what is much less noticed and examined, however, is regional inequality as a *driving force* of China's overall economic success.

For comparativists, this chapter also suggests a new approach to conducting subnational analyses. The traditional goal of comparative research is to "account for variation in outcomes among political units,"[4] as David Laitin writes in *Political Science: The State of the Discipline*. This traditional focus on variation fits the traditional goal in social science of positing and testing linear causal theories; in other words, we leverage variation across units to glean evidence of whether given independent variables cause given dependent variables of interest. In a complexity view of social realities, however, variables are *interdependent*; so are units of observation.[5] My approach of comparing localities as moving trajectories suggests that we cannot study *variation* across subnational units without also attending to their *connections*. Changes in one regional path can spill over into changes in other regional paths and cumulatively impact national outcomes.

First Movers vs. Laggards

At Blessed County, I hopped into a taxi and asked the driver to take me to the most dilapidated place in the county. About twenty minutes later, we arrived at a town that would soon be razed. I stopped at a row of old brick houses that flanked a river, along which a few women were washing vegetables. It was a quaint scene that reminded me of old pictures of southern China. There was some rubbish strewn around, and houses spray-painted with the word "demolish" sat eerily abandoned, but it really wasn't that bad. On my way back, the taxi driver boasted with genuine native pride: "Here in Blessed there are no poor people. Even the people living in the old houses you saw, don't assume they are poor. They are sitting on assets worth hundreds of thousands of dollars."

Blessed County represents a class of local political economies that I term *first movers*. Many coastal cities, such as Shenzhen and Xiamen, were designated by the central government as special economic zones (SEZs) in the 1980s. Not only were they the first to embrace world trade and foreign investments, these locales also led the way in capitalist reforms, from privatization to the creation of stock markets. Among the coastal provinces, Zhejiang is further distinguished by its model of "bottom-up capitalism."[6] This province is famous for having a strong private sector and relatively laissez-faire local states.[7] About 80 percent of Zhejiang's GDP is generated by private firms,[8] which excel in making light consumer goods such as "lighters, small hardware, shoes, and apparel."[9] By comparison, Jiangsu

A "dilapidated" part of Blessed County that would soon be razed

Province, an adjoining coastal powerhouse, follows a state-dominant growth model with a higher share of heavy manufacturing.[10]

Blessed County displays many of the quintessential qualities of the Zhejiang model. Geographically, this county has constraints. Unlike Forest Hill in Fujian, Blessed County does not possess natural resources. Historically its population has been dense and the supply of farmland has been tight. Yet precisely because of these limitations, "the people of Zhejiang were forced to take either one of two routes: study or trade."[11] Indeed, in Blessed County, you'll find a park that memorializes the large corps of scholars since the Song Dynasty who have passed the imperial examinations. For centuries, locals traveled widely and traded with merchants from as far away as Japan and Indonesia. In sum, the most significant advantages of this county are its coastal location and entrepreneurial history.

Turning to Humble County, in the central province of Hubei, we find a drastically different scenario. Prior to 1949, Humble County was an agrarian economy with almost no signs of industrial production.[12] Locals recall small-scale trade of agricultural produce but not long-distance commerce of the type in pre-1949 Blessed County.[13] Even today, as one official remarked, "Our urban residents don't even have a proper place to take a stroll. Put bluntly, this is quite a desolate place."[14] Humble County represents a different class of localities, which, for lack of better term, I call *laggard* states. By laggard, I certainly do not imply that the locals were intrinsically deficient. The term simply reflects the reality of economic and institutional "backwardness" (a common Chinese term for underdevelopment) in inland China vis-à-vis the coast.

Compared to Zhejiang, Hubei Province is much poorer, more populous, and less industrialized. In 2012, Hubei's GDP per capita was only about 61 percent of Zhejiang's. Agriculture made up 13 percent of Hubei's GDP, compared to only 5 percent in Zhejiang.[15] Since the beginning of market reforms, central provinces like Hubei have been neglected like the middle child of a family. Provinces on the east benefited from their coastal location and early exposure to global capitalism. Provinces on the west received generous fiscal transfers from the center because their hinterland geography and large ethnic minority populations posed national security concerns. Sandwiched between the two extremes, central provinces were long "caught in an awkward position" of being "neither eastern nor western," a state press report noted.[16] As a result, many locales in the central region actually faced fewer growth opportunities than those in the far west.

In terms of development, Humble County is constrained by disadvantages that are common to inland locales. Far from the coastline, landlocked counties have difficulty trading and exporting. Inland regions also lack entrepreneurial legacies and large networks of emigrant merchants found in Zhejiang. Moreover, because local markets in the central regions are small, it is difficult to cultivate home-grown entrepreneurs.[17] Fortunately, Humble County has some advantages. The county is only an hour's drive from Wuhan, the capital city of Hubei Province. It is accessible by three national railway lines constructed in the 1950s. Its topography has more flatland than hills, making it possible to build factories. The county also boasts an ample supply of wood and stone. In addition, during the socialist period, Mao chose to set up industrial bases in inland cities to ensure China's self-sufficiency in the event of foreign invasions. Thus, even before market opening, the county already had a number of small, state-owned factories in operation. This industrial history distinguishes Humble County from other inland locales, such as Upstart County of Jiangxi (featured in chapter 1), which was a predominantly rural economy that saw minimal industrial growth until the 1990s.

Figure 6.1 provides a stark illustration of the differences in tax wealth between the two counties. In Blessed County, tax revenue per capita, which started growing at a robust pace during the 1980s, climbed almost vertically upward starting from the mid-2000s. Commenting on the county's economic status, Yan, a finance bureaucrat, coolly said, "We have a strong base of enterprises. For example, Century Corp [one of the county's largest enterprises] generated 200 million yuan in taxes last year. Even in times when we were under financial stress, we were still relatively well-off in the whole province."[18] Next to Blessed, Humble's fiscal growth looks almost completely flat. But that is because the phenomenal

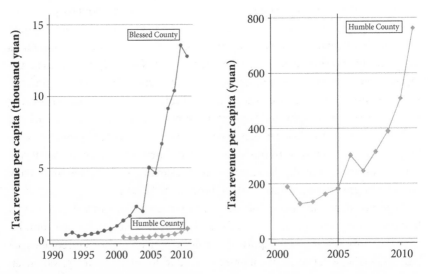

FIGURE 6.1 Fiscal growth in Blessed County vs. Humble County. Yearbooks of Blessed County and Humble County.

scale of Blessed's growth completely dwarfs the changes in Humble. If we look at Humble's fiscal statistics alone (on the right side of figure 6.1), we see a distinct upward swing from 2005 onward. As we will later see, the source of this belated takeoff can be traced to the impressive growth among first-mover states like Blessed County.

Table 6.1 summarizes the class of local political economies represented by each of the three cases featured in chapters 5 and 6, as well as the underlying conditions that define each case. Figure 6.2 shows their locations. On the surface, it may seem that given the vastly different geographic and historical endowments in Blessed County and Humble County, it is no surprise that the paths of the two diverge. If so, skeptics may ask: Why does it matter then if their paths were linear or coevolutionary? No matter what governments did or which changes occurred along the way, the two counties were destined to arrive at where they are today, right?

Wrong. Starting points and endowments clearly matter for development outcomes; given similar policies and efforts, Blessed County will always race ahead of Humble County. Yet even in Blessed County, developmental success was not

FIGURE 6.2 Location of Fujian, Zhejiang, and Hubei Provinces. The exact locations of the local cases are not indicated.

TABLE 6.1 Comparison of three local coevolutionary paths

	FOREST HILL, FUJIAN	BLESSED COUNTY, ZHEJIANG	HUMBLE COUNTY, HUBEI
Class of local state represented	Between first-mover and laggard state; resource-dependent industrial economy	First-mover state; private-sector dominant economy	Laggard state; some state-owned enterprises left over from socialist period
Defining conditions	Located in a coastal province but hill-locked; abundant natural resources (coal, wood, metals)	Located in a coastal province, directly on the coast, and close to Shanghai; no significant natural resources; long entrepreneurial history and extensive network of émigré merchants	Located in an inland province; access to national railways and some natural resources (wood and stone)
Speed of development	Goldilocks case: neither too fast nor too slow	Early takeoff and most rapid reforms; "real" FDI took off in the early 2000s	Late takeoff and slow reforms; did not succeed to attract (domestic) investments until after 2005
Economic role of the state	State played prominent role in attracting initial wave of capital and in supporting resource-intensive and heavy manufacturing industries	State evolved from secondary supportive role, with market actors taking the lead, to a more interventionist role, especially in urbanization	Initially, state had limited financial and human resources to promote growth; but its interventionist role became prominent after 2005
Target of development policies	Did not pick winners from the start; initially welcomed all industries and only later selected a few key industries for targeted support	Also did not pick winners from the start; directed state support ex-post to private firms that succeeded; most recently, directed state support at high-tech firms	After takeoff, still jack-of-all-industries; although government recently announced policy to target a few selected industries, in practice, it still welcomed all investments

a foregone conclusion. The process of market building was politically fraught. Initially, there was no formal protection of private property rights, and both central and local governments even deliberately discriminated against domestic enterprises in favor of foreign companies. How local private enterprises managed to flourish under such initially trying circumstances is central to the county's subsequent economic boom. Also essential to Blessed County's present-day outcome is the state's evolving economic role and its choice of developmental policies as new demands of governance arose. Turning to Humble County, local authorities were initially unable to engineer an economic miracle largely because of its locational disadvantages. The effects of geography, however, are not immutable; they vary situationally with the surrounding environment. As markets in neighboring regions evolved, opportunities that did not previously exist unexpectedly emerged.

The Coevolutionary Path of Blessed County

To compare two cases in this chapter, my discussion of each case will not go into as much detail as I did for Forest Hill in chapter 5. Instead, I will focus on the coevolution of markets and developmental strategies from the early 1980s to the present day. One central pattern that emerges from mapping the coevolutionary path of Blessed County is the dramatic transformation of the economic role of the state before and after the 2000s. Before the 2000s, county authorities were relatively noninterventionist; their job was mainly to provide a supporting environment for the blossoming of an incipient private economy. After the private sector exploded, however, this early growth produced new bottlenecks, so from the 2000s onward, the county government took on a highly interventionist and sometimes coercive role to reshape local markets. The main lesson is this: Even in a locale blessed with exceptionally favorable geographical and historical conditions, the state did not simply sit back, relax, and let nature take its course.

An Early Start to Market Opening

For locales like Blessed County, whose immense capitalist potential was stifled by political restrictions, the reformist patriarch Deng was literally their patron saint. A memoir that reviewed the county's thirty years of reform opened with a grand invocation of Deng's signature mottos: "Grounded in the essence of new thinking in the party, namely, the ideas of 'emancipating our minds' and 'seeking truth from facts,' our cadres embarked on a course of intellectual innovation and changed the priorities of our work."[19]

Like in many parts of coastal China, the first and most visible changes in the economy of Blessed County were the proliferation of TVEs (township and village enterprises). Many of these TVEs "wore red hats," that is, they were collectively owned in name but in practice were operated by enterprising individuals who "had relatives in various party-state departments," noted Officer Yan.[20] Recalling chapter 5, Forest Hill had also undergone a similar process of rural industrialization through TVEs. But even though both Forest Hill and Blessed County were coastal locales, there were striking differences in the type, scale, and success of TVEs. In Forest Hill, the TVEs were mostly small factories that produced paper and cement with minimal technology. On the other hand, the TVEs in Blessed County made a wide variety of products, primarily for exports, from electronics, apparel, textiles, and processed food to construction materials. In Blessed, industrial production grew a stunning thirty-three-fold between 1978 and 1992, while the value of exports more than quadrupled from 1988 to 1992, reaching over 800 million yuan by 1992.[21]

One reason for the differences is that whereas the TVEs in Forest Hill could only start by exploiting the locale's natural resources (trees and sand in the case of paper and cement manufacturing), Blessed County was poised for light export manufacturing. Its proximity to the metropolis of Shanghai provided important advantages in sourcing for early customers. Officer Luo, who manages human resources and is a native of the county, related, "During the early days, professionals like engineers and doctors would travel to Blessed County during the weekends [many of whom had family in town] and then return to Shanghai for work on Monday. Anyone from a village in our county can go to Shanghai and round up seven or eight people for any given business venture."[22] In addition to tapping kinship networks, many young people from Shanghai were "sent down" to the countryside in Blessed County during the Cultural Revolution. When markets opened, locals sought the help of these sent-down youths to bring business opportunities back from Shanghai. "Costs in the city were high, while over here we could process products like candy, biscuits, and boxes cheaply," a former civil servant turned businessman named Song recalled.[23] "Entrepreneurship runs in our blood," he added.

Another important difference is early efforts by state authorities in Blessed County to promote technological upgrading among TVEs, primarily through the transfer of physical and human capital from the local SOEs (state-owned enterprise). Officer Hu, who has served in both the county and township governments for many years, said, "Many of our county's TVEs were paired with SOEs. Old equipment from SOEs was passed down to TVEs in a ladder-like transfer."[24] In addition, technicians from SOEs were invited to impart skills to TVE workers. Local cadres also organized young villagers to intern in the SOEs in order to bring knowledge back to the rural enterprises. In other words, as early as the 1980s, the county government began to nurture the collective—and incipient private—sector by tapping into the resources of the formal state sector. This was decades before the concept of upgrading even entered the minds of officials in Forest Hill.

Blessed County also had a precocious start to property rights reforms. Even before the central party-state formally endorsed private ownership, officials in Blessed County had already begun to experiment with various hybrid management forms among TVEs, albeit short of explicit privatization. By 1988, nearly half of the county's TVEs operated on a "contract responsibility system" (enterprises were contracted to individual managers), another 15 percent were "rented," 4 percent tried an "assets rental system," and the remainder carried out shareholding reforms.[25] Then in 1992, the government of Blessed County undertook the task of "double accounting:" accounting first for the asset value of all the TVEs and second for their revenue and profits. It also introduced a standardized accounting system for the entire county.[26] These measures provided the foundation for a remarkably rapid wave of privatization the year after.

The Founding of Private Wealth

Even though Blessed County boldly tinkered with property rights structures, state and market actors alike were at constant risk of political reprisals. Property rights were neither wholly private nor secure. That is why local cadres gushed with excitement when they recalled the significance of Deng's Southern Tour and his "courage and strength" in calling for the deepening of capitalist reforms.[27] As Officer Hu said, "the risks of enterprise restructuring were tremendous," by which he meant the *political* risks.[28] Without firm endorsement from the top leadership, it would not be possible for local experiments to go any further.

Following the central government's decision in 1993 to establish a socialist market economy, the changes that followed in Blessed County were swift and dramatic. The party committee issued a directive that stipulated concrete guidelines on the "transformation of management among TVEs." Exceptionally large and promising TVEs were restructured into shareholding, private limited or conglomerate enterprises, while small-scale TVEs were auctioned off to individuals and turned into sole proprietary companies. Following the party committee's guidelines, the county government established an ad hoc "TVEs restructuring office" to oversee the implementation of ownership transfers.[29]

Within two years, between 1993 and 1995, more than ten thousand TVEs were privatized through various channels,[30] an impressive feat for a county with only slightly more than 700,000 residents. This outcome stands in sharp contrast to Russia, where en masse privatization of state-owned enterprises enriched a tiny handful of oligarchs who came to monopolize natural resource industries like oil and natural gas. In this county, which occupied only a small corner of China, en masse privatization benefited a much larger group of entrepreneurs (even though they were still a minority of the whole population). Additionally, the transfer of ownership was concentrated in light manufacturing industries, where barriers to entry by new market participants were much lower than in oil and natural gas industries. In other words, in parts of coastal China like Blessed County, the fruits of private wealth were far more broadly distributed than in post-communist Russia. This in turn may be credited to the earlier creation of TVEs, which provided market access to a large number of participants at the lowest grassroots levels.

Just as TVEs were being privatized en masse, many party-state officials and state enterprise managers quit their jobs and took the plunge into private business between 1993 and 1995. This widespread phenomenon was known as "plunging into the sea."[31] Many former civil servants benefited from their prior work experience and personal networks in the government, but this should not be simplistically interpreted as corruption. Rather, this was a time of market formation where small initial advantages—of which political connections were especially salient—could later snowball into tremendous market advantages, sometimes in ways not even anticipated by their beneficiaries.

The story of Mr. Song, a former civil servant turned entrepreneur, provides an illustrative example.[32] Song "unintendedly" left government in 1992 out of spite that his supervisors had not promoted him. Initially, he did not dare tell his family that he had quit his job. Instead, he related, "I pretended to go to work every day, riding my bike around town from morning to 5 p.m." He had no savings of his own, but three months later, he borrowed a hefty sum of 500,000 yuan from the county bank and started a real estate company, one of the first in the whole province. Why was the bank willing to lend so generously to him? Because when Song had been a township official, he had successfully helped the bank collect millions of dollars in bad debt, so the bank was both grateful to and trusted him. Upon setting up his company, Song set himself the personal goal of earning 500,000 yuan in profits over a lifetime, "which was a spectacular sum at that time," he stressed.[33] Surprising himself, he reached the goal *within a year*. Today he is a billionaire.

Paradoxically, the germination of a private economy through en masse privatization of TVEs and a wave of "plunging" civil servants coincided with state policies that were, in hindsight, oddly discriminatory against Chinese private companies. In a bid to attract foreign investments, the county government provided preferential tax breaks and subsidies to foreign invested enterprises (FIEs), but not to locals. This was not unique to Blessed County. As Huang relates in

Selling China, the national government advanced a political hierarchy of companies that stretched from large state-owned firms at the top, followed by FIEs, and then to private domestic enterprises.[34] Nationwide, for example, FIEs enjoyed a lower corporate tax bracket of as low as 15 percent, while Chinese companies were taxed at the full 33 percent. Such discriminatory treatment was partly politically driven. As Gallagher observes, it was ideologically safer for Chinese officials to encourage capitalist investment from foreigners than locals.[35] A private entrepreneur from Blessed expressed a similar logic: "Those who courted domestic investments risked being accused of stirring capitalism among natives. But foreigners are already capitalists, so it was safe to ask them to come and invest."[36]

In addition to offering a preferential incentive package, Blessed County attracted foreign investments through strong recruitment efforts. In the first few years of the 1990s, all the townships (but not the county agencies) were mobilized to enlist investors. A township cadre described the methods of investment promotion as follows:[37]

> That was a period of "all people join in courting investments." If you could bring in an investor, you would personally receive 2 to 5 percent of the investment value as a reward. . . . One method of attracting investors was through hometown reunions. Another was to recruit competent individuals to serve in the township, meaning people who had personal connections overseas. During the socialist days, these people were attacked as "rightists" because they had relatives in Hong Kong and Taiwan.

But this campaign ended quickly and was turned over to a team of economic offices and industrial park committees. Unlike Forest Hill, Blessed County did not embark on a prolonged, all-county "beehive" campaign to prospect investors because as one cadre plainly stated, "there wasn't a need to do so."[38] The county already had an extensive network of emigrant merchants, spread throughout Shanghai, Hong Kong, and even further, who were eager to return home and invest in a promising market. Even more important, Blessed County already had a strong base of local private entrepreneurs.

Facing discriminatory treatment, local entrepreneurs adapted simply by pretending to be foreign. This was phenomenon was known locally as "fake FDI."[39] One private entrepreneur related how it worked: "We prepared U.S. dollars, sent them to Japan, and then got someone from Japan to wire them back. That way, it's possible to get preferential treatment. Everyone was achieving the same ends in a variety of ways."[40] In order to successfully disguise themselves as foreign firms, however, domestic firms needed county officials to "open one eye and close the other."[41] This context provided fertile ground for collusion and corruption, but it also allowed local private firms to survive and thrive in an otherwise taxing policy environment and uneven playing field.

During the 1990s, Blessed County saw a Schumpeterian period of creative destruction, whereby intense competition among a large number of private firms weeded out weaker enterprises. Prior to 1998, the county government did not pick winners. Only by 1998 did it announce the industrial policy of "supporting the strong and excellent." Departing from the national developmental states of East Asia, which picked winners at the outset, the Blessed government threw its support behind winners that emerged triumphant from an early period of market competition. One private entrepreneur related:[42]

> During the first ten years of my firm's operations [1988–1998], neither the state nor society supported private enterprises like mine. We lived in the cracks, with SOEs and TVEs on top of us. We were left to survive and die on our own.... By 1998, our scale of operation exceeded a million dollars in revenue.... Well, once our enterprise grew big, the government would of course lend support.... When we bought this land for a new factory, the government provided assistance, along with some subsidies for product innovation.

By 2000, Blessed County had built a vibrant bottom-up economy, with private enterprises spread out throughout the various townships. By this point, a new and compelling contingency arose: the market was a mess. Throughout its thousands of years of history reaching back to the imperial ages, the county had always been "a county without a city at its core." There wasn't a central location where state and commerce could congregate to do business. Nor was there coordinated zoning of various industries and of the secondary and tertiary sectors. Rural and urban overlapped haphazardly. As enterprising as they were, local businesses could not reorganize the economic geography of the county on their own. Such an effort required the coercive power of the state. In 1999 Cai took office in Blessed County as deputy party secretary. Remembered admirably by locals as a leader "who has left deep imprints on Blessed's development,"[43] Cai made the creation of a new central business district the keystone of his legacy.

The Making of a Central Business District

State planning for a new central business district (CBD) had begun as early as 1995. But growing pressures for coordinated zoning and Cai's prioritization of this project accelerated its implementation. In 2002 Cai rose to the top seat of power as the county party secretary. That same year, the county demarcated a large area of more than seventy square kilometers as the CBD. Clearing this area for new construction proved an obvious challenge as it was filled with factories and warehouses. To remove the existing occupants, the county introduced a policy dubbed "retreating the secondary industry and advancing the tertiary sector." Those who owned property in the demarcated area were required to relocate to industrial parks, which were newly and simultaneously constructed in the suburban zones, in exchange for compensation. Alternatively, they could retain ownership of the land in the CBD area but had to transform its use from manufacturing to services or lease it to new occupants. Through this policy, factories and warehouses were moved out and replaced with new party-state complexes, hotels, shopping malls, and office towers in finance, real estate, and other services.

This process of exchanging industries for services did not, of course, happen without friction. In one instance reported in the media, an entrepreneur who had recently constructed a factory in the demarcated zone resisted state mandates to relocate. One day, officers from the county Urban Management Offices marched forcibly into her factory grounds and tried to demolish her property. The owner fought with them and set herself on fire in a fit of protest. Despite such incidents, the county government forged ahead with its urban renewal plans. As locals emphasize, timing was key to the success of the project. During the early 2000s, requisitioning land was still relatively affordable and not as politicized as it would become a decade later. Officer Luo concluded, "Our leaders seized the right moments."[44] Echoing the importance of strong leadership, a local entrepreneur similarly remarked, "Such reforms take courageous leaders, who dare to shoulder political responsibilities for taking bold steps."[45]

The completion of a CBD, inaugurated by the county offices' relocation into the area, marked a turning point in Blessed's development. This is evident from the fiscal chart in figure 6.1. Once the construction of the CBD was completed, tax revenue climbed vertically upward. This is because, as Officer Hu explained, "We evolved from industrialization only to the merger of industries and commerce, and then, further on, to a 'virtual' economy."[46] By "virtual" economy, he meant the rise of a financial market, with companies operating in banking, real estate, insurance, and so on. These are the service sectors that typically fetch the highest value in advanced capitalist economies. Also, once previously industrial land was turned into downtown commercial properties, many entrepreneurs saw their assets soar in value. As another official recounted, "There were two waves of private wealth creation. The first was en masse privatization of the TVEs. And the second came from the creation of the CBD."[47] Consistent with the pattern seen in Forest Hill, the lifting of political restrictions on entrepreneurial activities may initially stimulate a *mini* growth spurt, but a *spectacular* growth spurt, like the one seen in Blessed County from the mid-2000s onward, comes from the remolding of market structure.

The central business district of Blessed County

The redoubled rise of the private economy fed back to the county's policies for promoting FDI. In 2004 county officials introduced a policy innovation they named "mobilizing local private businesses to attract FIEs."[48] As we earlier saw in Forest Hill, local governments relied on local cadres to recruit investors because cadres typically had more connections and influence than regular citizens. But for Blessed County, given its stronghold of private entrepreneurs, recruiting market actors—rather than state actors—as the county's sales force was a better fit, as an experienced economic bureaucrat explained:[49]

> From our perspective on the front line, the best way to attract capital and investments is to use investors to attract investors and foreigners to attract foreigners. The government sets up the platform, but businesses should be the ones putting up the show. . . . I learned through my experiences promoting the county around the world that people still don't trust the government much. They rather trust enterprises. Ten thousand words spoken by the government does not even compare to a single good word spoken by a firm who has invested here.

Whereas FDI in the past likely came predominantly in the form of "fake FDI" (local private companies disguised as foreign), "the real spring of FDI" arrived belatedly in Blessed County from the mid-2000s.[50] By around this time, central discriminatory policies against domestic enterprises were also abolished. In 2006 the central government officially equalized corporate income taxes between domestic and foreign firms, ending decades of discriminatory policy. Domestic private companies no longer had to pretend to be foreign. As the existing domestic market was already developed, Blessed County was certainly not desperate for investments of any type. Instead, county officials started with a high bar for investments, selecting only those they deemed of high quality. Thus, whereas most locales typically attracted FDI from neighboring East Asia in low-end manufacturing, Blessed County in the 2000s lured many projects from the United States and Western Europe in high-value sectors. Today, of the more than 130 high-tech companies in the county, a third of them are foreign invested.[51]

Figure 6.3 summarizes the coevolution of markets and development strategies, as mapped out in the preceding sections. As we clearly saw, the focus and type of development strategies evolved as markets grew. *Before* and *when* the private-sector economy was being built, the county government's main role was to clarify property rights and to guide the process of ownership transfer from public to private hands. *After* the private sector had taken off and demand for economic restructuring and commercial zoning rose, the state shifted to a highly interventionist role, employing its top-down planning and coercive powers to relocate businesses into designated zones. Consistent with the core theme of chapter 5, the package of strategies required for *building* and *preserving* markets were different, even in an exceptionally blessed county.

Compared to other locales throughout China, Blessed County is certainly in an enviable position. But its development challenges are far from over. Given its current level of GDP per capita, the county comfortably qualifies as a middle-income economy. Its journey toward becoming an advanced capitalist economy, however, is still long. Climbing the value-added chain requires design, innovation, and financial skills, which are only starting to develop. Much of Blessed's economy is still powered by export-oriented, light manufacturers, who were hit hard by the 2008 global financial crisis (when orders from other countries abruptly shrank), and even more seriously, by steadily rising factor costs at home. To give an example, one apparel producer reported that it cost about 3,500 yuan per month, with social security included, to hire an average factory worker in the county, a steep rise from only 2,000 yuan five years ago. To cut costs, this producer turned to mechanization; already 40 percent of garment sewing at his factory was done by machines.[52] Yet another option is simply to move away to cheaper locations. Where? This question leads us to the life path of a completely different locale.

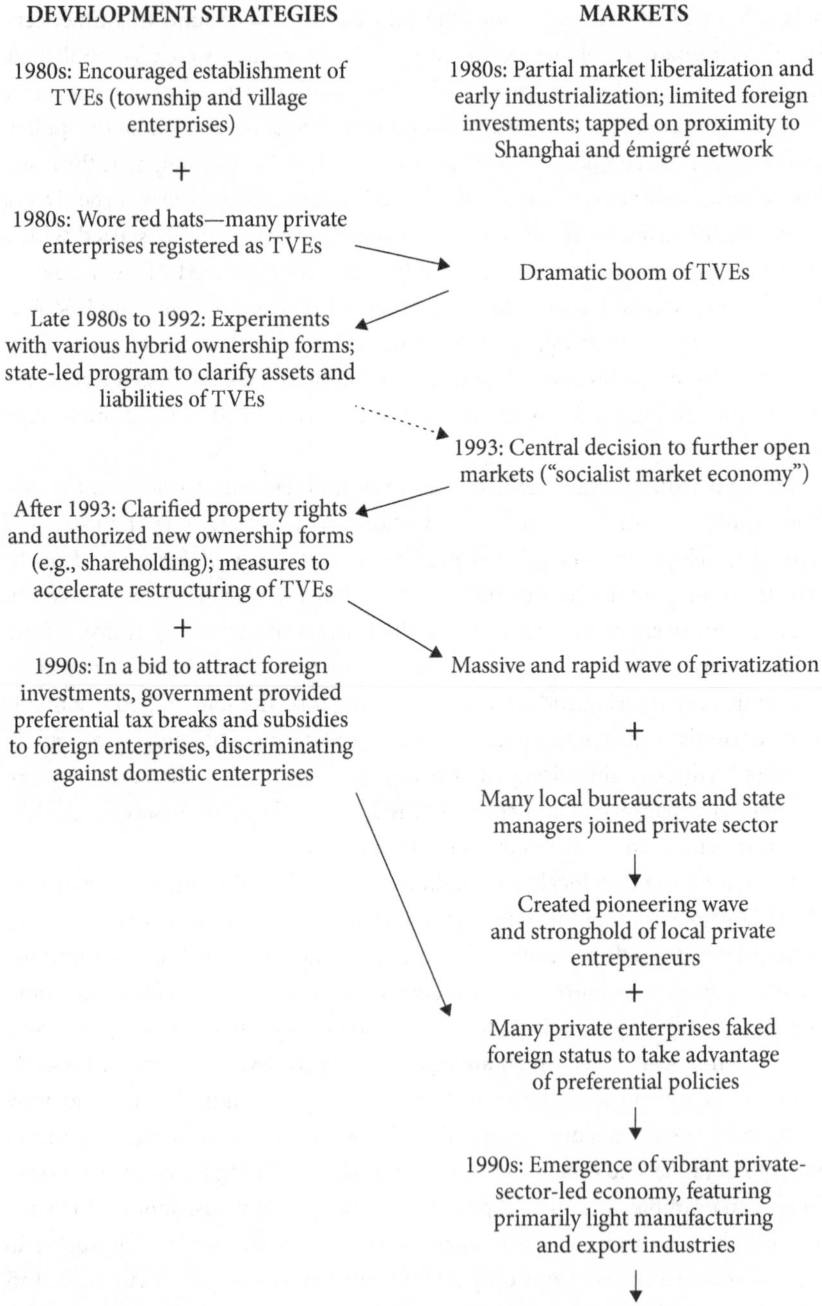

DEVELOPMENT STRATEGIES	MARKETS

1980s: Encouraged establishment of TVEs (township and village enterprises)

1980s: Partial market liberalization and early industrialization; limited foreign investments; tapped on proximity to Shanghai and émigré network

+

1980s: Wore red hats—many private enterprises registered as TVEs

Dramatic boom of TVEs

Late 1980s to 1992: Experiments with various hybrid ownership forms; state-led program to clarify assets and liabilities of TVEs

1993: Central decision to further open markets ("socialist market economy")

After 1993: Clarified property rights and authorized new ownership forms (e.g., shareholding); measures to accelerate restructuring of TVEs

+

1990s: In a bid to attract foreign investments, government provided preferential tax breaks and subsidies to foreign enterprises, discriminating against domestic enterprises

Massive and rapid wave of privatization

+

Many local bureaucrats and state managers joined private sector

↓

Created pioneering wave and stronghold of local private entrepreneurs

+

Many private enterprises faked foreign status to take advantage of preferential policies

↓

1990s: Emergence of vibrant private-sector-led economy, featuring primarily light manufacturing and export industries

↓

FIGURE 6.3 Coevolution of development strategies and markets in Blessed County

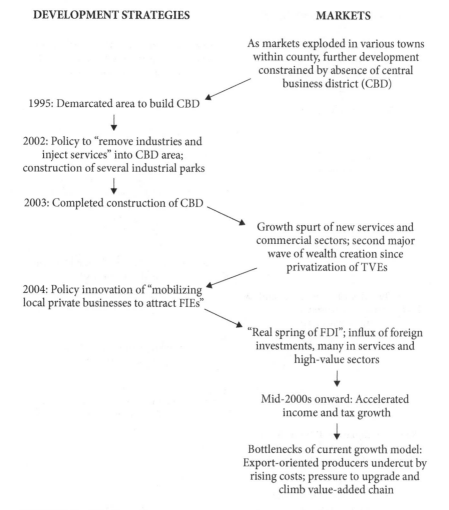

| DEVELOPMENT STRATEGIES | MARKETS |

As markets exploded in various towns within county, further development constrained by absence of central business district (CBD)

1995: Demarcated area to build CBD

2002: Policy to "remove industries and inject services" into CBD area; construction of several industrial parks

2003: Completed construction of CBD

Growth spurt of new services and commercial sectors; second major wave of wealth creation since privatization of TVEs

2004: Policy innovation of "mobilizing local private businesses to attract FIEs"

"Real spring of FDI"; influx of foreign investments, many in services and high-value sectors

Mid-2000s onward: Accelerated income and tax growth

Bottlenecks of current growth model: Export-oriented producers undercut by rising costs; pressure to upgrade and climb value-added chain

FIGURE 6.3   (Continued)

The Coevolutionary Path of Humble County

If the coevolutionary story of Blessed County was a movie played on fast-forward mode, Humble County's was put on pause mode for much of the first twenty-five years of reform. According to locals, the first signs of a growth spurt arrived in the county around 2005, which is reflected in the county's income and fiscal statistics (see figure 6.1). What explains this belated takeoff? One of the first cadres interviewed replied that it was because "the local officialdom suddenly awakened to the fact that our county can develop."[53] But people do not suddenly awaken. What

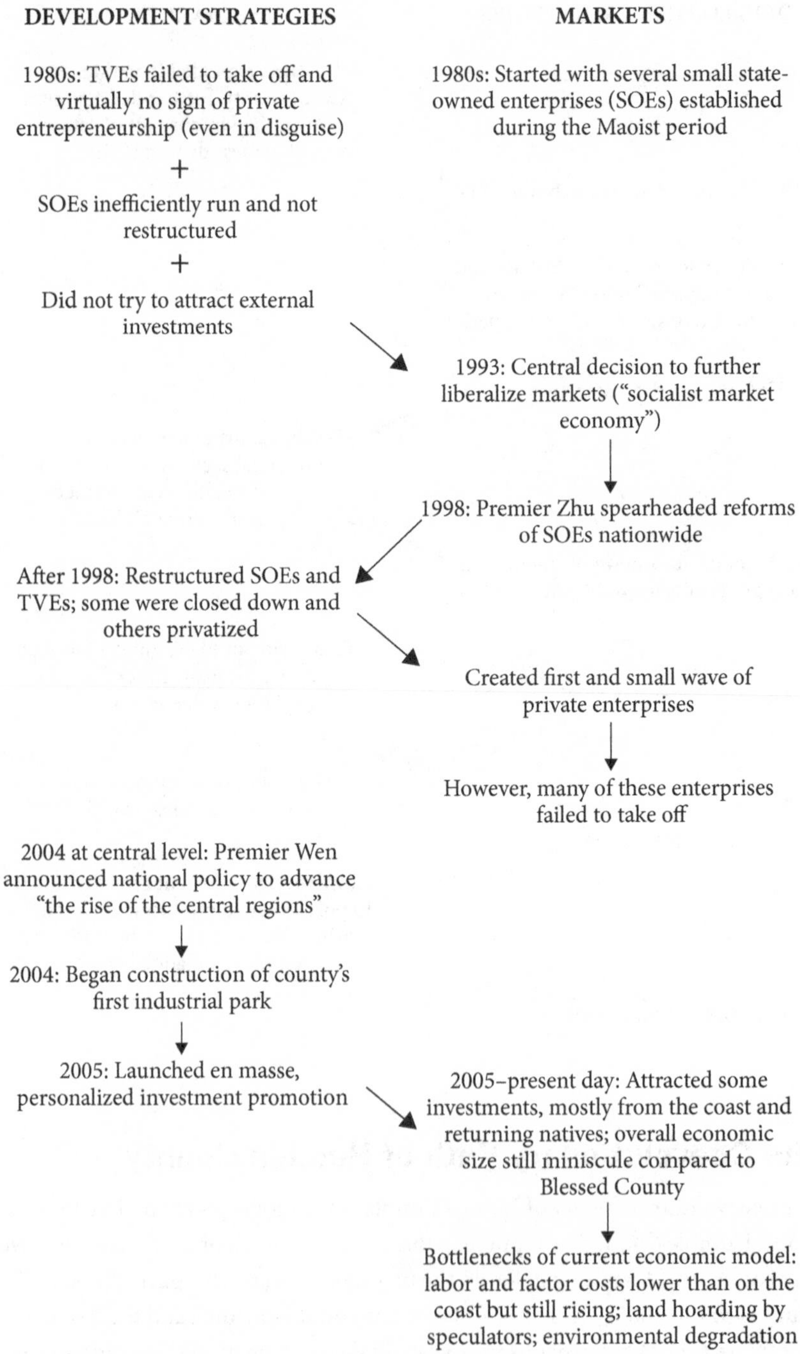

DEVELOPMENT STRATEGIES	MARKETS

DEVELOPMENT STRATEGIES

1980s: TVEs failed to take off and virtually no sign of private entrepreneurship (even in disguise)

+

SOEs inefficiently run and not restructured

+

Did not try to attract external investments

After 1998: Restructured SOEs and TVEs; some were closed down and others privatized

2004 at central level: Premier Wen announced national policy to advance "the rise of the central regions"

↓

2004: Began construction of county's first industrial park

↓

2005: Launched en masse, personalized investment promotion

MARKETS

1980s: Started with several small state-owned enterprises (SOEs) established during the Maoist period

1993: Central decision to further liberalize markets ("socialist market economy")

↓

1998: Premier Zhu spearheaded reforms of SOEs nationwide

Created first and small wave of private enterprises

↓

However, many of these enterprises failed to take off

2005–present day: Attracted some investments, mostly from the coast and returning natives; overall economic size still miniscule compared to Blessed County

↓

Bottlenecks of current economic model: labor and factor costs lower than on the coast but still rising; land hoarding by speculators; environmental degradation

FIGURE 6.4 Coevolution of development strategies and markets in Humble County

explains this awakening? After more digging, we soon arrived at a more concrete answer: "The reason for the post-2006 spurt is that industries from beyond our county transferred here. The takeover of these industries created many opportunities, resulting in rapid growth afterward."[54] In mapping the development of Humble County, one clear theme emerges: even though the laggard and first-mover regions are at least twenty years apart, economically and institutionally, their paths are *interdependent*. Neither could take off without the other.

A Slow Start to Market Opening

In both Forest Hill and Blessed County, the 1980s was a decade of vigorous market building, propelled by the proliferation of TVEs. Humble County too had established TVEs, but the way these TVEs operated and the results they produced were worlds apart. The business manager of one of the few TVEs that survived in Humble County and was later privatized recounted the situation in the 1980s as follows: "Mobilized by the local government, several natives in our township started a small linen factory. . . . All property was collectively owned. The factory made losses because it did not adhere closely to the market. What the factory produced did not meet the demands of the market."[55]

TVEs on the coast benefited from their coastal location. With easy access to export markets and opportunities to take over low-cost, labor-intensive manufacturing from more advanced economies in East Asia, TVEs sparked a rural industrial boom in this part of China. Inland locales like Humble County, however, were too far from major cities and even farther from the coast. Moreover, decades of extreme poverty and socialist rule had shriveled consumer markets in the region. On top of these geographic limitations, Humble County also lacked a pre-existing stock of managerial talent that was abundant in Blessed County. "One of the most important factors of entrepreneurial success is the management skills of the leadership. In our county, these skills were generally lacking. Leaders were not able to successfully start and maintain enterprises,"[56] said Fan, an economic bureaucrat who had served in the county for nearly thirty years.

Thus even though local officials and natives in Humble County were as eager as their coastal peers to stimulate the economy through TVEs, their efforts proved disappointing and even disastrous. Pressured by top-down targets, local officials rushed to create TVEs despite the lack of feasibility. Many of these TVEs ultimately failed, leaving the county government to clean up a morass of debts. "Everyone wanted to join the drive to set up TVEs, but the reality was not on our side. Even assigning targets was useless," Officer Fan stated.[57] This instance makes it clear that the effects of fiscal and career incentives in spurring initial growth were geographically limited.[58] Incentives could not create miracles in the absence of basic factors like access to export markets and the presence of locals with entrepreneurial experience, as abundantly found in Blessed County.

The Lost Decades

For much of coastal China, the central decision of 1993 (to establish a socialist market economy) opened a second bold chapter in its reform history. In both Forest Hill and Blessed County, TVEs and SOEs were privatized rapidly and en masse after the 1993 decision. In Humble County, however, the 1990s through early 2000s were lost decades. The county dragged its feet on the restructuring of TVEs and SOEs, which was not actualized until the early 2000s.

Why was Humble County so slow to restructure? One frequently cited reason was the risk-averse mindset of local leaders. As Zhu, another bureaucrat who had been in office since 1990 and was also a native of the county related:[59]

> We waited until the national government gave orders before we restructured. Such reforms require strong leadership. Not everyone wants to be the first to eat crabs. Everyone is fearful of creating a political mess. Anything that touches on ownership must be explicitly approved by the national government before we dare move ahead. We are not as forward looking as the coastal areas.

The list of political fears ran long. County leaders were worried that private individuals would not want to take over loss-making enterprises and that state workers would protest if they lost their "iron rice bowls" (lifetime employment). They also did not know how to clean up the enormous debts incurred by collective and state-owned enterprises.

But what in turn explains the prevalence of conservatism among leaders in the inland regions? By contrast, as we saw in the preceding cases, leaders on the coast seemed much more daring at initiating reforms and went boldly ahead to make changes even in the face of political resistance. One reason for this regional difference is that the payoffs of risk-taking are high on the coast, given its huge market potential. If local leaders succeed in creating a private economy or bustling commercial downtown, such efforts will generate tremendous benefits for the county, the bureaucracy, and themselves. Additionally, as Officer Zhu pointed out, economic reforms tended to generate quick and visible results on the coast, thus generating momentum for further change:[60]

> Markets on the coast are large, so restructuring will likely turn around loss-making enterprises within a year or two. In this way, the results are persuasive. Over here, we tried for so long to restructure, but only a few

enterprises made it. And even among those that did, they only recently begun to see some positive results. At the end of the day, our markets are small and consumption is weak.

Indeed, whereas the privatization of TVEs produced a founding batch of private entrepreneurs in Forest Hill and Blessed County, the same reforms in Humble County forced many TVEs to go bankrupt. When these enterprises were collectively owned, they could at least rely upon the county government for subsidies and debt relief. But as soon as they were privatized, these enterprises collapsed en masse, leaving only a handful that survived. In other words, just as the growth-promoting effects of strong bureaucratic incentives were geographically limited, so too was the creation of secure private property rights.[61]

> Clear property rights can bring many benefits, but once state support was removed, our enterprises could not adapt to the market on their own and thus failed. Rapid growth on the coast rested not only upon the clarification of property rights, but also locational advantages. Today, Humble County does not have any state-owned enterprises, as they have all been restructured. But aren't we still poor? Privatization alone does not guarantee success.

While the restructuring of collective and state-owned enterprises dragged along, local officials did try in the 1990s to attract investments, as Forest Hill did. But throughout the 1990s in Humble County, "courting capital and investments was mostly talk but few actions were actually taken," Zhao, a bureaucrat who worked on target setting, recounted.[62] The simple reason was that "nobody knew this place," said Liu, another official in charge of commercial promotion. "Businesses would not foolishly invest in a place they did not know."[63] Not only was Humble County remote and unheard of by foreign investors, it lacked basic physical infrastructure, such as transportation and electricity, to attract investors. So even when local leaders tried in earnest to recruit investors, they were snubbed, as economic Officer Fan recalled:[64]

> In 1996 I accompanied several of our county leaders to an investment recruitment meeting at Wuhan. A business owner had originally agreed to meet us there. But when we arrived, he made up some excuse and said he couldn't come. Instead, he sent a few of his assistants to meet with our leaders. He obviously looked down on us. But what could we do? We indeed did not have the right assets to attract investors to our county.

The county's double failure to nurture homegrown enterprises or to attract investors fed a vicious cycle of poverty and weak governance. County finances were in terrible shape, and local agencies were severely underfunded (even today they are still pitifully underfunded compared to agencies on the coast). Officer Zhao related, "Back when we were poor, our situation could not even qualify as eating [rice] budget," which refers to situations where local tax revenue was exhausted on paying cadre salaries. "It was more accurately described as 'thin gruel budget'.... We had no extra funds left to promote development. The government could hardly sustain itself, and this had a negative effect on political stability."[65] During this period, Humble County epitomized poor and predatory states. Street-level bureaucrats extracted arbitrary payments from local residents and companies, both to supplement low office budgets and to line their own pockets. A disciplinary officer recalled, "During that time, society loathed our agencies. Incidents of 'eat, extract, obstruct, and extort' were frequent. But businesses had no recourse whatsoever."[66] In turn, the lack of credible growth opportunities reinforced a sense of hopelessness and laziness among local cadres. As Officer Liu, the commerce veteran, expressed, "Back then, we lacked an appreciation of markets. We could not imagine that markets could grow so quickly and be so dynamic."[67]

A Late Growth Spurt

At long last, around 2005 locals reported a discernible break in the county's path. Economic growth and investment started to climb steadily for the first time since market opening (see figure 6.1). Simultaneously, a wave of changes swept the bureaucracy, from the assignment of targets, structure of incentives, compensation levels, fee collections, and cadre training to administrative slogans. There were signs of a virtuous cycle sparked by this unprecedented growth spurt. As Officer Zhao described, "Economic development certainly benefits the bureaucracy; funding for the agencies increased. Consequently, the government is even more motivated to promote the economy, and in order to do so, we are in the midst of transitioning from a control- to service-oriented administration."[68]

A principal source of this growth spurt, as I earlier revealed, is the transfer of industries from the coast. The burning question regards timing. Why around 2005? Why not much earlier or later? These changes in Humble County stemmed from a long-term accumulation of incremental shifts in the national market and policy environment. To stay on track of Humble County's trajectory, I will leave my discussion of the national government till later. For now, it suffices to know two key contributors to Humble's late catch-up.

First, in an effort to narrow widening regional disparities, the central state sought to accelerate economic growth in the central and western regions, primarily through infrastructure investments. In March 2004, Premier Wen Jiabao introduced the campaign of "The Rise of the Central Regions" in his delivery of the Annual Work Report of the State Council (similar to the State of the Union address in the United States). This initiative was subsequently elevated to the agenda of the CCP Politburo in 2006. A few years before Wen's 2004 pronouncement, the central government had already started to channel fiscal transfers to the interior regions to finance the construction of cross-regional transportation projects, such as highways, railroads, and airports. These centrally funded, large-scale transportation networks greatly increased access to previously landlocked locales and facilitated commerce between the coast and the interior.

One might ask: If central infrastructure investments could stimulate growth in the interior regions, then why did the central state not do so in the 1980s and 1990s? The answer is simple: it could not afford it then. Deng Xiaoping put it starkly when he told the leaders of Guangdong Province in 1979, approving their request to form special economic zones, "The party center has no money. So we will give you a policy that allows you to charge ahead and cut through your own difficult road."[69] During the founding decades, the coastal provinces received policy autonomy—rather than money—from the center. For locations like Blessed County, autonomy was sufficient to activate the tremendous capitalist potential in these places. After the coast grew rich and the center recentralized revenue through the 1994 fiscal reforms, the national government then had money to redistribute to the interior regions. Restated as an analogy of a family, the center was like a parent who first gave his abler children autonomy to leave home and make their own fortune, and after they succeeded, the parent then took contributions from the wealthier children to subsidize the poorer ones who had been left behind.

Second, as first movers transitioned from low- to middle-income economies, they were hit by rising factor costs, such as labor, land, rental, and costs of living. Furthermore, industrial land has become a scarce commodity. Even when investors are keen to build factories in coastal locales, local officials complain that there is little land left to accommodate the demand. Compare the cost of industrial land on the coast relative to the central regions (including Hubei Province). As shown in table 6.2, in 2002 and 2007, the average price of land on the coast consistently exceeded the national average, while the cost in the central regions was only 70 percent and 80 percent of that on the coast in the two years.

Next compare industrial labor costs. Table 6.3 shows gross payroll as a share of industrial value added in eight industries that are labor- or resource-intensive. In the coastal regions, the share of labor costs rose in nearly all these sectors from 2002 and 2007. In footwear and furniture production, previously the staple of Zhejiang producers, the jump in labor costs was especially high. In 2002, relative labor costs were lower in the central region than in the coastal region, except for

TABLE 6.2 Comparison of average price of industrial land

	SOUTHEASTERN REGIONS (YUAN/M²)	CENTRAL REGIONS (YUAN/M²)	NATIONAL AVERAGE (YUAN/M²)
Provinces included	Zhejiang, Shanghai, Jiangsu, Guangdong, Hainan	Hubei, Jiangxi, Anhui, Hunan, Chongqing	NA
2002	544	379	456
2007	575	457	507

Source: Adapted from Jiang, "Firm Relocation in East China" (2013, 201).

TABLE 6.3 Comparison of gross payroll as a share of industrial value-add

	2002		2007	
INDUSTRIES	COASTAL REGION (%)	CENTRAL REGION MINUS COASTAL REGION (% POINTS)	COASTAL REGION (%)	CENTRAL REGION MINUS COASTAL REGION (% POINTS)
Footwear and luggage	34.50	−21.57	41.15	−28.88
Toy and office supplies	40.88	−15.76	44.52	−19.12
Sawmills, plywood	17.95	−1.58	20.40	−7.73
Wood and metal furniture	26.14	−12.04	36.42	−21.24
Paper and paperboard	14.49	1.62	19.46	−9.87
Tire manufacturing	23.65	−4.85	25.22	−15.85
Plastic sheet and parts	21.29	−5.49	25.91	−14.79
Cement	23.03	−0.49	21.00	−8.96

Source: Adapted from Jiang, "Firm Relocation in East China" (2013, 199).

in paper, and by as much as twenty-one percentage points lower in footwear and luggage production. By 2007, the relative labor cost advantage of central over coastal regions increased in all eight sectors. In addition, some of the sectors listed below are heavily polluting industries, such as tire and cement manufacturing. Recall that in the case of Forest Hill, the city jump-started its industrial economy in the 1980s with small paper and cement factories. But since the late 1990s and until today, the government has been trying to kick these "backward" (its own word) factories out of the city.

Driven by these changing market conditions, factories on the coast started to search for alternative sites. Many started to migrate to the interior, inspiring the term "industrial transfer."[70] Pressures to move are especially intense among low-end, labor-intensive and resource-intensive sectors, no longer welcomed by wealthy local states that now prioritize quality of growth. To be clear, there wasn't a sharp starting point to this migration. Nor did private producers on the coast wait passively for state directions before adjusting their business plans. Instead it was the opposite; planners in Beijing reacted belatedly to this gradual movement of industries from the coast to the interior, as I will later discuss. Indirectly, however, central investment in the expansion of physical infrastructure in the central regions, as earlier described, helped places like Humble County be shovel-ready to take over manufacturing from the coastal first movers.

The emergence of domestic investors and central policy encouragement spurred the leadership in Humble County into renewed action. In 2004 Humble County began construction of its first industrial park, which would provide a dedicated space to house factories. Each locale was responsible for financing infrastructure projects, including industrial parks, within its own jurisdiction, as central grants were dedicated to financing cross-regional transportation like interstate highways. In this regard, like in other parts of China (including Forest Hill in chapter 5), land proceeds were an indispensable source of start-up capital for the county. The industrial park cost more than two billion yuan to construct. Higher-level governments provided partial budgetary support, but the bulk of finances came from leasing land to private capitalists.[71] Emphasizing the contribution of land finance to local development, Liu, the commerce bureaucrat, said:[72]

> Without a doubt, land finance provided our county a large sum of capital for infrastructure construction, for example, new roads, treated rivers, and public parks.... Once our urban facilities were built up, we could start to promote tourism.... And it is especially important for attracting investments too. Our industrial park is fully equipped with manufacturing facilities, transportation links, water and electricity supply. Only with these facilities in place would investors be willing to come. Without capital to build an industrial park, Humble County's development would be nowhere close to where it is today.

Later, as we shall see in chapter 7, this reliance among Chinese local governments on using land proceeds to finance infrastructure closely mirrors the strategy of "taxless public finance" among state governments in America during the early nineteenth century.[73] These states also resorted to using nontax revenue to construct canals, railways, and mega-projects that connected regional economies. Despite the risks and problems that stem from land financing (see chapter 1), the role it plays in building markets cannot be ignored or dismissed.

Consistent with the approach of directed improvisation, central policy makers authorized major shifts but delegated local actors to fill in the details. As Officer Zhu, the economic planner, expressed, "The central did not order us to build an industrial park. Rather, based on our understanding of the 'spirit' of broad directions provided by the center, we made plans according to local conditions."[74] One benefit of being a late developer was that Humble County did not have to start from scratch; instead, it could learn from the past experiences of coastal locales. Local officials took study trips to Jiangsu and Zhejiang to "collect scriptures from them," mainly in the areas of "management, design of industrial parks, and investment promotion policies," Zhu elaborated. He emphasized, however, that blind copying was not possible because local conditions varied immensely. In his words, "Whereas Zhejiang had mostly export manufacturers, we didn't have these. And their customer base and advantages were different from ours, so we were unable to transplant some of their investment promotion methods."[75] For example, Blessed County mobilized its stronghold of local private companies to recruit foreign investors from overseas, but Humble County was only to starting to cultivate its own private sector, which targeted mainly the domestic market. So even among locales, lessons from the coast had to be adjusted to fit realities in the interior.

Following efforts to construct an industrial park, the next step was to recruit investors to populate the park. How? Starting in around 2005, Humble County launched its own version of the beehive campaign that began a decade earlier in Forest Hill. All the townships and county agencies were assigned targets to attract a certain amount of investment each year. Similar to practices adapted in Forest Hill in the 1990s through early 2000s, these assignments came with high-powered incentives. Agencies that successfully attracted projects worth more than thirty million yuan were awarded 0.1 percent of the investments in the form of additional budget allocations. On top of rewards for agencies, an additional bonus of 100,000 yuan (about US$15,000) was offered to individual cadres for bringing in large projects valued at more than 100 million.[76] "The drive to recruit investors is led by the chief of each agency. But whoever has resources is also expected to contribute,"[77] said Officer Zhao, who managed targets.

To court investors, local bureaucrats relied, as their coastal peers had in the past, on personal connections, a method locally termed as "using intimate ties to court investments."[78] As Zhao elaborated, "The fact that [businesses] are here reflects a relationship of trust with particular officials, who will of course be willing to serve the businesses they personally recruited."[79] Again, reminiscent of Forest Hill in the 1990s, such personal connections provided a necessary substitute for formal property rights protection, especially since the bureaucracy in Humble County, still underfunded and underregulated, was rife with petty predation; this was a problem on which the leadership of a poor locale had to make compromises as much as it wished to eradicate it immediately. Realistically, only strong personal ties with particular officials gave investors sufficient confidence that they could overcome red tape and bureaucratic harassment.

Unlike Forest Hill and Blessed County, Humble County attracted *domestic*, rather than foreign, investors after 2005. One group comprised low-end manufacturers from the coastal regions and moderately wealthier central provinces like Hunan. For example, a ceramics factory had relocated from Guangdong Province to Humble County to take advantage of its ample land and cheaper labor.[80] Another source of investors was returning natives who had migrated to work in the coastal cities from the 1980s through 2000s. Some of these natives acquired technical skills and picked up entrepreneurial ideas after working many years in metropolises like Shenzhen and Shanghai. Emotionally attached to their hometowns and more adept than outsiders at navigating the local environment, these natives were eager to return to Humble County to start up new businesses. In recent years, several furniture companies have been started by this group of investors, who used to work in the furniture-making hubs of cities in Guangdong.[81] This provides yet another interesting parallel with first-mover states like Blessed County, which kick-started investments in the 1990s by tapping their networks of emigrant merchants and the Chinese diaspora, spread throughout Taiwan and Hong Kong. Humble County did not have the privilege of accessing such a network in the early decades, but today it does, in the mutated form of returning migrant workers from the coast.

Once credible growth opportunities came within reach, a coevolutionary chain reaction was belatedly triggered, reminiscent of what coastal locales had experienced one to two decades earlier. It changed mindsets, spurring among local cadres a desire not to be poor and backward anymore. Officer Zhao said, "From 2006, we charged ahead. Why is that? We were poor! Poverty forced us to change."[82] Spurred by competition within the province among late-developing locales, all yearning for a share of new domestic investors, growth promotion in Humble County today operates in a feverish mode. In 2012, the party secretary issued a directive on "Improving the Business Environment" to all the agencies. Its dedication to capitalism was enshrined in an almost religious-sounding slogan: "Investors are God; investment recruiters are heroes; bureaucrats are public servants; and those who harm business interests are sinners."

Comparing the coevolutionary paths of Forest Hill, Blessed County, and Humble County, my study reveals a pattern of *lagged* replication from richly to poorly endowed regions. This pattern is different from a vast literature on policy experiments and policy diffusion in China, which describes either the selection of "test points" by central reformers to try out certain policies before extending them nationwide (as in case of Special Economic Zones) or the diffusion of local innovations across regions, where economic preconditions are not relevant.[83] In contrast, as my comparative analysis uncovers, the replication of certain institutions and strategies that were first adopted on the coast is conditional upon the level of economic growth. For instance, Forest Hill had by 2014 already replaced the beehive campaign with technocratic specialization and operations. But Humble County cannot yet skip to this step, as Li, an investment officer, explained:[84]

> The initial work of investment promotion among localities on the coast is almost complete, so they no longer need to mobilize the entire bureaucracy. These locales have already accumulated enough capital and experience, so their focus now is to select quality enterprises from the available supply. It is the investors who must meet standards set by the bureaucracy, rather than the bureaucracy that has to beg investors to come. For them, the demand-and-supply relationship has changed. But Humble County does not yet have enough enterprises, so we must continue to mobilize everyone in the bureaucracy to recruit investors.

From this instance, we realize that it is one thing to observe and learn from what the first movers did, but another to have the necessary capacity and market conditions to replicate their strategies. Evidently, even within China, subnational laggards cannot blindly copy first movers; to succeed, they too had to adopt practices and policies that fit their stages of development and tasks at hand. This underscores the fallacy of recommending that Third World countries skip ahead and emulate the current practices and norms of developed nations.[85]

Kicking Away the Subnational Ladder?

In the future, will laggard states replicate the exact steps taken by first movers? It is unlikely. Even though the laggard states like Humble County appeared to have hopped onto the development train and have indeed begun to adapt both economically and institutionally, the national conditions that prevail today are drastically different from what coastal locales encountered in the 1980s and 1990s. So even though we observe many lagged parallels in the coevolutionary paths of the two regions, it is too simplistic to assume that the laggard will—or should—exactly copy the first mover's history.

Laggard states face several mounting challenges that may obstruct the sustainability of development in this region. First, even though factor costs are on average lower in the interior than in wealthy coastal cities, costs are nevertheless rising even in the former.[86] A bureaucrat who manages Humble's industrial parks noted, "Labor costs are rising, so we must move into high value-added industrial production soon."[87] Yet compared to Blessed County, Humble County has no advantage yet in high-end manufacturing; it is now merely taking over industries that the coast sought to discard. In Upstart County of Jiangxi (featured in chapter 1), also an inland locale, a bureaucrat from the Investment Bureau, Wang, expressed a similar worry. He said, "Labor costs are sharply rising, especially in the past few years. In our industrial parks, workers now cost at least two thousand yuan a month."[88] Worse, rising costs are not the only problem. As reports of labor strikes in recent years suggest, Chinese workers are becoming increasingly rights-conscious and assertive.[89] As Officer Wang from Upstart County further noted, "It is hard to recruit workers these days. Our advantage in supplying cheap labor is quickly expiring. Moreover, the post-1990s generation is unable to bear hardship."[90]

Second, although the supply of industrial land is more ample in the central and western regions than on the coast, it remains a finite resource. Even worse, this finite resource appears to be rapidly depleted and in many instances wasted by speculative behavior. During the 1990s, when economies were just being kick-started in the coastal regions, land had only begun to be traded, and the real estate market had not taken off. By the 2010s, however, land is perhaps the hottest commodity in China, driving speculators to snap up parcels of land in the hope of making quick gains from its appreciation. In this context, intense economic competition among inland locales inadvertently exposed desperate local officials to "fake investors" who seek to "hoard land" for speculative gains, rather than to actually build factories, employ workers, and generate tax revenue.[91] These opportunistic speculators demand that local governments grant them land with promises of making genuine investments. Then, upon receiving land titles, they leave, waiting to sell the empty plots for lucrative profits when prices spike.

A manager of Upstart County's industrial parks, Fu, elaborated on the plight facing inland locales desperate for investments:

> Our county has neither a port nor natural resources to attract investors. Over here, attracting capital and investments is a political assignment. Hence, many investors who are brought in only invest in name; in reality, they are empty. For example, an enterprise may only need 20 *mu* of land, but it will demand 150 *mu* from the county. Since land is cheap, it is given away. This can happen in three different ways. The investor asks for more land than he needs and then leaves it to waste; he constructs some production facilities for show; or he takes the land ownership certificate elsewhere and swindles others into thinking he has a big business.[92]

Worse, whereas personal connections played a constructive role in recruiting productive investors and substituting for formal property rights in the 1990s among coastal locales, these connections today have become a major barrier among inland locales to evicting fake investors. Officer Fu elaborated, "There is nothing we can do about it. These enterprises came here through our leaders; there are affective personal relationships involved. We can't afford to confront these enterprises. It's quite obvious which factories are empty. Some occupy over 100 *mu* of land but have only a few workers."[93] The long-term consequence of speculative land hoarding is that the county may not have sufficient land to accommodate productive projects in the future. If that happens, as Officer Wang expressed, "We have truly wasted our land quota allocation."[94]

Third, there is the problem of environmental degradation, probably the most widely discussed controversy associated with industrial transfer. Some worry that industrial transfer is merely a disguised scheme of "pollution transfer" to underdeveloped and investment-hungry areas. One Chinese commentary writes, "For example, Guangdong Province has moved ceramics producers that heavily pollute air and water to Hunan and Jiangxi. . . . Backward regions have become the sanctuary of polluting industries."[95] In written guidelines, central authorities insisted that industrial transfer should not occur at the expense of environmental protection. Local officials, too, maintained that they forbade polluting enterprises from entry. For example, Officer Wang from Upstart County declared, "Dangerous and resource-intensive production, such as fireworks and chemicals, are required to pass an environmental assessment. Those who fail are universally barred from entry."[96] Upstart County also issued an internal circular to its agencies stating that polluting factories (e.g., brick, sand, and cement producers) would not count toward fulfilling departmental investment targets.[97]

For start-up locales that offer few attractions, however, being selective about investments remains a luxury. A commerce bureaucrat from Humble County stated, "Our locale does not have a big population, is a small place and not yet urbanized. So how could we reject any investment project?" He added, "Honestly speaking, I think our county still focuses more on pursuing quantity than quality of growth. Having both quantity and quality is ideal, but that is very difficult to achieve in reality."[98] In this context, intense regional competition may have a perverse effect of accelerating a race to the bottom.

The preceding discussions culminate in a basic observation: not all of China can become Shanghai. Further, I should add, perhaps not all of China *wants to* become Shanghai. This observation is adamantly expressed by cadres in Upstart County, which had the least attractive factor endowments among the cases studied (not only is this county landlocked, it was almost entirely rural up until the 1990s). One local cadre expressed, "I feel that every place should develop based on its own reality and not follow the same old path of industrialization. . . . We have to find our own comparative advantage and the beautiful natural environment we possess is our comparative advantage."[99]

First movers went through a wrenching process of economic and institutional change that ultimately transformed these localities from poor to middle-income and from rural to urban. As fields made way for factories, this great leap wrought tremendous environmental damage and sometimes untold human costs, but at least the great transformation was partially achieved in locales like Forest Hill and Blessed County. But some locales like Upstart County are not fundamentally suited for industrialization, and, as locals pointed out, a pristine environment is probably their greatest asset. The worry is that when pressured to conform to an industrial path of development, Upstart County may both destroy its environment and continue to stay poor.

National and Domestic Flying Geese

We may now take a few steps back to understand how several layers of regional interdependence fit together. China's coastal development is inseparable from East Asia's development. First coined by Japanese scholar Akamatsu, the theory of "flying geese" proposed a regionally tiered pattern of development.[100] It is envisioned that Japan, like the first goose in a V-shaped formation, would lead a flock of lower-tier economies like Taiwan and Singapore. Then, as Japan successfully industrialized and moved up the value-added chain, it would pass down investment opportunities, technology, and know-how to the remaining geese. In many ways, this pattern has played out as predicted in the past three decades. During the 1960s and 1970s, the East Asian tigers took off by first undertaking labor-intensive export manufacturing. Then, by the 1980s and 1990s, facing rising factor costs at home, manufacturers in East Asia (primarily Hong Kong and Taiwan) chose to relocate low-end production to China's coastal provinces to take advantage of their abundant cheap labor and weak environmental and labor protection. East Asian companies moved upward into higher-end manufacturing and services sectors.

The takeoff in China's coastal economies was fueled not only by a surge of investments from East Asia, but also by the supply of cheap raw materials and labor from the interior provinces. For example, Blessed County in Zhejiang had benefited from a vast flow of migrant workers from laggard states like Humble County in the central and western regions. Without this abundant supply of cheap rural labor, it would not have been possible for export manufacturers on the coast to be so competitive on the international market.[101] Central regions also provided raw materials like agricultural produce, wood, metals, and coal at low prices to the coastal regions for processing. One estimate placed the annual losses that Gansu and Yunnan Provinces incurred from selling underpriced raw materials at 3.3 to 5 billion yuan respectively in the 1980s, more than half their income from industry.[102] Quoted in *The Economist*, an official from the National Development and Reform Commission (NDRC) summed up: "The resource-rich cities have made tremendous contributions to China's economic take-off, but the sacrifice they made is also huge."[103] As endowed as Blessed County may be, its economy could not have taken off without "sacrifices" made by laggard states.

Then, by the mid-2000s, as we learned from the preceding narratives, a pattern of *domestic* flying geese unfolded within China's national market. At present, coastal manufacturers have taken over the role played by East Asian manufacturers a few decades ago, while returning migrant workers from the coast substituted for Chinese diasporic businesses who built factories on the coast during the early years of market reforms.

Putting the pieces together, we arrive at a picture of nested layers of regional interdependence. China's economy is inextricably tied to those of its neighbors. And within China, the coevolutionary paths of subnational political economies cannot be studied independently from one another; their *variations* are as salient as their *connections*.

Was the pattern of domestic flying geese intended by China's central leaders? What was the role of the central government in regional development since market opening? What is especially surprising about the phenomenon of domestic flying geese is that it was not foreseen or engineered by any central planner, not even the visionary patriarch Deng himself. In fact, over the past thirty years of reform, central authorities sometimes blundered in their attempts to mold regional development in desired ways. Central efforts to promote industrial transfer in the 2000s were reactive rather than proactive.

To understand the origins and evolution of central policies toward regional development, a cursory review of history is in order. Under Mao's leadership, from the 1950s to 1970s, the center deliberately pumped resources into the central and western regions and suppressed market development on the coast, which Justin Lin would describe as "defying the comparative advantage (determined by the existing endowment structure)" of the respective regions.[104] Mao's policies were motivated by his anticapitalist ideology and his belief that propping up industries in the interior was necessary for national security defense.[105]

When Deng came to power, he reversed Mao's policy. Realizing that it made economic sense to harness rather than to defy regional comparative advantages, Deng pushed the coastal regions to leverage their geographic proximity to export markets and entrepreneurial legacies "to get rich first." It appears that Deng already had a vision of domestic flying geese in mind, which was termed a ladder-stepped strategy of development.[106] An official from Fujian described it as such: "The development of our country is sequential. The coastal areas develop first and then the process extends inward. Inland provinces will gradually be influenced by development in the more prosperous areas."[107]

In the 1980s, though, Deng's vision did not pan out as he hoped. Inland regions did not want to give up precious raw materials cheaply to the coastal provinces for processing, which would allow them to reap higher profits. Consequently, a regional "commodity war" broke out. Each province erected trade barriers to block the outflow of raw materials to other regions and the inflow of processed goods into their borders.[108] This period of duplicative industries and protectionism led some pessimists to predict a perpetual state of regional market fragmentation and even political breakdown.[109]

Such naysaying predictions turned out to be premature. Although the central government could not curb local protectionism by command, market forces came into play. Following the 1993 central decision to further liberalize markets, competition stepped up, over time eliminating weak industries and firms.[110] During the Seventh Five-Year Plan (1986–1990), the central party-state urged the coastal, central, and western regions to develop industries compatible with their respective endowments, namely "the restructuring of traditional industries, new industries, and consumer goods production" on the coast; energy, construction, and mining in the central regions; and agriculture and processing in the west. Economic and institutional disparities across the regions continued to widen throughout the 1990s and into the 2000s precisely because the coastal provinces dominated the valuable ranks of the national production chain. Contrary to the optimistic expectations of Deng's ladder-stepped model, the geographic dispersion of wealth and progress did not appear automatic, at least not during these decades.

Arriving in office in 2003, the Hu-Wen administration made balancing regional development a top priority. As earlier mentioned, Premier Wen officially launched the program of "The Rise of the Central Regions" in 2004, encompassing the provinces of Hubei (location of Humble County), Jiangxi (location of Upstart County), Henan, Hunan, Anhui, and Shanxi.[111] This political agenda coincided with a trend of industrial transfer that was already emerging, so the central government chose to push it along. In 2006, the Ministry of Commerce was tasked to oversee the program of "ten thousand businesses advance westward."[112] The ministry provided market training to more than a hundred thousand technical workers, managers, and state personnel annually; it also organized an annual high-profile convention, known as the Expo Central China, to match coastal manufacturers with inland governments.[113] In 2008, the NDRC, a powerful ministry, was enlisted to craft a set of policies to invigorate the central economies, signaling the elevated significance of this agenda.

While the idea of promoting regional complementarities is not new to central policy, the emphases of the current decade is different from those of the past. During the Seventh Five-Year Plan (1986–1990), the central government urged different regions to "leverage their respective advantages." At that time, the national goal was to "speed up development on the coast," while the inland regions would "support and accelerate coastal development." As the language indicates, central planners at that time envisioned a static geographic distribution of industries based on factor endowments, rather than a dynamic transfer of production and capabilities. Also, their policies were overtly biased toward benefiting the coast before the interior. By contrast, the State Council Circular of 2010 on "Guiding Principles on Industrial Transfer" eschewed a policy of asymmetrical sacrifice, stressing instead the merits of mutually beneficial exchanges between unequal regions:[114]

> The central and western regions offer an abundant supply of natural resources, low factor costs, and huge potential for market growth. The enthusiastic takeover of domestic and international industries will not only accelerate the process of new industrialization and urbanization in the interior and enhance harmonious regional development, but will also promote economic restructuring and upgrading on the coast. This will ultimately contribute to a refined division of labor in the national economy.

The central government's reorientation of regional development policy took China's evolving niche in the international market into serious consideration. Explaining the motivations of the State Council Circular of 2010, an official from the NDRC commented at a press conference, "Industrial transfer is an irreversible trend of development under the influence of a globalized economy."[115] The Chinese leadership was especially shaken by the global financial crisis of 2008, which abruptly shrank factory orders and threatened to put many workers on the coast out of jobs. The center was forced to respond with an unprecedented fiscal stimulus package, totaling four trillion yuan.[116] The crisis made it clear that continued reliance on cheap export manufacturing was not only unsustainable for the coastal locales, but would place China's national economy and political stability at the mercy of global market fluctuations.[117] Thus, whereas efforts to encourage regional cooperation used to be symbolic, uncoordinated, and underfunded,[118] this agenda was now to be taken seriously. As a *Xinhua* (the state press) report declared, "ladder-step industrial transfer has been elevated to the status of a national strategy."[119]

As NDRC officials emphasized, China today is a market economy, and "the state cannot make firms relocate."[120] Nevertheless, central authorities can foster this process by sending affirmative policy signals to local officials and market actors. The changes in investment patterns are visible. Since 2004, the central provinces have seen a steady rise in domestic investment (i.e., investment from

TABLE 6.4   Domestic investment in five central provinces (billion yuan)

	HUBEI	JIANGXI	HUNAN	HENAN	ANHUI	TOTAL DOMESTIC INVESTMENT IN FIVE CENTRAL PROVINCES	TOTAL FDI INFLOW TO CHINA
2008	95	110	123	185	323	836	1,045
2011	338	258	209	402	418	1,624	1,706
Change from 2008 to 2011	+355%	+234%	+170%	+217%	+130%	+194%	+163%

Source: Domestic investment from annual work reports of the provincial governments; FDI statistic from World Bank Indicators, converted from current US$ into billion yuan.

provinces within Mainland China, excluding Hong Kong, Taiwan, and Macau), as illustrated in table 6.4.[121] In 2004, among the six central provinces, only Hunan and Anhui mentioned domestic investment in their annual provincial government work reports. By 2008, this statistic was highlighted in all the provincial reports, except for Shanxi Province, whose economy is dominated by coal and resource extraction rather than manufacturing. In Hubei, the value of domestic investment more than tripled between 2008 and 2011. To put these numbers in perspective, I compare them to FDI inflows in table 6.4. In 2008, domestic investment in the five central provinces combined was about 80 percent the value of FDI that flowed into all of China. Three years later, the two numbers were almost equivalent. Clearly, whereas FDI had fueled early takeoff on the coast, domestic investment has taken over as the new growth engine of the interior.

Among the first movers, Zhejiang Province (the location of Blessed County) has been an especially rich source of industrial transfer to other provinces. According to the Zhejiang Economic and Technological Cooperation Office, Zhejiang businesses invested more than a trillion yuan across China in 2006, equivalent to the province's entire GDP in 2005.[122] Deng's expectations about a ladder-step pattern of regional development were actually correct. Alas, he did not live long enough to witness precisely how his expectations would play out in the twenty-first century.

In this chapter, I compared the coevolution of markets and development strategies in two contrasting locales. Then I situated their intertwining paths in the broader national and international contexts. My analysis generates three main lessons, highlighted below.

Lesson 1: Endowments are situationally significant but not deterministic.

For countries and locales alike, geographical conditions (such as location, topography, and availability of natural resources) and history (past experiences, pre-existing institutions)—broadly termed "endowments" here—are certainly important factors of development. Such factors, however, are situationally significant, rather than always deterministic.[123] Take for example Blessed County, which has the privilege of a coastal location but completely lacks natural resources. In the context of a globalized market economy, the absence of natural resources did not constrain its development; if anything, it actually had the benefit of turning the county toward commerce and trade, rather than resource extraction. Another example is Humble County, which is landlocked and has some natural resources. For the first twenty-five years or so, Humble County's development seemed doomed by its inland location and lack of prior experience in private entrepreneurship. Yet new and unanticipated opportunities arrived when the economy of its neighboring regions changed. After 2005, it was precisely its inland location that provided Humble County the attractions of ample industrial land and low factor costs.

Lesson 2: Political economies (national or local) are moving paths, not static models.

As we've learned from the three local cases I presented, even a single case can fit several competing descriptions depending on *when* observations are made. Proponents of minimalist governments that limit their role to protecting private property rights may champion Blessed County in the 1990s as their "model." Yet those who privilege the activist role of government in accelerating growth processes may also invoke the same case in the 2000s as their "model." Units of observation, therefore, cannot be characterized by snapshots taken only at certain points in time. Rather, they are better characterized by their evolutionary trajectories over an extended period of time.

In other words, my analysis advances a different way of doing comparative analysis. The conventional approach to comparative politics or political economy is to first identify variation in certain outcomes and then test factors that cause or correlate with this variation. This logic has been extended in a growing literature on subnational comparisons within China, which Rithmire calls "new regionalism." As she describes, this literature centers on how "local-level variables determine different local economic realities."[124] Yet whether at the national or subnational levels, variation must be understood in light of regional connections and not only "local-level variables." Political units are almost always interdependent, and this is especially true for subnational units, whose paths unfold within certain shared national parameters. As this chapter shows, by studying regions as connected moving paths, rather than as static models, we may observe not only variation in outcomes but also differences and similarities in processes. In addition, the timing of changes is also interdependent; whether a particular adaptation is adopted or works in one area depends on the evolving conditions of its neighbors. By comparing paths, rather than snapshots, we are more likely to notice spillover across cases, which over and beyond "local-level variables" can also profoundly shape outcomes. I have illustrated this dynamic comparative approach at a subnational level in this chapter, but this approach can obviously be applied to cross-national analyses too.

Lesson 3: Regional inequality is not only a consequence but also a strategy of development.

Regional inequality as a consequence of market opening and development is well-known among observers of China.[125] It is less noticed and understood, however, that regional inequality is also a strategy of China's national development. As this chapter illuminates, a key element of China's overall development success has been to exploit highly unequal endowments across coastal, central, and western regions. As an NDRC official pointed out, China's large size and regional diversity distinguishes its constraints and alternatives from East Asia, where regional inequalities are not as salient. He said, "Conversely, in China, regional tiers are sharp, providing room for maneuvering and relocation."[126]

Indeed, in the developmental state literature based on East Asian states like Japan and South Korea, entire countries are treated as single and homogeneous observations. In China, on the other hand, regional inequalities present a double-edged sword, problematic but also potentially advantageous. Therefore, the study of China's national development must take into account the issue of niche creation, the crafting of distinct and complementary roles for unevenly endowed members within a complex system.

Whether China can effectively harness regional inequalities in the coming years will impact the repositioning of its niche in the international market. Can inland regions take over labor-intensive manufacturing from the coast? Can coastal China really scale the global value-added chain? Understood as such, even if we have never known about Blessed County and Humble County, we are each distantly connected to these corners of China.

HOW DEVELOPMENT ACTUALLY
HAPPENED *BEYOND* CHINA

> **One of the handicaps of the twentieth century is that we still have
> the vaguest and most biased notions, not only of what makes Japan
> a nation of Japanese, but of what makes the United States a nation
> of Americans, France a nation of Frenchmen, and Russia a nation of
> Russians.**
>
> **The study of comparative cultures too cannot flourish when men are
> so defensive about their own way of life that it appears to them to be
> by definition the sole solution in the world.**
>
> —Ruth Benedict, *The Chrysanthemum and the Sword*

Are coevolutionary processes of development unique to China? Looking at the
existing literature, one would think that they must be. Most accounts of successful development are linear causal stories, usually of something done right
followed by spectacular growth. For example, several influential political economists invoke the case of England after the Glorious Revolution in 1688 as evidence that formal limits on state power led to capitalist success.[1] Similarly, in
the case of East Asian NIEs, the establishment of Weberian state apparatuses is
depicted as a necessary precursor to state-led economic boom.[2] These accounts
capture important but partial truths. They capture only snapshots of long zigzag paths, zooming in on one causal direction, thus reinforcing impressions that
development indeed goes from good institutions to prosperity.

In this concluding chapter, though, I present further evidence that development *is* a coevolutionary process, not only in China but also in other parts of the
world and in recent and historical periods. Development means the radical and
simultaneous transformation of states and markets, entailing many actors, many
dimensions, and many steps. If such a complex process unfolds neatly in one
direction, we should be surprised, indeed astounded.

My discussion in this chapter will be divided into three parts. First, based on
several existing accounts, I revisit segments of history in the rise of the West from
a coevolutionary perspective. My analysis reveals that so-called good or strong
(market-preserving) institutions that are widely embraced today as universal

causes of economic growth were in fact *not* the institutions that *built* markets in early Western societies. Parallel to my findings in contemporary China, medieval Western Europe and nineteenth-century America sparked growth through particular market-building institutions (some of which were uncannily similar to those seen in post-1978 China), which subsequently evolved into market-preserving institutions. Next, I apply the coevolutionary approach to analyze the unlikely boom of the film industry in Nigeria since the early 1990s, also known as Nollywood. Despite vastly different circumstances and institutional innovations, we also find a consistent pattern of economic and institutional coevolution within Nollywood, as I have traced on a national scale in reform China.

Finally, the chapter will conclude with what the China "model" really comprises and whether this model can last. My central message is that the underlying "cause" of economic development, if indeed we had to name one, is the construction of an adaptive environment that empowers relevant actors to improvise solutions to continuously evolving problems. Whether it is in Western Europe, the United States, East Asia, China, or Nigeria, particular solutions work only when they *fit* the particular demands of their environments. Therefore, it is futile and even self-defeating to search for one replicable model believed to work always and everywhere. The lessons to be learned from China's capitalist revolution are not particular solutions, which were improvised at certain times or in certain parts of the country, but rather lessons on strategies of directing improvisation.

Coevolutionary Dynamics in the Rise of the West

Beyond China, we can trace coevolutionary paths of development most vividly in the history of political economies that are *already developed*; being developed indicates that political and economic systems had undergone significant mutual adaptations. If we look carefully, evidence of development as a coevolutionary process actually exists in the literature, but the relevant accounts are not identified as coevolutionary. Below I conduct an exercise in historical reconstruction. Applying the analytic approach I used in preceding chapters to map out transformative paths in China, I retell two scenarios of Western development in coevolutionary terms: the expansion of trade in late medieval Europe followed by the revolution of public finance in the antebellum United States.

The Expansion of Trade in Late Medieval Europe

Avner Greif's research on the role of informal institutions in development, focusing largely on medieval European traders, has received much acclaim among economists.[3] He is well-known for his ideas that informal reputational mechanisms can effectively substitute for formal mechanisms of contract enforcement at early stages of development. In a coauthored article with political scientist David Laitin, they extended these ideas into "a theory of endogenous institutional change," arguing that in certain instances, self-enforcing institutions may actually undermine themselves in the long term.[4]

Greif and Laitin point to a long-standing problem in the study of institutional change. According to game theory approaches, institutions are by definition equilibrium outcomes; they arise because "each player's behavior is a best response."[5] According to this logic, once in place, institutions should self-reinforce and persist. Yet we know as a matter of fact that institutions sometimes change. Why and how do institutions change? Traditionally, social scientists have looked to exogenous causes (or shocks) as explanations. Greif and Laitin, however, argue that endogenous institutional change is possible. In their words, "It is appropriate to inquire whether the institution—which we analyze as a game theoretic equilibrium—endogenously affects aspects of the situation apart from behavior in the transaction under consideration. Such aspects should be considered as parametric in studying self-enforceability but as endogenously determined— and thus variable—in the long run."[6] While Greif and Laitin's theory speaks usefully to game theorists, I would like to suggest a more straightforward expression of their logic. In the context of political economies, endogenous institutional change happens when an initial institutional adaptation successfully kick-starts markets and the resulting economic growth motivates further institutional change. *In other words, states and markets coevolve.*

Below, I reconstruct Greif's account of the community responsibility system in late medieval Europe by highlighting the feedbacks between contract-enforcement institutions and markets. A coevolutionary causal map is summarized in figure C.1.

In premodern societies, commercial activities began on a geographically limited scale within the boundaries of home communities. Within villages and small towns, local residents bartered goods and later on used currency to buy and sell from one another. In these primitive settings, which are still seen among rural and poor communities today, exchanges are supported by personal reputations. For example, transacting farmers from the same village can generally trust one another because if one party cheats, the whole village will soon know and will avoid doing business with the cheater. In this way, concern for personal reputation deters players from dishonest behavior. Such mechanisms, however, work only in close-knit communities where everyone knows everyone. As Chinese sociologist Fei Xiaotong stresses, "These methods cannot be used with a stranger."[7] Transactions in modern markets occur among *strangers* who never have met and may

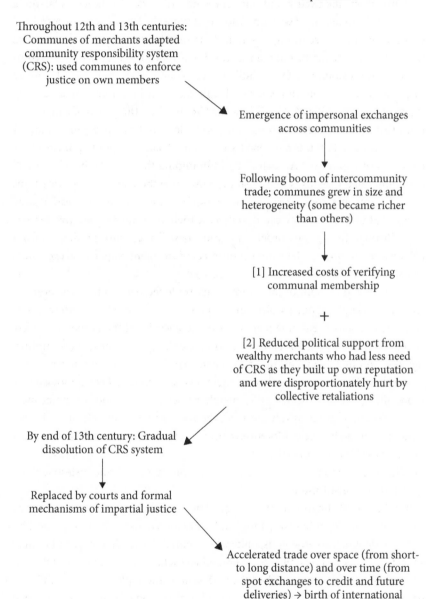

CONTRACT ENFORCMENT
INSTITUTIONS   MARKETS

Small markets within home community,
with exchanges based on personal
reputation

Throughout 12th and 13th centuries:
Communes of merchants adapted
community responsibility system
(CRS): used communes to enforce
justice on own members

Emergence of impersonal exchanges
across communities

Following boom of intercommunity
trade; communes grew in size and
heterogeneity (some became richer
than others)

[1] Increased costs of verifying
communal membership

+

[2] Reduced political support from
wealthy merchants who had less need
of CRS as they built up own reputation
and were disproportionately hurt by
collective retaliations

By end of 13th century: Gradual
dissolution of CRS system

Replaced by courts and formal
mechanisms of impartial justice

Accelerated trade over space (from short-
to long distance) and over time (from
spot exchanges to credit and future
deliveries) → birth of international
trade and financial markets

FIGURE C.1   Coevolution of institutions and markets in medieval Europe

never meet again after a transaction is made. Thus, according to standard institutional economics, modern markets require third-party enforcement of contracts by centralized regulatory states.[8] But how does the transition from personal to impersonal exchanges occur? Greif's study fills this gap.

Throughout the twelfth and thirteenth centuries, merchants across far-flung corners of Europe traded with one another despite the lack of strong centralized states at the time. According to Greif, these merchants were able to overcome transaction problems through an institutional innovation known as the community responsibility system (CRS). In this system, each merchant belonged to a self-governed commune, a social unit that "fell into a grey area between states and communities."[9] This is how the CRS worked. Imagine that a merchant from Commune A refused to pay for goods delivered by his business partner from Commune B. If this happened, Commune B had the right to punish all the members of Commune A, such as by impounding their goods. In this way, all communes had incentives to punish their own members for contract violations against merchants from other communes, not because the commune leaders were altruistic, but because they cared to protect their commune's collective reputation. Through this "public-order, reputation-based" mechanism,[10] distinct from personal reputation mechanisms of contract enforcement, impersonal exchanges across communities flourished in Europe.

Over time, the boom of intercommunity trade fed back to the institution of CRS that brought about its birth in the first place. As communes grew in size and heterogeneity (i.e., some merchants became wealthier than others), two key changes occurred. First, the ease of cheating and the costs of verifying communal membership increased. Dishonest merchants could escape from one commune to another. Also, as the number of members increased, it became logistically more difficult to track down every member's behavior. Second, wealthier merchants benefited progressively less from the CRS as they could rely on their own reputation to do business. Moreover, compared to smaller merchants, they had a lot more to lose from collective retaliations against their commune. Thus wealthy merchants began to withdraw their political support for CRS and instead lobbied for alternative institutions.

By the end of the thirteenth century, signs of disintegration appeared in the CRS. For example, in England, more and more merchants opted to register their personal debt in the Close Rolls, under the common law. Individuals, rather than collectives, took responsibility for commercial exchanges. In 1275, the Statute of Westminster I officially abolished the CRS system and replaced it with "individual responsibility, territorial law, central administration of justice, and personal collateral." Greif notes that this replacement process was not a clean, sharp transition but "took time to devise, implement, and perfect."[11]

Nevertheless, Greif asserts, the outgrowth of formal contract enforcement mechanisms from the CRS laid the foundation for an acceleration of trade over space (from short to long distance) and over time (from spot exchanges to credit and future deliveries). From this point onward, he declares, "international trade was born." Even though the CRS system was eventually abolished and replaced by formal institutions such as courts and the rule of law, Greif concludes that "by supporting intercommunity impersonal exchange," the CRS was "central to the development of Europe's financial markets" and "the emergence and development of the first European multinationals." Further, he stresses that "the modern European state's involvement in contract enforcement was not a precondition to impersonal exchange."[12] Rather, it was an intermediate form of impersonal exchange—intercommunity exchange—that gave impetus to centralized state interventions, which then made international trade possible.

This discussion reviews, in several zigzag steps, the coevolution of markets and contract-enforcement institutions in late medieval Europe. Note that this coevolutionary process, which laid down a skeletal foundation for the rule of law, financial markets, multinationals, and long-distance trade, preceded the Glorious Revolution of 1688 by more than three hundred years! The events of 1688 presented a structural break that pushed England's economy from a market-building to a market-expansion stage.[13] But as a coevolutionary remapping of Greif's account makes clear, formal limits on centralized states and parliamentary institutions were not the institutions that built markets in Europe's early history.

The Revolution of Public Finance in the Antebellum United States

Today, America is almost universally regarded as a beacon of democratic and capitalist success. Following Acemoglu, Johnson, and Robinson, the standard story asserts that English colonists had brought institutions of good governance with them to American soil, "providing secure property rights to a broad cross section of society" and thereby planting the seeds of long-term economic success.[14] This story posits that "the European form of good institutions protecting private property" is the "root cause" of development.[15]

But was this how development *really* happened in America? Setting aside the violent expropriation of other populations that simultaneously took place,[16] did a democratic tradition prevent corruption and the extraction of economic gains by a minority of elites among the descendants of European settlers? Did America, upon the ratification of the Constitution in 1789, begin with a complete package of good institutions—ranging from legal systems, uniform taxation codes, and

rules on corporate governance, to hard budget constraints on state governments—
that is today celebrated as the foundation of modern capitalism? How did governments raise funds to build massive transportation projects that connected
vast swaths of undeveloped land and thereby enable interstate commerce?

John Wallis's studies of the historical development of public finance in America shed nuanced light on these questions. Like Greif, Wallis never once used
the word "coevolution" in his accounts, yet the coevolutionary logic he traces is
unmistakable. In "Constitutions, Corporations, and Corruption," Wallis opens
with this rhetorical question: "Did state government efforts to provide the physical and commercial infrastructure lead to changes in, or follow from, existing
economic and political institutions?"[17] His answer is that causality ran both ways,
just as we saw in the expansion of trade in medieval Europe and in the capitalist revolution of post-1978 China. Borrowing from Wallis's accounts, below,
I reconstruct a trajectory of mutual causal change between America's state constitutional rules and markets during the antebellum period. This narrative is
summarized in figure C.2.

As Wallis points out, in 1790 American state governments did not pronounce
constitutional rules on public debt issuance or the creation of corporations. Yet
by 1852, eleven states revised their constitutions to include laws not only on
public financing but also on corporatization, two issues that at first glance seem
unrelated. To understand how this political change originated and interacted
with markets, we must go back to the early 1800s and a fundamental problem:
state governments were eager to spur rapid economic growth through infrastructure projects but could not raise local taxes. (This is a familiar problem for
present-day China. As I related in chapters 3, 5, and 6, it mirrors the conundrum
facing local governments after fiscal recentralization in 1994.)

By the 1820s, Wallis writes, the expansion of democratic institutions and vot-
ing rights for white males intensified pressures on state governments to deliver
visible economic results to their constituents. At the time, the most vital means of
growth promotion was construction of cross-state transportation, such as canals
and railways. Vast expanses of undeveloped land stood to appreciate many times
in value once transportation was constructed.[18] Moreover, if people could travel
easily from coast to coast, commerce would surely boom.

However, democracy posed a constraint on development ambitions. Local
residents did not want to pay taxes for cross-state projects that would benefit
other states. Exacerbating this free-rider problem was geographic mobility. If a
state insisted on raising taxes, its residents could simply move elsewhere. In order
to build massive infrastructure without taxing local populations, state governments came up with what seemed like a perfect solution; Wallis calls it "taxless
finance."

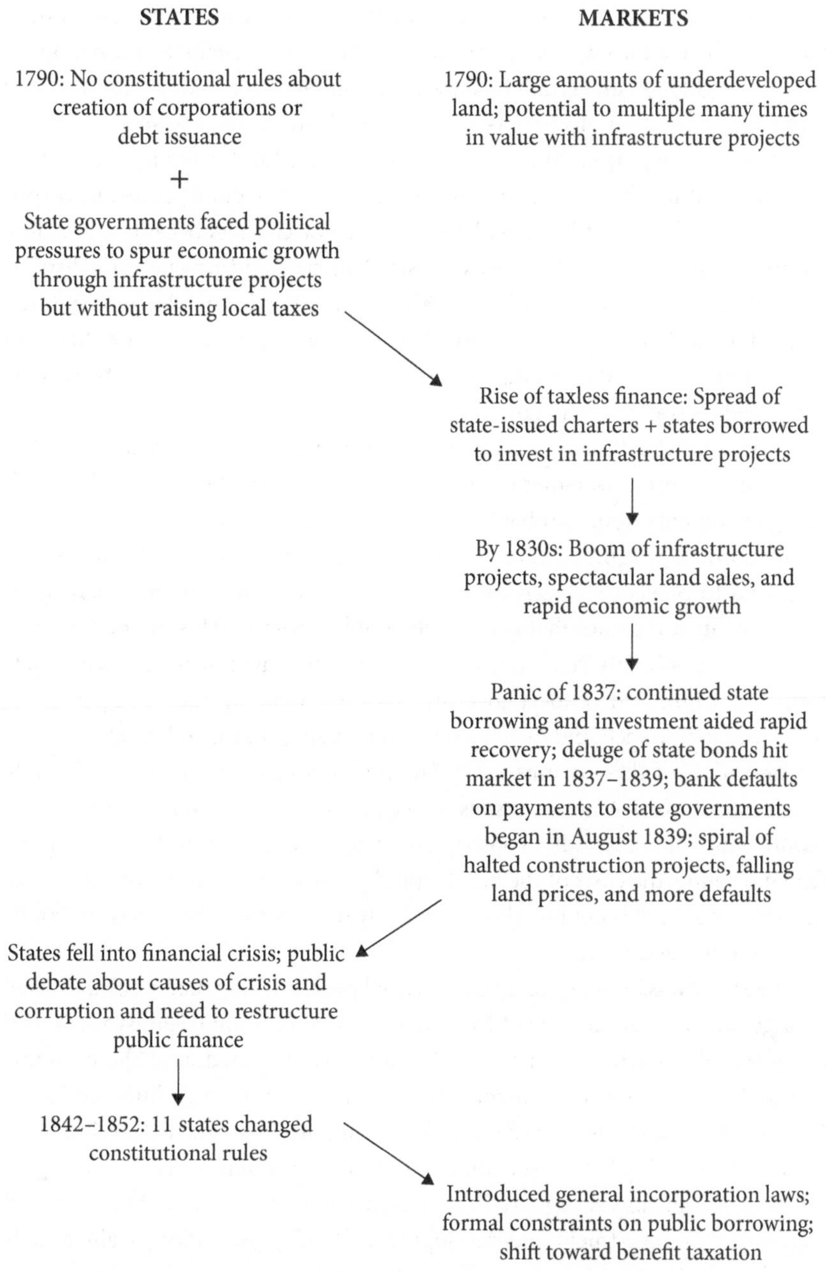

STATES	MARKETS
1790: No constitutional rules about creation of corporations or debt issuance	1790: Large amounts of underdeveloped land; potential to multiple many times in value with infrastructure projects

+

State governments faced political pressures to spur economic growth through infrastructure projects but without raising local taxes

Rise of taxless finance: Spread of state-issued charters + states borrowed to invest in infrastructure projects

By 1830s: Boom of infrastructure projects, spectacular land sales, and rapid economic growth

Panic of 1837: continued state borrowing and investment aided rapid recovery; deluge of state bonds hit market in 1837–1839; bank defaults on payments to state governments began in August 1839; spiral of halted construction projects, falling land prices, and more defaults

States fell into financial crisis; public debate about causes of crisis and corruption and need to restructure public finance

1842–1852: 11 states changed constitutional rules

Introduced general incorporation laws; formal constraints on public borrowing; shift toward benefit taxation

FIGURE C.2   Coevolution of states and markets in the antebellum United States

Instead of raising taxes, state governments issued charters to private companies in exchange for ownership interest. Charters were essentially monopoly or exclusive rights to run certain businesses, among which banking was especially profitable. The value of charters rested on exclusivity, but the more exclusive the charters, the greater "the possibility of creating (and charging for) private rents by limiting charters against the benefits of wider public access to corporate forms and lines of business." The issuance of charters became a breeding ground for grand corruption between state officials and private capitalists, as Wallis describes: "In New York, the Albany Regency headed by Martin Van Buren granted bank charters only to its political allies. In Arkansas, the state chartered a bank and capitalized it by issuing state bonds, and then allowed the bank to be controlled by two powerful families."[19]

Aside from charters, state governments also borrowed and then invested in infrastructure projects, either directly or through banks. Riding on public faith that governments would probably not default on loans, state governments could easily secure large sums of money for construction by issuing bonds, which were then sold to banks (which in turn brokered them on the London market) or reinvested in companies that constructed public projects. This method of public financing is highly reminiscent of current-day "investment financing platforms" in China, where local governments rush to set up shell companies for infrastructure projects and then borrow money using land as collateral to finance the operation of these companies.[20] The problem of taxless financing in early nineteenth-century America, just as we see in China today, is that taxpayers bore "contingent liabilities."[21] If a construction project succeeded and generated sufficient revenue, the costs of the bonds could be covered. But if the project failed, the debt would fall on public shoulders. Early on, however, the American public received only rave news.

The 1830s was boom time. The Erie Canal proved wildly successful and raked in large fortunes for the state of New York.[22] Elsewhere, Ohio, Pennsylvania, and Maryland also started building canals. Land prices soared, and the economy surged. By 1836, state governments had chartered more than six hundred banks. Between 1790 and 1860, they spent $425 million on infrastructure improvements, outstripping federal spending of $54 million. Wallis sums up, "State governments, by any measure, played a central role in the promotion of financial and transportation investment and development."[23] This observation, again, exactly describes local state-led growth in present-day China.

But boom soon turned into bust. Financial troubles struck in 1837, marking the start of "America's first great depression."[24] In 1837, restrictive lending policies in Britain, combined with the decline of cotton prices, forced American banks to suspend payments. But as Wallis recounts, the economy quickly rebounded after the Panic of 1837. By 1839, prices and trade recovered to pre-1837 levels and land sales peaked. Driving this rapid recovery was aggressive borrowing and investment among state governments. Lured by the land boom, states continued to borrow heavily from banks to finance infrastructure projects, despite the financial panic in 1837. Canal and railroad construction increased the price of land, stimulating land sales as well as the economy and spurring yet more borrowing. This frenzy of construction and borrowing extended from commercial centers in the northeast to states in the south and west.

A deluge of state bonds hit the market after 1836.[25] In addition to debts issued by established states like New York and Pennsylvania, other new players borrowed through nascent investment banks. "This was an enormous amount of debt to put on the market in a very short period of time," Wallis observes.[26] As a result, it became increasingly difficult for banks to sell these bonds. In August of 1839, the Morris Canal and Banking Company, to whom the state of Indiana had sold bonds, became the first bank to default on payments to state governments. As construction projects came to a screeching halt, a downward spiral of falling land prices and more defaults followed. The depression lasted four years, and states fell into deep financial holes.

The financial crisis stirred heated public and legislative debates about its causes, the scourge of corruption, and the need to restructure public finance. Wallis describes a process of critical self-reflection that strikes me as perhaps uniquely American. Instead of pointing fingers at particular individuals for the crisis, "states, in general, decided that bad institutions were the cause of the crisis."[27] States had gotten into this mess through taxless finance, so to prevent the problem from recurring, legislators changed their constitutions to limit taxless finance.

Within ten years from 1842, eleven states changed their constitutions, enshrining in law a body of rules that are today hailed as quintessential market-supporting institutions. These included a general incorporation law that allowed free entry to all lines of businesses, restrictions on the amount and procedures of public borrowing, and uniform property tax codes. A general shift toward benefit taxation decentralized fiscal responsibilities so that by the 1900s, city rather than state governments took the lead in providing infrastructure for public utilities (water, gas, sewage). As Wallis stresses, the Crisis of 1839 was not an exogenous shock but endogenous to earlier methods of taxless finance. It was the onset of crisis that forced politicians to make a difficult transition from taxless to tax-based public financing. Through this winding journey, punctured by a major depression, America entered the twentieth century with an impressive fleet of physical infrastructure and a scaffolding of rules fit for a modern market economy.

When viewed from a coevolutionary perspective, it becomes clear that the United States did not in fact acquire a complete package of market-supporting institutions upon independence. Instead, the components of this package were evolved following independence, propelled by the economic depression that grew out of a period of rapid market building. It would be too simplistic to equate democracy with good institutions and to draw a linear causal arrow from democracy itself to capitalist success. As we learn from revisiting America's past, democracy offers certain benefits for development (e.g., public deliberation on mitigating corruption and financial risks), but it also imposes certain constraints (e.g., inducing politicians to provide public goods without raising taxes). American history presents a story about a collective of politicians and people who *learn* to make democracy work, not a statement that democracy always and by itself works. To recommend that other countries replicate the current-day institutions of America is to ignore the rich and dynamic lessons provided by American history.

Coevolutionary Dynamics in the Unlikely Rise of Nollywood

Do we expect to find coevolutionary dynamics in other parts of the contemporary developing world? Being underdeveloped or still developing by themselves indicates that states and markets have yet to coevolve. Developing countries are akin to Humble County in the Chinese context; we cannot trace extended coevolutionary chains in Humble's history precisely because little change occurred in the first two decades and the first few steps of coevolution had only been recently taken. Nevertheless, if we look carefully within developing countries, we can find *pockets* of coevolutionary change in the most unlikely places, hidden in plain sight. One extraordinary instance is the rise of the filmmaking and creative industry in Nigeria—known as Nollywood—within a burst of twenty years.

Social scientists typically associate Nigeria with poverty, state failure, endemic corruption, and oil-derived wealth for the few. It is rarely noticed that Nigeria has produced the second-largest film industry in the world, behind Hollywood and ahead of Bollywood in terms of production volume. From its humble beginning as low-budget movies produced by amateurs and sold informally in the Alaba market of Lagos, Nollywood has generated US$800 million in revenue as of 2013,[28] making it the second-largest export sector after oil.[29] Unlike the oil industry, the fruits of the movie industry are widely spread through job creation for millions of Nigerians, especially aspiring and creative young people. It is also prized among viewers throughout Africa and the African diaspora as a conduit for telling African stories. In recent years, the industry has attracted millions of dollars in foreign investment and even Hollywood actors. *Half a Yellow Sun*, which made its debut on global markets in 2014, starred Oscar nominee Chiwetal Ejiofor from *12 Years A Slave*. The success of Nollywood has spread to other African countries, inspiring an emergent Gollywood in Ghana and Riverwood in Kenya.

Nollywood succeeded despite seemingly impossible odds. During the early twentieth century, filmmaking was introduced to Nigeria by British colonizers and subsequently caught on among the local population. By the 1980s, however, the film industry had all but collapsed. The Nigerian economy was in shambles after currency devaluation in 1986. The spread of violence after the end of the civil war forced people to stay home, eliminating audiences at movie theaters. There was no institutional funding or formal training grounds for moviemakers, much less state subsidies. In an environment where basic law and order was lacking, the protection of intellectual property rights (IPR) was of least concern to the Nigerian authorities and people. How could a film industry emerge and thrive within two decades under such ominous conditions?

In 1992 the moribund industry was unexpectedly revived by a confluence of regional technological shifts and one entrepreneur's enterprising idea. The early 1990s was a time when markets in Asia were actively replacing VCDs and VHSs with new technological devices. These obsolete products were cheaply exported and sold to Nigerian traders, one of whom was named Kenneth Nnubue. After he purchased a large shipment of blank tapes from Taiwan, Nnubue thought that if content was added to the tapes, they would sell better. So, investing his own funds, he made a video titled *Living in Bondage*, a story about a man who sold his soul to witchcraft in exchange for wealth, described as "the first movie to ever depict modern Western Africa through Nigerian lens."[30] The video became a blockbuster, selling more than 750,000 hard copies, which Nigerians could watch in the relative safety of their homes. This success inspired numerous others to follow, launching a new era of film production in a home video format.

Given rampant piracy and the absence of formal distribution channels, how could producers turn a profit on projects in which they had invested their own money? The answer was to make movies quickly and cheaply and then distribute them widely through informal channels. Even by the 2000s, Nollywood movies were produced with as little as $15,000 and churned out in approximately a week.[31] Filmmakers sold their movies directly to traders (known as "marketers") stationed in the major electronics markets. Movies were copied onto blank discs and then sold through the marketers' informal networks, including to homes and small parlors, where movies were shown for minimal fees. Pirates ripped off releases in about two weeks,[32] so movies had to be sold in large volume at great speed in order to outrun piracy. Another adaptive strategy was to immediately remake popular films into multiple sequels. Consequently, Nollywood movies were generally of poor quality and catered slavishly to popular tastes. A *New York Times* article described them as mostly "awful, marred by slapdash production, melodramatic acting and ludicrous plots."[33] Veteran Nigerian director Eddie Ugbomah agreed: "You don't produce 20 films a week. You must be producing rubbish."[34]

Yet even though piracy forced moviemakers to produce low-quality movies hurriedly and cheaply, it served a constructive role in spurring an initial wave of demand for Nollywood movies, what in Chinese may be termed "earning the first pot of gold." Rutschman describes the emergence of a "parallel circuit" of distribution where legal copies of the movies were simultaneously sold alongside pirated copies. Precisely because it was informal and ran at low costs, this wide distribution network reached out to tens of millions of consumers within a short time, which "catapulted [the emerging industry] to unprecedented levels of popularity, thereby increasing demand for both legitimate and illegitimate copies."[35] Arewa adds that widespread unauthorized distribution helped to build brand recognition "among a wide network of Africans on the continent and in the diaspora," such that later on, "losses from sales were ameliorated by increases in the intangible value of the Nollywood brand."[36]

The emergence of a market triggered the gradual replacement rather than the reinforcement of the original operational strategies that germinated demand for films. In the 2000s, as Nollywood movies became more popular and profitable, moviemakers started to attract formal funding from external sources. One of them was the BBC World Service Trust, which collaborated with Nigerian filmmakers in 2004 to produce a soap opera series with an educational message on AIDS.[37] Nollywood also evolved toward professionalization. At the founding stage, most participants were self-taught, like director Lancelot Imasuen, who proudly proclaimed in an interview: "I have no godfather. I am a product of myself and God. So I can categorically say today, I picked up the art of filmmaking from the street."[38] Over time, Nollywood developed a corps of full-time personnel and an array of acting, directing, and production schools. By 2002, the Actors Guild grew to five thousand members, a tenfold increase from 1996.[39] Then in 2005, a powerful new technology was introduced to Nigeria: YouTube. Unauthorized postings of movies appeared, producing a new piracy threat but also a new business opportunity.

As operations readapted to environmental shifts, Nollywood entered a phase of market bifurcation and consolidation. Rutschman points to the emergence of a two-tier consumer base, each served by a distinct production and dissemination model: "a low-budget tier, in which the paradigms and dynamics of old

Nollywood persist; and a top-tier, which higher budgets and better technical quality leading to an aesthetic revision of cinematographic patterns."[40] The higher-end market led the way toward formalization, digitization, and globalization. One member of this vanguard was director Kunle Afolayan, whose 2009 movie *The Figurine* was screened in theaters alongside Hollywood features. The *New York Times* wrote optimistically that "people have begun to speak of an emerging movement—New Nollywood—that has captivated a new generation of would-be filmmakers."[41]

Moving on to the recent decade, we observe further state and market adaptations motivated by the emergence of a new Nollywood during the 2000s. The state, conspicuously missing from the industry in the previous twenty years, belatedly stepped in to offer a helping hand. In 2010 the government invested 200 million naira (US$1.23 million) in a loan program for filmmakers. Still more recently, the Nigerian president pledged more funds to sponsor a training program for Nollywood practitioners and subsidies for private institutions that offered training and certification services in film production. On the market front, Jason Njoku, an English entrepreneur of Nigerian descent, founded iRoko, the African version of Netflix, which streams movies to subscribers. After iRoko received a multimillion-dollar investment from an American company in 2011, it became the largest distributor of Nollywood movies, reaching a global online audience.[42]

As Nollywood evolved toward formalization, demand for stronger enforcement of IPR stepped up among regulators and top-tier producers. While unauthorized distribution helped the industry take off at a founding stage, Arewa qualifies that "Nollywood has reached a point where higher levels of copyright enforcement would be beneficial to further development of the industry."[43] In 2006 the government transferred the Nigerian Copyright Commission from the Ministry of Culture to the Ministry of Justice,[44] signaling the agency's shift in function from cultural promotion to IPR enforcement. Today, the website of the commission prominently advertises raids on pirated goods and penalties against convicted pirates. Nollywood's experience suggests that IPR protection was the product—rather than precursor and cause—of an emerging creative industry. Figure C.3 summarizes my analysis of the coevolution of operational strategies and markets in Nollywood.

While the particulars of Nigeria's industry-specific case and China's political-economic transformation since 1978 obviously make up two different worlds, a comparison of the two reveals striking parallels in coevolutionary dynamics and market-building strategies. First, both the Nigerian and Chinese cases reveal a process of market coevolution that may be divided into three distinct stages: building, consolidation, and expansion. In Nollywood, the domestic market for

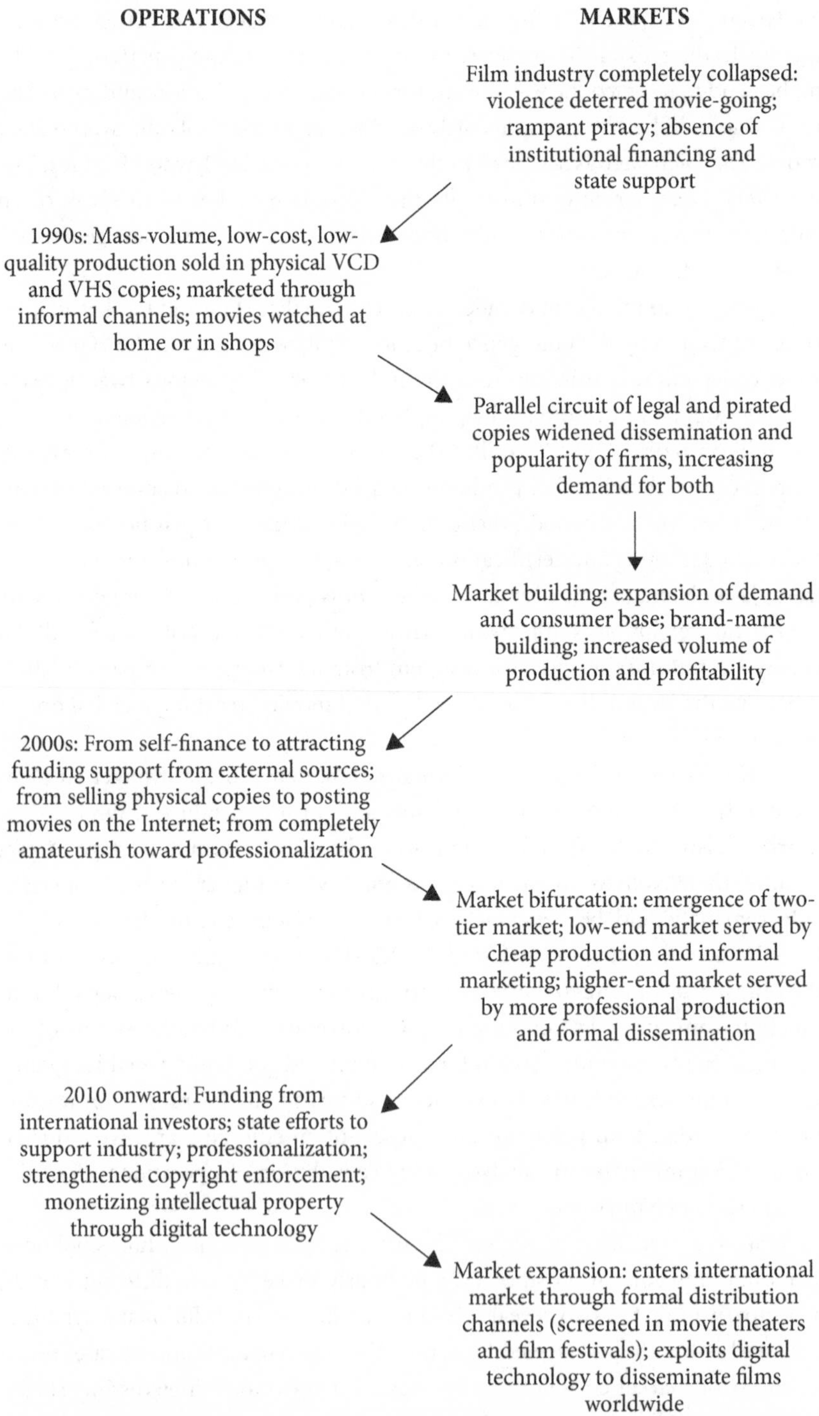

OPERATIONS   **MARKETS**

Film industry completely collapsed:
violence deterred movie-going;
rampant piracy; absence of
institutional financing and
state support

1990s: Mass-volume, low-cost, low-
quality production sold in physical VCD
and VHS copies; marketed through
informal channels; movies watched at
home or in shops

Parallel circuit of legal and pirated
copies widened dissemination and
popularity of firms, increasing
demand for both

Market building: expansion of demand
and consumer base; brand-name
building; increased volume of
production and profitability

2000s: From self-finance to attracting
funding support from external sources;
from selling physical copies to posting
movies on the Internet; from completely
amateurish toward professionalization

Market bifurcation: emergence of two-
tier market; low-end market served by
cheap production and informal
marketing; higher-end market served
by more professional production
and formal dissemination

2010 onward: Funding from
international investors; state efforts to
support industry; professionalization;
strengthened copyright enforcement;
monetizing intellectual property
through digital technology

Market expansion: enters international
market through formal distribution
channels (screened in movie theaters
and film festivals); exploits digital
technology to disseminate films
worldwide

FIGURE C.3 Coevolution of operational strategies and markets in Nollywood

a movie industry was built over the 1990s, bifurcated and consolidated over the 2000s, and then expanded to regional and international audiences in the 2010s. Recalling the coevolutionary paths of coastal locales in China (Forest Hill and Blessed County), we find a similar pattern. Markets were built during the 1980s and early 1990s; then chaotic markets settled around winners who had trumped competition and emerged dominant; and finally successful homegrown businesses began to invest outward. In each of these stages, functionally and qualitatively different institutions were employed to promote markets.

Second, in both the rise of Nollywood and China's capitalist economy, pre-existing weak institutions were adapted to build markets. In Nollywood, unauthorized distribution of films, regarded in developed economies as violation of IPR and a sign of weak state capacity, catapulted Nollywood films into unprecedented popularity throughout Africa, generating consumer demand where none previously existed. As Rutschman acutely sums up, "Low levels of intellectual property, when combined with a loose regulatory framework, may create an environment that *best fosters* the growth of incipient creative industries in the global South and ultimately pave the way for future formalization."[45] Weak institutions by themselves, however, do not build markets; it is the adaptive and ingenious responses of ground-level actors that activate their constructive potential. Nollywood filmmakers improvised their production and distribution strategies to fit changing environmental conditions. Likewise but in a different context, China's local officials also adapted property rights structures and growth-promotion policies to suit evolving demands and resources as income levels rose.

Third, regional connections spurred development in both the Nigerian and Chinese cases. Nollywood benefited from the transfer of outdated technology (VHSs and VCDs) from Asia to Africa. The abundant flow of cheap blank tapes from Asia provided an essential fuel for the Nigerian film industry, sparked by an entrepreneurial idea to put content onto the tapes. This dynamic parallels the migration of unwanted industries from coastal to inland China that stimulated late growth spurts in the latter. Additionally, as the case of Nollywood suggests, regional transfer of opportunities may actually work better than charity in helping locals make their own success. A case in point is 1 Million Shirts, a charity founded by American businessman Jason Sadler that asked for donations of old T-shirts to send to Africa. As the founder said in an interview with *Time*, his was an altruistic initiative "to motivate people to get off their butts, get off the couch and do something to help."[46] But instead of helping and earning the gratitude of Africans, Sadler's good intentions drew outrage, especially from African businesses. *Time* explains, "Flooding the market with free goods could bankrupt the people who already sell them."[47] Another study also reports that the textiles industry in many African countries was hit hard by bales of free clothing coming from the West. In Zambia, textiles workers staged protests against the import of donated garments that threatened their livelihoods.[48]

Why did donated T-shirts hurt the textiles market while exported cheap tapes sparked the film market? Because those free T-shirts were donated under the false presumption that Africans lacked shirts to wear or could not make their own shirts. As Olopade points out in her critique of charity-making companies like TOMS, which donates a pair of free shoes to poor communities for every pair of shoes bought: "Unfortunately, the model ignores the fact that plenty of poor people have shoes, both on their feet (like T-shirts) and available for local purchase. In the end, it exploits shoeless victims as a brand differentiator."[49] Asian exporters were not trying to "help" when they sold tapes cheaply to African markets; they were merely trying to get rid of obsolete products and earn some income from selling them. For African traders, the tapes they bought were cheap but not free. So like market actors everywhere, they were motivated to add value to the tapes to sell them for profits. This is why, ironically, while business as usual may stimulate growth opportunities, charitable gifts may end up inadvertently disrupting fragile markets in the Third World. In other words, no charity could be better than thoughtless charity.

Summing up the three cases I have explored—medieval Europe, the antebellum United States, and Nollywood—we see further evidence that development *is* a coevolutionary process. As many developing countries feature highly fragmented state power and lack a single authoritarian party to launch reforms nationwide (as seen in post-1978 China, post-independence Singapore, and post-1961 South Korea), we are likely to find coevolutionary processes only in pockets of these political economies, as in the case of Nigeria's movie industry. Aside from Nigeria, another example is Indonesia, where a local hail-a-ride business, known as Go-Jek (similar to Uber), has experienced "crazy growth," in the words of its founder. This business succeeded precisely because of poor transportation, constant traffic congestion, and weak governmental regulation.[50] Similar to the experiences found in Nigeria and China, which tapped upon unlikely resources to launch markets (weak IPR enforcement in Nigeria and a combination of patronage ties and communist political norms in China), the Indonesian case also illustrates the creative exploitation of weak conditions to tackle the distinct challenges of poor societies. With Indonesia, Nigeria, and China combined— three of the world's largest emerging markets—one can scarcely claim that such experiences are exceptional.

Acknowledging the reality that development is a coevolutionary process has far-reaching implications for the type of questions we ask, the methods we employ, the causation we trace, and the policies we make. On the theoretical front, it raises new questions: How do state and markets interact and change together over time? And what are the underlying conditions that enable and facilitate coevolutionary processes? These are the two main questions I have tried to address, as a first step of a larger and long-term agenda, through an examination of China's capitalist revolution since 1978. In my attempt to answer these questions, I lay out the conceptual and analytic building blocks of a coevolutionary framework. This framework, as I suggest through the preceding narratives, may be broadly applied to other national and temporal contexts.

What Is the China Model?

What is the China model, if indeed there is one? And what should we learn from it? For a long time, pundits have searched for particular models of economic success; the common assumption has been that if the right model can be replicated in other settings, growth will follow. The Washington Consensus prescribed a list of policy recommendations that is presumed to work magic everywhere. In its heyday, Japan's economic miracle motivated an eager search for the secrets of the Japanese model. Today, with China's rise, attention has shifted to uncovering the China model or the Beijing Consensus, as some call it. This desire for a one-size-fits-all formula is understandable. The point of my book, however, is that this is precisely the wrong target of search.

The universal model of success does not comprise particular structures and strategies found in particular contexts at particular times, be it the United States, Western Europe, Japan, or China. As I have shown in this book, particular solutions for market promotion vary over the course of development, within countries, and even within locales of a single country. In China, the list of particular policies, strategies, and institutions that evolved after 1978 runs very long, including everything from export-driven manufacturing, dual-track pricing, hybrid property rights, fiscal contracting, state capitalism through mega-SOEs, and capitalism from below to you-name-it (as James Palmer aptly notes, "because China is so vast, its successes can be attributed to whatever your pet cause is").[51] Yet all these features prevail only in certain times and in certain parts of China. If by "model" we mean a set of characteristics that are consistent over space and time, then none of these particular features make up the China model. One may cite single-party authoritarianism as a consistent structural feature, but this condition describes a regime type that is also found in North Korea, so it hardly serves as a useful model.

Rather, what is consistent over time and across space in reform-era China is the adaptive approach of *directed improvisation*; this is the China model of the past thirty-five years. The post-Mao generation of central reformers, starting with Deng, crafted a set of conditions that empowered primarily local state but also market actors to pursue development adaptively. It is these ground-level actors who improvised numerous particular solutions to continuously changing problems, specific to their locale and income level, thereby fueling a coevolutionary process of development. These adaptive responses interacted with an unequal distribution of growth opportunities and endowments across regions, producing a variety of subnational coevolutionary paths. While some like Blessed County sped ahead economically and institutionally, others like Humble County lagged behind. These divergent trajectories of change spilled into one another and cumulated to revolutionize the entire political economy.

That effective adaptation is desirable and ought to be encouraged is obvious, but this observation is not useful by itself. This study has gone further to identify the sources of adaptive capacity. Unlike several others, I do not attribute these sources solely to history. I agree that past experiences impact the starting points of nations and their arsenals of ideas and tools for problem solving. But history is not destiny. Nor does it cause or foreclose adaptive capacity. Like individual creativity, societal adaptability is not a gift endowed to some lucky few but an attribute that can be cultivated. The uplifting message of China's story is that even when fortune deals a poor hand of cards, it is possible to shape conditions that foster adaptive responses to ever-evolving challenges.

The conditions that promote adaptation are what I call *meta-institutions*, distinguished from institutions in general. Institutions are particular solutions to particular problems. For instance, one way to deter business partners from reneging on promises is to sign written contracts, backed by a formal judiciary. This is one possible remedy, but it is not the only or best one. There are many ways to resolve or mitigate any given problem. Meta-institutions are institutions that guide the processes and methods of problem solving within and across communities. Expressed in North's terms, such institutions are "the underlying forces shaping the process of change."[52]

One essential step toward promoting adaptation is to distinguish *control* from *influence*. In complicated situations where the range of problems and solutions can be predicted in advance, principals seek to exercise control over agents in order to achieve desired outcomes. But in complex settings—exemplified by all political economies—the possible scope of problems and solutions and even preferences lies beyond human anticipation and planning. In these situations, seeking to exert full control is futile and may even foreclose useful solutions. Nevertheless, there is room to exert influence so as to direct bottom-up adaptation toward constructive and collective purposes.

In the context of reform-era China, central reformers exercised influence by targeting three universal problems of adaptation, which I group under the themes of variation, selection, and niche creation. Each of these three problems manifests as follows: how to balance variety and uniformity in localized policy implementation (variation); how to clearly define and reward success within the bureaucracy (selection); and how to encourage distinct roles and beneficial exchanges among highly unequal regions (niche creation). Chapter 3 illuminates why seemingly modest incremental reforms nonetheless produced spectacular changes that revolutionized the entire political economy. Chapter 4 explores the micro-foundation of unusually entrepreneurial behavior among China's public agents and explains why such behavior, though generally growth- and revenue-promoting, also incurred widespread public resentment. Chapter 6 underscores the time-variant contributions of unequally endowed locales to one another's development, which in turn impacts China's national competitiveness. By tracing the state's responses to each of three main problems of adaptation, we arrive at a sharper understanding of why China's great transformation has displayed three distinct patterns: broad, bold, and uneven.

Stated in generic terms, my analysis of China and the other three national cases suggest six lessons on enhancing localization and adaptive output, summarized below.

1. Delimit boundaries of experimentation and flexibility

It is well-known that the Chinese leadership makes ample use of experimentation in policy making;[53] what I further emphasize is that effective experimentation has to be *bounded*. Free-for-all experimentation invites chaos, not adaptability. As examined in chapter 3, central commands in the CCP hierarchy are usually but not always ambiguous. Vague commands allow local flexibility and improvisation, generating feedback for central policy adjustments. On certain important national prohibitions, however (e.g., enforcement of land quotas), commands are clear. And on affirmative endorsements of a particular course of action (e.g., privatization), commands are clear. The mixture of vague and clear commands from the top signals to local agents which lines they cannot cross, how far they can experiment, and when they can boldly march forward.

2. Activate incremental changes across connected domains simultaneously

Incremental changes mean modifications of the preceding state, for example, from complete price control to partial price liberalization, then from partial to full price liberalization. Incremental changes are not necessarily small changes; some can radically transform political economies, depending on the preceding steps already taken. Activating incremental changes across many connected domains simultaneously is more likely to stimulate systemic changes of the type seen in China.

Recommendations that developing countries modestly target reforms in only one or a few areas may seem pragmatic, but they may not be effective.[54] To illustrate, if state-owned firms are allowed to sell surplus goods on the market but prices remain fixed by plan, then the consumer goods market is unlikely to take off. In another example, if public wages are raised but little is done to strengthen disciplinary mechanisms, then higher wages alone are unlikely to elicit a less predatory bureaucracy. As this book shows, China's reforms were multipronged even when they were carried out incrementally. Thus understood, what is needed for reforms in poor and weak societies is not replacement of the standard good-governance package with something "easier,"[55] but rather with a different package tailored to the tasks and constraints of market building. The latter would likely involve improvising strategies that defy orthodox prescriptions.

3. In the beginning, define success narrowly

The Chinese experience suggests that in order to achieve visible and rapid results, start by defining success narrowly. Focusing narrowly on a few goals (i.e., ends) should not be confused with making a few changes (i.e., means). The post-Mao leadership launched market reforms by initially defining bureaucratic success narrowly as economic success, deliberately de-emphasizing other goals; achieving rapid economic results, however, required reforms across a broad range of issues. It should be noted that narrow definitions of success may come at a political price when applied to the public sector.[56] Whereas companies may pursue profits single-mindedly, governments usually have to cater to multiple conflicting demands from society. Any reform program must thus consider who the primary agents of change are (e.g., government, companies, or nonprofit organizations) and whether success for these agents can be narrowly and clearly defined.

4. Give everyone a personal stake in the development process

States are massive organizations. Strong and motivated leaders cannot produce miracles by themselves if their teams are feeble and weakly incentivized. Distinctively in China, everyone in the bureaucracy, down to street-level regulatory officers and even schoolteachers, is given a personal stake in the development process. Their personal payoffs are linked to the fiscal performance of their locale and hiring unit. This is an adaptation of prebendalism, typically equated with corruption, to fuel bureaucratic entrepreneurism in the pursuit of profit-oriented goals. For local leaders, in addition to monetary rewards, career and reputational rewards are also tied to the development process.

However, once markets flourish, as we've seen in many parts of coastal China, this economic change spawns a different incentive for maintaining growth, one that may be more powerful than top-down assigned rewards: local leaders can derive extravagant personal rents by commanding power over booming economies. When poor, state agents at all ranks are inclined to extort and steal. When capitalist markets successfully take off, more lucrative and smarter avenues to trade power for money also emerges. Indeed, advanced market economies like the United States are not in fact free from corruption.[57] Rather, they are distinguished by grand and even legalized modes of corruption that provide some privileged players access to the game of fabulous wealth creation.[58]

5. Let some get rich first but pair up the poor and the rich

Opposite to Mao's attempts to suppress coastal development and prop up industries in the interior, Deng chose to open markets and let the natural comparative advantages of the coast work their magic. First-mover coastal locales "got rich first," coevolving larger markets and stronger institutions before the rest. They became the front engine of China's phenomenal growth. But not to forget, the interior provinces were the rear engines that supplied cheap labor and underpriced raw materials to the coast for manufacturing and export to the world. Going forward, central reformers aim to promote the migration of low-end industries from the coast to the interior, while pushing the coast to go upmarket onto higher ranks of the global value chain.

6. Harness weak institutions to build markets

Whether in the cases of reform-era China, medieval Europe, the antebellum United States, or Nollywood, adaptive agents deployed pre-existing "weak" institutions—weak from the perspective of modern formalized standards—to build markets, producing unorthodox and surprising solutions. Through the case of Forest Hill, chapter 5 has listed and examined a variety of market-building and market-preserving institutions in reform-era China. Table C.1 summarizes the two institutional varieties found in the other country cases.

The idea of building markets with weak institutions is counterintuitive, even paradoxical, because we normally think that weak institutions are impediments against economic development. Therefore, as this logic goes, we must first turn weak institutions into strong institutions that approximate those found in rich countries before it is possible to pursue growth. This logic then becomes entangled in a chicken-and-egg problem of how we can obtain strong institutions if growth is lacking in the first place.

My comparative analysis of coevolutionary paths across contexts points to a consistent and (in hindsight) obvious way out of vicious cycles of poverty and weak state capacity: make creative use of whatever is available. We miss the obvious because standard binary labels of "weak/strong" and "good/bad"

TABLE C.1 Examples beyond China of harnessing weak institutions to build markets

	"WEAK" INSTITUTIONS FOR BUILDING MARKETS	"STRONG" INSTITUTIONS FOR PRESERVING MARKETS
Late medieval Europe	Contract enforcement through communal responsibility and reputation mechanisms	Contract enforcement through individual responsibility and third-party regulation via centralized states
Antebellum United States	Taxless finance: use charters and state borrowing without taxation to finance infrastructure projects	Tax-supported finance: General incorporation laws and state borrowing backed by taxation
Nigeria's Nollywood	Use rampant piracy and informal channels to distribute films widely and cheaply	Enforcement of intellectual property rights and new digitized modes of dissemination

blinds us to the potential of nonmodern, nonformal, non-rule-of-law, and nondemocratic institutions. Our conventional and strongly rooted bias that the norms of the developed West are universally best leads us to regard any deviation from these norms only as weaknesses.[59] Consequently, institutions in developing societies are routinely identified by what they *are not* rather than by what they *are.*

Conventional theories that posit accelerated growth as a result of strong institutions are tailored to middle- and high-income economies. Poor countries begin with an abundance of so-called weak institutions; they need theories of development that occur *through* weak institutions.

Despite vastly different time periods and particular circumstances among the earlier examined cases of medieval Europe, the antebellum United States, and Nigeria's Nollywood vis-à-vis post-1978 China, we can trace some similar meta-conditions that facilitated or spurred adaptive responses. For example, after the financial crisis, American legislators chose to revise the constitutions across multiple connected domains, including corporatization, public borrowing, and taxation. It would not be possible to eliminate taxless finance by addressing only debt issuance without at the same time tackling complications created by the lack of uniform tax codes and the corruption inherent in chartering. This wide scope of legislative changes that swept American states from 1842 to 1852 does not fit the advice offered by some policy experts to present-day developing countries to limit reforms pragmatically to a few changes. Similar to the formulation of national reform packages in China (see chapter 3), America overhauled its public financial system in the early nineteenth century through multipronged reforms in intertwined domains. In both the Chinese and American cases, however, such reforms did not skip straight from one starting point to an ideal predetermined outcome. Systemic changes in both instances took place over multiple steps.

Where interventions that foster adaptive processes cannot be provided, it helps to at least *not* have the wrong interventions. As the evolution of the CRS in medieval Europe and Nollywood in Nigeria suggest, the *absence* of hegemonic external interventions allowed local improvisation to take place. Imagine a scenario where foreign consultants traveled back in time to twelfth-century Europe and saw the CRS in action. Following standard policies prescribed to developing countries today, these consultants would tell the medieval European merchants, "Your system of communal contractual enforcement is primitive. We have come from the future and can tell you definitively that the best system for capitalism is secure private property rights and centralized regulatory states. So abolish what you have now and replace it with the system of the future." The medieval merchants would probably stare at these well-meaning, sophisticated consultants with incredulity. How could they skip straight to centralized regulatory states in the twelfth century? And why should they abandon a system that is currently working for them?

When foreign experts enter developing contexts and insist that there is one universal standard of good institutions—namely, that found in wealthy capitalist societies—this by itself imposes a lethal impediment against localized adaptation. Imagine "good governance" in medieval European communes being measured according to how closely they approximated institutions of the future. Then imagine foreign consultants dispensing praise and conditional aid to these European communes based on how well they score in good governance alongside contemporary countries; such an index could be titled "Worldwide and Timeless Governance Indicators" (WTGI). Further imagine medieval commune leaders and merchants being herded into classrooms to be taught about the technicalities of replicating institutions from the future in their current communities. Could this be an environment that empowers medieval actors to improvise fitting solutions for the needs of their time?

Nollywood may have emerged and thrived in Nigeria precisely because this is a sector of the economy that neither foreign experts nor the government had expected to boom. Filmmakers, actors, and marketers were completely left to their own means. Initially, film producers defined success narrowly as selling movies en masse and quickly by catering to popular tastes (reminiscent of beehive campaigns launched by local officials in China to recruit investors of all types, regardless of quality). Early on, Nollywood movies were, as described by *The New York Times*, "awful." But Nigerian moviemakers didn't care because their consumers, mostly the poor, liked and bought their movies. After the film industry took off, the aesthetic preferences of suppliers and consumers evolved, and without needing advice or urging from outsiders, local production readapted to changing preferences. Imagine if foreign experts had introduced a program in the 1990s to help Nigerians produce quality films fit for a sophisticated audience, enforced IPR protection, and eliminated informal distribution channels. Would such a program have created a Nollywood? We may only speculate. But it is instructive to ponder the comments of a Nollywood director about Western-inspired movies shown in film festivals (which was the dominant mode of production during the colonial period):[60] "It cannot be sold. No African will pay a dime to buy it."[61]

Indeed, the relevance of this book need not be limited only to other developing countries; it may also extend to the reform of foreign aid institutions. As reviewed in chapter 2, there has been a growing chorus in the policy and aid community for adaptive programs that value local knowledge and are tailored to diverse local conditions.[62] A report by the Carnegie Endowment terms this shift a "second generation" of governance aid that "strives for best fit rather than best practices."[63] This promising agenda of localizing foreign aid and improvising fitting solutions is in essence similar to China's localized and adaptive style of market reforms. Before foreign experts can effectively go local, however, they need to first acquire and accumulate deep knowledge of local contexts in the Third World (just as local cadres in China must first grasp the fine-grained details of their communities before they can adaptively implement central policies). Without such contextual knowledge, it is not possible for aid technocrats to know the solutions that might fit particular problems in the communities they seek to help.

But while "going local" is widely embraced in principle, actualizing it is easier said than done. Aid professionals are long accustomed to prescribing best practices based on a universalistic assumption of good governance. They hail from similar backgrounds in finance and economics, trained at a small number of elite programs.[64] Their careers do not rest on evaluations by local aid recipients. And even if sympathetic to local voices, technocrats are constrained by organizational deliverables, where large projects with visible and scalable results are preferred over localized initiatives with uncertain payoffs.[65] All these conditions impede the adoption of adaptive approaches *within* aid agencies. The Harvard Kennedy School has tried to encourage adaptive approaches by urging practitioners to sign manifestos pledging support to "do development differently."[66] This is an important symbolic step, but actualizing meaningful change, as shown in this book, requires that we tackle concrete organizational impediments to change.

In a separate essay titled "Making Details Matter: How to Reform Aid Agencies to Generate Contextual Knowledge,"[67] I apply insights from this book to suggest some concrete guidelines for empowering and motivating aid agencies to care about the details of developing communities, a prerequisite for replacing best practices with best fit programs. This essay won the Global Development Network 2014 Essay Contest on the Future of Development Assistance, held in partnership with the Bill and Melinda Gates Foundation to "invite fresh thinking related to the future of aid." I hope this effort further suggests that the most valuable lessons offered by the Chinese experience are lessons on directing improvisation, not on whether its particular measures can be copied. Furthermore, these lessons need not apply only to other countries. Crafting meta-institutions for effective adaptation is a universal problem of human development.

Will China Stay Adaptive?

On a concluding note, it is worth speculating on the momentous question of whether China can stay adaptive. Already China has risen from low- to middle-income status. This escape from the poverty trap ushers in a set of novel challenges, encapsulated in the term "middle-income trap."[68] During the past decades, China successfully adapted institutions to build emerging markets, attract foreign investments, and become the factory of the world. Moving on, to advance from middle-income to sustainable long-term prosperity, it would have to evolve its economic methods and at the same time coevolve its existing administrative and political institutions.

Rather than to hazard simplistic predictions of whether China will succeed or fail, it is more useful to highlight some specific fault lines that have surfaced. One concern is whether the new leadership under Xi Jinping has the political muscle to pull off broad reforms necessary to address the range of problems that have accumulated since 1994. As I have argued, reforms in China were incremental yet broad in scope. The 1993 decision comprehensively tackled various distortions stemming from partial market reforms during the pre-1993 period. By now, new pressures have mounted to a near tipping point. Such problems include severe vertical fiscal imbalance, hidden debts incurred by local governments, overly rapid state-led urbanization, environmental degradation, a brewing real estate bubble, and, as I write this conclusion, an ongoing stock market meltdown that has wiped out stock values about ten times the size of Greece's economy.

As China develops a larger and more complex market economy, the problems that emerged have grown larger in stake and impossible to disentangle. An internal report distributed to Chinese leaders wrote, "There are so many problems now, interlocked like dogs' teeth."[69] The analogy of interlocked teeth expresses the difficulty of tackling one problem without simultaneously tackling other intertwined problems. When China was poor and had yet to open its door to global markets, there was relatively little to lose in trying out reforms; failures could be contained. Today, however, reforming a complex and open economy is like playing an extremely high-stakes game of Jenga; the pieces are stacked very tall, and a wrong move could topple the whole system.

Yet another concern is whether the Chinese leadership can evolve a new system of bureaucratic evaluation and incentives to suit an era of sprawling governing objectives. During the early decades of market building, the CCP state unambiguously defined bureaucratic success as economic success and lavished rewards upon those who delivered measurable results. This system worked to spur growth, but rising economic wealth forced priorities of governance to change. Today, local officials are expected not only to deliver material prosperity but also to maintain social harmony, protect the environment, supply public services, respond to public complaints, and even to promote happiness.[70]

On the surface, these developments appear to signal a more responsive and multitasking authoritarian state. But when implemented on the ground, the effects may be paralyzing. Zhao Shukai, a researcher at the State Council, provides an insightful assessment. In the example of petitioning, he observes that higher-level governments hold subordinates firmly accountable to complaints and petitions lodged by citizens. Officials at the grassroots are subject to hard targets that assess their performance by the number of petitions lodged in their jurisdiction.[71] But the higher levels pay little regard to "whether the grassroots governments have the responsibility or due power to deal with petitioning." The result, Zhao concludes, is that "the assessment system for maintaining social stability not only damages grassroots governments' trust for their superiors," but also incites opportunistic citizens to "take advantage of this unreasonable assessment system."[72] In other words, if this trend continues, local authorities would become neither formally accountable to society nor free to act single-mindedly toward narrow goals. This political mutation combines the worst of authoritarianism and populism.[73]

Moreover, President Xi's unprecedented, forceful crackdown on corruption at all ranks has exacerbated a palpable sense of paralysis within the bureaucracy. As emphasized in this book, corruption goes hand-in-hand with growth promotion. For local officials, the most lucrative stream of corruption comes not from brute extraction of private wealth but from greasing access to emerging and booming markets. Cozy state-business ties and collusive deals are often what it takes to assure entrepreneurs of their property rights and to entice investments. Moreover, setting aside corrupt dealings, all policy innovations entail political risks;

officials could easily be charged for corruption on the grounds of doing what has not been explicitly authorized. The crackdown on corruption as it is currently done indirectly stifles bureaucratic risk taking, innovation, and state-led growth.

The challenges facing China in the coming decades differ from those of the past in that they undermine the very meta-institutions that have made China so remarkably adaptive since 1978. This implies that in the future China needs to find new sources of adaptability and innovation. Instead of relying on the bureaucracy as an agent of change, as it has done in the past, the CCP must release and channel the immense creative potential of Chinese society. It is simplistic to assume that such a change has to involve formal democratization. It would also be unimaginative to think that we have exhausted all possibilities of political systems, that is, either multiparty democracy or single-party autocracy. Aside from introducing elections, there can be other ways to activate social creativity. Academic freedom is a clear place to start. Resisting social change in a globalized, open age is futile; Chinese leaders may only move with it.

If China fails to adapt to the twenty-first century, economic stagnation could stir domestic political instability that may in turn threaten international peace and order. The United States is unlikely to benefit from unrest in China given the inextricable ties between the two economies. If China succeeds, it will be a turning point in human history. For the first time in more than three hundred years, a non-Western nation may surpass the economic and political might of the West, and the balance of global power would be radically altered.

We bear witness to this critical juncture.

Appendix A

STEPS FOR MAPPING COEVOLUTION

Coevolution is a particular form of change involving adaptive mechanisms among two or more parts of a system.[1] In order to map this form of change, we will need to generate a panel dataset that captures institutional features in states and markets (or any pair of domains) over time. Generating such datasets poses significant challenges, especially in developing and authoritarian countries, where formally recorded data are sparse or guarded with secrecy.[2] This appendix describes four basic steps I follow in collecting data to map coevolutionary processes of development and how I adapted my fieldwork and structure of interviews to fit this analytic objective. Furthermore, I offer some suggestions for combining this method of multistep process tracing with quantitative tests. I describe these steps based on my research in China, but the procedures suggested may also be applied to a broad class of problems and contexts.[3]

1. *Identify two or more domains of significance*

"Domains" can encompass two (or more) populations, institutions, or spheres of action, for example, teachers and students, businesses and bureaucracies, state and economy, repression and resistance. These two domains coexist within a larger environment, which is termed a "system."

Governance or state capacity has multiple dimensions. Throughout this book, I focus on the bureaucracy for a compelling reason: it is the bureaucracy that executes decisions made by power holders.[4] Whether the bureaucracy has the incentives and ability to perform its assigned tasks, as well as how it interprets its tasks, is thus central to state capacity.[5]

Bureaucracy itself is still a complex cluster variable with many attributes. My research disaggregates the domain of bureaucracy into finer strands. A few examples include the assignment of tasks and targets, rewards and penalties associated with performance, and the interpretation of rules and what constitutes rule-breaking behavior.

Each of these subdomains is then converted into a template of semistructured interview questions. One needs to have sufficient contextual knowledge in order to translate abstract themes like "rules" into actual questions that respondents would be willing and indeed keen to discuss. For example, I studied the evolution of rules by focusing on the rules of bureaucratic financing (revenue generation and spending). I knew that this particular context would allow me to probe indirectly into extractive practices, such as fees and fines collection, and notions of property rights within bureaucracies, but it is not as sensitive as a conversation on corruption, which is normally out of bounds. Furthermore, by itself, bureaucratic financing is a neutral activity, neither good nor bad. When designing and asking questions, I focus simply on understanding what people do and why, rather than impose judgments that certain actions are by definition corrupt.

On the economy, I highlight industrialization and investments, setting aside higher-order economic arenas like financial markets and corporate governance. This is because in start-up economies like China, capital injection and conversion of agriculture to industry are the primary avenues of economic development. Institutions of corporate governance and financing usually come later.

2. Identify significant time periods

The second step is to identify the significant time periods of analysis. At the national level in China, the first obvious starting point is 1978, when the central leadership under Deng Xiaoping opened markets. The second is 1993, when the post-Deng leadership announced the decision to transition from partial to full-fledged market reforms. A subsequent policy break occurred in 2003, when the Hu-Wen leadership, emphasizing "harmonious development," took office.

At the local levels, the significant periods are deeply influenced by policy breaks at the central level, but they are not always identical. As a former county leader explained, "At the national level, you can clearly demarcate distinct stages, because every stage is defined by important meetings and policy pronouncements. . . . But at the grassroots, our implementation of policies is continuous, flowing from one administration into another."[6] In other words, the phases of reform and development among subnational units should be seen as being divided by approximate, rather than clear-cut, markers.[7]

To identify the significant periods of analysis for each local case, my research team and I began by asking several experienced cadres, "In your view, what are the significant periods of development in your locale?" We also asked about the characteristics of each period, whether and when watershed events or structural breaks occurred, the tenure and signature agenda of leaders, and so forth. These responses were checked against written sources, such as yearbooks, websites, and secondary accounts, and then used to guide the implementation of step 3, which is to document how the selected domains (step 1) manifested at each significant phase (step 2).

3. *Identify dominant traits in the significant periods*

My third step is to document the dominant traits of the selected domains at the significant periods of analysis. In undertaking this step, two points deserve elaboration. First, in political-economic settings, significant changes are often *qualitative* (or *structural*) rather than *quantitative* in nature. It is misleading to reduce different qualitative patterns to numbers on a continuous scale because such patterns constitute differences in *type* (A, B, C), rather than in *degree* (1, 2, 3).[8] For example, Thelen's *How Institutions Evolve* compares the sources of employee training, relationship between states and labor unions, and public policies toward the artisanal class across four advanced capitalist economies.[9] Her study shows that Germany's labor institutions are qualitatively *different* from those of the United States (A, B, C), not *more or less good* (1, 2, 3).

Yet when comparing developing and developed countries, the differences between the two are widely assumed to be differences in *degree*, not in *type*. From this perspective, developed countries are held up as the gold standard, while developing countries are measured by their distance from this ideal. Perhaps the most well-known example is the Worldwide Governance Indicators (WGI), an international index of the quality of governance issued by the World Bank. Numerous other organizations also offer their own cross-national indices, all assigning a single numerical score to each country.[10] Such indices lend themselves to rankings from the best to the worst and conveniently provide data for regression analyses. But such measurements assume the existence of one universal benchmark—as defined by the developed world—and by implication all variances from this benchmark are interpreted as deficiencies, rather than differences in functions and patterns.[11] Such indices, while highly fashionable and useful in certain ways, impede our ability to register and appreciate qualitative differences in institutions across low-, middle-, and high-income nations.

My work pays special regard to observing qualitative differences, that is, how particular arrangements function and operate in practice. I also collect statistical data (e.g., GDP, tax revenue, number of convicted corruption cases) where they are available and appropriate. But my primary focus is on structural features and dominant practices.

Second, following on my previous point, one of the key contextual differences between developing and developed countries is that informal politics dominate in the former. In most developing countries, enforcement of formal rules is weak; instead, informal norms are prevalent and strong.[12] Often it is the informal institutions that actually determine the distribution of power and outcomes of development. Unlike formal policies, informal politics are not neatly recorded in archives and ready-made datasets. The study of informal politics requires being deeply embedded in local contexts and gaining the trust of local respondents in order to find out, by speaking and interacting with them, what they actually care about, what they actually do, and how they do it.

Taking the previous two points into account, I chart qualitative historical changes by relying extensively on in-depth interviews primarily with veteran local bureaucrats and secondarily with local businesses, approximating an oral history approach. Where available, I supplement the interviews with archival and written materials collected at local sites. One advantage of oral over textual accounts is that we are more likely to learn both about formal policies and informal practices from conversations. Also, oral accounts are dynamic; people can respond to questions of how and why. Appendix B describes my coverage, strategies, and procedures of interviewing. Here I lay out how my interview questions were structured in order to trace coevolutionary dynamics over time.

Focusing on the bureaucracy and the economy, I design a general template of questions that elaborate on several dimensions of each domain, with examples listed below.

1. *Background*: political and economic characteristics of the locale; salient historical legacies; growth opportunities and constraints
2. *Development focus and economic reforms*: focus of development and reforms; creation of collective enterprises; process and outcomes of enterprise restructuring; origins of private sector
3. *Investment promotion strategy*: targets of investment; methods of recruitment; attractions and incentives provided
4. *Industrial strategy*: industrial composition; industrial promotion policies; efforts at selection, if any; process of transition to tertiary sectors
5. *Business environment*: most salient problems faced by local businesses; efforts to improve business environment
6. *Bureaucratic practices and reforms*: funding and salary levels; implementation of centrally initiated reforms; assignment of targets; anticorruption measures
7. *Other topics*: patterns of industrial relocation, tax collection practices, land-based financing

One innovation in my design of fieldwork is that instead of investigating the above dimensions only during the present period, which is the conventional practice,[13] I ask the same questions over each significant period of history, identified in step 2. In Pierson's terms, this approach generates a "moving picture" (that is, a sequence of snapshots over an extended period of time), instead of a single snapshot at one point in time. Or, expressed in statistical terms, it produces panel rather than cross-sectional data. This step is repeated for each subnational case, producing panels of qualitative-institutional data over the course of market reforms for the selected cases. Such data form the raw material for mapping out local coevolutionary paths, as seen in chapters 5 and 6.

Before moving to step 4, I would read the oral transcripts and supplemental materials several times and then extract and display the dominant patterns in a table format. Table 5.1 (the chapter on Forest Hill) provides an example, but it is not enough to stop here. While the table summarizes the associated economic and bureaucratic traits at each period, it does not "move."[14] To explain the transitions from stage to stage, we need to take further steps to investigate how and why changes happened.

4. Identify mechanisms of mutual influence at significant junctures

After collecting data on the dominant traits of targeted domains over several periods, my fourth step is to identify whether and how an observed trait in one domain in an earlier period might have influenced the patterns of its coupled domain in the next period. Addressing this issue requires returning to the field sites again, sometimes many more times, this time targeting my inquiries on why certain changes occurred and how these changes related to changes in the previous and next periods. In investigating why, my questions center on the evolutionary mechanisms of variation, selection, and niche creation: Was a new alternative generated, and by whom? Was a new selection made or recombined with existing traits? Did the selection criteria change? Was a previous selection retained or abandoned? How did different regions relate to one another?

Based on the information collected, the items initially arrayed in a table are then rearranged in a zigzag pattern (as illustrated in figure 1.4.), highlighting the direction and mechanisms of mutual influence between two domains of interest.[15] Realities, however, are messy and do not always conform to an "ideal" zigzag pattern of mutual influences. Causality may run in multiple directions: simultaneous, reciprocal, and lagged.[16]

My study certainly does not profess to have definitively proven each step of each coevolutionary chain I have mapped out. Nor is it my current objective to obtain precise point estimates of the causal effects of one particular variable on another.[17] For certain micro-questions, with limited interactivity and complex dynamics, arriving at precise estimates of linear causal effects is of course valuable. But in order to understand the long-term process of political and economic development, as well as the underlying forces of adaptive change, it is more useful—indeed essential—to chart dynamic patterns of mutual adaptation over time. My study suggests and demonstrates an essential *first* step toward tackling this extremely important task.

Each coevolutionary path traced in this study may be understood as a *sequence* of hypotheses between two *interdependent* variables, rather than a single hypothesis of a linear relationship between one dependent (outcome) and independent (explanatory) variable. In cases that successfully modernized, the economy changed not only quantitatively but also qualitatively over time, from emerging to established markets; political and administrative institutions also changed structurally over time, from one combination of functions and features into another. Both variables—states and markets—are moving targets that drive each other's evolution.

It would take an extraordinarily voluminous and fine-grained dataset to perform multiple tests of a connected sequence of steps,[18] rather than just one test of a linear relationship. Nevertheless, one may take smaller steps to test a particular link in a proposed coevolutionary chain. For example, in chapter 4 I mapped out the processes of coevolution between the economy and bureaucratic compensation practices (see figure 4.4). One link I proposed was that pegging bureaucratic pay and perks to the amount of revenue created dual incentives for local cadres to both promote the economy and to self-finance their offices. This, I propose, was an intermediate step between purely prebendal and fully salaried, Weberian bureaucracies. In a separate analysis (Ang 2012a), I collected an original dataset that estimated actual bureaucratic compensation (formal and informal combined) across 136 counties and examined its association with revenue as an indirect test of the structure of monetary incentives within the bureaucracy. On its own, data collection for this analysis is already painstaking, and it provides systematic evidence for only one snapshot, though an important one, in a long-term coevolutionary process I have mapped out. Nevertheless, this example showcases one method of combining coevolutionary narratives with quantitative tests of larger-n data.[19]

The efforts proposed here to combine process tracing with correlational tests relates to but departs from other multimethod approaches. A recent article by Humphreys and Jacobs proposes Bayesian integration of quantitative and qualitative data (BIQQ). My work shares their concern for integrating "causal inferences deriving from cross-case correlations ... with causal inferences deriving from within-case evidence of causal processes." Humphreys and Jacobs' method, however, is still premised upon the existence of "a single, binary causal variable and a binary outcome variable,"[20] which they illustrate with the example of the effects of a drug treatment on a diseased population. This is a classic instance in which reverse causality (i.e., the population affects the drug) is not relevant, and thus the methods they propose are appropriate and useful for their subjects of study. Where two complex variables mutually evolve, however, as in the case of political-economic development, we need to develop other multimethod approaches that capture this reality. My book aims to move this agenda forward by first tracing interactive processes within cases.

Appendix B

INTERVIEWS

The most valuable source of data for this book is a collection of more than four hundred interviews conducted between 2006 and 2015. Most of my interviews were with local bureaucrats, but some were with business owners, managers, central-level officials, and state researchers. I focus on local bureaucrats because China's development is distinctively state-centric and decentralized. This appendix describes the distribution of my interviews, how they were conducted, how I selected local cases, and how I managed and analyzed interview transcripts.[1]

While this appendix reports my interviewing experience in China specifically, two approaches discussed here are relevant to qualitative researchers in general. The first is my hybrid interviewing approach that combines interviews conducted by myself and trained natives. I will elaborate on why I selected this approach and how I implemented it. The second is my emphasis on systematically transcribing conversations in order to capture spoken words as data. This is a basic procedure, but it has surprisingly not received much attention in the methodological literature.[2]

My interviews are divided into three sets. The first was aimed broadly at understanding the politics and conditions that influence adaptive processes in China. I disaggregated this line of inquiry into three themes examined in the book: how central authorities interpreted national problems and issued directives to local authorities (variation); how bureaucratic evaluation and compensation worked and evolved over time (selection); how higher-level interventions reacted to and influenced regional patterns of development (niche creation).

This set of interviews began as part of my research from 2006 to 2009, which at that time studied only the second theme of bureaucratic incentives and controls. Over the years, I collected more interviews, with the final round completed in 2015. Chapters 3 and 4 draw largely on this body of research.

The second set of interviews centered on mapping the paths of state-and-market coevolution in four main localities: Forest Hill (Fujian), Blessed County (Zhejiang), Humble County (Hubei), and Upstart County (Jiangxi). The first three cases are featured at length. Unfortunately, because of space limitations, the fourth case appears only briefly in chapters 1 and 6. These interviews provide the raw material for chapters 5 and 6.

In addition to these two main sources, I also tapped into interviews conducted for two separate projects. The first was a joint project with Xiaojun Li on regulatory discrimination, for which we collected semistructured interviews with forty-six street-level regulatory officers. We studied whether and why regulatory officers might target certain businesses for inspections. The second was a joint project between the China Program at Stanford University and the National Development and Reform Commission (NDRC) on the challenges of urbanization. I was privileged to join the team for fieldwork in the city of Chengdu, Sichuan, during the summer of 2012, which gave me valuable opportunities to hear the views of officials about urbanization from the central to the lowest village levels.

Coverage of Interviews

There are a total of 375 interviews in the two main groups described above. Table B.1 divides them by geographic region, levels of government, and functional sectors within the party-state. Geographically, these interviews span coastal (e.g., Fujian, Zhejiang, Jiangsu), northern (e.g., Shandong), central (e.g., Hubei), and western (e.g., Sichuan) provinces. They also cover bureaucracies across a variety of party-state functions, including economic management (e.g., investment bureaus, planning commissions, and industrial park committees), political affairs (e.g., publicity and discipline departments), provision of public services (e.g., education and health bureaus, public schools, hospitals), legislation (People's Congress and consultative conferences), courts, and more.

In combination, the wide coverage of these interviews provided an aerial view of China's entire political economy, rather than only certain geographic regions or pockets of the bureaucracy, while the local case studies supplied deep and dynamic insights into the processes of state-and-market coevolution in different parts of China.

TABLE B.1 Distribution of interviews

	NUMBER OF INTERVIEWS
By province	
Central party-state	22
Fujian	22
Guangdong	10
Hubei	29
Hunan	12
Jiangsu	38
Jiangxi	9
Liaoning	8
Shandong	33
Shanghai	9
Sichuan	111
Tianjin	44
Zhejiang	17
Others	11
Total	**375**
By level of government	
Central	22
Province	24
City	46
County	223
Township and village	45
Companies	15
Total	**375**
By party-state function	
Administrative services center	9
Audit and discipline	6
Economic affairs	46
Education and health	32
Environment	21
Finance and tax	59
Land	12
Leadership or state secretariat	9
Judiciary and law enforcement	14
Legislature	7
Party organs[a]	18
Personnel management	37
Research	12

(Continued)

TABLE B.1   (Continued)

	NUMBER OF INTERVIEWS
By party-state function	
Others[b]	78
Companies	15
Total	**375**

[a] Organizations in this group include the Organization Department, Strategy Department, Discipline Committee, Publicity Committee, and Party School.

[b] Organizations in this group include, but are not limited to, the Civil Affairs Bureau, Statistical Bureau, Agricultural Bureau, Culture Bureau, Price Bureau, and Labor and Social Security Bureau.

Interview Channels and Strategies

The vast majority of my interviews were arranged through institutional contacts in China, mostly university professors who introduced me to agencies or companies based in the particular city or province of the university. After a general introduction was made, I was given the contact information of various organizations I requested to meet. Then I usually proceeded to set up appointments myself and conducted interviews without the company of a third party from the university or government. I was accompanied by research assistants whom I personally hired as note takers. This local-institutional channel of access allowed me to speak to entrepreneurs or bureaucrats from a variety of departments while maintaining research independence and some degree of informality.

Only my interviews in a county of Shandong Province were arranged through the Foreign Service Office. In this instance, a Foreign Service officer accompanied me to all the interviews. My first set of local interviews in 2006 was conducted in this setting. At the time, being a doctoral student with limited institutional and contextual knowledge of China, the experience was valuable, as interviewees were willing to patiently explain things to me. The limitations of such formal access, however, become apparent as one seeks to probe deeper into certain subjects, such as corruption or the politics of appointments.

Other than local institutional contacts, a smaller share of my interviews were arranged informally through personal friends who had family members or friends working in local governments. In these instances, I normally could speak only to a few bureaucrats my friends happened to know, rather than to interview many of them in one research trip. I found, however, that the narrowness of scope in these informal settings was made up for by the depth and candor of discussions.

For example, on investment promotion, a topic that virtually all officials welcome, the perspectives told varied by interview channels. In the most formal channel, such discussions would highlight the achievements of investment promotion, which were true but one-sided. Interestingly, respondents in formal settings sometimes spoke with innocent candor when they assumed their methods and practices must be perfectly "normal" and shared by others within and beyond China.[3] Such "innocence," however, was generally limited to cadres from low-level administrations (townships and villages) and less-developed inland regions, who had limited contact with foreigners. By comparison, through less formal channels, I learned both about the achievements and problems of investment promotion, sometimes even frank admissions about corrupt opportunities that accompanied growth-promoting activities.

My experiences in interviewing led me to think how I could better make use of local personal connections to maximize the richness of interviews while maintaining breadth of perspective. Ethnographers typically spend months and even years immersing themselves in one small location to approximate native or "insider" status.[4] I wanted to approach the wealth and depth of insights that one could gain from the ethnographic method. As a political scientist, though, I was equally interested in broad historical processes and comparisons across cases. Accumulating fieldwork experience no doubt enriched my contextual knowledge of China and sharpened my fluency in the subjects I studied. Yet no matter how immersed and fluent I strove to become, I—and indeed nobody—could be native (born, raised, and embedded in personal networks) to multiple particular locations at once.

The method of matched proxy interviewing, which I first learned about from Cammett's work in Lebanon,[5] provided a partial solution. To overcome the challenges of studying an extremely politically divisive environment, Cammett trained Lebanese university students to conduct semistructured interviews with nonelite residents from their particular religious group (Christian, Druze, Shi'i Muslim, and Sunni Muslim). Variants of this strategy were also used in surveys that matched surveyors with respondents from their own ethnic group in order to elicit candid responses about sensitive issues like political violence.[6] This literature gave me the idea of supplementing my own fieldwork and interviews with proxy interviews conducted by trained research assistants in their place of residence. This hybrid strategy would allow me to acquire simultaneously broad and deep perspectives into the politics of local development.

Proxy Interviewing

Adapting matched proxy interviewing to my study, I recruited and trained college students in China to conduct semistructured interviews in their home counties. For my doctoral research, I had some early experience in hiring students to conduct short interviews on specific questions with respondents they personally knew. Moving on, I wanted to refine this method and in particular to apply it to mapping local histories, as this is where the advantage of trained native interviewers lies. I conducted proxy interviewing in several waves over the years, both for the book and separate research projects. Through this process, I learned to improve my methods of recruitment, training, communication, and feedback, as well as the design of structured interviews. My joint project with Li also employed the proxy interviewing method, which provided a valuable opportunity to identify high-performing students. Out of the main body of 375 interviews, 130 were conducted by proxy and 77 contributed to the local history component.

In order for proxy interviewing to work, it was essential to spend tremendous time and care in selecting, training, and guiding the assistants when they conducted interviews. After carefully reviewing applications and interviewing candidates, the selected students were required to participate in a formal training session, lasting one to two full days. Students were trained on research protocol, procedures to ensure confidentiality, research objectives, interviewing techniques, and note-taking techniques, among others. After the formal training, the students were tasked to conduct a few interviews based on a narrower set of questions, both to test their abilities and commitment as well as to provide learning opportunities. They returned to their hometowns and arranged interviews with targeted respondents through personal connections and chain referrals. Fieldwork and interviewing is hard work, so the drop-out rate was high. Finally, I settled on a core team of four students for the local history component of the book. They met me again for a briefing and additional training session.

For the coevolutionary case studies, I designed a general template of interview questions (described in appendix A). When my assistants were on the ground conducting interviews, which typically took place over one to three weeks while they were home, they were required to inform me about their travel and interview schedule in advance. Every interview had to be typed up on the day it was conducted and sent to me (more on transcription in the next section). I usually read each transcript within a day of receiving it and marked detailed comments and questions on the transcripts. Where appropriate and possible, the students arranged follow-up interviews to address my questions.

The local case studies required several rounds of interviews. During the first round, the students and I sought to outline the defining traits of the location and the broad strokes of its history. Then with each subsequent round, we narrowed more closely on particular historical periods and questions of interest. So while I had a template of questions for the team of students, each student's questions would be revised and tailored according to the location's particular characteristics and the stage of research. All this was extremely time- and energy-consuming work. Proxy interviewing provides the advantage of native access and depth, not convenience or time savings.

Both the students and I collected written materials to supplement the interviews. These included local yearbooks, gazettes, government documents, websites, media reports, and secondary literature. To verify the accuracy of responses, portions of the interviews were repeatedly asked to several respondents and also checked against archival sources. Where interviews were conducted on my own and by my assistants in the same locale, this was deliberately done separately so that my presence as a nonnative would not affect the native's access or interview experience. The information we gathered was different and complementary. For example, my student's interviews with private entrepreneurs in one county consistently included references to "fake FDI" (domestic companies disguised as foreign companies to benefit from preferential tax breaks given to foreigners before 2006), which was an open secret among local businesses and officials. My interviews with private entrepreneurs in the same place were also informative, focusing mainly on the founding and history of these companies and industrial transfer to the interior, but never once was "fake FDI" mentioned. In another instance, my assistant's research shed useful light on urban development in her hometown but said little about villages, partly as she grew up in the urban area. My trip to the villages gave me a firsthand look into rural life and changes that widened the picture.

When the idea of mapping local coevolutionary paths dawned on me, I hoped to select cases that represented two extreme parts of China: the most prosperous places located directly on the coast and the much poorer ones in the interior provinces. I did not have the privilege of picking specific locations within these two regional blocs; instead, I took the pragmatic step of seizing whatever opportunities came along and pushing as far as I could go. In the end, taking into account my access, the availability of qualified research assistants, and the representative value of the cases, I settled on Forest Hill in Fujian (aka the Goldilocks case that coevolved neither too quickly nor too slowly), Blessed County in Zhejiang, and Humble County in Hubei as the three main cases featured in the book.

Transcription, Analysis, and Citation

In both the interviews I personally conducted and the proxy interviews, I paid particular attention to transcribing interviews as close to verbatim as possible. A lot of information is lost or distorted if the interviews are only summarily recorded and translated to English during note taking. Detailed transcripts are especially important for this study because every piece of recollection and response forms the raw material with which historical accounts are pieced together. In my experience, many pieces of data that did not seem salient during the interviews would later on become important at the analysis stage when more pieces of information were collected and compared. So if the interviews had not been recorded as they were spoken, such oral data would have been forgotten and lost.

Native Chinese writers are generally able to transcribe a significant portion of the interviews because of their language skills. For a nonnative Chinese writer like me, however, this is difficult to do. Hence, for my interviews, instead of using a recorder, I trained and brought student note takers with me. This was a far better alternative than using a recorder because elite respondents, understandably, prefer not to be recorded. In the Chinese context, though, it was perceived as appropriate for professors to bring their students along, and the student's note taking was seen more as an educational activity (like homework) than a recording. On some longer trips, I brought up to three note takers so that they could take turns and check one another's transcription.

I accumulated more than a thousand pages of interview transcripts in Chinese. How does one go about systematically analyzing so much data? I could spend an entire chapter answering this question. But my short response is that depending on the volume of transcripts and the objectives of research, the use of qualitative analysis software to code textual data can aid pattern recognition. All research, whether qualitative or quantitative, is about uncovering patterns. As David Apter comments, "Fieldwork is exciting. It is like working with the pieces of a jigsaw puzzle. One gradually discerns a pattern."[7] For a small amount of textual data, one may extract and display the dominant patterns simply on a Word document. But for more than a thousand pages of transcripts, I use Atlas.ti as a coding instrument. This software allows me to code the transcripts based on as many themes and subthemes as I choose; and it is able to output the quotations for each selected code (e.g., cadre bonus schemes in the 1990s). This device allows qualitative researchers to systematically search for and compare patterns.

It is important to maintain the anonymity of my respondents, as repeatedly emphasized by other China scholars.[8] This is especially the case for elite respondents like bureaucrats and entrepreneurs, who have been generous enough to share their valuable experiences that inform and enrich this study. I identify the interviewees by the year in which the first interview was conducted, followed by an ID. The letter B stands for bureaucrat, C for company, and REG for my joint project on regulation with Li. I also do not identify the name of the particular locations studied to avoid identifying individuals. Instead, I gave pseudonyms to the local cases and individual leaders mentioned in these cases.[9]

Notes

INTRODUCTION

1. Different disciplines employ different but overlapping terms in reference to the quality of governance and institutions. Most economists adopt the term "institutions," defined by North as "rules of the game" that structure social behavior (North 1990). Three common measures of institutions used by economists are "risk of expropriation by the government, government effectiveness, and constraints on the executive" (Glaeser et al. 2004, 273), which are all measures of governance. The term "good governance" has been widely used in the policy and aid community (Grindle 2004; IMF 1997; Jomo and Chowdhury 2012b). Invoking Douglass North's seminal work, the creators of the Worldwide Governance Indicators (WGI) at the World Bank define good governance as "norms of limited government that protect private property from predation by the state" (Kaufmann, Kraay, and Mastruzzi 2007a, 555). The WGI measures six dimensions of governance: voice and accountability, political stability, government effectiveness, regulatory quality, rule of law, and control of corruption. Political scientists and sociologists refer more commonly to state capacity and stress the ability of governments to actualize goals (Evans, Rueschemeyer, and Skocpol 1985; Migdal, Kohli, and Shue 1994). A recent volume, *States in the Developing World*, defines state capacity as "the organizational and bureaucratic ability to implement governing projects" (Centeno, Kohli, and Yashar, forthcoming). Some political scientists disagree that limited government defines good governance (Kurtz and Schrank 2007a, 2007b). Yet regardless of the different terms used and disagreements about definition, the general consensus is that the institutions found among successfully developed economies are a universal benchmark of good or strong institutions, also widely believed to be necessary for economic growth.

2. Boix and Stokes 2003; Inglehart and Welzel 2005; Lipset 1959.

3. For a case study, see Goldsmith 2012. For quantitative studies, see Glaeser et al. 2004; Kurtz and Schrank 2007b.

4. Sachs 2005; Sachs et al. 2004.

5. Sachs 2005, 73.

6. Burnside and Dollar 2000.

7. Deaton 2013; Easterly 2006b; Hubbard and Duggan 2009.

8. IMF 1997; 1998, 39–42; World Bank 1992, 1994, 2002b.

9. The belief that growth is preconditioned on good governance has provided strong rationale for conditional aid. As Collier sharply points out, however, "Conditionality turned out to be a paper tiger: governments discovered they only needed to *promise* to reform, not actually do it" (2007, 67). See also Pritchett and de Weijer 2011; Riggs 1964.

10. Andrews 2013, 35; Hendley 1999; Jensen 2003.

11. Pritchett and Woolcock 2004, 193. For similar views, see Riggs 1964; Fukuyama 2004; Lansing 2006; Rodrik 2007; Pritchett and de Weijer 2011; Andrews 2013.

12. Acemoglu, Johnson, and Robinson 2002; Handley 2008; Kohli 2004; Lange 2009; Mahoney 2010. Also see arguments about the long-lasting effects of state formation moments on economic and political outcomes (Levitsky and Murillo 2013; Vu 2010).

13. Acemoglu and Robinson 2012. For an earlier articulation, see Sokoloff and Engerman 2000.

14. See Przeworski's critique of the deterministic overtones of path-dependent arguments in a review of the literature. As he observes, "Indeed, I cannot find an explicit specification of alternative paths in any of the institutionalist writings" (2004, 172).

15. Acemoglu and Robinson 2012, 44.

16. Acemoglu and Robinson assert that countries can "break the mold" by "*quickly* developing inclusive economic and political institutions" (2012, 409–410, italics added), citing the case of postindependence Botswana, one of the few sub-Saharan African countries that are thriving today. Pushing their logic back one step, the obvious question is: why could Botswana "quickly" achieve good governance while many others could not? The authors reply, "Botswana *already* had tribal institutions that had achieved some amount of centralized authority and contained important pluralistic features" (413, italics added). They further compare this tribal system to the Magna Carta, a celebrated agreement of limited government between King John and the barons of England in the thirteenth century (407). So we are rerouted back to the original problem: if nations don't *already* have prototypes of good institutions like the Magna Carta, then how can they *quickly* develop good institutions in order to achieve economic success? Clearly, according to the logic of Acemoglu and Robinson, absent a long history of good institutions, poverty and weak governance will persist. And this, as the title of their book declares, is "why nations fail."

17. China's policy of "reform and opening" (*gaige kaifang*) was officially inaugurated under Deng's leadership at the Third Plenum held in December of 1978.

18. Also, see work by John Padgett and his collaborators for extraordinarily intricate accounts of the coevolution of political and economic networks during various periods of European history (Padgett and McLean 2011; Padgett and Powell 2012). Similarly, in an incisive historical analysis, Chang (2002) argues that developed countries did not in fact use "good" policies and institutions when they were in the process of developing. And as Ginsburg (2015), a legal scholar, points out, even the Magna Carta, popularly revered as an exemplary liberal institution, was in fact "a failure," "hardly constrained the monarch," and limited the rights of women and minorities.

19. More examples include personal patron-client ties, communal affiliations, rampant piracy, profit-oriented rather than service-oriented public administration, and taxless public finance (paying for public projects without formal taxation or transparent rules of public borrowing).

20. Acemoglu and Robinson recommend that the way to escape vicious cycles is by "*quickly* developing inclusive economic and political institutions" (2012, 409–410, italics added).

21. See Diamond (2005) on geography as the "ultimate" cause of divergence in human development.

22. Owen Barder, "The Implications of Complexity for Development," Kapuscinski Lecture, May 2012, http://www.owen.org/blog/5723.

23. Furthermore, prior to the establishment of the People's Republic of China in 1949, China had suffered more than a century of dynastic decline, foreign invasion, civil war, and famines (Schell and Delury 2013).

24. In 1980, measured by current U.S. dollars, China's GDP per capita was equivalent to Malawi's and only about 88 percent of Chad's and Bangladesh's. World Bank Database, http://data.worldbank.org/indicator/.

25. The "bottom billion" refers to the world's poorest countries (Collier 2007).

26. Brandt and Rawski 2008, 5; Lardy 1983, 148.

27. Feng 1996.

28. One example is the Organizational History Statistics (*zuzhishi ziliao*), an authoritative statistical source compiled by the Central Organization Department on the size of public employment.

29. Walder 2009, 1. See also Su 2011.

30. MacFarquhar and Schoenhals 2006, 2.

31. World Bank database, http://data.worldbank.org/indicator/.

32. Whether these institutions work like they do in the capitalist West is a different matter; the dramatic structural transformation of the economic system since 1978 is beyond doubt.

33. Manion 2004; Wedeman 2012.

34. Fujian city official, interview (REG-2012–020). To maintain the anonymity of my respondents, I do not identify their names or particular location. Instead, I identify the interviewees by the year in which the first interview was conducted, followed by an ID. For more on my coverage of interviews and citation protocol, see appendix B.

35. Also, in contradiction to Sachs's policy advice, China did not escape the poverty trap through massive foreign assistance.

36. Naysayer predictions about China's imminent collapse have long been made by others (Chang 2001; Pei 2006).

37. Acemoglu and Robinson 2012, 423, 440, 427.

38. See Woo 1999. For a similar argument in the context of East Asia, see Krugman 1994.

39. It would be equally simplistic to attribute China's turnaround solely to high investments. As Barry Naughton, an expert on the Chinese economy, explained, "High investment rates 'cause' economic growth, in a mechanical sense, but are also themselves a symptom of productivity improvements that are the ultimate source of economic growth" (2007, 148). Such "productivity improvements" were highly dependent on state policies and institutions. Moreover, whereas high investment rates during the socialist period reflected almost only state investments, investment decisions during the reform period were made by households, businesses, and government in response to "new areas in the dynamic Chinese economy" (Naughton 2015, 114).

40. Landry 2008; H. Li and Zhou 2005; Maskin, Qian, and Xu 2000.

41. Montinola, Qian, and Weingast 1995; Oi 1992, 1999; Walder 1995; Whiting 2001.

42. As Tsai observed, "Within a single province, evidence can be mustered for market preserving federalism, local state corporatism, and even klepto-patrimonialism" (2004, 18). See also Baum and Shevchenko 1999; Bernstein & Lü 2003.

43. Coase and Wang 2012; Lin, Cai, and Li 2003; Naughton 1995; Oi and Walder 1999; Rawski 1995; Shirk 1993.

44. Hausmann, Pritchett, and Rodrik 2005; Oi and Walder 1999; Qian 2003; Rodrik 2008.

45. Qian 2003, 323.

46. Also, this literature does not notice that so-called transitional institutions worked better in some parts of China than others and were replaced at different times. In chapters 1 and 6, I show and explain why the rate of institutional replacement varied across regions.

47. The term "authoritarian resilience" was coined by Nathan 2003.

48. Florini, Lai, and Tan, 2012; Gallagher 2005; Heilmann 2008.

49. Dimitrov 2013a; Mertha 2008; Nathan 2003; Tsai 2007.

50. Dickson 2008; Tsai 2007.

51. Duckett 2001; Lee 2014; Stockmann 2012.

52. Shambaugh 2008.

53. For recent edited volumes on adaptive governance and innovation in China, see Dimitrov 2013b; Heilmann and Perry 2011b; Teets and Hurst 2015; Naughton and Tsai 2015.

54. Heilmann and Perry 2011a.

55. In particular, see Perry's (2011) insightful discussion of the reconfiguration of Maoist campaigns for present-day economic policy implementation, which I find similar to the phenomenon of en masse investment recruitment by local agencies (more in chapter 1).

56. The literature on poverty traps is large enough to constitute an entire subfield. For a review, see Bowles, Durlauf, and Hoff 2006.

57. North, Wallis, and Weingast 2009, 26.

58. Ibid., 167.

59. Krasner 2014.

60. There had been efforts to introduce alternative regression models to capture highly interactive, nonlinear relationships (for example, in international conflict, see Beck, King, and Zeng [2000]), but such models have not generally entered mainstream analyses and graduate training. Statistical (or machine) learning offers a promising array of new tools for modeling nonparametric relationships. This book seeks to provide a qualitative-historical foundation for studying complex interactions and reciprocal causation on a macro level that would complement the micro tools of statistical learning.

61. This is a series of essays published in *The Journal of Politics* (Kaufmann, Kraay, and Mastruzzi 2007a, 2007b; Kurtz and Schrank 2007a, 2007b). For another debate, see Kaufmann and Kraay 2002; Lora 2002; Pritchett 2002.

62. Kaufmann, Kraay, and Zoido-Lobatón 1999, 1. For other econometric analyses offering evidence that good governance or institutions cause growth, see Acemoglu, Johnson, and Robinson 2002; Kaufmann and Kraay 2002; Kaufmann, Kraay, and Mastruzzi 2007b; Knack and Keefer, 1995; Mauro 1995; Rodrik, Subramanian, and Trebbi 2004.

63. Kurtz and Schrank 2007b, 540.

64. Kaufmann, Kraay, and Mastruzzi rebut by faulting their critics for not complying with "the best-practice frontier" in growth empirics (2007a, 555). Tellingly, their rebuttal was focused on the technicalities of regression analysis rather than the process of political-economic change. Despite acknowledging that growth regressions are "intrinsically dynamic," feedbacks between growth and governance were treated as an endogeneity problem that could be statistically fixed (2007a, 561).

65. Przeworski 2004, 185, emphasis added.

66. Axelrod and Cohen 1999, 7–15; Page 2011, 7.

67. Miller and Page 2007, 10.

68. Introductory guides to complex adaptive systems include Axelrod and Cohen 1999; Holland 1996; Miller and Page 2007; Mitchell 2009. The Santa Fe Institute is a center dedicated to the study of complexity.

69. Pierson 2004, 2; see also Hall 2003.

70. Pierson 2004, 2.

71. Fine-grained insights into actual practices and structural patterns are not conveniently recorded in available datasets. Thus my study relies heavily on interviews with more than four hundred veteran bureaucrats and businesses and in-depth fieldwork in selected localities that cover coastal, central, and western regions.

72. Axelrod and Cohen 1999; Holland 1996; Ostrom and Basurto 2011. Yet another mechanism of coevolution is retention, namely, propagation and abandonment of previous selections. Retention will feature prominently in my micro-level analyses of coevolutionary paths (in particular, see chapters 1, 5 and 6). Retention, however, is set aside in my current examination of meta-institutions that structure adaptive processes. Instead, this book focuses on the meta-institutions that influence the processes of variation (chapter 3), selection (chapter 4), and niche creation (chapters 5 and 6). I discuss the conditions that influence the retention and replacement of initial selections in a separate work.

73. Mahoney and Thelen 2015; Mahoney and Thelen 2010; Streeck and Thelen 2005; Thelen 2004.

74. Holland 1996, 9. In complexity terms, an agent "has the ability to interact with its environment, including other agents" (Axelrod and Cohen 1999, 4). Thus, a cog in a machine is not an agent, but a human is an agent. Organizations and communities may be considered populations of agents.

75. Pierson 2004, 82.

76. This is Blessed County from Zhejiang Province, which is featured in chapter 6.

77. Amsden 1989; Evans 1995; Johnson 1982; Wade 1990; Woo-Cumings 1999.

78. In *Bringing the State Back In*, Evans, Rueschemeyer, and Skocpol highlight state autonomy as essential to state capacity. By autonomous states, they mean "collectivities of career officials . . . [who] are likely to launch distinctive new state strategies in times of crisis" (1985, 9). In this instance of the Chinese county, however, state actors did not respond to an externally imposed crisis, but rather to an endogenous consequence of their earlier development strategies.

79. Kaufmann, Kraay, and Mastruzzi 2007b; Kaufmann, Kraay, and Zoido-Lobatón 1999.

80. Oi & Walder 1999, 24.

81. This use of communal affiliations to create property rights finds striking parallels with the case of medieval Europe, as originally documented by Greif (2006a) and which I discuss in chapter 7.

82. To clarify, this instance does not indicate that coevolutionary processes must start with communal institutions and end with activist state interventions. The particular contents of each step are unique to each place. What is generalizable is the pattern of mutual causation that emerges from the particulars.

83. Aoki 2010; Hall and Soskice 2001.

84. North 1990.

85. North and Weingast 1989.

86. Weingast 1995.

87. Acemoglu and Robinson 2012.

88. Inglehart and Welzel 2005.

89. One notable exception is the literature on various measures of partial market reforms in China prior to 1993.

90. North 2005, 13.

91. Ibid., 70.

92. Axelrod and Cohen 1999, xiv.

93. This is apparent from a common saying in politics: "You can't please everyone." See, for example, "In Challenger, a Chastening for Emanuel," *New York Times*, Feb. 25, 2015.

94. Page 2011.

95. North 2005, 70.

96. Axelrod and Cohen 1999, 114.

97. On the challenges of localizing foreign aid, see Ang 2014b.

1. MAPPING COEVOLUTION

1. B2013–329.

2. B2013–325.

3. Analytic narratives combine narratives with abstract reasoning. This approach seeks to distill "the logic of the processes that generate the phenomena" from the "thick descriptions" of particular cases (Bates et al. 1998, 14).

4. For a review, see Lustick 2011.

5. The zigzag pattern reflects an "ideal" reciprocal pattern of coevolution. Coevolutionary paths, however, often in fact run in multiple directions: reciprocal, simultaneous, and lagged (Lewin and Volberda 2003, 584).

6. The intellectual roots of this school can be traced back to Polanyi (1957), Gerschenkron (1962), and Hirschmann (1958). All three observe that "economically backward" nations require the state to do more than protect property rights and instead actively organize markets through a repertoire of policy tools.

7. Evans 1995.

8. In Weber's own words, a key feature of professional bureaucracies is the establishment of a "sphere of competence subject to impersonal rules" (1968, 229).

9. Today, we still see nonspecialized functions practiced but only among "primitive" economic entities like small family businesses.

10. Simon 1957, 7. Likewise, a textbook on public administration states, "Specialization is a key tenet of public administration, and government agencies are designed around specialties" (Frederickson 1991).

11. Similarly, North views the specialization of functions as a measure of the complexity of economic transactions and hence broadly the level of societal development (1990, 34–35). North, Wallis, and Weingast (2009) also regard "impersonal exchanges" as a key feature of advanced "open access" societies.

12. Professionalism also means not using personal resources for organizational needs. For example, public and corporate employees are generally not expected to use their own funds to pay for office expenditure. But as we will see in the Chinese context, local cadres use their personal connections to advance the collective development goals of their locales.

13. As Chinese sociologist Fei Xiaotong (1992) insightfully notes, there is little meaningful separation between private and public spheres in small, rural communities because residents in these contexts are accustomed to growing up and living around others with whom they are deeply familiar.

14. Woo-Cumings 1999.

15. Johnson 1982, 32.

16. Even after the Asian financial crisis, the developmental state model was not entirely discredited. Indeed, some cite the difficulty of maintaining Weberian qualities as a cause of the financial crisis (Yusuf 2001).

17. Lecture at the Dili Convention Centre, Feb. 18, 2015. A transcript of the lecture is available on the personal website of Mahbubani at http://www.mahbubani.net/articles.html.

18. Quah 2010, 191.

19. Kohli 2004.

20. Quoted in Huff 1999, 220.

21. Oi 1995, 1113.

22. Oi 1999, 3, emphasis added.

23. Blecher 1991, 2008; Blecher and Shue 1996, 2001; Oi 1999; Walder 1995.

24. The Chinese term is 一窝蜂.

25. The Chinese term is 全民招商.

26. Upstart is a pseudonym for the county. All locations and individuals are identified by pseudonyms.

27. Kung and Chen 2012.

28. Lieberthal 1995, 183; World Bank 2002a, 34–35.

29. In terms of GDP per capita, Jiangxi Province is ranked twenty-fifth out of thirty-one provinces in 2012 (China Data Online).

30. Edin 2003; Whiting 2001.

31. The Chinese term for subdistricts is 街道.

32. As Moe, an authority on bureaucracy, states, "The typical bureau receives a budget from governmental superiors and spends all of it supplying services to a nonpaying clientele" (1984, 763). See also Wildavsky 1964.

33. Ang 2009b.

34. The Chinese term for "personal (or social) connections" is *guanxi*. There is a substantial literature on *guanxi* by sociologists and anthropologists (Gold, Guthrie, and Wank 2002; Michelson 2007; Yang 1994).

35. B2010–195.

36. B2011–216.

37. B2013–340; B2014–343; B2014–347.

38. B2012–309.

39. Patron-client relations between local officials and entrepreneurs are well-documented (Tsai 2007; Wank 1996; Xin and Pearce 1996).

40. B2014–343. The Chinese term for "affective relationships" is *renqing*, a stronger term than *guanxi*.

41. Unless otherwise indicated, I use the exchange rate in January of 2014, which was US$1 = 6.09 yuan. The rate is from http://www.oanda.com/currency/historical-rates/.

42. B2013–340.

43. B2012–304.

44. B2013–341.

45. B2010–190.

46. Kang 2002.

47. On the enmeshing of *guanxi* with legal institutions in China, see Ang and Jia 2014; Michelson 2007.

48. B2013–325.

49. B2013–318.

50. Lü 2000; McCormick 1990.

51. Hui puts it well: "When we take the European experience as the norm and non-Western experiences as abnormal, we are led to 'search for what went wrong in other parts of the world'" (2005, 9). See also Wong 1997, 210.

52. Lü 2000, 22.

53. Lu 2000, 289–90.

54. Failed development in sub-Saharan African countries has been widely attributed to the persistence of patrimonial rule, that is, the failure to Weberianize (Evans 1995; Kohli 2004; Van de Walle 2001).

55. Heilmann 2009; Jefferson and Rawski 2001, 258; Oi and Walder 1999; Rawski 1995; Rodrik 2007, 24.

56. Qian 2003.

57. Heilmann 2008.

58. Holland 1996, 2.

59. Kaufmann, Kraay, and Zoido-Lobatón 1999; World Bank 1993.

60. Evans 1995; Johnson 1982; Wade 1990.

61. Sachs (2005) recommends injecting massive foreign aid to lift poor countries out of poverty traps, while Mao tried to use central state investments to accelerate industrial growth in China. Both methods have been described as "Big Push" plans (Easterly 2006a; Naughton 2007, 55–82).

62. This instance illustrates that reforms are not merely a matter of political will or incentives (Acemoglu 2008; Geddes 1994). To quote Collier, "it is also a technical matter, and in the bottom billion there is a chronic shortage of people with the requisite knowledge" (2007, 67).

63. Huang (1998) provides a vivid ethnographic account of how a village leader mobilized his personal connections to launch village enterprises.

64. Rodrik 2008.

65. On the geographically limited success of rural industrialization, see Naughton 2007, 284; Oi and Shimizu 2010; Ong 2012.

66. Local bureaucrats describe their two primary concerns as "eat" (吃饭) and "work" (工作). In poor localities, where the budget is entirely consumed by cadre wages and benefits, leaving little for developmental projects, the situation is described as "eating budget" (吃饭财政).

67. Bardhan 1997; Kaufmann and Wei 2000; Manion 2004, 105.

68. The case of America during the Gilded Age provides an instructive parallel. The process of economic rebuilding after the Civil War was rife with corruption, yet it produced corporate titans like J. P. Morgan, John D. Rockefeller, and Andrew Carnegie (Brands 2010).

69. Another illustration at the international level are ongoing debates over whether developing countries should be obliged to reduce carbon emissions in light of global warming.

70. Acemoglu and Robinson 2006; Inglehart and Welzel 2005.

71. Many studies on China have shown that bureaucratic changes, even in the absence of formal democratization, could restrain power-holders and alter incentives and norms (for example, see Oi 1999; Whiting 2001; Yang 2004; Lee 2014).

72. Grindle 2004, 152.

73. Krasner 2013. See also Lake 2016.

74. Rodrik 2008.

75. Pierson 2004, 49; see also Thelen 1999, 319.

76. Here is where I depart from Collier's pointed critique of institutional arguments. He writes, "Good governance and policy ... cannot generate opportunities where none exists. ... Even the best governance and policy are not going to turn Malawi into a rich country—it just does not have the opportunities" (2007, 64). Collier's comments would apply just as well to China's inland locales during the early decades of reform, when they "just [did] not have the opportunities." Yet opportunities did emerge later on, when markets on the coast took off and then began to saturate (see chapter 6). In short, although some places would always have more opportunities than others, few places are permanently deprived of opportunities.

2. DIRECTED IMPROVISATION

1. "Complex adaptive systems" is an interdisciplinary field dedicated to the study of complex scenarios where intense interaction among multiple adaptive agents generates tremendous uncertainty.

2. I thank Jonathan Bendor for underscoring this insight. See also North 2005, 66.

3. One notable exception is a strand of literature in American politics that focuses on the politics of influence.

4. See my discussion of central policy making in chapter 3 for an elaboration.

5. Holland 1996, 9.

6. Axelrod and Cohen 1999, 7.

7. This particular process of selecting and recombining various components to form new permutations has been named by some as "syncretism" (Berk, Galvan, and Hattam 2013; Kushida, Shimizu, and Oi 2014). While syncretism describes the process of selection and recombination, it does not explain where alternatives come from (sources of variation), why certain traits are chosen over others (the selection criteria), why certain selections are retained or replaced over time (changes in selection criteria), and the relationship of each unit to other units in a system (niches). By itself, syncretism is also not a theory about the underlying sources of adaptive capacity.

8. Lustick 2011, 3.

9. More precisely, to *adapt* is to respond to an immediate and specific contingency, whereas to *evolve* is to undergo a sequence of adaptations that transform key properties of the original form. For example, a fish may adapt to a new predator by hiding. But when

the creature develops a new physical trait after numerous iterative adaptations, such as by growing legs and migrating to shore, I interpret this as evolution.

10. For example, see Acemoglu and Robinson 2012; Engerman and Sokoloff 2006; Kohli 2004; Skocpol 1979. In this view, institutional changes via shocks are expected to persist until another shock throws the system into disarray. Krasner (1988) labels this type of change "punctuated equilibrium," a term first proposed by Eldredge and Gould (1972) in the context of biological changes.

11. Mahoney and Thelen 2010; Streeck and Thelen 2005.

12. Moreover, Mahoney and Thelen's framework identifies four types, rather than mechanisms, of gradual change (the authors specifically used the term "types") (2010, 16). Consider "layering," one of the four types of gradual change they identify. Humans evolved from apes in a layering manner, that is, through the accretion of numerous modifications over a long period of time. But one may push further back and ask: How does this layering process occur? The answer is traced to the basic mechanisms of variation, selection, and retention. It is these mechanisms, rather than types of gradual change, that constitute the building blocks of evolution.

13. Axelrod and Cohen 1999, 7. Similarly, North notes that human intentionality distinguishes social evolution from biological evolution through natural selection. In his words, "it is the intentionality of the players as expressed through the institutions they create which shapes performance" (2005, 66).

14. For explications of the differences between risk and uncertainty, see (Knight 1921; North 2005, chap. 2; Seybert and Katzenstein 2015). I thank Peter Katzenstein for a stimulating conversation that clarified my thinking about these issues.

15. The limits of human cognition lie at the heart of the "bounded rationality" tradition of Herbert Simon (for recent extensions, Bendor 2010). In my understanding, however, the bounded rationality paradigm differs from complexity in certain consequential ways. Simon stresses human limitations in making precise calculations about optimal strategies; the implication of this premise is that institutions (such as habits and routines) are developed to cope with cognitive limitations and the "bottleneck of attention" (1957, 90). On the other hand, complexity theorists like Axelrod and Cohen underscore the difficulty of predicting surprising outcomes like the information revolution, which does not stem from limitations in calculation or attention but from the fact that certain outcomes are *simply unthinkable*. Thus, in the complexity perspective, institutions are designed not merely to cope with cognitive limitations but rather to activate and harness the creative potential of the unknowns. This chapter elaborates on this particular view of institutional design.

16. Another simple example of a marvelous possibility—a positive uncertainty—is falling in love. We can never fully anticipate the exact people with whom our lives may become closely connected.

17. Perhaps this is why Albert Einstein is famously quoted as saying, "Imagination is more important than knowledge. For knowledge is limited to all we now know and understand, while imagination embraces the entire world, and all there ever will be to know and understand."

18. For an argument against the common fixation with control in international politics, see Seybert and Katzenstein 2015. See also Scott's probing analyses of the failures of control among modern state planners in *Seeing Like a State* (1998).

19. Axelrod and Cohen 1999, xvi.

20. North 2005, 1, italics added.

21. North 2005, 70.

22. For a review, see Carothers and de Gramont 2011. Pritchett and Woolcock (2004) provide an especially sharp critique of the good-governance approach, which they aptly characterize as "skipping straight to Weber."

23. Andrews 2013; Grindle 2004; Jomo and Chowdhury 2012b; Rodrik 2007.

24. Evans 2004; Fukuyama 2004; Rodrik 2007, 45.

25. Grindle 2011, 563.

26. Andrews 2013.

27. As Rodrik concedes, "This literature appears to have had very little impact on operational practices" (2008, 100). Similarly, a report by the Carnegie Endowment concurs: "Fully operationalizing these [second-generation] insights and overcoming the uncertainties will be hard" (Carothers and de Gramont 2011, 11).

28. Grindle 2011.

29. The DDD Manifesto is published on the website of the Harvard Kennedy School. To date, it includes hundreds of signatories, including representatives from aid organizations and major NGOs. http://buildingstatecapability.com/the-ddd-manifesto/.

30. Axelrod and Cohen 1999, xiv.

31. In a separate work, I suggest some concrete steps for reforming aid agencies in order to generate the necessary contextual knowledge to tailor aid programs to local contexts (Ang 2014b).

32. Axelrod and Cohen 1999, 32.

33. Ibid., 43–44; see also March 1991.

34. Pritchett and de Weijer 2011; Pritchett and Woolcock 2004.

35. Kohli 2004.

36. Andrews 2013, 193.

37. The classroom setting provides a straightforward illustration. Instructors can strongly influence how students choose to learn by defining and rewarding success. If instructors define success as giving the right answers according to a given checklist, this criterion will herd students toward rote memorization rather than creative thinking. Hence, "how success is defined affects the chances for learning" (Axelrod and Cohen 1999, 122).

38. Stephen, Fotini, and Thier 2010.

39. Stephen Walt, "Mission Creep in Afghanistan," *Foreign Policy*, July 20, 2009.

40. Andrews 2013, 173.

41. Holland 1996, 27.

42. Page 2011.

43. Miller and Page 2007, 105.

44. Gray 2011; Topping 1996; Munley, Garvey, and McConnell 2010.

45. Garrett 2004; Doner 2009, 11–14.

46. Evans 1995, 319.

47. Amsden 1989; Evans 1995; Wade 1990.

48. Axelrod and Cohen 1999, xii.

49. Lansing 2006.

50. Bransford 2000.

51. Rodrik 2007, 166.

52. Sen 1999, 291.

53. Evans 2011; Evans and Heller 2013.

54. Evans 2004, 31.

55. Ibid., 43.

56. Providers of order need not only be the state but could also include civic organizations. For example, see my comparison of "I-paid-a-bribe" (a crowdsourcing platform of bribery reports) in China and India (Ang 2014a).

57. On public deliberative institutions in China, see Fishkin et al. 2010; He and Warren 2011.

58. Moreover, deliberative and bargaining processes have been an enduring feature of the Chinese bureaucracy (Lieberthal and Lampton 1992; Lieberthal and Oksenberg 1988).

Also, social actors and policy entrepreneurs exert growing influence on bureaucratic decision making (Mertha 2008, 2009).

59. Evans 2004.

60. Ober 2008.

61. Hamilton, Madison, and Jay 2012, 28.

62. Katzenstein 1985, 29.

63. Evans 1995; Johnson 1982.

64. This strategy was long ago employed by imperial governments in China. Civil service examinations brought large networks of educated men into "the orbit of the state" (Bossler 1998, 53).

65. Lim 2014.

66. Mertha 2009.

67. Landry 2008.

68. Axelrod and Cohen 1999, 32.

69. Edin 2003; Huang 1996; Landry 2008; Naughton and Yang 2004.

70. The Chinese term for "tailor your methods to local contexts" is 因地制宜.

71. Rodrik 2007.

72. Wilson 1989, 115.

73. Ibid., 117.

74. Kelman and Friedman 2009.

75. Miller and Page 2007, 105.

76. Davis and Feng 2009; Fan, Kanbur, and Zhang 2009; Li, Sato, and Sicular 2013.

77. OECD 2013, 113. In China the central government provides equalization grants, but its scale is far from sufficient to bridge overwhelming gaps in tax income across regions (Lou and Wang 2008, 141).

78. Miller and Page 2007, 105.

79. B2015–297.

80. The role of regional competition in China's development has already been widely discussed (Coase and Wang 2012, 148; Montinola, Qian, and Weingast 1995; Li, Li, and Zhang 2000; Xu 2011), but that of complementarities among unequal regions has received much less attention.

81. McMillan and Naughton 1992, 131.

82. Nathan 2003, 13.

83. Heilmann and Perry 2011b.

84. Tsai 2006.

85. Conference on "Adaptive Authoritarianism: China's Party-State Resilience in Historical Perspective," organized by Elizabeth Perry and Sebastian Heilmann, Harvard University, July 14–16, 2008. The term is also cited in "China's Internet: A Giant Cage," *The Economist*, April 6, 2013.

86. Nathan and Scobell 2012, 349; Stockmann 2012; Weller 2008.

87. Breznitz and Murphree 2011.

88. Heilmann and Perry 2011a, 6.

89. Rawski 2011; Shambaugh 2008.

90. Blanchard and Shleifer 2001.

91. Landry 2008, 79.

92. Ang 2015.

93. For more on franchising versus direct ownership, see Brickley and Dark 1987. The differences between the two organizational forms extends on an earlier discussion of the trade-offs between market transactions and hierarchical structures (Coase 1937; Williamson 1975).

94. Rejecting overly ambitious good-governance reforms that attempt to skip straight from bad to good governance, many experts recommend the opposite, which is that pragmatic reforms should "target few changes" (Grindle 2004, 545). See also Jomo and Chowdhury 2012a; Rodrik 2007, 5.

95. Wedeman 2003; Yang 1997; Young 2000.

96. Naughton 2003.

97. Akamatsu 1962.

98. Similarly, resource and factor endowments do not by themselves cause growth, just as eggs, sugar, and flour do not by themselves turn into cake. Ingredients don't make cake; people do.

3. BALANCING VARIETY AND UNIFORMITY

1. Huang 1998, 136–137.

2. While this chapter is focused on the reform period, the tragedy of the Great Leap Forward provides another stark illustration of the limitations of dictators. Mao wavered on setting grain and production targets, confusing his subordinates, and he seemed oblivious to the enormity of disaster until millions of peasants had perished (Chan 2001, 191–194; Bernstein 1984).

3. Miller 1992; Moe 1984; Williamson 1985.

4. See for example Chung 2000; Huang 1996; Landry 2008; Oi 1999.

5. Florini, Lai, and Tan 2012; Heilmann 2008.

6. Tsai 2006.

7. B2007–53.

8. See for example Lieberthal and Oksenberg 1988; Lin, Cai, and Li 2003; Naughton 1995.

9. Goldstein 1995, 1105.

10. McMillan and Naughton 1992.

11. Goldstein 1995, 1106.

12. Jomo and Chowdhury 2012a, 26, italics added.

13. Ibid., 18, italics added.

14. For other arguments for "good enough" or "just enough" governance, see Krasner 2013; Lake 2016; Levy and Fukuyama 2010.

15. Grindle 2004, 545, italics added.

16. Rodrik 2007, 5.

17. Aoki 1994; Hall and Soskice 2001.

18. Hall and Soskice 2001, 17.

19. The Chinese term for "policy complementarity" is 配套.

20. Oksenberg and Tong 1991.

21. Naughton 2007, 59–60.

22. Schurmann 1966.

23. For a village-level account of "opportunistic" cadres placed in office, see Huang 1998, 44.

24. Vogel 2011, 248.

25. Ibid., 354.

26. Shirk 1993. See also Oi 1999; Walder 1996.

27. Naughton 1995.

28. Coase and Wang 2012, 47.

29. Oi 1999, 1.

30. Coase and Wang 2012, 53.

31. Osnos 2014, 14.

32. Coase and Wang 2012, 54.

33. Oi 1992, 1999; Walder 1995.

34. Edin 2003; Whiting 2001.

35. Naughton 2007, 70.

36. Actions taken by local officials to promote the TVEs included serving as guarantors for bank loans, mobilizing funds and customers through connections, and pooling and redistributing income, to name a few (Oi 1999).

37. Brandt and Rawski relate a telling encounter with the manager of a state-owned factory in the 1970s: "A visitor asked, '[So] you just sit there and wait for instructions?' To which the director responded, 'Yes, that's our job. The upper level issues plans, and we implement them'" (2008, 15).

38. Vogel 2011, 465.

39. Klein 2007, 281–82.

40. Vogel 2011, 448.

41. Gallagher 2005.

42. Vogel 2011, 465.

43. Qian and Wu 2003, 33.

44. Shirk 1993, 18.

45. Qian and Wu 2003, 35.

46. Ibid., 36.

47. "How Reforms Were Relaunched" (*Zhongguo gaige shi zeme chongqide*), *China Reform* (*Zhongguo Gaige*) 12 (2012): 23.

48. Schell and Delury 2013, 336.

49. For a comprehensive review of these reforms, see Yang (2004).

50. A recent study of changes in the patterns of corruption finds that while the scale of bribery has climbed unabated, corruption in the forms of embezzlement and misuse of public funds has steadily declined over the years, reflecting the effects of capacity-building reforms since 1993 (Ko and Weng 2012).

51. Coase and Wang 2012, 147.

52. Oi and Zhao 2007; World Bank 2002a.

53. Man and Hong 2011, 167.

54. Kung and Chen 2012.

55. The Chinese term for "financing platforms" is 融资平台.

56. Bardhan 2010, 54–64.

57. Between 1996 and 2005, the national per capita road area has increased from 7.56 to 10.92 square meters, and the rate of wastewater treatment rose from 23.62 percent to 45.67 percent (Wu 2011, 49).

58. This is apparent in the locales featured in chapters 5 (a hill-locked city) and 6 (a landlocked county).

59. Naughton 2015.

60. Mikesell et al. 2011.

61. In 2011 Stephen Green, head of the research department at Standard Chartered Bank, predicted that more than 80 percent of China's local governments would not be able to service their debts, a statement that triggered fears of a financial crisis. See "Stanchart warns on China's local government debt," *Caixin*, September 21, 2011.

62. Wallis 2005.

63. Vogel 2011, 465.

64. Brandt and Rawski 2008, 16.

65. Ministry of Land and Resources of the People's Republic of China, "A Summary of Plans for National Land Use" (*Guoguo tudi liyong zongti guihua gangyao*), *Xinhua News Agency*, Oct. 24, 2008.

66. "Shrinking arable land adds concern on China's grain security," *Xinhua*, October 18, 2010.

67. "Explaining the Policy of the Ministry of Land Resources" (*Guotu ziyuanbu zhengce jiedu: 18 yimu gengdi, yimu buneng shao*), *Renmin Ribao*, July 23, 2008.

68. "A canal too far," *The Economist*, Sept. 27, 2014.

69. State Council, "Decision on Accelerating Regulation of Water Consumption" (*guanyu jiakuai shuili gaige fazhan de jueding*), Dec. 31, 2010.

70. "China to Check Water Consumption," *China Daily*, Sept. 14, 2011.

71. State Council, Dec. 31, 2010.

72. See Article 86 of Government of the People's Republic of China, "PRC Law on Land Management" (*zhonghua renmin gongheguo tudiguanli fa*), Jan. 1, 1999.

73. "Construction of a technological system for monitoring land" (*tudi zhengzhi zonghe jianguan jishu tixi jianshe zaiji*), *China Land Resources News*, Dec. 27, 2013.

74. B2010–201.

75. B2010–200.

76. B2011–281.

77. For example, one article wrote, "In China the state would just requisition the land, and let farmers go hang" ("A Chance to Fly," *The Economist*, Feb. 21, 2015).

78. Findings in this section are based on my field research with a team of researchers from Stanford University and the NDRC (National Development and Reform Commission) in Chengdu, Sichuan Province, in August 2012. We interviewed officials in the departments of land, finance, and development and reform, among others, at the provincial, city, county, and township levels.

79. Officials from Chengdu estimated the one-time costs of relocation at 250,000 to 400,000 yuan per resident, including the construction of new housing and social security payments but not including the long-term costs of public services provision.

80. Interview with the Coordination Agency of Chengdu City, 2012. Such transactions took place through state-established organizations called "Rural Property Rights Transfer Centers" (农村产权交易所).

81. Tsai 2006, 118.

82. Vogel 2011, 364.

83. Ibid., 364.

84. Ibid., 386, 390. Similarly, American presidents can shape public opinion by exercising their power of the "bully pulpit."

85. Ibid., 441.

86. Coase and Wang 2012, 50.

87. Vogel 2011, 443–445.

88. B2011–279.

89. State Council, "Provisions on Several Issues in the Development of Commune and Brigade Enterprises" (*guanyu fazhan shedui qiye ruogan wenti de guiding*), July 3, 1979.

90. In Chinese, the phrase is 要有一个大发展.

91. In Chinese, "availability of local resources and demand" is 根据当地的资源和需求, "self-independent" is 自力更生, "according to local conditions" is 因地制宜, "for those localities that have the right conditions" is 有条件的地方, and "based on need and feasibility" is 根据需要和可能.

92. In Chinese, the term for "relevant departments" is 有关部门 and "based on their assessments of the pros and cons" is 权衡利弊确定.

93. See section 6 on "Ownership."

94. See section 10 on "Pricing Policy."

95. B2011–279.

96. Central Committee of the Chinese Communist Party, "Notice on Agricultural Work for 1984" (*guanyu yijiu basi nian nongcun gongzuo de tongzhi*), Document No. 1, Jan. 1, 1984. As the Shandong official reiterates, that instructions to promote TVEs appeared in the No. 1 directive was itself a strong signal of the party's resolution. In other words, numbers on policy directives serve a signaling function.

97. See section 3 on "Employment."

98. The China Statistical Yearbooks only reported the number and output of collective enterprises in the industrial sectors, but not in the tertiary sector.

99. Vogel 2011, 390.

100. Tsai 2007, 58–59. It is probably impossible to know from the available official statistics exactly how many collective enterprises were de facto private operations. But it suffices to know that the line between collective and private ownership was deliberately fuzzy.

101. Tsai 2006, 130.

102. Ibid., 131. See also Dickson 2003; Qian and Wu 2003.

103. Tsai 2006, 136–37.

104. Qian and Wu 2003, 37.

105. Tsai 2007, 55.

106. "Private sector contributes over 60% to GDP," *CCTV* (English), Feb. 6, 2013.

107. Lardy 2014.

108. B2012–308. The Chinese term is 吃透上级文件.

109. Oksenberg 1970.

110. Axelrod and Cohen 1999, 32.

111. Grindle 2011, 200.

112. Jomo and Chowdhury 2012b; Rodrik 2007, 5.

113. Padgett and Ansell 1993.

114. Huber and Shipan 2002.

115. As elaborated in chapter 2, I differentiate *uncertainty* (indeterminate outcomes that cannot be anticipated in advance) from *risks* (probabilistic outcomes that are within anticipation).

4. FRANCHISING THE BUREAUCRACY

1. Wilson 1989, xviii.

2. Quoted in "No Golf, Long Days Are New Norm for India's Bureaucrats," *The Washington Post*, July 11, 2014.

3. Duckett 1998, 2001; Lee 2014; Oi 1992, 1999; Walder 1995.

4. North 2005, 70.

5. Axelrod and Cohen 1999, chap. 4.

6. The concepts of high-powered vs. low-powered incentives are traced back to transactional theories of economics (Coase 1937; Williamson 1975). Public bureaucracies are assumed to be low-powered organizations (Dixit 1997; Moe 1984).

7. "As China Awaits New Leadership, Liberals Look to a Provincial Party Chief," *New York Times*, Nov. 5, 2012.

8. "Mayor of Chinese City Is Held by Communist Party Investigators," *New York Times*, Oct. 16, 2013.

9. "A Muddy Tract Now, But by 2020, China's Answer to Wall Street," *New York Times*, April 2, 2014.

10. "China Suspends Family Planning Workers After Forced Abortion," *New York Times*, June 15, 2012.

11. "Years After Revolt, Chinese Village Glumly Returns to Polls," *New York Times*, April 1, 2014.

12. Wilson's (1989) classic study divides the American bureaucracy into three layers: executives, managers, and operators.

13. Baum and Shevchenko 1999, 334.

14. For example, see Huang 1996; Kostka and Yu 2014; Landry 2008.

15. Ang 2012b, 692. In Chinese, extra-bureaucracy is termed 事业单位. The pop-up box in figure 4.1 lists the extra-bureaucracies under the charge of the Culture Bureau.

16. Ibid., 691.

17. In a separate article, I discuss the meaning of "cadre" and its evolution from the revolutionary period to the present day. I also clarify the distinction between "civil servants" (a modern administrative term that came into official use after 2006) and other public employees who are not civil servants (Ang 2012b).

18. Walder 2004, 195. In Chinese, these political elites are sometimes referred to as 领导干部.

19. Specifically, they are appointed by the Organization Department (a party organ) at the next higher level of administration (B2010–211, B2010–212).

20. Manion 1985.

21. The Chinese term for "local leadership" is 地方领导.

22. "A Summary of Local Leadership," official website of the PROC Central Government, http://www.gov.cn/test/2008–02/26/content_901628.htm.

23. B2011–236; B2011–241. Recent studies find that the average tenure length of local party secretaries and state chiefs has shortened over the years (Guo 2009; Landry 2008).

24. Olson 2000.

25. B2007–107.

26. B2011–237.

27. B2011–237; B2011–239; B2011–240. Exceptions are the positions of party secretary, chief of government, chief of organization, chief of public security bureau, chief of discipline, chief of procuratorate, and chief of courts, which are required to be staffed by a nonnative of the locale, as these positions are powerful and susceptible to nepotism (B2011–236; B2011–237; B2011–263; B2011–239; B2011–240; B2011–241).

28. Lipsky 1980.

29. See also Edin 2003, 49.

30. B2011–236; B2011–221; B2011–222; B2011–225; B2011–239; B2011–240; B2011–237. One practical reason why natives are hired is that they can speak and work in local dialects, which is essential at the grassroots.

31. Lieberthal and Oksenberg 1988.

32. Huang 1996; Kung and Chen 2011; Li and Zhou 2005.

33. Kostka and Yu 2014; Landry 2008.

34. Guo 2009; Kung and Chen 2012; Lu and Landry 2014.

35. Wilson 1989, 117.

36. See Moe's (1989) contention that "American agencies are designed to fail."

37. Kelman and Friedman 2009.

38. This is also known as the "cadre responsibility" (干部责任) and "target responsibility" (目标责任) systems.

39. This is probably a main reason why actual documents on cadre evaluation are rarely shown and examined in the literature.

40. See references to the importance of cadre evaluation for economic development (Oi 1999, 49; Xu 2011), local policy implementation (O'Brien and Li 1999), dynamics of protest (Cai 2004; Takeuchi 2014), and enforcing bureaucratic discipline (Cai 2015).

41. Some have described items on cadre evaluation guidelines (Edin 2003; Heberer and Trappel 2013; Tsui and Wang 2004), but only a few studies have reproduced entire lists of targets (Whiting 2001; Ong 2012, 80–81; Wang 2015, 25–26). Table 4.4 shows a sample list of targets in greater detail than was previously seen.

42. Vogel 2011, 244.

43. Edin 2005, 39.

44. Whiting 2001, 106.

45. Edin 2003; O'Brien and Li 1999, 172.

46. B2011–254; B2011–257.

47. This strategy is known in Chinese as "skipping over water" (跳水). A subdistrict leader elaborated with an example: "Let's say we have collected nine million yuan in taxes. We will report only five million yuan this fiscal year and leave the remainder for next year's report. . . . If our results this year are lower, the higher levels will lower their targets correspondingly. With lower targets next year and a surplus that is already in place, our pressure for meeting next year's target will be lower" (B2011–229).

48. Chen, Li, and Zhou 2005; Li and Zhou 2005; Maskin, Qian, and Xu 2000.

49. Edin 2003, 45.

50. B2010–193.

51. Kung and Lin 2007.

52. Edin 2003; Oi 1999; Whiting 2001.

53. Even setting aside illegal bribes, my data on county governments in Shandong Province (1998–2005) find that bonuses constituted less than 1.4 percent of total compensation, including formal salary, allowances, bonuses, and other benefits. See Ang 2012a.

54. Whiting's study in 1989 reported that leaders of a top-ranked township received 17,500 yuan in bonuses, compared to only 6,000 yuan in the weakest performer (2004, 110).

55. Grand bribery rose in frequency and in scale in the recent decade (Ko and Weng 2012; Manion 2004; Wedeman 2012).

56. B2013–341; Zhang forthcoming.

57. Deng and Yang 2013; Mertha 2008.

58. Zhang 2010; Zhang forthcoming.

59. I collected a document from a city in Zhejiang Province titled "Energy Conservation Target Responsibility Contract in 2008" (节能目标责任书), which was signed by the mayor. In the contract, four pledges were made. (1) Reduce energy consumption as a ratio of GDP by 4.4 percent compared to the previous year; (2) Strengthen the implementation of energy conservation targets by the city agencies, (2) Strengthen and inspect energy conservation among local enterprises; (4) Seriously take into account energy conservation in cadre evaluation and consider it as a veto target.

60. For notable exceptions, see Zhang forthcoming; Zhao 2013.

61. In Chinese, the term for "overall economic efficiency" is 经济发展综合效益 and "development costs" is 发展代价.

62. Birney 2014.

63. O'Brien and Li 1999. See also Birney 2014.

64. O'Brien and Li 1999, 182.

65. Green 2013.

66. Wu et al. 2014, 21.

67. On the difficulties of verifying environmental outcomes, see Zhang 2010.

68. The Chinese term for subdistrict is 街道.

69. B2011–229.

70. This instance illustrates that tax revenue targets cannot be simply written off as targets of "fiscal extraction" (Lu and Landry 2014). Local leaders can influence the amount of tax revenue generated in two ways, which may take place simultaneously: one is to actively recruit businesses in order to expand the tax base; another is to collect more taxes from existing enterprises. The former activity is not extractive but actually growth-promoting (even if it is associated with corruption, as discussed in chapters 1 and 5).

71. Kostka and Yu 2014.

72. Ibid.

73. B2007–90, B2007–91.

74. B2010–188.

75. The nominal annual income of urban and rural residents is reported in the *China Statistical Yearbooks*. As for civil servants, I estimated mean formal wages by first collecting official wage scales from 1985 to 2006. Then, following statistical sources from the *Central Organization Department*, I computed formal wage levels for each rank and then divided total wages by the number of public employees to obtain an average for the entire civil service. The second step takes into account the fact that only a minuscule percentage of cadres occupy leading positions.

76. B2011–235. Furthermore, even though official wages were supposed to adjust annually for inflation, in practice they barely increased since the last increment in 2006 (B2011–221; B2011–222; B2012–308; B2013–311). In 2014 the central government finally announced a much-delayed decision to raise civil service salaries. Monthly standardized wages for the lowest-ranked bureaucrats rose from 630 yuan (US$103) to 1,320 yuan (US$217), while ministerial officials received 11,385 yuan (US$1,869) after the adjustment. See "Civil Servants to See 60 Percent Increase in Salary," *China Daily*, Jan. 18, 2015.

77. 1993, 122; Klitgaard 1988, 77.

78. Weber 1968, 231–235.

79. Parrillo 2013, 1.

80. Weber 1968, 221, 966.

81. Ibid., 1032, 1965.

82. For more on McDonald's franchising system, see Love 1995.

83. This is why outsourcing certain government services that involves coercion, such as policing and tax collection, is riskier than other services like garbage collection (Moe 1984). Thus, among modern public administrations, most regulatory agencies (such as the Internal Revenue Service) are fully state-funded and salaried, whereas only certain noncoercive services are outsourced to private providers.

84. Weber 1968, 965, 229.

85. Hickey 1991, 389.

86. B2013–326.

87. Xu 2007.

88. Chan and Ma 2011, 311.

89. Burns 2007, 19.

90. Whiting 2001, 117.

91. One study misinterprets supplemental items of compensation like "restaurant meals, alcohol, luxury cars, travel, and foreign tourism" as "embezzlement" (i.e., funds that are illegally stolen by public employees). It further argues that such embezzlement is "both illegal and tolerated" because central officials would rather local officials embezzle than take bribes (Fan, Lin, and Treisman 2010). This completely misunderstands the institutional context and fails to distinguish between supplemental compensation and illegally stolen funds, between elite and street-level bureaucrats, and between different time periods. Indeed, the authors themselves noted that "one of the strangest features of the phenomenon of consumption from the state budget in China is *how open it is*." Obviously, if local cadres had stolen from state treasuries and then openly paraded their crimes through brazen consumption, this would be political suicide, not corruption.

92. B2008–136.

93. The Chinese terms for "greasy" and "distilled water" departments are 油水衙门 and 清水衙门 respectively.

94. B2008–140.

95. B2007–128.

96. Xu 2007.

97. "Local Governments Do Whatever It Takes to Attract Investors" (*Guangdong bufen jiceng zhengfu wei zhaoshang buze shouduan*), *Southern Daily*, March 29, 2012.

98. Weber 1968, 965.

99. Ang 2009a. During that time, it was not strictly illegal for individual offices to set up multiple bank accounts on their own because a formal and centralized system of bank account management had yet been established. Because of the association of these accounts with arbitrary extraction, however, the former is widely perceived as "small treasuries" (小金库) and "illegal slush funds" (Tsai 2004; Wedeman 2000).

100. Lu 2000.

101. Weber 1968, 1095.

102. Yang 2004.

103. Given the amorphous and largely nonmonetized nature of supplemental pay and perks, this category of compensation is normally difficult to measure. My dataset makes innovative use of line-item budgets to reconstruct the monetized value of supplemental compensation, and allows us for the first time to view changes in compensation structures over time. Briefly described, I employ previously unavailable line-item budgets compiled by the finance authorities in Shandong Province. Unlike conventional budgets that list public spending in broad categories, line-item budgets detail spending by items (e.g., basic salary, vehicles, overtime pay). Using these line items, I reconstruct a measure for supplemental compensation, namely, spending items that constituted pay and benefits to local cadres. For more details, see Ang 2012a.

104. The Chinese term is 坐收坐支.

105. Ang 2009a.

106. The Chinese term is 非税收入一般缴款书.

107. B2010–196; B2011–226; B2011–227; B2011–228.

108. The Chinese term is 使用权.

109. B2007–114.

110. Ko and Weng, 2012.

111. Menes 2006. This will also be elaborated through a historical case study in chapter 5.

112. Andrews 2013, 3.

113. See Parrillo (2013) for a historical account of the movement away from profit motives and toward fixed salaries in America's bureaucracy from 1780 to 1940. China is still undergoing this process of transformation and moreover at different rates across the country.

5. FROM BUILDING TO PRESERVING MARKETS

1. Appendix B elaborates on the coverage of my interviews, interviewing methods, and citation protocol.

2. Kaufmann, Kraay, and Zoido-Lobatón 1999.

3. Woo-Cumings 1999.

4. Grindle 2004, 2011.

5. Chang 2002, 127. See also Doner 2009.

6. Rodrik 2007, 16.

7. Doner 2009; Noble 1998; Hamilton-Hart 2002; Biggs and Levy 1991. For a review of this literature, see Doner 2009, 15–16.

8. Andrews 2010, 2013; Grindle 2004; Jomo and Chowdhury 2012b.

9. Rodrik 2007, 39, italics added. Likewise, attempting to make sense of China's stunning turnaround, Acemoglu and Robinson comment, "Such growth was feasible partly because there was a lot of catching up to be done. Growth under extractive institutions is *easier* when creative destruction is not a necessity" (2012, 440, italics added). Yet in fact, as

we shall later see through the case of Forest Hill, even a single locale within China clearly underwent creative destruction, not once but several times, during its catch-up stage.

10. Rodrik 2007, 39.

11. Grindle 2004, 545; Rodrik 2008.

12. Rodrik 2007, 44–50.

13. Indeed, the lack of distinction among the development strategies of low-, middle-, and high-income countries is especially odd when compared to corporate management; it is common knowledge that start-up companies cannot and do not adopt the same strategies as established corporations (Bhide 2000).

14. North and Weingast 1989. As a student of China, I am often asked, "What are the scope conditions in China?" that is, what are the conditions that limit the generalizability of China's experiences? It is useful to extend this question and also consider the scope conditions of England at the time of the Glorious Revolution. For a start, England in the seventeenth century was an emerging colonial power, while most contemporary developing countries are postcolonial states dragged into modernization. Obviously, the world politics and domestic socioeconomic realities in conquering and conquered regions and in two contexts that are three centuries apart could not be more different. Yet it is often taken for granted that experiences from Western history are generalizable, whereas experiences from other parts of the world are exceptional. For example, Tilly's (1992) famous study of Western Europe's state-building experiences has been widely embraced as a universal theory of state building, but a few scholars have contested this view (Wong 1997; Centeno 2002; Hui 2005).

15. Acemoglu and Robinson (2012) also invoke the Glorious Revolution as evidence that inclusive and nonextractive institutions are the universal causes of economic boom. They extend this logic to argue that twentieth-century Botswana had successfully developed because it had tribal institutions that were already "a primitive form of pluralism." According to them, Botswana escaped the poverty trap by "quickly developing inclusive economic and political institutions after independence," described as a critical juncture that "exhibited many parallels to England on the verge of the Glorious Revolution" (2012, 407, 410).

16. Greif 2006a, 232.

17. Weingast 1995.

18. Oi & Walder 1999.

19. The biographies of America's capitalist titans provide another illustration. Describing J. P Morgan at a young age, Brands wrote, "The Civil War disrupted much of the transatlantic trade . . . [but] Morgan learned to fish in troubled waters" (2010, 73). Those who were adept at navigating the treacherous environment of market rebuilding after the destruction of the Civil War during the Gilded Age ultimately became fabulously rich.

20. B2013–295. This official noted that only after "the basics were taken care of" did businesses start to care about the legal system. Their most recent concern, he added, was the protection of intellectual property rights.

21. An official from the Ministry of Finance told me that his ministry could not directly remit fiscal grants to township governments across the country because "some townships didn't even have a post office, much less a bank." Even in a high-growth economy like China, basic infrastructure is still lacking in parts of the country, especially at the lowest level of administrations (B2006–6).

22. The Chinese term is 第一桶金.

23. Grindle 2011, 208, 218, italics added.

24. One well-known example of the use of personal connections in rural communities to spur entrepreneurial activities is microfinance. Muhammad Yunus, founder of the Grameen Bank in Bangladesh, changed the lives of millions of poor people by offering

microloans. Each borrower joins a small group of borrowers from the same village that share collective responsibility for repaying the loans (cited in Axelrod and Cohen 1999, 10). When he first started, though, Yunus's initiative was roundly rejected by conventional banks, who pronounced that "it was impossible to lend money to the poorest of the poor" ("Interview with Nobel Laureate Muhammad Yunus, Spiegel Online, Dec. 7, 2006). Another example from Bali is the use of religious rituals among farmers to coordinate and enforce informal water-sharing arrangements (Lansing 2006).

25. Qian and Xu 1993. See also Donnithorne 1972.

26. World Bank and State Council 2013, 100.

27. B2012–291.

28. Yuen Yuen Ang, "What Is the Party in China's Political System?" Working Paper, University of Michigan, 2015.

29. It is also worth highlighting that although the party and the state are depicted as two parallel hierarchies in textbook accounts, they are not in fact separate entities. Personnel flows between party and state hierarchies, and especially at the elite levels, officials typically straddle both party and state roles. For example, city mayors (chiefs of state) are members of city party committees and sometimes simultaneously serve as deputy party secretaries. Thus, when asking about the role of the party in local development, it is necessary to clarify if one means by "party" the formal organization, which is static, or the individuals who occupy party positions, who move fluidly between or coexist in party and state hierarchies.

30. These are known in Chinese as 事业单位. For more background, see Ang 2012b.

31. In 2012, Fujian ranked ninth in terms of GDP per capita among the thirty-one provincial units.

32. Vogel 2011, 418.

33. Forest Hill Statistical Yearbooks and the World Bank Database.

34. B2015–362.

35. B2015–363.

36. B2013–326.

37. See "Left-Behind Children of China's Migrant Workers Bear Grown-Up Burdens," *Wall Street Journal*, Jan. 17, 2014.

38. As Officer Tian analyzed in Marxist terms, "Marx is correct; the accumulation of capital is a bloody process." Commenting on the earlier days of chaotic markets and smuggling in Xiamen (Fujian's provincial capital city), he added that "this was part of the stage of factor accumulation" (B2013–326).

39. Oi and Walder 1999; Qian 2003; Whiting 2001.

40. Nee 1989.

41. Oi and Walder 1999. See also Oi 1992, 1999.

42. Local actors were highly sensitive to central signals. In the case of Forest Hill, TVEs were started right after 1979 but boomed after the central leadership resoundingly endorsed TVEs in a No. 1 Directive issued in 1985 (as discussed in chapter 3). A county official recalled: "TVEs suddenly burst into the scene after 1985. Shortly afterward, Star Township won the honor of being the first '100 million Yuan' township" (B2015–360).

43. B2013–326.

44. B2015–360.

45. C2015–356; B2013–324.

46. B2013–326.

47. Kung and Lin 2007.

48. See my discussion of local leadership evaluation criteria in chapter 4.

49. B2013–324.

50. B2013–327.

51. As I discussed in chapter 3, the bottlenecks resulting from the partial market reforms of the 1980s contributed to but were not the singular cause of the 1993 decision. Much credit must be given to Deng, who outmaneuvered party conservatives through his Southern Tour of 1992. His swan-song act steered China firmly back on the path of capitalism.

52. B2013–325.

53. The Chinese term for "restructure" is 改制 and "privatize" is 私有化.

54. B2013–326.

55. Ibid.

56. A distinctive feature of China's FDI compared to other developing countries is that it came mostly from the "China Circle," especially Hong Kong and Taiwan but also Singapore, South Korea, and Japan (Wang 2015; Ye 2014).

57. B2013–326.

58. Lü 2000.

59. Bardhan 1997; Kaufmann and Wei 2000; Manion 2004, 105.

60. B2013–326. "Preparing an envelope" is a euphemism for paying a bribe or presenting a gift.

61. Montinola et al. 1995, 58.

62. According to Naughton, manufacturing accounted for 70 percent of FDI inflows in 2003 and 2004 (2007, 419).

63. REG-2012–019; REG-2012–020.

64. See also Tsai 2007; Wank 1996; Xin and Pearce 1996.

65. C2015–351.

66. This was reported in the *Fujian Daily News*, 2011.

67. On political co-optation of private capitalists, see Dickson 2008; Tsai 2007.

68. During the 1st City People's Congressional Meeting in 1997 (the year Forest Hill officially attained municipal status), 33 of the 376 delegates were business owners or managers.

69. At a national level, see Ang and Jia 2014; Truex 2014.

70. Tsai 2006, 139.

71. For more details, see chapter 4.

72. B2015–361.

73. B2013–324.

74. The Chinese term for "release" is 松绑. Osnos translates the term as "unfettered" (2014, 11).

75. B2013–326.

76. C2013–328.

77. B2013–326.

78. For a quantitatively based argument, see Kurtz and Schrank 2007b.

79. This was reported in the *Fujian Online News*, 2014.

80. There is an abundant collection of books on grand corruption in the United States and other wealthy economies. In particular, see Genovese and Farrar-Myers 2010; Whyte 2015. On rent-seeking in Asia, see Khan and Jomo 2000.

81. I discuss the national policies and local responses leading to this phenomenon in chapter 3.

82. Evans 1995; Johnson 1982, 318; Wade 1990.

83. Blecher and Shue 2001; Oi 1999; Walder 1995.

84. The term in Chinese is 粗放.

85. B2013–326.

86. Kohli 2004; Sasada 2013.

87. B2015–360.

88. Fei 1992, 43.

89. The term in Chinese is 熟人社会.

90. Fei 1992, 44.

91. Perry 2011, 43, 49.

92. B2013–323.

93. B2015–359.

94. B2013–323.

95. B2013–324.

96. B2015–367. The term in Chinese is 普遍现象.

97. B2015–367.

98. B2015–369.

99. B2015–370.

100. B2013–326.

101. B2013–324.

102. Ibid.

103. Amsden 1989; Evans 1995; Wade 1990, 334.

104. B2015–325.

105. C2013–328.

106. B2013–323.

107. B2015–325.

108. The Chinese term for "quality" is 质量.

109. In Chinese, the term for "method of economic growth" is 经济增长方式 and "method of economic development" is 经济发展方式.

110. B2013–324.

111. Ibid.

112. The term in Chinese is 龙头企业.

113. This was reported in the *Fujian Daily News*, 2011.

114. B2013–324.

115. This variety of investment targets is still assigned in Upstart County, an inland locale, as featured in chapter 1.

116. B2013–325.

117. Ibid.

118. REG-2012–019.

119. The term "middle-income trap" appeared in the World Bank's 2030 Report (World Bank and State Council 2013). The report interprets "middle-income trap" as the inability to advance from middle-income to high-income levels, according to the World Bank's classifications. This could result from having exhausted the advantages of early development (such as low cost and technological imitation) but not yet having acquired the high technologies and institutions required for advanced capitalist development.

120. Grindle 2004, 152. See also Krasner 2013; Lake 2016; Levy and Fukuyama 2010.

121. Doner 2009, 4.

122. Ibid., 69, italics added.

123. Diamond 2005.

124. Schell and Delury 2013.

6. CONNECTING FIRST MOVERS AND LAGGARDS

1. Consistent with chapter 5, I do not identify specific locations or individuals in order to maintain the anonymity of my respondents. Instead, for ease of narration, I assign pseudonyms to several respondents who are frequently quoted.

2. B2015–373.

3. Ibid.

4. Laitin 2002, 630.

5. On interdependence among countries in world politics, see Katzenstein 1975.

6. Nee and Opper 2012.

7. Even though local governments in Zhejiang are widely considered noninterventionist by Chinese standards, they are still omnipresent and highly interventionist by American standards. As one official from Blessed County related, "One time, I accompanied our county leaders to visit a county in the state of Washington. The county had about a million residents . . . but only eight thousand civil servants. Our county has almost a million residents, but we must have about twenty thousand civil servants. [In America] the county leader can take vacations every year. But our county leaders can never rest. They don't even have enough time to eat" (B2012–310).

8. "To Understand Xi Jinping, Pay Attention to the Zhejiang Model," *Hexun*, April 24, 2014.

9. B2013–327.

10. For a comparison of the economic models in Zhejiang and Jiangsu, see Huang 2007.

11. B2013–327.

12. B2015–373.

13. B2015–372.

14. B2013–331.

15. Author's calculation from China Data Online.

16. "The Strategy of China's Regional Development" (*zhongguo quyu fazhan geju*), *Xinhua*, July 2, 2009.

17. Porter (1990) views the size of domestic markets as one of the key conditions of creating competitive firms.

18. B2012–311.

19. Central Party School, "Report on 30 Years of Blessed County's Development," 2008, 8 (hereafter "Party School Report").

20. B2012–311.

21. "Party School Report," 75.

22. B2015–349.

23. C2015–354.

24. B2012–308.

25. County Archives Office, "Report on Blessed County's Private Sector Development," 75 (hereafter "Archives Office Report").

26. "Archives Office Report," 64.

27. B2012–308.

28. Ibid.

29. "Archives Office Report," 90.

30. B2012–310.

31. The Chinese term is *xiahai* (下海). For more on *xiahai*, see also Dickson 2003, 136.

32. C2015–354.

33. Ibid.

34. Huang 2003.

35. Gallagher 2005.

36. C2012–314.

37. B2012–309.

38. B2015–350.

39. The Chinese term is 假外资. See also Tsai 2007, 184.

40. C2012–313.

41. Ibid.

42. C2012–315.

43. B2015–349.

44. B2015–350.

45. C2015–352.

46. B2012–308.

47. B2015–350.

48. "Party School Report," 160.

49. B2012–310.

50. Ibid.

51. "Party School Report," 160.

52. C2015–351.

53. B2013–329.

54. B2013–331.

55. C2015–374.

56. B2015–373.

57. Ibid.

58. See for example Li and Zhou 2005; Montinola, Qian, and Weingast 1995; Oi 1992.

59. B2015–372.

60. Ibid.

61. Ibid.

62. B2013–329.

63. B2013–331.

64. B2015–373.

65. B2013–329.

66. B2013–334.

67. B2013–331.

68. B2013–329.

69. Vogel 2011, 399.

70. The term in Chinese is 产业转移.

71. B2015–372; B2015–373; B2015–375.

72. B2013–331.

73. Wallis 2005.

74. B2015–372.

75. Ibid.

76. B2013–330.

77. B2013–329.

78. B2013–330; B2015–373. The term in Chinese is 以亲招商 or 亲情招商.

79. B2013–329.

80. B2013–331.

81. B2015–375; See a report on furniture-making hubs in Guangdong Province, "New Frontiers," *The Economist*, Jan. 14, 2014.

82. B2013–329.

83. See for example Florini, Lai, and Tan 2012; Heilmann 2008; Teets and Hurst 2015; Vogel 2011, chap. 14.

84. B2013–330.

85. For a sharp critique of the approach of "skipping straight to Weber," commonly adopted by international aid agencies, see Pritchett and Woolcock 2004.

86. Rising labor costs reflect shrinking labor supply, which results from the one-child policy, preferential policies for the agricultural sector in the recent decade, and institutionalized discrimination against migrant labor through the *hukou* (household registration) system (Kuruvilla, Lee, and Gallagher 2011).

87. B2015–375.

88. B2013–340.

89. Kuruvilla, Lee, and Gallagher 2011. See also Mary Gallagher, "We Are Not Machines: Teen Spirit on China's Shopfloor," *The China Beat*, Aug. 23, 2010.

90. B2013–329.

91. The Chinese term for "hoarding land" is 圈地.

92. B2014–343.

93. Ibid.

94. B2013–340.

95. One of the investment projects in Humble County that came from Guangdong Province was a ceramics factory. "Severe pollution: The negative consequences of industrial transfer" (*zhujiang liuyu zhongda wuran chanye zhuanyi de eguo*), *Huaxia*, July 18, 2013.

96. B2013–340.

97. Document from Upstart County, "Investment Targets," 2013.

98. B2014–337.

99. B2013–341.

100. Akamatsu 1962. For a revisionist view of the flying geese theory after the economic crisis of the 1990s, see Hatch 2010.

101. Cai and Wang 2008.

102. Yang 1997, 67.

103. "Not So Grim Up North-West," *The Economist*, Jan. 11, 2014.

104. Lin 2012, 243.

105. Yang 1997, chap. 2.

106. Ibid., 27.

107. B2013–325.

108. Wedeman 2003.

109. Young 2000.

110. Naughton 1995, 158.

111. *Xinhua*, July 2, 2009. Together these six provinces make up 28 percent of China's population and one-third of its rural population.

112. Wei and Bai 2013, 80.

113. "The Ministry of Commerce takes seven measures to promote industrial transfer" (*shangwu jiang caiqu qixiang cuoshi tuidong chanye zhuanyi cujin zhong bu jueqi*), *Xinhua*, April 26, 2008.

114. This focus on mutually beneficial relationships between unequally endowed members brings to mind peer tutoring between novice and advanced students in classrooms, as I discussed in chapter 2.

115. NDRC, "Refining the Industrial Division of Labor" (*youhua chanye fengong geju*), transcript of press conference, 2010.

116. The package stalled the recession, but the sudden infusion of trillions of dollars into the economy fed a frenzy of public borrowing and construction, leaving behind the current mountain of local government debt (Lardy 2012).

117. State Council, "Guiding Principles on Industrial Transfer to the Central and Western Regions" (*guowuyuan guanyu zhongxibu diqu chengjie chanye zhuanyi de zhidao yijian*), Document No. 28, Aug. 31, 2010.

118. For instance, Yang describes the East-West Rural Enterprise Cooperation Project of 1994, which was led by the Ministry of Agriculture, as a politically weak and poorly funded bureaucracy. Local governments were asked to raise their own money for cooperation projects (1997, 110).

119. *Xinhua*, July 2, 2009.

120. B2015–297; also B2015–296; B2015–298.

121. The term *shengwai zijin* (省外资金) is defined as investments from domestic sources beyond one's province, excluding investments from Hong Kong, Taiwan, and

Macau. See "Definition of statistical terms in beyond-province investment reports" (*Hubei sheng yinjin shengwai zijin tianbiao shuoming*), 2008, Issued by the Hubei Provincial Commerce Bureau.

122. Wei and Bai 2013, 80.

123. While geography may determine long-term economic outcomes leading to the rise of human civilizations (Diamond 2005), my analysis suggests that its effects are moderated in the present age by regional economies, globalization, and infrastructural developments.

124. Rithmire 2014, 167.

125. Davis and Feng 2009; Fan, Kanbur, and Zhang 2009; Li, Sato, and Sicular 2013.

126. B2015–297.

CONCLUSION

1. Acemoglu and Robinson 2012; D. North and Weingast 1989.

2. Amsden 1989; Evans 1995; Johnson 1982; Kohli 2004; Wade 1990.

3. Greif 2006b.

4. Greif and Laitin 2004.

5. Ibid., 633.

6. Ibid., 634.

7. Fei 1992, 44.

8. Dixit 2004; North 1991.

9. Greif 2006a, 223.

10. Ibid., 232.

11. Ibid.

12. Ibid., 232–234.

13. Brewer 1988; Dincecco 2011; North and Weingast 1989.

14. Acemoglu, Johnson, and Robinson 2002, 1235.

15. Acemoglu 2003.

16. As critics pointed out, while the English colonists might have provided property rights to their own members, the article by Acemoglu, Johnson, and Robinson fails to mention that these settlers also deprived other segments of society, most notably indigenous populations, of their pre-existing rights. Khan writes, "The emergence of stable property rights . . . emerged in these societies *after* the critical transformations in economic, social, and political structures had already been carried out, in these cases through processes of enormous violence" (Khan 2012, 71–72; see also Kurtz and Schrank 2007b, 543).

17. Wallis 2005, 211.

18. This was also seen in the case of Blessed County, where the construction of a new central business district dramatically increased the asset holdings and wealth of many local entrepreneurs (chapter 6).

19. Wallis 2005, 215, 214.

20. See my discussion in chapter 3.

21. Wallis 2005, 213.

22. Ibid., 216.

23. Ibid., 226.

24. Roberts 2012.

25. Wallis 2001, 19.

26. Ibid.

27. Wallis 2005, 234.

28. Rutschman 2015, 693.

29. Arewa 2011, 9.

30. Rutschman 2015, 691.

31. Arewa 2011, 25.

32. Andrew Rice, "A Scorsese in Lagos: The Making of Nigeria's Film Industry," *New York Times*, Feb. 23, 2012.

33. *New York Times*, Feb. 23, 2012.

34. Eddie Ugbomah, interviewed in *Nollywood Babylon* (2008).

35. Rutschman 2015, 690.

36. Arewa 2011, 24.

37. Andrew Holz, "Dateline Nigeria (Part 2)," *Scriptdoctor: Medicine in the Media*, May 10, 2008.

38. Lancelot Oduwa Imasuen, interviewed in *Nollywood Babylon* (2008).

39. Norimitsu Onishi, "Step Aside, L.A. and Bombay, for Nollywood," *New York Times*, Sept. 16, 2002.

40. Rutschman 2015, 696.

41. *New York Times*, Feb. 23, 2012.

42. Rutschman 2015, 695, 696–697.

43. Arewa 2011, 24.

44. "About NCC-Historical Background," Website of the Nigerian Copyright Commission, http://www.copyright.gov.ng/index.php/about-us/ncc-historical-background.

45. Rutschman 2015, 701, italics added.

46. Nick Wadhams, "Bad Charity? (All I Got Was This Lousy T-Shirt!)," *Time*, May 12, 2010.

47. *Time*, May 12, 2010.

48. Olopade 2014, 53.

49. Ibid.

50. "Roll out the Welcome Mat," *Economist*, Feb. 27, 2016.

51. James Palmer, "For American Pundits, China Isn't a country. It's a Fantasyland," *The Washington Post*, May 29, 2015.

52. North 2005, 13.

53. For example, see Florini, Lai, and Tan 2012; Heilmann 2008; Vogel 2011.

54. See my discussion in chapter 3.

55. Rodrik 2007, 39; Acemoglu and Robinson 2012, 440. See my discussion in chapters 3 and 5.

56. For example, a recent volume ponders the challenges of simultaneously pursuing and balancing multiple goals in developing countries (Centeno, Kohli, and Yashar, forthcoming).

57. Genovese and Farrar-Myers 2010; Glaeser and Goldin 2006.

58. Normally, when we think about elite capture and corruption, countries like Russia come to mind. While it is certainly true that America provides wider economic opportunities to its citizens than does Russia, it is also well-known that America is one of the most unequal countries in the world today (Gilens 2012).

59. Ang 2015.

60. Rutschman 2015, 690–691.

61. Lancelot Oduwa Imasuen, interviewed in *Nollywood Babylon* (2008).

62. In particular, see Andrews, Pritchett, and Woolcock 2013; Rodrik 2007.

63. Carothers and de Gramont 2011, 10.

64. Weaver 2008, 77.

65. George and Sabelli 1994, 43. Cited in Weaver 2008, 85.

66. http://buildingstatecapability.com/the-ddd-manifesto/.

67. Ang 2014b. The GDN Essay Contest selected thirteen winning essays from 1,470 submissions worldwide and was judged by a panel of international development experts. For a summary of this essay, see "Crafting Institutions for Localized Aid," *Ideas For*

Development (blog hosted by the French Development Agency), June 9, 2015, available in English and in French.

68. World Bank and State Council 2013.

69. "Vaunting the Best, Fearing the Worst," *The Economist*, Oct. 27, 2012.

70. See my discussion in chapter 4. Guangdong Province has introduced a "happiness index" that measures the level of happiness across cities and that will be used to evaluate local leaders. See the website on the Guangdong Happiness Index System, hosted by *Southern Daily*: www.economy.southcn.com.

71. This explains the determined and sometimes coercive efforts of local officials to "retrieve" petitioners who visit higher-level governments and Beijing (Li, Liu, and O'Brien 2012, 330).

72. Zhao 2013, 8.

73. On recent discussions of populist authoritarianism, see Dickson 2005; Goldman 2006; Liebman 2011; Heilmann and Perry 2011a; Gallagher forthcoming.

APPENDIX A

1. See chapter 2 for a review of the distinct mechanisms of coevolution and how this form of change is distinguished from change via exogenous shocks and incremental changes in general. On coevolutionary causal maps, see Murmann 2013.

2. On the numerous political challenges of conducting research in authoritarian China, see Carlson et al. 2010; Heimer & Thøgersen 2006.

3. For example, management scholars have applied the coevolutionary approach to study the mutual interaction between firm strategies and their environments (Murmann 2013). Also, see research by network theorists on the coevolution of social, political, and economic networks (Padgett and McLean 2011; Padgett and Powell 2012).

4. Evans 1995; Evans and Rauch 1999; World Bank 1993.

5. A recent volume focuses on state capacity as the quality of bureaucracy, "independent of whether it is deployed and to what end" (Centeno, Kohli, and Yashar forthcoming).

6. B2013–325.

7. Also, across subnational cases, the timing and length of stages can vary dramatically, as we saw in the paired comparison of a coastal and inland county in chapter 6. For example, in Blessed County (Zhejiang), local respondents considered the two years between 1993 and 1995 as one significant stage because private property rights were established during this short period of time, laying the foundation for rapid private-sector growth afterward. Contrastingly, in Humble County (Hubei), some locals lumped the 1990s to the mid-2000s as one chunky stage because they did not see that much had changed during these years.

8. If different qualitative patterns are coded, they should be coded as categorical rather than continuous variables.

9. Thelen 2004. See also the *Varieties of Capitalism* literature (Hall and Soskice 2001).

10. Another popular example is the Corruption Perception Index (CPI), which assigns a single numerical score of corruption to each country. One of the many problems of the CPI is that the scores do not distinguish among different *types* of corruption. And because the scores are based on perception, sophisticated corrupt activities, such as buying the influence of legislators to pass favorable laws (Gilens 2012), are less likely to be perceived as corrupt compared to bribery or lawless extortion. The scores then generate the misleading impression that rich countries are virtually free of corruption (Whyte 2015).

11. Ang 2015.

12. Riggs 1964; Helmke and Levitsky 2004.

13. As Pierson notes, "contemporary social scientists typically take a 'snapshot' view of political life" (2004, 2).

14. For example, Aoki's fascinating analysis of the coevolution of bureaucratic and economic structures in postwar Japan ends at providing a summary table of simultaneously occurring features (1997, 245). My study aims to take the further step of understanding why certain traits appeared together and how their mutual emergence relates to features or measures that precede and follow each observed period.

15. For an application in the context of corporate management, see Murmann 2013.

16. Lewin and Volberda 2003, 584.

17. According to Mahoney and Thelen, demonstration of detailed case knowledge is a key criterion for establishing causal mechanisms in qualitative research. In their words, "The real requirement is that CHA [comparative historical analysis] researchers successfully identify linking processes concretely and in sufficient detail to persuade others—including case experts—that the initial set of hypothesized causal factors actually contributed to the outcome" (2015, 16).

18. Such data are rare even in the study of firms, where micro-level data is much more abundant than in the study of political economies. As a review of the management literature concludes, "Empirical coevolution research requires longitudinal methods of analyses and time series data.... Efforts at creating such data sources are still in their infancy" (Lewin and Volberda 2003, 586).

19. Padgett and his collaborators have also combined qualitative and quantitative approaches to map coevolution using network data (Padgett and McLean 2011; Padgett and Powell 2012).

20. Humphreys and Jacobs 2015, 655.

APPENDIX B

1. I thank Xuehua Zhang and Xiaojun Li for sharing their own experiences in fieldwork that informed my own approach. Melani Cammett kindly shared insights into her proxy interviewing experience over the phone.

2. Several recent works offer useful insights into ethnographic research (Schatz 2009) and the practicalities of interviewing in political science (Rathbun 2008), as well as interview strategies specific to China's context (Carlson et al. 2010), but they do not discuss the nuts and bolts of interview transcription, an essential step in qualitative data collection. For an exception, see Mosley 2013.

3. One example discussed in the book is the case of a local official from Humble County (Hubei), who incorrectly assumed that his county's current methods of en masse investment promotion must be being conducted across the country. In his words, "Anyway, the whole country is doing this" (see chapter 1). Another example that appeared in the opening of chapter 4 is the case of a public school principal in a county who candidly shared his outlandish methods of fundraising with me. His assumption was that I would be impressed by his entrepreneurial ideas. It did not occur to him that foreigners or even visitors from the coastal cities in China might find his methods problematic. Hence, from these experiences, I learned the importance of not bringing my own normative biases into fieldwork and to separate my observations during the process of interviews from my later analyses of these observations.

4. Geertz 2000.

5. Cammett 2012.

6. Scacco 2009.

7. Apter 1973, 5; cited in Schatz 2009, 3.

8. For example, see Shirk 1993, 20; Oi 1999, 205–210; Heimer and Thøgersen 2006.

9. Tsai (2007) also uses pseudonyms.

References

Acemoglu, Daron. 2003. Root causes: A historical approach to assessing the role of institutions in economic development. *Finance and Development, 40(2)*, 27–30.
———. 2008. Interactions between governance and growth. In *Governance, growth, and development decision-making*. Washington, D.C.: World Bank.
Acemoglu, Daron, Johnson, Simon, and Robinson, James. 2002. Reversal of fortune: Geography and institutions in the making of the modern world income distribution. *Quarterly Journal of Economics, 117*(4), 1231–1294.
Acemoglu, Daron, and Robinson, James. 2006. *Economic origins of dictatorship and democracy*. Cambridge: Cambridge University Press.
———. 2012. *Why nations fail: The origins of power, prosperity and poverty*. New York: Crown Publishers.
Akamatsu, Kaname. 1962. A historical pattern of economic growth in developing countries. *The Developing Economies, 1*(1), 3–25.
Amsden, Alice H. 1989. *Asia's next giant: South Korea and late industrialization*. New York: Oxford University Press.
Andrews, Matt. 2010. Good government means different things in different countries. *Governance, 23*(1), 7–35.
———. 2013. *The limits of institutional reform in development: Changing rules for realistic solutions*. Cambridge: Cambridge University Press.
Andrews, Matt, Pritchett, Lant, and Woolcock, Michael. 2013. Escaping capability traps through problem driven iterative adaptation (PDIA). *World Development, 51*, 234–244.
Ang, Yuen Yuen. 2009a. Centralizing treasury management in China: The rationale of the central reformers. *Public Administration and Development, 29*(4), 263–273.
———. 2009b. *State, market, and bureau-contracting in reform China*. PhD dissertation, Stanford University, Palo Alto, Calif..
———. 2012a. *Bureaucratic incentives, local development, and petty rents*. Working paper. Department of Political Science. University of Michigan.
———. 2012b. Counting cadres: A comparative view of the size of China's public employment. *China Quarterly, 211*, 676–696.
———. 2014a. Authoritarian restraints on online activism revisited: Why 'I-Paid-A-Bribe' worked in India but failed in China. *Comparative Politics, 47*(1), 21–40.
———. 2014b. Making details matter: How to reform aid agencies to generate contextual knowledge. Winning Essay of the GDN Essay Competition on The Future of Development Assistance, available on the website of Global Development Network.
———. 2015. Beyond Weber: An alternative ideal-type of bureaucracy and why we need one. Working Paper. Department of Political Science. University of Michigan.
Ang, Yuen Yuen, and Jia, Nan. 2014. Perverse complementarity: Political connections and the use of courts among private firms in China. *The Journal of Politics, 76*(2), 318–332.

Aoki, Masahiko. 1994. The Japanese firm as a system of attributes: A survey and research agenda. In M. Aoki and R. Dore (Eds.), *The Japanese firm: The sources of competitive strength.* Oxford: Oxford University Press.

——. 1997. Unintended fit: Organizational evolution and government design of institutions in Japan. In M. Aoki, H.-K. Kim, and M. Okuno (Eds.), *The role of government in East Asian economic development: Comparative institutional analysis.* New York: Clarendon Press.

——. 2010. *Corporations in evolving diversity: Cognition, governance, and institutions.* Oxford: Oxford University Press.

Apter, David. 1973. *Political change: Collected essays.* London: Cass.

Arewa, Olufunmilayo. 2011. The rise of Nollywood: Creators, entrepreneurs, and pirates. University of California, Irvine, Legal Research Paper Series 2011–12.

Axelrod, Robert M., and Cohen, Michael D. 1999. *Harnessing complexity: Organizational implications of a scientific frontier.* New York: Free Press.

Bardhan, Pranab. 1997. Corruption and development: A review of issues. *Journal of Economic Literature, XXXV,* 1320–1346.

——. 2010. *Awakening giants, feet of clay: Assessing the economic rise of China and India.* Princeton, N.J.: Princeton University Press.

Bates, Robert, Greif, Avner, Levi, Margaret, Rosenthal, Jean-Laurent, and Weingast, Barry. 1998. *Analytic narratives.* Princeton, N.J.: Princeton University Press.

Baum, Richard, and Shevchenko, Alexei. 1999. The "state of the state." In M. Goldman and R. MacFarquhar (Eds.), *The paradox of China's post-Mao reforms.* Cambridge, Mass.: Harvard University Press.

Beck, Nathaniel, King, Gary, and Zeng, Langche. 2000. Improving quantitative studies of international conflict: A conjecture. *American Political Science Review, 94*(1), 21–35.

Bendor, Jonathan. 2010. *Bounded rationality and politics.* Berkeley: University of California Press.

Berk, Gerald, Galvan, Dennis, and Hattam, Victoria. 2013. *Political creativity: Reconfiguring institutional order and change.* Philadelphia: University of Pennsylvania Press.

Bernstein, Thomas. 1984. Stalinism, famine, and Chinese peasants: Grain procurements during the Great Leap Forward. *Theory and Society, 13*(3), 339–377.

Bernstein, Thomas P., and Lü, Xiaobo. 2003. *Taxation without representation in rural China.* Cambridge: Cambridge University Press.

Besley, Timothy, and McLaren, John. 1993. Taxes and bribery: The role of wage incentives. *Economic Journal, 103*(416), 119–141.

Bhide, Amar. 2000. *The origin and evolution of new businesses.* Oxford: Oxford University Press.

Biggs, Tyler, and Levy, Brian. 1991. Strategic interventions and the political economy of industrial policy in developing countries. In D. Perkins and M. Roemer (Eds.), *Reforming economic systems in developing countries.* Cambridge, Mass.: Harvard University Press.

Birney, Mayling. 2014. Decentralization and Veiled Corruption under China's "Rule of Mandates." *World Development, 53,* 55–67.

Blanchard, Olivier, and Shleifer, Andrei. 2001. Federalism with and without political centralization: China versus Russia. *IMF Staff Papers, 48,* 171–179.

Blecher, Marc. 1991. Developmental state, entreprenuerial state. In G. White (Ed.), *The Chinese state in the era of economic reform: The road to crisis.* London: Macmillan.

——. 2008. Into space: The local developmental state, capitalist transition, and the political economy of urban planning in Xinji. *City, 12*(2), 171–182.

Blecher, Marc, and Shue, Vivienne. 1996. *Tethered deer: Government and economy in a Chinese county*. Stanford, Calif.: Stanford University Press.

———. 2001. Into leather: State-led development and the private sector in Xinji. *The China Quarterly, 166*(166), 368–393.

Boix, Carles, and Stokes, Susan C. 2003. Endogenous democratization. *World Politics, 55*(4), 517–549.

Bossler, Beverly Jo. 1998. *Powerful relations: Kinship, status, and the state in Sung China*. Cambridge, Mass.: Harvard University Press.

Bowles, Samuel, Durlauf, Steven, and Hoff, Karla Ruth. 2006. *Poverty traps*. Princeton, N.J.: Princeton University Press.

Brands, H.W. 2010. *American colossus: The triumph of capitalism, 1865–1900*. New York: Doubleday.

Brandt, Loren, and Rawski, Thomas G. 2008. *China's great economic transformation*. Cambridge: Cambridge University Press.

Bransford, John. 2000. *How people learn*. Washington, D.C.: National Academy Press.

Brewer, John. 1988. *The sinews of power: War, money, and the English state, 1688–1783*. Cambridge, Mass.: Harvard University Press.

Breznitz, Dan, and Murphree, Michael. 2011. *Run of the red queen: Government, innovation, globalization, and economic growth in China*. New Haven, Conn: Yale University Press.

Brickley, James, and Dark, Frederick. 1987. The choice of organizational form: The case of franchising. *Journal of Financial Economics, 18*(2), 401–420.

Burns, John P. 2007. Civil service reform in China. *OECD Journal on Budgeting*, 1–25.

Burnside, Craig, and Dollar, David. 2000. Aid, policies, and growth. *The American Economic Review, 90*(4), 847–868.

Cai, Fang, and Wang, Dewen. 2008. Impacts of internal migration on economic growth and urban development in China. In J. DeWind and J. Holdaway (Eds.), *Migration and development within and across borders*. New York: Social Science Research Council.

Cai, Yongshun. 2004. Managed participation in China. *Political Science Quarterly, 119*(3), 425–451.

———. 2015. State and agents in China: Disciplining government officials. Stanford, Calif.: Stanford University Press.

Cammett, Melani. 2012. Positionality and sensitive topics: Matched, proxy interviewing as a research strategy. In L. Mosley (Ed.), Interviewing research in political science. Ithaca, N.Y.: Cornell University Press.

Carlson, Allen, Gallagher, Mary, Lieberthal, Kenneth, and Manion, Melanie (Eds.). 2010. Contemporary Chinese politics: New sources, methods, and field strategies. New York: Cambridge University Press.

Carothers, Thomas, and de Gramont, Diane. 2011. Aiding governance in developing countries: Progress amid uncertainties. Carnegie Endowment for International Peace.

Centeno, Miguel. 2002. Blood and debt: War and the nation-state in Latin America. University Park: Pennsylvania State University Press.

Centeno, Miguel, Kohli, Atul, and Yashar, Deborah. Forthcoming. States in the developing world: Cambridge: Cambridge University Press.

Chan, Alfred. 2001. Mao's crusade: Politics and policy implementation in China's Great Leap Forward. Oxford: Oxford University Press.

Chan, Hon S, and Ma, Jun. 2011. How are they paid? A study of civil service pay in China. *International Review of Administrative Sciences, 77*(2), 294–321.

Chang, Gordon. 2001. *The coming collapse of China*. New York: Random House.

Chang, Ha-Joon. 2002. *Kicking away the ladder: Development strategy in historical perspective*. London: Anthem.

Chen, Ye, Li, Hongbin, and Zhou, Li-An. 2005. Relative performance evaluation and the turnover of provincial leaders in China. *Economics Letters, 88*(3), 421–425.

Chung, Jae-ho. 2000. *Central control and local discretion in China: Leadership and implementation during post-Mao decollectivization*. Oxford: Oxford University Press.

Coase, Ronald. 1937. The nature of the firm. *Economica, 4*(16), 386–405.

Coase, Ronald, and Wang, Ning. 2012. *How China became capitalist*. Houndmills, Basingstoke: Palgrave Macmillan.

Collier, Paul. 2007. *The bottom billion: Why the poorest countries are failing and what can be done about it*. Oxford: Oxford University Press.

Davis, Deborah, and Feng, Wang. 2009. *Creating wealth and poverty in postsocialist China*. Stanford, Calif.: Stanford University Press.

Deaton, Angus. 2013. *The great escape: Health, wealth, and the origins of inequality*. Princeton, N.J.: Princeton University Press.

Deng, Yanhua, and Yang, Guobin. 2013. Pollution and protest in China: Environmental mobilization in context. *China Quarterly, 214*(214), 321–336.

Diamond, Jared M. 2005. *Guns, germs, and steel: The fates of human societies*. New York: Norton.

Dickson, Bruce J. 2003. *Red capitalists in China: The party, private entrepreneurs, and prospects for political change*. Cambridge: Cambridge University Press.

———. 2005. Populist authoritarianism: The future of the Chinese Communist Party. Paper presented at the Conference on "Chinese Leadership, Politics, and Policy," Carnegie Endowment for International Peace.

———. 2008. *Wealth into power: The Communist Party's embrace of China's private sector*. Cambridge: Cambridge University Press.

Dimitrov, Martin. 2013a. Vertical accountability in communist regimes: The role of citizen complaints in Bulgaria and China. In M. Dimitrov (Ed.), *Why communism did not collapse*. New York: Cambridge University Press.

———. 2013b. *Why communism did not collapse: Understanding authoritarian regime resilience in Asia and Europe*. New York: Cambridge University Press.

Dincecco, Mark. 2011. *Political transformations and public finances: Europe, 1650–1913*. Cambridge: Cambridge University Press.

Dixit, Avinash. 1997. Power of incentives in private versus public organizations. *American Economic Review, 87*(2), 378–382.

———. 2004. *Lawlessness and economics: Alternative modes of governance*. Princeton, N.J.: Princeton University Press.

Doner, Richard. 2009. *The politics of uneven development: Thailand's economic growth in comparative perspective*. Cambridge: Cambridge University Press.

Donnithorne, Audrey. 1972. China's cellular economy: Some economic trends since the Cultural Revolution. *The China Quarterly, 52*(52), 605–619.

Duckett, Jane. 1998. *The entrepreneurial state in China: Real estate and commerce departments in reform era Tianjin*. London: Routledge.

———. 2001. Bureaucrats in business, Chinese-style: The lessons of market reform and state entrepreneurialism in the People's Republic of China. *World Development, 29*(1), 23–37.

Easterly, William. 2006a. The Big Push deja vu: A review of Jeffrey Sachs's The End of Poverty. *Journal of Economic Literature, 44*, 96–105.

———. 2006b. *The white man's burden: Why the West's efforts to aid the rest have done so much ill and so little good*. New York: Penguin Press.

Edin, Maria. 2003. State capacity and local agent control in China: CCP cadre management from a township perspective. *The China Quarterly, 173*(173), 35–52.

———. 2005. Remaking the Communist Party-State: The cadre responsibility system at the local level in China. *China: An International Journal, 1*(1), 1–15.

Eldredge, Niles, and Gould, Stephen Jay. 1972. Punctuated equilibria: An alternative to phyletic gradualism. In T. J. M. Schopf (Ed.), *Models in Paleobiology*. San Francisco: Freeman Cooper, 82–115.

Engerman, Stanley L., and Sokoloff, Kenneth L. 2006. The persistence of poverty in the Americas: The role of institutions. In S. Bowles, S. N. Durlauf, and K. R. Hoff (Eds.), *Poverty traps*. Princeton, N.J.: Princeton University Press.

Evans, Peter. 1995. *Embedded autonomy: States and industrial transformation*. Princeton, N.J.: Princeton University Press.

———. 2004. Development as institutional change: The pitfalls of monocropping and the potentials of deliberation. *Studies in Comparative International Development, 38*(4), 30–52.

———. 2011. The capability enhancing developmental state: Concepts and national trajectories. Paper presented at the Princeton Conference State Building in the Developing World: Latin America, São Paulo, Brazil.

Evans, Peter, and Heller, Peter S. 2013. Human development, state transformation and the politics of the developmental state. In S. Leibfried, F. Nullmeier, E. Huber, M. Lange, J. Levy and J. D. Stephens (Eds.), *The Oxford Handbook of Transformations of the State*. Oxford: Oxford University Press.

Evans, Peter, and Rauch, James. 1999. Bureaucracy and growth: A cross-national analysis of the effects of "Weberian" state structures on economic growth. *American Sociological Review, 64*(5), 748–765.

Evans, Peter, Rueschemeyer, Dietrich, and Skocpol, Theda. 1985. *Bringing the state back in*. Cambridge: Cambridge University Press.

Fan, Chengze Simon, Lin, Chen, and Treisman, Daniel. 2010. Embezzlement versus bribery. NBER Working Paper 16542.

Fan, Shenggen, Kanbur, S. M. Ravi, and Zhang, Xiaobo. 2009. *Regional inequality in China: Trends, explanations and policy responses*. London: Rouledge.

Fei, Xiaotong. 1992. *From the soil: The foundations of Chinese society (A translation of Fei Xiaotong's Xiangtu Zhongguo)* (G. Hamilton and Z. Wang, Trans.). Berkeley: University of California Press.

Feng, Jicai. 1996. *Ten years of madness: Oral histories of China's Cultural Revolution*. San Francisco: China Books and Periodicals.

Fishkin, James, He, Baogang, Luskin, Robert, and Siu, Alice. 2010. Deliberative democracy in an unlikely place: Deliberative polling in China. *British Journal of Political Science, 40*(2), 435–448.

Florini, Ann, Lai, Hairong, and Tan, Yeling. 2012. *China experiments: From local innovations to national reform*. Washington, D.C.: Brookings Institution Press.

Frederickson, George. 1991. Toward a theory of the public for public administration. *Administration and Society, 22*(4), 395–417.

Fukuyama, Francis. 2004. *State-building: Governance and world order in the 21st century*. Ithaca, N.Y.: Cornell University Press.

Gallagher, Mary. 2005. *Contagious capitalism: Globalization and the politics of labor in China*. Princeton, N.J.: Princeton University Press.

———. Forthcoming. *Authoritarian Legality: Law, Workers, and the State in China*. Cambridge: Cambridge University Press.

Garrett, Geoffrey. 2004. Globalization's missing middle. *Foreign Affairs, 83*(6), 84–96.

Geddes, Barbara. 1994. *Politician's dilemma: Building state capacity in Latin America*. Berkeley: University of California Press.

Geertz, Clifford. 2000. *The interpretation of cultures*. New York: Basic Books.

Genovese, Michael, and Farrar-Myers, Victoria. 2010. *Corruption and American politics*. Amherst, N.Y.: Cambria Press.

George, Susan, and Sabelli, Fabrizio. 1994. *Faith and credit: The World Bank's secular empire*. London: Penguin.

Gerschenkron, Alexander. 1962. *Economic backwardness in historical perspective*. Cambridge, Mass.: Belknap Press of Harvard University Press.

Gilens, Martin. 2012. *Affluence and influence: Economic inequality and political power in America*. Princeton, N.J.: Princeton University Press.

Ginsburg, Tom. 2015. Stop revering Magna Carta. *The New York Times*, June 14.

Glaeser, Edward, and Goldin, Claudia. 2006. *Corruption and reform lessons from America's economic history*. Chicago: Chicago University Press.

Glaeser, Edward, La Porta, Rafael, Lopez-De-Silanes, Florencio, and Shleifer, Andrei. 2004. Do institutions cause growth? *Journal of Economic Growth*, 9(3), 271–303.

Gold, Thomas, Guthrie, Doug, and Wank, David. 2002. *Social connections in China: Institutions, culture, and the changing nature of guanxi*. Cambridge: Cambridge University Press.

Goldman, Merle. 2006. Authoritarian populists: China's new generation of leaders. *Yale Journal of International Affairs*, 20, 20–26.

Goldsmith, Arthur A. 2012. Is governance reform a catalyst for development? In K.S. Jomo and A. Chowdhury (Eds.), *Is good governance good for development?* London: Bloomsbury Academic.

Goldstein, Steven M. 1995. China in transition: The political foundations of incremental reform. *The China Quarterly*, 144(144), 1105–1131.

Gray, Peter. 2011. The special value of children's age-mixed play. *American Journal of Play*, 3(4).

Green, Stephen. 2013. China—masterclass: What makes 10 million local government officials tick? Standard Chartered Bank Research Report.

Greif, Avner. 2006a. History lessons: The birth of impersonal exchange: The community responsibility system and impartial justice. *The Journal of Economic Perspectives*, 20(2), 221–236.

——. 2006b. *Institutions and the path to the modern economy: Lessons from medieval trade*. New York: Cambridge University Press.

Greif, Avner, and Laitin, David D. 2004. A theory of endogenous institutional change. *The American Political Science Review*, 98(4), 633–652.

Grindle, Merilee. 2004. Good enough governance: Poverty reduction and reform in developing countries. *Governance*, 17(4), 525–548.

——. 2011. Good enough governance revisited. *Development Policy Review*, 29(1), 533–574.

Guo, Gang. 2009. China's local political budget cycles. *American Journal of Political Science*, 53(3), 621–632.

Hall, Peter. 2003. Aligning ontology and methodology in comparative research. In J. Mahoney and D. Rueschemeyer (Eds.), *Comparative historical analysis in the social sciences*. New York: Cambridge University Press.

Hall, Peter, and Soskice, David. 2001. *Varieties of capitalism: The institutional foundations of comparative advantage*. Oxford: Oxford University Press.

Hamilton, Alexander, Madison, James, and Jay, John. 2012. *Selected Federalist Papers*. Mineola, N.Y.: Dover Publications.

Hamilton-Hart, Natasha. 2002. *Asian states, Asian bankers: Central banking in Southeast Asia.* Ithaca, N.Y.: Cornell University Press.

Handley, Antoinette. 2008. *Business and the state in Africa: Economic policy-making in the neo-liberal era.* Cambridge: Cambridge University Press.

Hatch, Walter. 2010. *Asia's flying geese: How regionalization shapes Japan.* Ithaca, N.Y.: Cornell University Press.

Hausmann, Ricardo, Pritchett, Lant, and Rodrik, Dani. 2005. Growth accelerations. *Journal of Economic Growth, 10*(4), 303–329.

He, Baogang, and Warren, Mark. 2011. Authoritarian deliberation: The deliberative turn in Chinese political development. *Perspectives on Politics, 9*(2), 269–289.

Heberer, Thomas, and Trappel, Rene. 2013. Evaluation processes, local cadres' behaviour and local development processes. *Journal of Contemporary China, 22*(84), 1048–1066.

Heilmann, Sebastian. 2008. From local experiments to national policy: The origins of China's distinctive policy process. *China Journal, 59*(59), 1–30.

——. 2009. Maximum tinkering under uncertainty. *Modern China, 35*(4), 450–462.

Heilmann, Sebastian, and Perry, Elizabeth. 2011a. Embracing uncertainty: Guerilla policy style and adaptive governance in China. In S. Heilmann and E. Perry (Eds.), *Mao's invisible hand: The political foundations of adaptive governance in China.* Cambridge, Mass: Harvard University Press.

——. 2011b. *Mao's invisible hand: The political foundations of adaptive governance in China.* Cambridge, Mass: Harvard University Press.

Heimer, Maria, and Thøgersen, Stig. 2006. *Doing fieldwork in China.* Honolulu: University of Hawaii Press.

Helmke, Gretchen, and Levitsky, Steven. 2004. Informal institutions and comparative politics: A research agenda. *Perspectives on Politics, 2*(4), 725–740.

Hendley, Kathryn. 1999. Rewriting the rules of the game in Russia: The neglected issue of demand for law. *East European Constitutional Review, 8*(4), 89–95.

Hickey, Paul C. 1991. Fee-taking, salary reform, and the structure of state power in late Qing China, 1909–1911. *Modern China, 17*(3), 389–417.

Hirschman, Albert. 1958. *The strategy of economic development.* New Haven, Conn.: Yale University Press.

Holland, John H. 1996. *Hidden order: How adaptation builds complexity.* Cambridge, Mass.: Perseus Books.

Huang, Shu-min. 1998. *The spiral road: Change in a Chinese village through the eyes of a Communist Party leader* (2nd ed.). Boulder, Colo.: Westview Press.

Huang, Yasheng. 1996. *Inflation and investment controls in China: The political economy of central-local relations during the reform era.* Cambridge: Cambridge University Press.

——. 2003. *Selling China: Foreign direct investment during the reform era.* Cambridge: Cambridge University Press.

——. 2007. Ownership biases and FDI in China: Evidence from two provinces. *Business and Politics, 9*(1), 1–45.

Hubbard, R. Glenn, and Duggan, William R. 2009. *The aid trap: Hard truths about ending poverty.* New York: Columbia Business School Pub.

Huber, John D., and Shipan, Charles R. 2002. *Deliberate discretion: The institutional foundations of bureaucratic autonomy.* New York: Cambridge University Press.

Huff, Gregg. 1999. Turning the corner in Singapore's developmental state? *Asian Survey, 39*(2), 214–242.

Hui, Victoria Tin-bor. 2005. *War and state formation in ancient China and early modern Europe*. New York: Cambridge University Press.

Humphreys, Macartan, and Jacobs, Alan. 2015. Mixing methods: A Bayesian approach. *American Political Science Review, 109*(4), 653–673.

IMF (International Monetary Fund). 1997. *Good governance: The IMF's role.* Washington, D.C.: IMF.

———. 1998. *Annual report 1998.* Washington, D.C.: IMF.

Inglehart, Ronald, and Welzel, Christian. 2005. *Modernization, cultural change, and democracy: The human development sequence.* Cambridge: Cambridge University Press.

Jefferson, Gary, and Rawski, Thomas. 2001. Enterprise reform in Chinese industry. In R. Garnaut and Y. Huang (Eds.), *Growth without miracles: Readings on the Chinese economy in the era of reform.* Oxford: Oxford University Press.

Jensen, Erik G. 2003. The rule of law and judicial reform: The political economy of diverse institutional patterns and reformers' responses. In E. G. Jensen and T. C. Heller (Eds.), *Beyond common knowledge: Empirical approaches to the rule of law.* Stanford, Calif.: Stanford University Press.

Jiang, Yuanyuan. 2013. Manufacturing firm relocation in east China: Tendency and mechanism. In H. Wei, Y. Wang and B. Mei (Eds.), *The micro-analysis of regional economy in China: A perspective of firm relocation.* Singapore: World Scientific.

Johnson, Chalmers. 1982. *MITI and the Japanese miracle: The growth of industrial policy, 1925–1975.* Stanford, Calif.: Stanford University Press.

Jomo, K. S., and Chowdhury, Anis. 2012a. Introduction: Governance and development. In K. S. Jomo and A. Chowdhury (Eds.), *Is good governance good for development.* London: Bloomsbury Academic. Published in association with the United Nations.

———. 2012b. *Is good governance good for development?* London: Bloomsbury Academic. Published in association with the United Nations.

Kang, David C. 2002. *Crony capitalism: Corruption and development in South Korea and the Philippines.* Cambridge: Cambridge University Press.

Katzenstein, Peter. 1975. International interdependence. *International Organization, 29*(4), 1021.

———. 1985. *Small states in world markets: Industrial policy in Europe.* Ithaca, N.Y.: Cornell University Press.

Kaufmann, Daniel, and Kraay, Aart. 2002. Growth without governance. *Economia: Journal of the Latin American and Caribbean Economic Association, 3*(1), 169–229.

Kaufmann, Daniel, Kraay, Aart, and Mastruzzi, Massimo. 2007a. Growth and governance: A reply. *The Journal of Politics, 69*(2), 555–562.

———. 2007b. Growth and governance: A rejoinder. *The Journal of Politics, 69*(2), 570–572.

Kaufmann, Daniel, Kraay, Aart, and Zoido-Lobatón, Pablo. 1999. Governance matters. World Bank Policy Research Working Paper 2196. http://info.worldbank.org/governance/wgi/pdf/govmatters1.pdf.

Kaufmann, Daniel, and Wei, Shang-Jin. 2000. Does "grease money" speed up the wheels of commerce? IMF Working Papers (64), 1–20.

Kelman, Steven, and Friedman, John. 2009. Performance improvement and performance dysfunction: An empirical examination of distortionary impacts of the emergency room wait-time target in the English National Health Service. *Journal of Public Administration Research and Theory: J-PART, 19*(4), 917–946.

Khan, Mushtaq. 2012. Governance and growth challenges for Africa. In A. Noman, K. Botchwey, H. Stein and J. Stiglitz (Eds.), *Good growth and governance in Africa: rethinking development strategies*. Oxford: Oxford University Press.

Khan, Mushtaq, and Jomo, Kwame. 2000. *Rents, rent-seeking, and economic development*. Cambridge: Cambridge University Press.

Klein, Naomi. 2007. *The shock doctrine: The rise of disaster capitalism*. New York: Metropolitan Books.

Klitgaard, Robert E. 1988. *Controlling corruption*. Berkeley: University of California Press.

Knack, Stephen, and Keefer, Philip. 1995. Institutions and economic performance: Cross-country tests using alternative institutional measures. *Economics and Politics, 7*(3), 207.

Knight, Frank. 1921. *Risk, uncertainty and profit*. New York: Houghton Mifflin and Co.

Ko, Kilkon, and Weng, Cuifen. 2012. Structural changes in Chinese corruption. *China Quarterly, 211*, 718–740.

Kohli, Atul. 2004. *State-directed development: Political power and industrialization in the global periphery*. Cambridge: Cambridge University Press.

Kostka, Genia, and Yu, Xiaofan. 2014. Career backgrounds of municipal party secretaries: Why do so few municipal party secretaries rise from the county level? *Modern China, 41*(5), 467–505.

Krasner, Stephen. 1988. Sovereignty: An institutional perspective. *Comparative Political Studies, 21*(1), 66–94.

——. 2013. Seeking 'good-enough-governance'—not democracy. *Reuters*, Sept. 23.

——. 2014. State building outside in: Development theories and policy implications. Paper presented at the University of Michigan Center for Chinese Studies Annual Conference on "Building State Capacity in China and Beyond," Oct. 17, 2014.

Krugman, Paul. 1994. The myth of Asia's miracle. *Foreign Affairs, 73*, 62.

Kung, James Kai-Sing, and Chen, Shuo. 2011. The Tragedy of the Nomenklatura: Career incentives and political radicalism during China's Great Leap famine. *American Political Science Review, 105*(1), 27–45.

Kung, James Kai-Sing, and Chen, Ting. 2012. Behind the "China Miracle": Revenue incentives of local leaders. Paper presented at the Ann Arbor, Mich., Lecture, CCS Research Seminar, University of Michigan.

Kung, James, and Lin, Yimin. 2007. The decline of township-and-village enterprises in China's economic transition. *World Development, 35*(4), 569–584.

Kurtz, Marcus, and Schrank, Andrew. 2007a. Growth and governance: Models, measures, and mechanisms. *The Journal of Politics, 69*(2), 538–554.

——. 2007b. Growth and governance: A defense. *The Journal of Politics, 69*(2), 563–569.

Kuruvilla, Sarosh, Lee, Ching Kwan, and Gallagher, Mary (Eds.). 2011. *From iron rice bowl to informalization: Markets, workers, and the state in a changing China*. Ithaca, N.Y.: Cornell University Press.

Kushida, Kenji, Shimizu, Kay, and Oi, Jean. 2014. *Syncretism: The politics of economic restructuring and system reform in Japan*. Stanford, Calif.: Stanford APARC.

Laitin, David. 2002. Comparative politics: The state of the sub-discipline. In I. Katznelson and H. Milner (Eds.), *Political science: The state of the discipline*. New York: Norton; American Political Science Association.

Lake, David. 2016. *The statebuilder's dilemma: On the limits of foreign intervention*. Ithaca, N.Y.: Cornell University Press.

Lampton, David. 2014. *Following the leader: Ruling China, from Deng Xiaoping to Xi Jinping*. Berkeley: University of California Press.

Landry, Pierre. 2008. *Decentralized authoritarianism in China: The Communist Party's control of local elites in the post-Mao era*. Cambridge: Cambridge University Press.

Lange, Matthew. 2009. *Lineages of despotism and development: British colonialism and state power*. Chicago: University of Chicago Press.

Lansing, Stephen. 2006. *Perfect order: Recognizing complexity in Bali*. Princeton, N.J.: Princeton University Press.

Lardy, Nicholas R. 1983. *Agriculture in China's modern economic development*. Cambridge: Cambridge University Press.

——. 2012. *Sustaining China's economic growth after the global financial crisis*. Washington, D.C.: Peterson Institute for International Economics.

——. 2014. *Markets over Mao: The rise of private business in China*: Washington, D.C.: Institute for International Economics.

Lee, Charlotte. 2014. *Training the party: Party adaptation and elite training in reform-era China*. Cambridge: Cambridge University Press.

Levitsky, Steven, and Murillo, Victoria. 2013. Building institutions on weak foundations. *Journal of Democracy, 24*(2), 93–107.

Levy, Brian, and Fukuyama, Francis. 2010. Development strategies integrating governance and growth. World Bank Policy Research Working Paper 5196.

Lewin, Arie, and Volberda, Henk. 2003. The future of organization studies: Beyond the selection-adaptation debate. In C. Knudsen and H. Tsoukas. (Eds.), *The Oxford handbook of organization theory*. Oxford: Oxford University Press.

Li, Hongbin, and Zhou, Li-An. 2005. Political turnover and economic performance: The incentive role of personnel control in China. *Journal of Public Economics, 89*(9), 1743–1762.

Li, Shuhe, Li, Shaomin, and Zhang, Weiying. 2000. The Road to Capitalism: Competition and Institutional Change in China. *Journal of Comparative Economics, 28*(2), 269–292.

Li, Lianjiang, Liu, Mingxing, and O'Brien, Kevin. 2012. Petitioning Beijing: The high tide of 2003–2006. *China Quarterly, 210*(210), 313–334.

Li, Shi, Sato, Hiroshi, and Sicular, Terry. 2013. *Rising inequality in China: Challenges to a harmonious society*. New York: Cambridge University Press.

Lieberthal, Kenneth. 1995. *Governing China: From revolution through reform*. New York: W. W. Norton.

Lieberthal, Kenneth, and Lampton, David. 1992. *Bureaucracy, politics, and decision making in post-Mao China*. Berkeley: University of California Press.

Lieberthal, Kenneth, and Oksenberg, Michel. 1988. *Policy making in China: Leaders, structures, and processes*. Princeton, N.J.: Princeton University Press.

Liebman, Benjamin. 2011. A return to populist legacy? Historical legacies and legal reform. In S. Heilmann and E. Perry (Eds.), *Mao's invisible hand: The political foundations of adaptive governance in China* (viii). Cambridge, Mass: Harvard University Asia Center: Distributed by Harvard University Press.

Lim, Linda. 2014. Singapore's success: After the miracle. In R. E. Looney (Ed.), *Handbook of emerging economies*. London: Routledge, Taylor and Francis Group.

Lin, Justin Yifu. 2012. *The quest for prosperity: How developing economies can take off*. Princeton, N.J.: Princeton University Press.

Lin, Justin Yifu, Cai, Fang, and Li, Zhou. 2003. *The China miracle: Development strategy and economic reform*. Rev. ed. Hong Kong: Chinese University Press.

Lipset, Seymour Martin. 1959. Some social requisites of democracy: Economic development and political legitimacy. *The American Political Science Review, 53*(1), 69–105.

Lipsky, Michael. 1980. *Street-level bureaucracy: Dilemmas of the individual in public services*. New York: Russell Sage Foundation.

Lora, Eduardo. 2002. Growth without governance: Comments. *Economia: Journal of the Latin American and Caribbean Economic Association, 3*(1), 216.

Lou, Jiwei, and Wang, Shuilin. 2008. *Public finance in China: Reform and growth for a harmonious society*. Washington, D.C.: World Bank.

Love, John F. 1995. *McDonald's: Behind the arches*. New York: Bantam Books.

Lu, Xiaobo. 2000. Booty socialism, bureau-preneurs, and the state in transition: Organizational corruption in China. *Comparative Politics 32*(3), 273–294.

Lü, Xiaobo. 2000. *Cadres and corruption: The organizational involution of the Chinese Communist Party*. Stanford, Calif.: Stanford University Press.

Lu, Xiaobo, and Landry, Pierre. 2014. Show me the money: Interjurisdiction political competition and fiscal extraction in China. *American Political Science Review, 108*(3), 706–722.

Lustick, Ian S. 2011. Taking evolution seriously: Historical institutionalism and evolutionary theory. *Polity, 43*(2), 179–209.

MacFarquhar, Roderick, and Schoenhals, Michael. 2006. *Mao's last revolution*. Cambridge, Mass.: Harvard University Press.

Mahoney, James. 2010. *Colonialism and postcolonial development: Spanish America in comparative perspective*. Cambridge: Cambridge University Press.

Mahoney, James, and Thelen, Kathleen. 2010. *Explaining institutional change: Ambiguity, agency, and power*. Cambridge: Cambridge University Press.

——. 2015. *Advances in comparative-historical analysis*. Cambridge: Cambridge University Press.

Man, Joyce Y., and Hong, Yu-hung. 2011. *China's local public finance in transition*. Cambridge, Mass.: Lincoln Institute of Land Policy.

Manion, Melanie. 1985. The cadre management system, Post-Mao: The appointment, promotion, transfer and removal of party and state leaders. *China Quarterly, 102*(102), 203–223.

——. 2004. *Corruption by design: Building clean government in mainland China and Hong Kong*. Cambridge, Mass.: Harvard University Press.

March, James. 1991. Exploration and exploitation in organizational learning. *Organization Science, 2*(1), 71.

Maskin, Eric, Qian, Yingyi, and Xu, Chenggang. 2000. Incentives, information, and organizational form. *The Review of Economic Studies, 67*(231), 359.

Mauro, Paulo. 1995. Corruption and Growth. *Quarterly Journal of Economics, 110*(3), 681–712.

McCormick, Barrett L. 1990. *Political reform in post-Mao China: Democracy and bureaucracy in a Leninist state*. Berkeley: University of California Press.

McMillan, John, and Naughton, Barry. 1992. How to reform a planned economy. *Oxford Review of Economic Policy, 8*(1), 130–143.

Menes, Rebecca. 2006. Limiting the reach of the grabbing hand: Graft and growth in American cities. In E. Glaeser and C. Goldin (Eds.), *Corruption and reform: Lessons from America's economic history*. Chicago: University of Chicago Press.

Mertha, Andrew. 2008. *China's water warriors: Citizen action and policy change*. Ithaca, N.Y.: Cornell University Press.

——. 2009. "Fragmented Authoritarianism 2.0": Political pluralization in the Chinese policy process. *The China Quarterly, 200*(200), 995–1012.

Michelson, Ethan. 2007. Lawyers, political embeddedness, and institutional continuity in China's transition from socialism. *American Journal of Sociology, 113*(2), 352–414.

Migdal, Joel S., Kohli, Atul, and Shue, Vivienne. 1994. *State power and social forces: Domination and transformation in the Third World*. Cambridge: Cambridge University Press.

Mikesell, John, Ma, Jun, Ho, Alfred, and Niu, Meili. 2011. Financing local public infrastructure: Guangdong province. In J. Man and Y.-h. Hong (Eds.), *China's local public finance in transition*. Cambridge, Mass.: Lincoln Institute of Land Policy.

Miller, Gary J. 1992. *Managerial dilemmas: The political economy of hierarchy*. Cambridge: Cambridge University Press.

Miller, John H., and Page, Scott E. 2007. *Complex adaptive systems: An introduction to computational models of social life*. Princeton, N.J.: Princeton University Press.

Mitchell, Melanie. 2009. *Complexity: A guided tour*. Oxford: Oxford University Press.

Moe, Terry M. 1984. The new economics of organization. *American Journal of Political Science, 28*(4), 739–777.

——. 1989. The politics of bureaucratic structure. In J. E. Chubb and P. E. Peterson (Eds.), *Can the Government Govern?* (267–329). Washington, D.C.: The Brookings Institution.

Montinola, Gabriella., Qian, Yingyi, and Weingast, Barry. 1995. Federalism, Chinese style—The political basis for economic success in China. *World Politics, 48*(1), 50–81.

Mosley, Layna (Ed.). 2013. *Interview research in political science*. Ithaca, N.Y.: Cornell University Press.

Munley, Vincent, Garvey, Eoghan, and McConnell, Michael. 2010. The effectiveness of peer tutoring on student achievement at the university level. *The American Economic Review, 100*(2), 277–282.

Murmann, Johann Peter. 2013. The coevolution of industries and important features of their environments. *Organization Science, 24*(1), 58–78.

Nathan, Andrew. 2003. Authoritarian resilience. *Journal of Democracy, 14*(1), 6–17.

Nathan, Andrew, and Scobell, Andrew. 2012. *China's search for security*. New York: Columbia University Press.

Naughton, Barry. 1995. *Growing out of the plan: Chinese economic reform, 1978–1993*. New York: Cambridge University Press.

——. 2003. How much can regional integration do to unify China's market? In N. Hope, D. T. Yang, and M. Yang Li (Eds.), *How far across the river?: Chinese policy reform at the millennium* (xxii). Stanford, Calif.: Stanford University Press.

——. 2007. *The Chinese economy: Transitions and growth*. Cambridge, Mass.: MIT Press.

——. 2015. Economic rebalancing. In J. deLisle and A. Goldstein (Eds.), *China's challenges*. Philadelphia: University of Pennsylvania Press.

Naughton, Barry, and Yang, Dali L. 2004. *Holding China together: Diversity and national integration in the post-Deng era*. New York: Cambridge University Press.

Naughton, Barry, and Tsai, Kellee. 2015. *State capitalism, institutional adaptation, and the Chinese miracle*. New York: Cambridge University Press.

NDRC Industrial Economy Research Center. 2013. *Report on Industrial Development in China* (*Zhongguo chanye fazhan baogao*). Beijing: Economic and Management Publishing House.

Nee, Victor. 1989. A theory of market transition: From redistribution to markets in state socialism. *American Sociological Review, 54*(1), 663–681.

Nee, Victor, and Opper, Sonja. 2012. *Capitalism from below: Markets and institutional change in China*. Cambridge, Mass.: Harvard University Press.

Noble, Gregory. 1998. *Collective action in East Asia: How ruling parties shape industrial policy*. Ithaca, N.Y.: Cornell University Press.

North, Douglass. 1990. *Institutions, institutional change, and economic performance.* Cambridge; New York: Cambridge University Press.

———. 1991. Institutions. *Journal of Economic Perspectives, 5*(1), 97–112.

———. 2005. *Understanding the process of economic change.* Princeton, N.J.: Princeton University Press.

North, Douglass, Wallis, John, and Weingast, Barry. 2009. *Violence and social orders: A conceptual framework for interpreting recorded human history.* Cambridge: Cambridge University Press.

North, Douglass, and Weingast, Barry. 1989. Constitutions and commitment: The evolution of institutional governing public choice in seventeenth-century England. *The Journal of Economic History, 49*(4), 803–832.

O'Brien, Kevin J., and Li, Lianjiang. 1999. Selective policy implementation in rural China. *Comparative Politics, 31*(2), 167–186.

Ober, Josiah. 2008. What the ancient Greeks can tell us about democracy. *Annual Review of Political Science 11*(1), 67–91.

OECD. 2013. *Fiscal federalism 2014: Making decentralisation work.* Paris: OECD Publishing.

Oi, Jean. 1992. Fiscal reform and the economic foundations of local state corporatism in China. *World Politics, 45*(1), 99–126.

———. 1995. The role of the local state in China's transitional economy. *China Quarterly, 144*(144), 1132–1149.

———. 1999. *Rural China takes off: Institutional foundations of economic reform.* Berkeley: University of California Press.

Oi, Jean, and Shimizu, Kaoru. 2010. Uncertain outcomes of rural industralization. In T.-K. Leng and Y. Zhu (Eds.), *Dynamics of local governance in China during the reform era.* Lanham, Md.: Lexington Books.

Oi, Jean, and Walder, Andrew. 1999. *Property rights and economic reform in China.* Stanford, Calif.: Stanford University Press.

Oi, Jean, and Zhao, Shukai. 2007. Fiscal crisis in China's townships: Causes and consequences. In E. Perry and M. Goldman (Eds.), *Grassroots Political Reform in Contemporary China.* Cambridge, Mass.: Harvard University Press.

Oksenberg, Michel. 1970. Getting ahead and getting along in Communist China. In J.W. Lewis (Ed.), *Party leadership and revolutionary power in China.* Cambridge: Cambridge University Press.

Oksenberg, Michel, and Tong, James. 1991. The evolution of central-provincial fiscal relations in China, 1971–1984: The Formal System. *China Quarterly, 125*(125), 1–32.

Olopade, Dayo. 2014. *The bright continent: Breaking rules and making change in modern Africa.* New York: Houghton Mifflin.

Olson, Mancur. 2000. *Power and prosperity: Outgrowing communist and capitalist dictatorships.* New York: Basic Books.

Ong, Lynette H. 2012. *Prosper or perish: Credit and fiscal systems in rural China.* Ithaca, N.Y.: Cornell University Press.

Osnos, Evan. 2014. *Age of ambition: Chasing fortune, truth, and faith in the new China.* New York: Farrar, Straus and Giroux.

Ostrom, Elinor, and Basurto, Xavier. 2011. Crafting analytical tools to study institutional change. *Journal of Institutional Economics, 7*(3), 317–343.

Padgett, John, and Ansell, Christopher. 1993. Robust action and the rise of the Medici, 1400–1434. *American Journal of Sociology, 98*(6), 1259–1319.

Padgett, John, and McLean, Paul. 2011. Economic credit in renaissance Florence. *Journal of Modern History, 83*(1), 1–47.

Padgett, John, and Powell, Walter. 2012. *The emergence of organizations and markets.* Princeton, N.J.: Princeton University Press.

Page, Scott E. 2011. *Diversity and complexity.* Princeton, N.J.: Princeton University Press.

Parrillo, Nicholas R. 2013. *Against the profit motive: The salary revolution in American government, 1780–1940.* New Haven, Conn.: Yale University Press.

Pei, Minxin. 2006. *China's trapped transition: The limits of developmental autocracy.* Cambridge, Mass.: Harvard University Press.

Perry, Elizabeth. 2011. From mass campaigns to managed campaigns: "Constructing a new socialist countryside." In S. Heilmann (Ed.), *Mao's invisible hand: The political foundations of adaptive governance in China* (viii). Cambridge, Mass: Harvard University Asia Center. Distributed by Harvard University Press.

Pierson, Paul. 2004. *Politics in time: History, institutions, and social analysis.* Princeton, N.J.: Princeton University Press.

Polanyi, Karl. 1957. *The great transformation.* Boston: Beacon Press.

Porter, Michael. 1990. *The competitive advantage of nations.* New York: Free Press.

Pritchett, Lant. 2002. Growth without governance: Comments. *Economia: Journal of the Latin American and Caribbean Economic Association, 3*(1), 224.

Pritchett, Lant, and de Weijer, Frauke 2011. Fragile states: Stuck in a capability trap? World Development Report 2011 Background Paper.

Pritchett, Lant, and Woolcock, Michael. 2004. Solutions when the solution is the problem: Arraying the disarray in development. *World Development, 32*(2), 191–212.

Przeworski, Adam. 2004. The last instance: Are institutions the primary cause of economic development? *European Journal of Sociology, 45*(2), 165–188.

Przeworski, Adam, Alverez, Michael, Cheibub, Jose Antonio, and Limongi, Fernando. 2000. *Democracy and development: Political institutions and material well-being in the world, 1950–1990.* Cambridge: Cambridge University Press.

Qian, Yingyi. 2003. How Reform Worked in China. In D. Rodrik (Ed.), *In search of prosperity: Analytic narratives on economic growth.* Princeton, N.J.: Princeton University Press.

Qian, Yingyi, and Wu, Jinglian. 2003. China's transition to a market economy: How far across the river? In N. C. Hope, D. T. Yang, and M. Yang Li (Eds.), *How far across the river?: Chinese policy reform at the millennium* (1v). Stanford, Calif.: Stanford University Press.

Qian, Yingyi, and Xu, Chenggang. 1993. The M-form hierarchy and China's economic reform. *European Economic Review, 37*(2), 541–548.

Quah, Jon. 2010. *Public administration Singapore-style.* Bingley: Emerald.

Rathbun, Brian. 2008. Interviewing and qualitative field methods: Pragmatism and practicalities. In J. Box-Steffensmeier, H. Brady, and C. David. *The Oxford handbook of political methodology.* Oxford: Oxford University Press.

Rawski, Thomas G. 1995. Implications of China's reform experience. *China Quarterly, 144,* 1150–1173.

——. 2011. Human resources and China's long economic boom. *Asia Policy, 12*(1), 33–78.

Riggs, Fred Warren. 1964. *Administration in developing countries: The theory of prismatic society.* Boston: Houghton Mifflin.

Rithmire, Meg. 2014. China's "new regionalism": Subnational analysis in Chinese political economy. *World Politics, 66,* 165–194.

Roberts, Alasdair. 2012. *America's first Great Depression: Economic crisis and political disorder after the Panic of 1837.* Ithaca, N.Y.: Cornell University Press.

Rodrik, Dani. 2007. *One economics, many recipes: Globalization, institutions, and economic growth.* Princeton, N.J.: Princeton University Press.

——. 2008. Second-best institutions. *American Economic Review, 98*(2), 100–104.

Rodrik, Dani, Subramanian, Arvind, and Trebbi, Francesco. 2004. Institutions rule: The primacy of institutions over geography and integration in economic development. *Journal of Economic Growth, 9*(2), 131–165.

Rutschman, Ana Santos. 2015. Weapons of mass construction: The role of intellectual property in Nigeria's film and music industries. *Emory International Law Review, 29,* 673–740.

Sachs, Jeffrey. 2005. *The end of poverty: Economic possibilities for our time.* London: Penguin.

Sachs, Jeffrey, McArthur, John, Schmidt-Traub, Guido, Kruk, Margaret, Bahadur, Chandrika, Faye, Michael, and McCord, Gordon. 2004. Ending Africa's poverty trap. *Brookings Papers on Economic Activity, 2004*(1), 117–216.

Sasada, Hironori. 2013. *The evolution of the Japanese developmental state: Institutions locked in by ideas.* London: Routledge.

Scacco, Alexandra. 2009. Who riots? Explaining participation in ethnic violence in Nigeria. PhD dissertation, Columbia University.

Schatz, Edward (Ed.). 2009. *Political ethnography: What immersion contributes to the study of power.* Chicago: University of Chicago Press.

Schell, Orville, and Delury, John. 2013. *Wealth and power: China's long march to the twenty-first century.* New York: Random House.

Schurmann, Franz. 1966. *Ideology and organization in Communist China.* Berkeley: University of California Press.

Scott, James C. 1998. *Seeing like a state: How certain schemes to improve the human condition have failed.* New Haven, Conn.: Yale University Press.

Sen, Amartya. 1999. *Development as freedom.* New York: Oxford University Press.

Seybert, Lucia, and Katzenstein, Peter. 2015. Circulatory power in world politics. Working Paper.

Shambaugh, David L. 2008. *China's Communist Party: Atrophy and adaptation.* Washington, D.C.: Berkeley: Woodrow Wilson Center Press; University of California Press.

Shirk, Susan L. 1993. *The political logic of economic reform in China.* Berkeley: University of California Press.

Simon, Herbert A. 1957. *Administrative behavior: A study of decision-making processes in administrative organization* (2d ed.). New York: Macmillan.

Skocpol, Theda. 1979. *States and social revolutions: A comparative analysis of France, Russia, and China.* Cambridge: Cambridge University Press.

Sokoloff, Kenneth, and Engerman, Stanley. 2000. History lessons: Institutions, factor endowments, and paths of development in the New World. *Journal of Economic Perspectives, 14*(3), 217–232.

Stephen, Biddle, Fotini, Christia, and Thier, Alexander. 2010. Defining success in Afghanistan. *Foreign Affairs, 89,* 48–60.

Stockmann, Daniela. 2012. *Media commercialization and authoritarian rule in China.* Cambridge: Cambridge University Press.

Streeck, Wolfgang, and Thelen, Kathleen. 2005. Introduction: Institutional change in advanced political economies. In W. Streeck and K. Thelen (Eds.), *Beyond continuity: Institutional change in advanced political economies.* Oxford: Oxford University Press.

Su, Yang. 2011. *Collective killings in rural China during the cultural revolution.* New York: Cambridge University Press.

Takeuchi, Hiroki. 2014. *Tax reform in rural China: Revenue, resistance, and authoritarian rule.* Cambridge: Cambridge University Press.

Teets, Jessica, and Hurst, William. 2015. *Local governance innovation in China: Experimentation, diffusion, and defiance.* New York: Routledge.

Thelen, Kathleen. 1999. Historical institutionalism in comparative politics. *Annual Review of Political Science, 2*(1), 369–404.

——. 2004. *How institutions evolve: The political economy of skills in Germany, Britain, the United States, and Japan.* Cambridge: Cambridge University Press.

Tilly, Charles. 1992. *Coercion, capital, and European states, AD 990–1990.* Cambridge, Mass.: Wiley-Blackwell.

Topping, K. J. 1996. The effectiveness of peer tutoring in further and higher education: A typology and review of the literature. *Higher Education, 32*(3), 321–345.

Truex, Rory. 2014. The returns to office in a "rubber stamp" parliament. *American Political Science Review, 108*(2), 235.

Tsai, Kellee. 2004. Off Balance: The unintended consequences of fiscal federalism in China. *Journal of Chinese Political Science, 9*(2), 1–27.

——. 2006. Adaptive informal institutions and endogenous institutional change in China. *World Politics, 59*(1), 116–141.

——. 2007. *Capitalism without democracy: The private sector in contemporary China.* Ithaca, N.Y.: Cornell University Press.

Tsui, Kai-yuen, and Wang, Youqiang. 2004. Between separate stoves and a single menu: Fiscal decentralization in China. *China Quarterly, 177*(177), 71–90.

Van de Walle, Nicolas. 2001. *African economies and the politics of permanent crisis, 1979–1999.* New York: Cambridge University Press.

Vogel, Ezra F. 2011. *Deng Xiaoping and the transformation of China.* Cambridge, Mass.: Belknap Press of Harvard University Press.

Vu, Tuong. 2010. *Paths to development in Asia: South Korea, Vietnam, China, and Indonesia.* New York: Cambridge University Press.

Wade, Robert. 1990. *Governing the market: Economic theory and the role of government in East Asian industrialization.* Princeton, N.J.: Princeton University Press.

Walder, Andrew G. 1995. Local governments as industrial firms: An organizational analysis of China's transitional economy. *American Journal of Sociology, 101*(2), 263–301.

——. 1996. Markets and inequality in transitional economies: Toward testable theories. *American Journal of Sociology, 101*(4), 1060–1073.

——. 2004. The party elite and China's trajectory of change. *China: An International Journal, 2*(2), 189–209.

——. 2009. *Fractured rebellion: The Beijing Red Guard movement.* Cambridge, Mass.: Harvard University Press.

Wallis, John. 2001. What caused the crisis of 1839? NBER Working Paper 133.

——. 2005. Constitutions, corporations, and corruption: American states and constitutional change, 1842 to 1852. *The Journal of Economic History, 65*(1), 211–256.

Wang, Yuhua. 2015. *Tying the autocrat's hands: The rise of the rule of law in China.* New York: Cambridge University Press.

Wank, David L. 1996. The institutional process of market clientelism: Guanxi and private business in a South China city. *China Quarterly, 147*(147), 820–838.

Weaver, Catherine. 2008. *Hypocrisy trap: The World Bank and the poverty of reform.* Princeton, N.J.: Princeton University Press.

Weber, Max. 1968. *Economy and society: An outline of interpretive sociology.* New York: Bedminster Press.

Wedeman, Andrew. 2000. Budgets, extra-budgets, and small treasuries: Illegal monies and local autonomy in China. *Journal of Contemporary China, 9*(25), 489–511.
———. 2003. *From Mao to market: Rent seeking, local protectionism, and marketization in China*. Cambridge: Cambridge University Press.
———. 2012. *Double paradox: Rapid growth and rising corruption in China*. Ithaca, N.Y.: Cornell University Press.
Wei, Houkai, and Bai, Mei. 2013. Characteristics and tendency of enterprise relocation in China. In H. Wei, Y. Wang, and B. Mei (Eds.), *The micro-analysis of regional economy in China: A perspective of firm relocation*. Singapore: World Scientific.
Weingast, Barry. 1995. The economic role of political institutions: Market-preserving federalism and economic development. *Journal of Law, Economics, and Organization, 11*(1), 1–31.
Weller, Robert. 2008. Responsive authoritarianism. In G. Bruce and L. Diamond (Eds.), *Political change in China: Comparison with Taiwan* (117–143). Boulder, Colo.: Lynne Rienner Publishers.
Whiting, Susan. 2001. *Power and wealth in rural China: The political economy of institutional change*. New York: Cambridge University Press.
———. 2004. The Cadre evaluation system at the grass roots: The paradox of party rule. In B. Naughton and D. L. Yang (Eds.), *Holding China together: Diversity and national integration in the post-Deng era*. New York: Cambridge University Press.
Whyte, David. 2015. *How corrupt is Britain*. London: Pluto Press.
Wildavsky, Aaron. 1964. *The politics of the budgetary process*. Boston: Little.
Williamson, Oliver E. 1975. *Markets and hierarchies, analysis and antitrust implications: A study in the economics of internal organization*. New York: Free Press.
———. 1985. *The economic institutions of capitalism: Firms, markets, relational contracting*. New York: Free Press.
Wilson, James. 1989. *Bureaucracy: What government agencies do and why they do it*. New York: Basic Books.
Wong, Roy Bin. 1997. *China transformed: Historical change and the limits of European experience*. Ithaca, N.Y.: Cornell University Press.
Woo-Cumings, Meredith. 1999. *The developmental state*. Ithaca, N.Y.: Cornell University Press.
Woo, Wing Thye. 1999. The real reasons for China's growth. *China Journal* (41), 115–137.
World Bank. 1992. *Governance and Development*. Washington, D.C.: World Bank.
———. 1993. *The East Asian miracle: Economic growth and public policy*. New York: Oxford University Press.
———. 1994. *Governance: The World Bank's experience*. Washington, D.C.: World Bank.
———. 2002a. China: National development and sub-national finance: A review of provincial expenditures. Washington D.C.: World Bank.
———. 2002b. *World development report 2002: Building institutions for markets*. New York: Oxford University Press.
World Bank and State Council. 2013. *China 2030: Building a modern, harmonious, and creative society*. Washington, D.C.: World Bank.
Wu, Jing, Deng, Yongheng, Huang, Jun, Morck, Randall, and Yeung, Bernard. 2014. Incentives and outcomes: China's environmental policy. *Capitalism and Society, 9*(1), 1–41.
Wu, Weiping. 2011. Fiscal decentralization, infrastructure finance, and regional disparity. In J. Man and Y.-h. Hong (Eds.), *China's local public finance in transition*. Cambridge, Mass.: Lincoln Institute of Land Policy.

Xin, Katherine R., and Pearce, Jone L. 1996. Guanxi: Connections as substitutes for formal institutional support. *The Academy of Management Journal, 39*(6), 1641–1658.

Xu, Chenggang. 2011. The fundamental institutions of China's reforms and development. *Journal of Economic Literature, 49*(4), 1076–1151.

Xu, Songtao. 2007. *Looking back at 28 years of personnel reform (Huimou zhongguo renshi zhidu gaige 28 nian)*. Beijing: Zhongguo Renshi Press.

Yang, Dali. 1997. *Beyond Beijing: Liberalization and the regions in China*. London: Routledge.

———. 2004. *Remaking the Chinese leviathan: Market transition and the politics of governance in China*. Stanford, Calif.: Stanford University Press.

Yang, Mayfair. 1994. *Gifts, favors, and banquets: The art of social relationships in China*. Ithaca, N.Y.: Cornell University Press.

Ye, Min. 2014. *Diasporas and foreign direct investment in China and India*. Cambridge: Cambridge University Press.

Young, Alwyn. 2000. The razor's edge: Distortions and incremental reform in the People's Republic of China. *Quarterly Journal of Economics, 115*(4), 1091–1135.

Yusuf, Shahid. 2001. The East Asian miracle at the millennium. In J. Stiglitz and S. Yusuf (Eds.), *Rethinking the East Asian miracle*. Washington, D.C.: World Bank.

Zhang, Xuehua. 2010. Implementing China's energy-saving and emission-reduction targets: Verification and accountability. Unpublished manuscript.

———. Forthcoming. Implementation of pollution control targets in China. *China Quarterly*.

Zhao, Shukai. 2013. Rural China: Poor governance in strong development. Stanford University CDDRL Working Paper No. 134.

Index

Page numbers in italics refer to figures and tables.